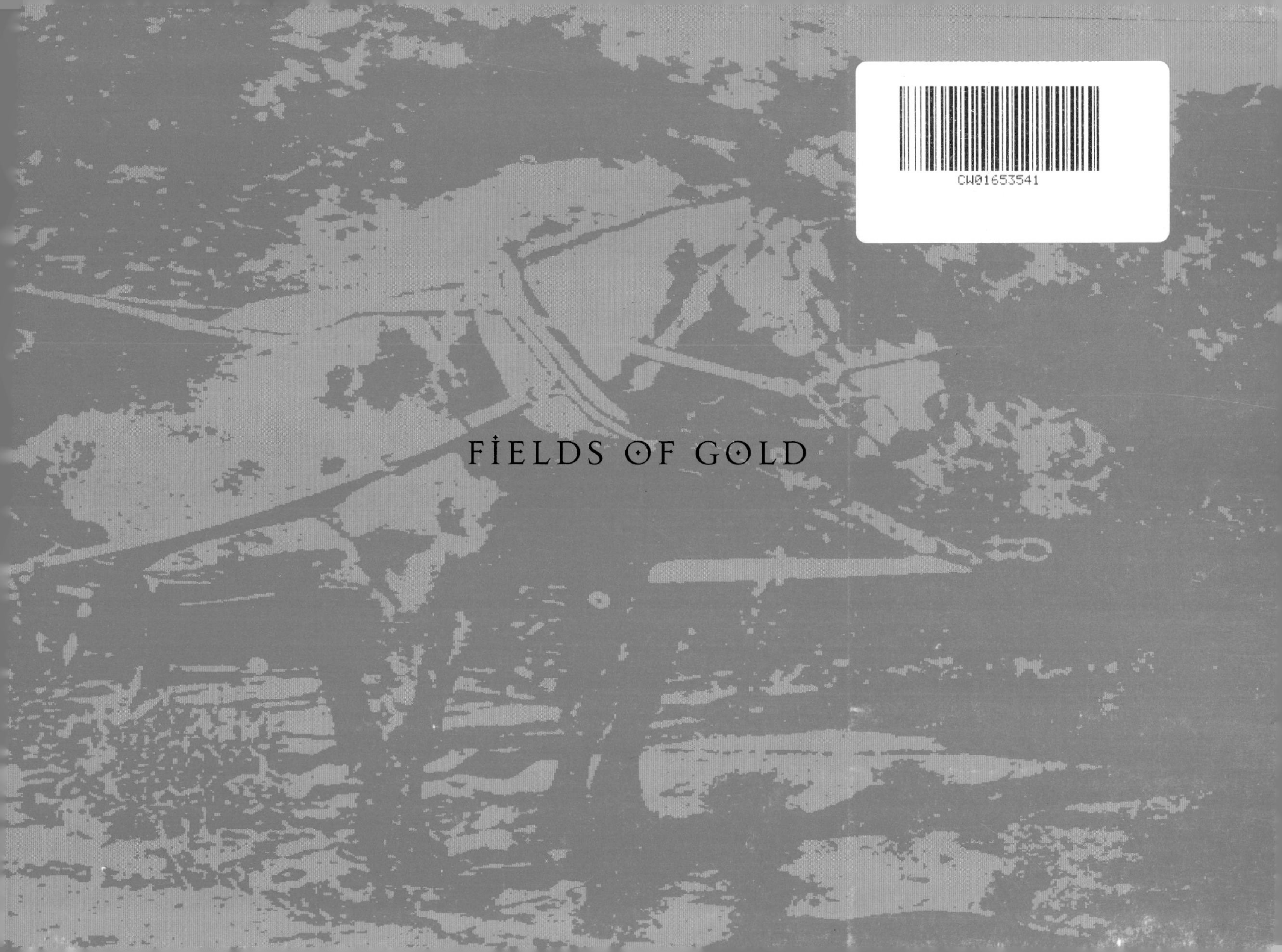

# FIELDS OF GOLD

1. Mother Gabriel Gill, Foundress of the Dominican Sisters in Western Australia

# FIELDS OF GOLD

A history of the Dominican Sisters
in Western Australia

Ruth Marchant James

Published and distributed in Australia by
Dominican Sisters of Western Australia
31 Williamstown Road
Doubleview WA 6018



National Library of Australia
Cataloguing-in-Publication data

James, Ruth Marchant.
Fields of gold ; a history of the Dominican Sisters in Western Australia.

Bibliography.
Includes index.
ISBN 978 0 646 37319 5.

1. Mother Mary Gabriel Gill, 1837-1905. 2. Dominican sisters - Western Australia - History. 3. Catholic schools - Western Australia - History. 1. Title.

255.972009941

Designed and produced by Street Design, West Leederville, WA
Copy-edited by Victor Publishing Consultants, Inglewood, WA
Printed and bound in Western Australia by Frank Daniels Pty Ltd, Perth, WA

*This book is dedicated in gratitude to the memory of*
*John James Jensen*
*a life-time friend and generous benefactor*
*of the Dominican Sisters*

# Foreword

The Irish-Australian link is very evident in the composition of the colonial clergy and religious who served the expatriate Catholic Irish in far off Australia, well removed from the fields of green of their childhood. Even so there was an international flavour. Religious congregations had bonds that led back to the continent. The earlier English penal laws as applied to Ireland had meant that the middle class Irish could only secure a Catholic education for their offspring if they sent them abroad, often to France or Spain. This was the background of the first Irish Dominican Sisters.

The gold strikes of the 1880s and 1890s in Western Australia attracted people from around the world. The goldfields of the Murchison, the 'Cross, and along the famed golden mile of Kalgoorlie generated both adrenalin and challenges to those charged with the spiritual and cultural development of the new communities. In 1899 the Dominican Sisters arrived in the vast Geraldton diocese to commence their educational apostolate among the rural and mining towns.

How could an enclosed teaching order whose traditions dated to the time of the Inquisition and Renaissance Italy be reconciled to the dynamics of an Australian goldfield? Ruth Marchant James skilfully unveils the mysteries and the myths often associated with convent life. The reader grasps not only the sense of vocation and mission that drove the Dominican Sisters to an amazing array of localities, but also comes to appreciate these Sisters as women, as teachers and as community figures. Ruth ably strikes an authentic note as she plays across the range of personalities and places. The resonant chord is a tribute to her finely honed literary expertise and to her adroit use of diaries, reminiscences, oral history techniques, government and ecclesiastical reports and other secondary sources that span a century of change.

The proponents of equal opportunity had had their contests in Western Australia. The equality of claim on the government purse for per capita contribution for the education of children – regardless of attendance at either a government or a non government school – had been contested keenly. Yet the debate did not produce the sectarian divide experienced in the eastern colonies. By the time the Dominican Sisters arrived in the diocese of Geraldton in 1899 the population explosion and changing demographics caused by the gold rushes had swept aside many local differences. The Bishop wanted to staff schools in areas that had been barely taken up as pastoral leases, let alone support a township. Ruth details how the Sisters undertook the challenge, teaching children of all denominations and winning the general support of the community – as was evident at Day Down at the occasion of Mother Gabriel's untimely death. She was mourned as a public figure, as her local involvement and her pioneering role in leading the first group of Irish Dominican Sisters to both New Zealand and Western Australia, well deserved.

Ruth Marchant James, a Fellow of the Royal Western Australian Historical Society and member of Council, has made a significant contribution to the genre of community history in Western Australia already. Her readers will not be disappointed in this well crafted and sensitive portrayal of a group of Sisters formerly cloaked in the anonymity of their religious habits. Through their commitment to 'Truth, Love and Knowledge', they emerge as personable and capable women, adapting to local conditions and circumstances, confirming that 'where there is change there is life'.

*Clement Mulcahy, M Phil, B A Hons. Dip Ed*
*Past President and Chairman of Council, RWAHS*

# Preface

Fields of Gold traces the history of the West Australian Dominican Sisters from their arrival at Dunedin, New Zealand in February 1871, Greenough in June 1899, to the present day. Unfortunately, exigences of space has not allowed me to cover in detail, every branch house, school and Dominican Sister who made an impact on the people of this State. Having to be selective was a difficult, but necessary task.

The reader may wonder at the consistent use of the title Sister, rather than Mother, when it is obvious that the religious person concerned held a senior position in the community. The decision to refer to all religious throughout the work as Sister, with the exception of earlier Mother Prioresses, was made with the Dominican Sisters' approval to save confusion. It is impossible to individually name all those who contributed to the publication, however, I can assure you that their support has been gratefully appreciated. Special and sincere thanks to Sister M. Perpetua Gill OP, who kindly made herself available at all times. Her reliable interest, knowledge and input has been a vital part of the production.

Acknowledgements are also due and thankfully given to the following:

Sister M. Antoninus Campbell OP for the active role she took in the final stages of selecting and assisting with the photographs. Pat Adamson, who freely gave her time and expertise during the early correction stages of the draft. Clement Mulcahy who kindly read and commented on the manuscript. Natalie and Vic Greaves who edited and proof-read the final work. Sisters M. Augustine McCarthy OP (NZ), who read and approved the chapter on New Zealand. Archivists, Sisters Theresa Rougham OP (NZ), Judith McGinley OP (NZ), Frances Stibi PBVM (Perth Catholic Archives), Sister Elizabeth Quirke PBVM (Geraldton Catholic Archives), Pat Gallaher (Geraldton librarian) and Shirley Scotter (Irwin Historical Society). For their support and assistance Damien and Robyn James, Helen Jolly, Sisters Joan Carville OP, M. Albeus Fahey PBVM, Flora Ricupero PBVM and all members of the Dominican community.

Finally, my eternal gratitude to my husband for his selfless assistance and encouragement during the writing and research, and to our family for their patient understanding.

RMJ

# Metric and other Conversions

**CURRENCY**

| | | |
|---|---|---|
| 12 pence | equivalent to | 1 shilling |
| 1 shilling | equivalent to | 10 cents |
| 20 shillings | equivalent to | 1 pound |
| 1 pound | equivalent to | 2 dollars |

(A Sovereign was a gold coin valued at 1 pound)

**LENGTH**

| | | |
|---|---|---|
| 1 inch | equivalent to | 25.4 mm |
| 1 foot | equivalent to | 30.5 cm |
| 1 yard | equivalent to | .914 m |
| 1 mile | equivalent to | 1.61 km |

**AREA**

| | | |
|---|---|---|
| 1 acre | equivalent to | .405 hectares |

**TEMPERATURE**

| | | |
|---|---|---|
| 32 degrees Farenheit | equivalent to | 0 degree Celsius |
| 100 degrees Farenheit | equivalent to | 37.8 degrees Celsius |

**SCHOOL CLASSES/YEARS**

| Primary School | | Secondary (High) School | |
|---|---|---|---|
| Grade 1 (Infants) | Year 1 | Grade 8 | Year 8 |
| Grade 2 | Year 2 | Grade 9 | Year 9 |
| Grade 3 | Year 3 | Junior | Year 10 |
| Grade 4 | Year 4 | Sub Leaving | Year 11 |
| Grade 5 | Year 5 | Leaving | Year 12 |
| Grade 6 | Year 6 | | |
| Grade 7 | Year 7 | | |

# CONTENTS

# List of Illustrations

# Prologue

A span of almost 700 years separates the foundation of the original Dominican Convent, Our Lady of Prouille, in the south of France and Rosary Convent, the first Dominican foundation formed at Greenough in Western Australia. From that first ancient convent founded by Domingo de Guzman (later St Dominic) in 1206, grew a highly-respected religious order with thousands of members, both male and female, involved with education and care across the globe.

Domingo de Guzman, founder of the Order of Friars and Preachers, was born c.1170 at Calaruega in north-eastern Spain. The son of Castilian nobleman, Don Felix Guzman and his revered wife Jane of Aza, he entered the university at Palencia in the old city of Castile at an early age, where he completed his theological studies. Later, he became a canon and sub-Prior of the Chapter at Osma Cathedral, where he remained for 10 years leading the life of a contemplative under the Rule of St Augustine. A young man of great integrity, Dominic showed the caring and charitable side of his nature when the city of Palencia was devastated by famine in 1191. Unable to contribute ready money to assist the poor and needy, he sold his personal possessions, including his much-loved books and manuscripts, to provide for some of their needs.

Christians in a number of European countries, particularly southern France, were pressured in the early part of the 13th century by the enormous changes that had taken place in religion. People, dissatisfied with traditional doctrines and critical of the example set by some members of the clergy, began to seek other articles of faith on which to base their beliefs. Attracted to a less complicated, simpler lifestyle, many Catholics became indoctrinated with the heretical teachings espoused by itinerant preachers in anti-Church groups. Their involvement over the years gave rise to the powerful Albigensian, or Catharist heresy movement, and put at risk the very fabric of the Christian Church.

Dominic was first acquainted with the threat of heresy when he accompanied Bishop Diego on a diplomatic mission to Denmark. It was said that during a stopover at Toulouse he successfully argued against the heretical beliefs put forward by an innkeeper, then later converted the man to Catholicism. By the time Dominic had returned to France, he had decided that his future vocation lay in preaching the gospel. He was convinced that by taking up an apostolate, similar to that of the early apostles, he might be able to reinforce the teachings of true

Christian faith and convert non-believers and wayward Catholics corrupted by the evils of heresy.

In 1203, Dominic and Bishop Diego set out on an evangelical mission to preach against the Albigensian heretics in Languedoc. As mendicants they adopted a simple lifestyle and, following the narrow, winding paths that led to various French villages, made contact with the populants and relied upon the villagers' generosity for food and shelter. Forever on the move, they continued to preach the teachings of Christ in the market places, town squares and churches. Concentrating on areas between the dioceses of Carcassonne and Toulouse, the preachers visited the towns of Montreal, Laurac, Mirepoix and Fanjeaux, where the majority of inhabitants were known to favour Catharism. Dominic later chose Prouille, near Fanjeaux, as the centre from which he would base his work.

During the Middle Ages, it was not unusual for women to be left unprotected for long periods whilst their menfolk fought in wars or travelled on the continent. At that time, a number of noblemen, impoverished by mounting debts, were unable to maintain their estates and employ sufficient household staff. Weakened by these circumstances, they readily succumbed to offers made by wealthy heretics who were willing to support and educate their daughters. In 1206, Diego and Dominic converted a group of noblewomen who had earlier embraced the strict ascetic lifestyle promoted by members of the heretical movement. These well-educated women formed the nucleus of a new religious community and, after receiving approval from the Bishop of Toulouse, Dominic formally founded a convent within Albigensian territory, near St Mary's Church, in the vale of Prouille.

Dominic duly appointed a Prioress and prayed that other recruits would also make lifelong commitments to serve God. The nuns, who lived an enclosed life, wore a white tunic, a black veil and, for warmth, an outer cloak of unbleached wool. They spent the majority of their time in prayer, whilst the remaining hours were spent spinning and weaving. Just like the heretics, who offered education to the children of believers, Dominic persuaded the families he had converted to place their daughters with the nuns at Prouille for instruction. As the religious group's spiritual director and superior, Dominic was a frequent visitor to the convent, and on the death of Bishop Diego at the end of 1207, he assumed sole responsibility for their welfare. With the building of a new convent in 1212, discussions took place involving enclosure and a suitable Rule for the Order, and it is interesting to note that the guidelines eventually introduced by St Dominic became the basis on which the Dominican Constitutions were later formed.

When the Bishop of Toulouse authorised Dominic and his companions to 'root out corrupt heresy, drive out vice, teach the faith and encourage in men sound morals', he handed them a poisoned chalice. Not only did they have to confront wide-spread ignorance among the people of southern France, but also they had to dispel the heresies put forward by a great many itinerant preachers. These heretics, driven by an unshakeable belief in the existence of two opposing forces – good and evil – persuaded their followers that whilst goodness emanated from the spirit, evil came from everything associated with the body and material goods. Staunch devotees were advised to practise celibacy and live a spartan existence, devoid of all possessions. In contrast, other believers, unable to cope with such a stringent lifestyle, led debauched, nihilistic existences.

The Albigensian leaders were clever debaters and far from ignorant; whilst most of the arguments presented by religious academics were often beyond the comprehension of the common people and, consequently fell upon deaf ears. In view of such opposition, Dominic eventually came to the conclusion that only a trained body of intellectual preachers would be capable of routing the heretics and putting an end to their evil influence.

By 1216, an order of Dominican friars, the Order of Preachers, was founded at Toulouse and within a year the monks, as well as the Dominican nuns, had successfully opened a number of houses in other parts of Europe. Prior to St Dominic's death, on 6 August 1221, and 13 years before his canonisation, a decision was made at General Chapter to send a group of friars to Britain. This move resulted in a Dominican house being set up at Oxford in 1221, followed three years later by a similar foundation in Ireland.

Keen to assist the Dominican friars in their new undertaking, the Cistercian monks of St Mary's Abbey in Dublin agreed to lease the Dominican community an adjoining piece of land on the northern bank of the River Lee. A church and monastery were later built on this property and by the end of the 13th century some 20 Dominican houses had taken root throughout Ireland. By the time Henry VIII had commenced the dissolution of the monasteries in 1539, at least 38 foundations had been established in that country.

The first known foundation of Dominican nuns in Ireland was established at Galway in 1644. At first, the foundation was successful, but the Cromwellian invasion of Galway aborted any plans the nuns might have had for the future. Members residing in the convents and monasteries were ordered to leave the country or return to their families. Rather than disperse, the Galway Sisters chose exile in Spain and arrangements were made for them to join the Dominican nuns of the second order at Toledo and Bilbao. In 1686, when Father John Browne, Master-Provincial of Ireland, requested the Sisters' return to Galway to re-establish their convent, the only two survivors of the original exiled group were Sisters Julian Nolan and Mary Lynch. At that stage, James II was King of England and Catholics regarded the future with optimism; however, any hope they may have cherished to reside in peace was short-lived after William of Orange took over the throne in 1689. By 1697, the worsening political situation between the English landlords and the Irish people had reached a point where regular religious orders were again under threat of banishment and it was decreed, by an Act of Parliament, that all bishops and members of religious communities, prior to going into exile, were to sell their properties and settle any outstanding debts by the following May.

Instead of carrying out their initial intention to settle in France, the Dominican Sisters, who had previously led a cloistered life, were persuaded to go underground. Secret accommodation was provided by various sympathetic friends and relatives and the nuns carefully avoided the civil authorities by disguising themselves as seculars and using the title 'Mrs'. The nuns regrouped after remaining dispersed for some time and when 90-year-old Sister Julian died, towards the end of 1701, Sister Mary Lynch succeeded her as Prioress. From these uncertain beginnings in Galway, two other groups were eventually formed in Ireland, one at Drogheda and another in Dublin.

Despite the tenuous position of Catholics in Ireland and the strict civil laws that existed, the Dominicans never failed to seek new opportunities. In March 1717, eight members of the Galway foundation withdrew to Dublin. Disguised as dressmakers, the women lived temporarily at Fisher's Lane before taking up residence in a convent originally built for the Benedictine nuns at Channel Row. That same year, two members of the group, Sisters Catherine and Mary Plunket, departed for Belgium. Sister Catherine remained on the continent for five years and, on her return to Ireland, successfully founded the Siena Convent at Drogheda. Although their living arrangements were unusual, the Sisters in Dublin lived in strict accordance with the Rule and Constitutions of the Dominican Order. For the sake of anonymity, the community was often referred to as 'Mrs Bellew's family', Bellews being the name of one of the professed Sisters. Unfortunately, little headway was made and only three or four members stayed behind when the community moved to Clontarf in 1808. Three years after re-establishing their convent, the Sisters experienced the long-forgotten joy of again wearing the Dominican habit and, as a group, began to look forward to more enlightened times.

Contrary to expectations, the new community at Clontarf was not a great success. The loss of many benefactors, due to the harsh Penal Laws and other restricting factors, had a marked effect on the foundation's financial status. During the 11 years that the Sisters persevered with the foundation, only four ladies entered the convent and lack of support eventually forced the closure of the Dominican boarding and day schools. On 12 December 1819, the remaining five Sisters moved to St Mary's Convent at Cabra in Dublin. In the beginning, the community managed to survive on an income received from parlour boarders. The introduction of the Catholic Emancipation Act in 1829, however, brought about many changes including an increase in the number of novices. Consequently, in 1835, a new Dominican boarding school was opened at Cabra to replace the one closed earlier at Clontarf. During those early years of struggle, no one could have predicted that this convent was destined to become a major Dominican centre.

Between 1832 and 1842, 22 novices made their profession and the Sisters, encouraged by the rise in vocations, continued to operate a successful boarding school. New-found confidence later resulted in a decision being made to establish yet another foundation in Dublin. On 24 October 1836, the Sisters moved into a house at 39 Lower Mount Street and, shortly afterwards, took up permanent residence at Sion Hill, Blackrock, Dublin. St Catherine's, Sion Hill, a large three-storey building set in nine acres of heavily wooded grounds, attracted a large number of religious recruits as well as parents wishing to enrol their daughters as boarders and day scholars.

The foundation's continuing growth meant that, by August 1867, the Dominican Sisters at Sion Hill were in a strong enough position to accept an invitation to found their first mission outside of Ireland at Port Elizabeth, South Africa. Three years after establishing the South African community, another group of volunteers set out to open a similar foundation in the newly-created bishopric of Dunedin, on the South Island of New Zealand. Leading this mission was Dublin-born Mother Mary Gabriel Gill, dedicated and respected foundress of the Dominican Order in New Zealand and later, in Western Australia.

CHAPTER 1

# Aotearoa, land of the Long White Cloud

When New Zealand's first Dominican Prioress* Mother Mary Gabriel Gill and her nine companions left Ireland in 1870, they little realised that the new foundation established by them at Dunedin would also be the fountainhead of the Dominican Order in distant Western Australia.

Victoria Margaretta Gill, who became a member of the Dominican community at Sion Hill, Dublin, in 1853, was well-educated, responsible and devout. She was born in 1837 at Grosvenor Park, Rathmines, Dublin, the eldest daughter of well-to-do brewer Andrew Gill and his wife Ellen Maria. In keeping with her family's social position, a private governess initially tutored the child at home. This early form of education was followed by a brief period at the Loreto Convent, Rathfarnham, Dublin, after which, at the age of 10, Victoria was enrolled as a boarder at the Sion Hill Dominican Convent at Blackrock, Dublin. [1] Nineteenth century society placed great emphasis on

*equivalent to the current Mother-General

female refinement and respectability and, like most convent-educated ladies of that period, young Victoria would have been taught, among other accomplishments, elegance of manners, deportment, a foreign language, needlework, painting, singing and music, as well as the usual basic educational skills. By the time she had completed her formal education and returned from abroad with her parents, Victoria had developed a great deal of self-confidence and, judging by future events, appears to have become a determined young woman, very much in control of her own life.

Although Victoria Gill came from a privileged background and was brought up in a loving and happy environment, her youthful years were sometimes touched by personal sadness. Not only would she have been concerned about the precarious state of her mother's health, but she also would have shared her parents' anguish at the premature loss of some of their children. [2] Equally, she would have been disturbed and saddened at the adult decision she felt she must make when she was just 15 years old. Unfortunately, no extant diaries or correspondence fully explain the reason why the teenage girl hastily decided to withdraw from society and enter a convent without first seeking her parents' blessing. The contents of a letter written by Mother Gabriel, 34 years after she left her family home, seem to offer at least one logical explanation:

*RMS Orizaba*
*December 1887,*

*All my thoughts are turning towards Rome; once again, for the second time in my life, I turn away while within reach of the accomplishment of my greatest desire in the way of sight-seeing. The evening before I fled from my home to enter Sion Hill, my parents had matured plans for spending Holy Week in Rome – Another plan for my future though I was only fifteen years of age was also to be decided on the Tuesday following – To escape the latter I felt myself bound to sacrifice the former – and in the depth of January – the ground covered with snow thickly frozen, I fled from my home and all I loved for Him who called me to be his spouse.* [3]

It is obvious that, in 1887, Mother Gabriel's life-long dream to visit Rome had failed yet again when the vessel did not dock at Naples. In her own words, earlier arrangements were shattered in 1853, when, in order to avoid a delicate situation, she sacrificed a planned family visit to Italy. One might assume from her guarded comments that her parents, no doubt acting in good faith, might have been engaged in drawing up a marriage agreement, which their headstrong young daughter found totally unacceptable. Victoria, dressed in readiness to attend a fashionable ball in Dublin, apparently seized a God-sent opportunity to escape an unwelcome obligation. Cancelling the evening's social engagement, and still wearing the gown she had chosen to wear to the ball, the young woman went instead to the Dominican convent at Sion Hill to seek admission. Clearly she felt trapped. Perhaps she had earlier considered a religious vocation and her parents, wishing to see her settled with a family, were not impressed.

By the time Miss Gill received the Dominican habit and the religious name Sister Mary Gabriel on 17 August 1853, the initial opposition displayed by her parents appeared to no be longer an issue. The young novice's reception ceremony was conducted by the Vicar-General of the Dublin Archdiocese, the Very Reverend W. Gore, and, on 18 May the following year, Sister Gabriel made her profession in the presence of the Dominican Prioress, Mother Mary O'Brien Butler, and members of the congregation. [4] As both a novice and later a professed nun, Sr Gabriel Gill proved to be a dependable and prayerful member of the community and the leadership qualities she developed as a young nun were quickly recognised. She taught not only the basic subjects offered in the school curriculum, but in addition German, French and music. Sister Gabriel continued as Mistress of Schools until October 1867, when, at the age of 30, she was appointed Mistress of Novices. She occupied that role until she left Ireland some three years later to become the founder of the new Dominican foundation at Dunedin.

The future Bishop of Dunedin, Dr Patrick Moran, consecrated Bishop of the Titular See of Dardania in 1856, which also included the administration of the Eastern Vicariate of the Cape of Good Hope, South Africa, was a native of Rathdrum, County Wicklow. He proved to be a respected missionary, dedicated educationalist and, if the occasion warranted, an outspoken champion of lost causes. One of Bishop Moran's first appointments after being ordained was in the same parish as St Catherine's Convent, Sion Hill, which meant that he was familiar with the work carried out by the Dominican Sisters. During his South African term of office, he was responsible for the building of many churches, schools and convents and shortly after he appealed for a Dominican community to take over the schools, a band of six Sisters set out from Dublin in 1867 to found the order's first mission at Port Elizabeth, South Africa. [5]

Two years later in New Zealand, when Otago, Southland and Stewart Island were separated from the diocese of Wellington, the new bishopric of Dunedin was established and the city bearing that name was chosen as the seat of the new diocese. Bishop Moran, who was appointed Dunedin's first bishop, knew very little about New Zealand and its people, apart from the fact that most of the Maoris lived on the North Island and that the South Island was currently newsworthy because of its rich gold deposits. Dr Moran returned to Dublin on Sunday, 7 August 1870, hoping to recruit a group of priests and nuns willing to travel with him to New Zealand. Except for acquiring the services of Father William Coleman, he could not raise much interest among the clergy. His approach to the Dominican Prioress at Sion Hill, however, proved far from disappointing and after gaining a positive response, he successfully obtained the Archbishop of Dublin's approval for the nuns to leave Ireland. In the meantime, members of the community interested in volunteering for the overseas mission were asked to submit their names for consideration. The selection process was thorough, for, according to the strict Dominican procedure, the Sisters volunteering for the mission would first have to have their application examined by the Archbishop. He would then take into consideration any objections made privately by members of the community. From the candidates finally selected, the Mother Prioress and members of her council would choose a Superior to head the proposed foundation.[6]

Andrew Gill, on learning that his daughter had been appointed Superior of the New Zealand foundation, presented the new Dunedin-bound community with a gold ciborium. Inscribed in Latin were the words: *Sororibus Sti Dominici apud Dunedin in Nova Zealandia in honorem SSmi Sacramenti et in amorem carae suae filiae Victoriae dono me dedit Andreas Gill XII Kal. Oct. MDCCCLXX**. Translated the inscription read: 'To the Sisters of St Dominic in New Zealand in honour of the most Blessed Sacrament and as a token of love for his beloved daughter, Victoria, given by Andrew Gill 20 October, 1870'. [7] Besides 33-year-old Mother Gabriel Gill and the foundation's newly-appointed sub-Prioress, 59-year-old Mother Agnes Rooney, the Dunedin mission group included Sisters Francis Sullivan (45), Catherine Hughes (40), Vincent Whitty (37), Gertrude Dooley (33), di Ricci Kirby (33) and Bertrand McLaughlin (19). Two lay Sisters, Lucy Tracy and a recently professed 21-year-old nun, Sister Peter Jordan, were also members of the new community. Of the original pioneer group, only Sister di Ricci was to accompany Mother Gabriel when she founded another mission in Western Australia 29 years later.

2. The Gill Residence, Dublin, 1887
Courtesy Dominican Sisters, N.Z.

The 10 Dominican missionaries boarded the passenger ship SS *Glendower* at Plymouth on 9 October 1870, and in the company of Bishop Moran and Father Coleman,

*Amendment date is 20 September – 12 days before Roman Kalends (1 October)

set out for Sydney, New South Wales, en route to New Zealand. The first stage of the journey was less than encouraging, for, shortly after reaching the Channel, the steam ship ran headlong into a fierce gale off the coast of Torbay and lost two of its anchors. The threat of being swept onto the rocky shoreline became a distinct possibility and the long hours spent waiting and praying must have been a frightening experience for all concerned. When the vessel finally limped into Plymouth for repairs, the Captain of the SS *Glendower* had no option but to delay the sailing date for several weeks.

By the time the vessel finally cleared port, the Sisters had settled comfortably into shipboard life. For convenience sake whilst travelling, instead of wearing the customary Dominican cream habits, they wore black attire. The group was pleased to find that apart from the daily recitation of the Angelus, which suffered on account of set meal times, most of their religious duties and ceremonies were maintained on a regular basis. The strong, resilient and independent characteristics of Mother Gabriel Gill were evident during the long voyage southwards. Sometimes accused of having favourites, she was nevertheless extremely level-headed and despite disappointment, eternally optimistic. Comforting, cheering and encouraging her companions when their spirits needed uplifting, it was said that she constantly quelled any doubts they might have had by reminding them that their future in a new country was full of promise.

The SS *Glendower* eventually reached Sydney harbour on 2 February 1871, and the Sisters' arrival was greeted with a great deal of enthusiasm by well-wishers, some of whom had past links with the Dominicans at Sion Hill. After spending a few pleasant days in New South Wales, the Dunedin-bound passengers travelled to Melbourne to join the steamship SS *Gothenburg* on its regular run across the Tasman Sea to New Zealand. [8] As expected, the vessel entered Otago Harbour early in the morning on 18 February and the new arrivals were extremely touched by the warmth of the welcome awaiting them when the vessel docked at Port Chalmers. The momentous day had been eagerly anticipated and was greeted with great joy by the Catholics of Dunedin.

No railway then connected the port with the city, so various types of horse-drawn vehicles transported the new arrivals to their destination. Few Catholics owned carriages, but those who did willingly made them available for the day. Four Dominican Sisters were placed in the first and second carriages and the remaining two members of the community followed in an open barouche. As various coaches, buggies and an assortment of riders formed a procession to escort Bishop Moran, Father Coleman and the 10 Dominican Sisters into town, other residents and leading members of the congregation swelled the cavalcade. On reaching St Joseph's Church in Dowling Street, the party was met by Dunedin's parish priest, Father Moreau, who offered grateful thanks for their safe arrival in the form of a Te Deum and Benediction. [9]

Before Bishop Moran took up his appointment in New Zealand, Bishop Viard, the Bishop of Wellington, had unfortunately given the impression that Dunedin's Catholic community had collected a substantial sum of money and secured a suitable convent in anticipation of the Sisters' arrival. As it turned out, the information given prior to sailing was misleading. Hard-working Father Delphin Moreau, a member of the French Marist congregation and a priest greatly respected for his achievements on the South Island, was not always appreciated by some Irish members of the community who perhaps preferred English-speaking priests. He was, therefore, not entirely overjoyed when he first heard that a Dominican group from Ireland was planning to establish a foundation in the newly-established diocese. Obviously concerned about the lack of financial support for such a venture, the parish priest made an impetuous last minute attempt to persuade Bishop Moran to bring only one Dominican Sister with him from Sydney, daring to suggest that arrangements could be made for the remainder of the party to follow at a later stage. It did not occur to the priest that his request might not be granted. Convinced that he was about to receive just the one nun, a bishop and a priest, Father Moreau went ahead with plans to refurbish the presbytery for the men and to provide single accommodation at a lady's house for one female. Not until one member of the reception committee decided to telegraph those on board the SS *Gothenburg* did the facts become known. [10]

Father Moreau ultimately offered the vacant Robin Hood Hotel for use as a convent. As it was run-down and highly unsuitable for living quarters, the bishop refused to let the nuns take up residence in the old building. Instead, hasty arrangements were made to house the 10 Sisters in the Oregon timber, seven-room Catholic presbytery originally intended for the bishop. In the interim, Dr Moran and his assistant accepted a few days' hospitality from a local resident before moving into small, wooden, rented premises on Bell Hill. It was a difficult beginning by any stretch of the imagination. The French priest, who was struggling to make ends meet, had prematurely closed St Joseph's school prior to the nuns' arrival, and most of the children had been accepted into other schools. Wall maps and many of the school's requisites had been removed and, apart from a few remaining desks and benches, the building was left almost bare. The Dominican Sisters' desire to establish a high-class centre of learning in Dunedin was also hindered by the fact that a number of private ladies' schools existed in the town and the recently-opened government high school had an enrolment of some 87 pupils, many of whom were Catholics. [11]

The original Catholic school, St Joseph's, in Dunedin, opened in 1863, had been set up in a wooden, obsolete government building acquired by Father Moreau. The male and female classes were in different sections and, in 1870, the girls' school was run by a Mrs Conway and the boys' school by a Mr Shepherd. When the Dominicans assumed control of the girls' school they taught in a renovated coach house and stables, leaving the original premises to be used solely by males. The Sisters opened their first school in Dunedin on Monday, 20 February 1871, and for the first year Mrs Conway continued as a member of the staff. Within a week of the Sisters occupying the presbytery, one of the rooms in the temporary convent had been converted into a high school classroom to accommodate three senior day students seeking admittance. At the same time, the Sisters' belief in the future was re-kindled when Mr Murphy, proprietor of the Shamrock Hotel, enrolled his two nieces as pupils, for he not only paid their school fees in advance, but also made the first of many generous donations to the Sisters. [12]

The school curriculum offered a wide range of subjects with many extras included, and as the community was not then in a position to open a boarding school, day and private tuition fees were the main source of income. The Dominican staff were blessed with some very talented women. The sub-Prioress, Mother Agnes, originally from County Meath, was Dublin-educated and an excellent singer and linguist. Like the Prioress, Mother Gabriel, she was also an accomplished pianist. Foundation member, Sister Catherine Hughes, was another natural teacher. A great lover of literature, her childhood had been embodied in an educational environment; encouraged by a mother and sister who ran a top-class private school at Whitehall, Blackrock. The Hughes family was extremely musical and no expense was spared in bringing out the best of their children's talents. A former pupil of Chopin had, at one stage, taught Sr Catherine, and her sister, Lady Duffy, was a celebrated musician in her own right and renowned as a patron of the Irish theatre in Dublin in the 1920s. Sister Francis Sullivan was a skilled linguist and Sister Peter Jordan, one of the two lay Sisters looking after the domestic needs of the Dunedin community, had once been a lady's maid in Paris and spoke French fluently. The expertise provided by these teachers was extremely important. Indeed, the whole Dominican community gained from the additional financial assistance derived from increased enrolments in pianoforte, harp, French, German, Italian and Spanish lessons, as well as tuition in art, singing, painting, needlework and flower-making.

A large proportion of Dunedin's population was Scottish and, like the town's founding fathers, mainly Presbyterian. Catholics were very much in the minority and their spiritual needs were ministered by occasional visits from French Marists and English-speaking itinerant priests. Gold discoveries in 1861 saw an increase in the population and, because many of the new immigrants were Catholics, Father Moreau was appointed Otago's first resident priest. [13] The majority of early residents were poor and not highly-educated, and just as barriers existed between various religious bodies, likewise wide gaps existed between the different social classes. A combination of poverty, *laissez-faire* and family expectation often took its toll on the young, particularly where education was concerned. Notwithstanding the almost single-handed efforts earlier made by Fr Moreau, and the generosity shown to the nuns by the people of Dunedin, Bishop Moran was less than impressed to discover that the diocese was practically without means. The lack of financial assistance and its impact on the Dominican mission's survival was of great concern to the bishop who felt responsible for the nuns, having brought them half way around the world to establish new schools. On 3 March, the bishop, no longer able to restrain himself, delivered a damning pastoral:

*We have learned how deplorable is the state of religion here; and we have also learned, to our dismay, from various sources, that the information given us in Europe as to the resources of this Diocese and the preparation made for our coming, was most incorrect. We had been led to believe that there was a good Church in Dunedin, and eleven other Churches and Chapels in the country districts – a fair Episcopal residence – Schools – a large house for a Convent of religious ladies – all free from debt; and finally, funds in hand to start us in the great work before us. You will readily understand, therefore, how great has been our disappointment, and disgust, and discouragement, to discover on landing that there was scarcely even the remotest appearance of truth in the statements made to us.*

*On the faith of the information thus given, we brought with us ten Nuns to inaugurate the most important and essential work of Catholic education. In Ireland we entered into a contract with them to the effect that, provided they paid their own expenses to New Zealand, we would provide for them in Dunedin a suitable Residence and School-halls…We are prepared to make trial and see if possibly and happily the state of affairs may not be after all so hopeless as it appears at this moment.* [14]

An evening meeting, quickly organised in St Joseph's Church on the first Thursday in Lent, was intended to draw attention to the Sisters' most urgent needs. Voted to the chair, Bishop Moran informed those present that unless they accepted part of the financial burden and provided suitable school buildings and a convent for the Sisters, he would be obliged to send the Dominicans away. Consequently, a committee of 17, consisting of five clergymen and 12 parishioners, was appointed and the bishop's timely pleas resulted in pledges totalling £400, of which he contributed £100 and Father Coleman £20. [15]

As well as attending to their various church duties, the Sisters took it upon themselves to repair and make new vestments for the priests, to replace former worn and shabby items, and also to assist in other church requirements. Their first year in New Zealand involved not only long hours but a great deal of stress, and it was a matter of great concern when the Prioress Mother Gabriel Gill fell ill and was confined to her room for the months of September and October; however, despite initial set backs, a great deal of progress was made during 1871. School enrolments increased, parish conditions improved and the Sisters were slowly showing signs of becoming self-sufficient. In October that year, St Joseph's Church was re-opened after much-needed extensions and the Dominicans were justifiably proud when an exceptionally large group of children were confirmed there.

When Bishop Moran negotiated the purchase of two adjoining homes towards the end of 1871, the Sisters thought that they had found a permanent convent. Although the houses were smaller than the presbytery and lacked an 'exquisite view of the bay and surrounding hills', the surrounding grounds were ideal. Mother Gabriel, who was still convalescing, thought the property most desirable for a select school, not only on account of its situation, but because it was 'in the midst of the Aristocracy, and in a milder climate'. [16] The owner's refusal to negotiate was a disappointing blow to the Sisters, for the offer made by the bishop was considered more than fair and likely to succeed. Members of the Dominican community, however, sensibly looked upon the whole episode as yet another setback in a disastrous train of events and decided to raise funds for the erection of a school and convent. To inform the public that the Dominican Nuns of St Joseph's, Dunedin, intended to hold a bazaar during the Christmas Holidays, an announcement appeared in the *Otago Daily Times* on 25 November 1871. The response was overwhelming and the bazaar, which proved to be a huge success raised a total of £2000 – a large sum of money for those days.

During the second half of the nineteenth century, Dunedin, with its splendid, although steep position, was considered to be New Zealand's major port. The town, overlooking Otago Harbour, gradually spread out from its original site on the western side of the upper harbour, across the isthmus and along the slopes of the peninsula on the far side, to become the second principal city of the South Island. Apart from adjusting to a new climate and relentless winds that were 'very trying on the throat and eyes', [17] the Sisters found that the mornings and evenings were often cold and damp and the unexpected rain not unlike 'home'.

Extensions to the former presbytery in Dowling Street (now Tennyson Street) commenced on 13 February 1872, at a cost of £775. When the additions were completed three months later, the Sisters happily accepted their first intake of female boarders. Among the first to enrol at the Dominican Convent Boarding and Day School For Young Ladies were students from the towns of Christchurch, Tokomairiro, Invercargill and Oamaru and two Canadian sisters who had recently settled in Dunedin. Unfortunately, the Sisters' personal space was limited and because the building was not originally designed for either a school or a convent, members of the community were forced to share alternative meal times with boarders in the convent refectory. In October, the bishop, fully aware that the acquisition of more spacious quarters was a matter of prime importance, decided to spend an extra £200 on further improvements in the form of a laundry block and outbuildings.

As a result of Bishop Viard's death in June 1872, Bishop Moran was appointed Apostolic Administrator of Auckland. Although he willingly accepted the additional responsibilities that came with the position, he was often away, for the appointment included care of the Wellington Province as well as whole of the South Island. [18]

In 1873, the number of female students attending the Dominican Convent was recorded as 160 with a further 80 pupils enrolled at the boys' school. Encouraged by the progress made in less than two years, Bishop Moran once again considered the possibility of obtaining larger premises away from the city to re-establish the girls' boarding school. Consequently, when 'the Slopes', a country estate at Wakari on the outskirts of Dunedin, came on the market in November 1873, the bishop seized the opportunity to purchase the property. A spacious residence and well-established gardens were features of the 60 to 70 acre property, which had fine scenic views and extensive grounds suitable for playing fields. The freehold property was previously owned by a Dominican benefactor, Mr Murphy of the Shamrock Hotel in Dunedin, and included in the purchase price was farm stock as well as appliances. With foresight, the bishop also made arrangements to buy an additional 20 acres of land adjoining the estate and approval was given to make immediate extensions to the buildings in readiness for the school's opening in 1874. [19]

The first boarders to St Dominic's Priory, Wakari, were admitted on 27 January 1874. Waiting to greet them were members of the new community: Mother Gabriel Gill, Sisters Vincent Whitty and di Ricci Kirby and lay postulant, Jane Neylon who, when she later celebrated her reception as a novice at the Priory, took the name Sister Joseph.

Meanwhile, the Sisters still living in Dunedin continued to operate the increasingly popular day school in Dowling Street. Prior to taking on the new foundation, Mother Gabriel, a person of tireless energy, suffered yet another bout of illness and the bishop and her companions were increasingly fearful that the strain of the last three years was taxing her strength.

By mid-1875, there were 83 young ladies attending St Dominic's Priory at Wakari and 216 at their first foundation St Joseph's, Dunedin. Wakari, unfortunately, was some distance from the city, and for practical reasons did not continue as a boarding school after 1875. The property became a holiday centre for members of the Dominican community until it opened as a Jesuit College two years later. [20]

In spite of its disappointing beginning, the 1870s proved to be one of the Dunedin community's most progressive periods. During that decade, pupil numbers rose rapidly, new religious members arrived from Ireland and two former Dominican students were the first to enter the novitiate. In April 1876, a group of Christian Brothers from Melbourne took over the boys' school at Dunedin and, to the delight of both the bishop and nuns, the long-overdue Dominican Convent was completed and occupied in October 1877. The Catholic community also took great interest in the construction of a bell tower and additions

3. St Dominic's Priory, Dunedin
Courtesy Dominican Sisters, N.Z.

to St Joseph's Church. To allow for future expansion, Bishop Moran had earlier purchased a site below the original convent from Father Moreau for £300. Although the interior layout of the new three-storeyed wing was planned to suit the simple lifestyle of an enclosed religious order, Bishop Moran, Mother Gabriel and the architect, Mr Francis Petre, had taken a number of necessary comforts into account. The building was commodious, well-lit and cheerful and, after experiencing years of inconvenience, the nuns must have been pleased to find that a furnace room and piped heating service had been installed in the basement to take into account Dunedin's chilly climate. [21] Mother Gabriel Gill, who could never resist the opportunity to get involved personally with a project, remained at the convent during vacation time to oversee the choice of interior colours intended to suit a conventual lifestyle. One of the novices, Sister Rose, described the end result:

*The novitiate walls are azure blue, the windows overlook the garden, Seminary and hills in the distance, it is really a little gem. St Catherine's corridor, which is directly outside Novitiate is salmon colour, St Dominic's buff, along which are the novices' cells; the Blessed Virgin's celestial blue, Sacred Heart pink, Angel Guardian green. The staircase leading to the Community room and Hall also green; the Choir, parlour and Community room peach blossom colour and Nazareth mauve, the Refectory and kitchen cream colour.* [22]

After the Sisters finally moved into the Priory the former presbytery-cum-convent was converted into a school. The day-school was extended and the provision of newer, brighter classrooms and airy dormitories meant that, from January 1878, the Sisters were at last in a position to accept an increased number of boarders. Bishop Moran must have been impressed with the new arrangements when, upon his return to Dunedin, over 100 children from St Dominic's Seminary and pupils from St Joseph's School welcomed him. In the 'Select Senior Classroom' [23] he viewed individual concert items and was given a presentation of ten sovereigns towards the cost of erecting a new cathedral.

Mother Gabriel, who had for some time been keen to establish branch houses, decided, after six Dominican Sisters arrived from Ireland in 1881, that she could at last spare staff to open a second foundation. Accepting an invitation to commence a school at Invercargill, the Prioress and her companion, Sister di Ricci Kirby, left Dunedin in October to make the necessary arrangements. Foundation members Sisters di Ricci (Senior Sister), Bertrand, Raymond* and Peter left Dunedin on 12 January 1882, and boarded the SS *Albion* for the short journey south to Invercargill. [24] In accordance with the Dominican rule, the new branch house remained dependent on the mother house.

By the beginning of January 1882, there were 29 Dominican Sisters, including postulants, living on the South Island of New Zealand. [25] Besides their own establishments, the community also taught at St Patrick's school, South Dunedin, from 1882 to 1897, after which the Mercy Sisters from Australia took control. The Dominican Sisters' second branch house, Rosary Convent, was duly opened at Oamaru, North Otago, in September 1882. The parish school, temporarily accommodated in St Patrick's Church, had a combined enrolment of approximately 150 male and female primary pupils as well as 10 high school students. A good relationship existed between the Sisters and the people of Oamaru and the

*usually spelt Raymund

parishioners made a determined effort to clear the parish debt of £2000. This goal was achieved by 1884, when the bishop announced, during the blessing of the new Oamaru church-school, that all church property in the town was almost free of debt. [26]

In 1883, Queenstown, a future flourishing gold mining centre was chosen as the site for a new Dominican foundation. Mother Gabriel and a companion, accompanied by Bishop Moran and four foundation Sisters, left Dunedin on 8 February and journeyed to the beautiful shores of Lake Wakatipu. They boarded a paddle-steamer at Kingston, and from the southernmost point of the glacial lake made the three-hour trip up Lake Wakatipu to Queenstown where, despite the late hour, the nuns were given a rousing welcome. Stepping ashore to the strains of music provided by the Queenstown Brass Band, they were warmly greeted by the town's leading Catholics and a long line of local residents with children lighting the way with lanterns. Our Lady of the Sacred Heart Convent was officially blessed on the following Sunday, and the next day St Joseph's church-school opened for enrolments. Dominican author, Sister Mary Augustine McCarthy informed her readers:

*The latter was a day school for children under ten, English and the rudiments of French being taught, no doubt in addition to the usual subjects, for the fee of ten shillings a month. The 'School for Young Ladies' offered an English education in all its branches, Latin, French, German and Italian Languages and Literature, Music, Singing, Plain and Fancy work, Drawing and Painting. The fees for day pupils were £12 a year, and for boarders £40 a year.* [27]

Considering the enthusiastic fanfare and obvious delight at their appearance in the district, the Sisters were extremely disappointed by the initial lack of support. When Mother Gabriel returned to Queenstown some six weeks later enrolments had greatly improved. With the completion of a new school building in July 1883, pupil numbers continued to increase albeit slowly. By then, Sion Hill was no longer in a position to supply reinforcements to the South African and New Zealand foundations. In view of the scarcity of local vocations and the additional workload associated with branch houses, there was a need for the Dominican Sisters to re-assess the staffing situation. As a result, in 1884, the ever-pragmatic Mother Gabriel began to investigate the possibility of establishing a Dominican missionary novitiate in Ireland, where girls could be trained for mission work. [28]

There is no question that Mother Gabriel Gill was the linchpin around which the Dunedin Dominican community revolved. She had been re-elected Prioress in 1876, 1879 and in 1883 and by the time the sub-Prioress Mother Agnes succeeded her in January 1886, Mother Gabriel, affectionately referred to as 'Mother of the

Missions', had dominated the New Zealand scene for 15 interesting and progressive years. Her efforts to establish a novitiate in Ireland were strongly championed by Bishop Patrick Moran of Dunedin, and Dr Kirby, the Rector of the Irish College in Rome, who provided the foundress with the necessary testimonials and advice.

On 18 June 1886, after a long sea voyage, Mother Gabriel and her travelling companion, Sister Alphonsus Owens, arrived at Dublin. Seeing her father again, and meeting the Sisters she had previously known at St Catherine's Convent, Sion Hill, must have evoked many memories. The community in Ireland had been kept well-informed about the new mission and not only was there a warm welcome waiting, but a generous offer to transfer two Sisters from Sion Hill to Dunedin in the hope that their arrival might at least alleviate some of the immediate staffing problems. From the outset Mother Gabriel's quest to find a suitable residence in, or near, Dublin became increasingly more difficult and there were many anxious moments about the inconvenience caused to two postulants waiting to enter the proposed novitiate. The Irish community was extremely supportive, but at the time was unable to help with accommodation or finances. It was quite by chance that Father Marmion, a young, sympathetic professor visiting Sion Hill from the Holy Cross College at Cloncliffe, suggested the likelihood of Mother Gabriel taking over the property of a friend. To her delight, Mother Gabriel was offered, for two years rent-free, the use of Beaumont, an attractive Georgian residence set in 70 acres of grounds at Drumcondra, five miles from Dublin. [29]

Accompanied by Sister Paul Lyons, a companion on loan from Sion Hill, and three postulants, Mother Gabriel opened the Dominican training centre at Beaumont on 8 September 1886. By October, there were 12 young ladies in training at Beaumont and no lack of enquiries from others seeking admittance. The customary dowry was not introduced, however, and financial problems and other related concerns, were never far from the surface. Mother Gabriel briefly discussed some of these when she wrote to Bishop Reynolds of Adelaide in October 1886:

*...We are very poor – I was obliged to admit one-third of the number without any pension though I fixed only £25 per annum, according to your advice, for the annual sum to be paid by each. Last week letters from Dunedin announced that the nuns there do not wish me to establish a noviciate, the times having become much more depressed since I left, and so many of our Catholic people emigrating from N.Z. to Sydney and other parts of Australia, they fear it will be impossible for them to help me, and they dread debt will be the consequence. Of course they are not yet aware that I am here at Beaumont and that we have free quarters for two years. Thanks to Divine Providence and my father's generosity, I am not in debt,*

*but we are denying ourselves every comfort except the necessities of life. Twelve chairs which we move from room to room, one fender, one set of fire irons form the chief articles of furniture (besides beds) for 25 rooms!* [30]

Once again Bishop Moran came to the fore, and after allaying fears that the Dunedin community might have had about future debts arising from the new venture at Beaumont, he was able to convince Mother Gabriel's successor at Dunedin that a sum of £25 per annum should be sent to cover some of the costs incurred in the clothing and upkeep of the novices in Ireland. Although financially hard-pressed at that time, the bishop also offered to contribute £100 a year whilst the missionary novitiate was functioning. [31] In hindsight, Mother Gabriel's project might have been better delayed until other options were explored and the Archbishop of Dublin's acceptance of the scheme had been discussed in more detail. With her usual optimism, Mother Gabriel refused to consider the possibility of failure, yet, despite her receptivity to change the exercise was not a resounding success. Weighed down by strict Church procedure and used to dealing with a more relaxed and co-operative bishop, the Superior of Beaumont was forced to spend a great deal of time dealing with the status of the missionary novitiate.

Dr William Walsh, who succeeded Dr McCabe as Cardinal Archbishop of Dublin, was a stickler for formalities and appeared to be not overly sympathetic to Mother Gabriel's cause. Archbishop Walsh was displeased that she had consented to accept a year's free chaplaincy from a group of priests of the Oblates of Mary living at Belcamp, two miles from Beaumont. He was also not convinced that, should the mission fail, his diocese would not be responsible for any outstanding debts. Isolated by distance from her supporters, Bishop Moran and Dr Kirby, Mother Gabriel felt spiritually deprived when her confessor and early champion, Father Marmion, left Ireland to join a monastery in Europe. The future Benedictine Abbot and internationally acclaimed spiritual writer, Dom Columba Marmion, continued to advise her, but admitted that he was powerless to help. Whilst the advice he gave was supportive, it was balanced enough to include criticism. 'I must say the turn things have taken is an enigma for me', he wrote, 'to be candid when you said in one of your letters that you had got lay professors for the novices, I felt at once that you had committed a grave error – to my mind – I would have used all my influence with you to prevent this'. [32]

Acting on further advice from her current confessor and following, as she thought, the correct procedure, Mother Gabriel wrote to the Archbishop of Dublin on 15 October 1886, to request the presence of a delegate to examine three Beaumont postulants waiting to receive their habits. She was stunned when he refused and must have reached the depths of despair when she read his reason:

*...As matters stand, I am plainly not in a position of my own authority to make any recognition of your convent as a convent canonically established. Your settlement is not a permanent one. The whole arrangement of it rests with the Bishop of Dunedin. Of course it will give me great pleasure to do whatever may be necessary on my part to give effect to any wishes of his Lordship. As to receptions or professions, it is of course plain that ladies entering in your house are not to have any permanent connection with the diocese. They enter there with the intention of leaving the diocese as a matter of course. Thus we are obliged to fall back on your own Bishop's regulations whatever they may be.* [33]

It was originally thought that a disclaimer, signed by postulants prior to reception, would provide the proof needed to convince the Archbishop that no future member of the New Zealand community could make a claim against the diocese of Dublin. Yet a letter written by Archbishop Walsh on 26 January 1887, made it clear that this suggestion was not acceptable and further clarification was needed from Rome. He stated, 'I shall be happy to act for the Bishop of Dunedin as His Lordship's representative and delegate. But we must have a distinct acceptance of the responsibility by the Bishop on the part of his diocese – this acceptance being declared by Propaganda to be such as will leave this diocese free of all responsibility in the matter'. [34] Distance, and the length of time it took to send and receive letters, slowed the process considerably and placed added strain on those waiting. So it was with a sense of relief that the examination and confirmation of documents, eventually sent by Bishop Moran and the Holy See through Dr Kirby in Rome, put an end to the on-going saga.

4. Beaumont, Dublin

Subsequently, on 11 June 1887, five postulants from the missionary novitiate, Beaumont, were received at an impressive ceremony. The young ladies, receiving their religious names and exchanging their plaid postulant dresses and black, tulle-frilled veils for the flowing cream habit of a Dominican novice were the Misses Annie Mulcahy (Sr Cecily), Angela Warren (Sr Josepha), Fannie Cosgrove (Sr Jordan), Mary Rowe (Sr Pius), and Teresa

Mullany (Sr Antoninus). Another postulant, Maggie Crofts (Sr Thomas), was later received in New Zealand. One has to admire Mother Gabriel's fortitude in the face of such strong opposition, for, on the eve of her departure from Ireland, Archbishop Walsh let it be known in a letter to Dr Kirby that he was not impressed by her determination to proceed. In his opinion 'the Dominican nun from Dunedin' had 'proved herself so far to be a very troublesome person'. It seems that he was not keen to accept Bishop Moran's personal guarantee without further documentation. 'I have told her, over and over again', he continued, 'that before I can move a step, she must present to me a formal statement from her Bishop'. [35] Prior to leaving, Mother Gabriel received her final admonishment from the Archbishop: '…I must ask you to excuse me from seeing you. I should not wish to say to you on your leaving the country all that I should feel called upon to say if I were to see you'. [36]

In November 1887, Mother Gabriel and a party of nine left Ireland and in England boarded the RMS *Orizaba*, an Orient Line ship bound for Sydney, Australia. Two of these postulants, the Misses Ada O'Connor (Sr Benignus) and Rita Murphy (Sr Dominica) later joined the foundress in Western Australia. There is no doubt that the schools Mother Gabriel had founded at Dunedin 17 years earlier were always foremost in her thoughts. Before leaving England, Mother Gabriel purchased a variety of teaching aids such as scissors, drawing boards, paper, globes, books, embroidery cotton, basket-making frames, modelling boards, dumbbells and Indian clubs, as well as several small items of furniture.

The Dominican group eventually reached Port Chalmers, Dunedin, aboard SS *Waihora* on 26 January 1888, and was heartened by the appearance of Bishop Moran, who, with their fellow Dominicans, offered congratulations on the success of St Dominic's overseas novitiate.

Considering Mother Gabriel's experience in novitiate training at Beaumont, her return to the Priory was timely. On arrival she accepted the role of Mistress of Novices, replacing Mother Evangelist who had been suffering ill health for some time. A conscientious, precise teacher, she set out to oversee 'the training of all postulants and novices in virtue and science' and, according to one of her former pupils, she 'applied the brake' whenever her novices showed signs of becoming too lively. [37] Mother Gabriel's re-election to the office of Prioress in 1889 was not entirely unexpected and during the next three years much was achieved in the provision of new buildings.

The twentieth anniversary of the Dominican Sisters' departure from Sion Hill was celebrated with the opening of St Dominic's College in Dunedin on 5 October 1890. The buildings, which cost in the vicinity of £8500, provided the extra space and facilities needed to cater for an increased number of enrolments. The Dominicans set high standards and the college's academic achievements, plus the emphasis the Sisters placed on moral issues, deportment and culture, won over parents of all persuasions. A number of branch houses and schools had also been improved and extended over the years, and future foundations were under consideration. A Dominican primary school was opened at Milton, about 37 miles from Dunedin, in January 1891, and, in February 1893, a similar foundation was established at Lawrence, the site of yet another significant gold strike. Three years later, in 1895, a primary school was opened in North East Valley, a suburb of Dunedin, and, in 1899, the same year that Greenough was opened, another convent was established at Cromwell in the Otago diocese.

The convening, by Bishop Moran, of the First General Chapter of the New Zealand Dominican Sisters was an important milestone. Held on 17 December 1893, it was intended to review all aspects of administration and also to compile a book of constitutions suited to the requirements of the Dominican Sisters in New Zealand. Several important issues were raised, including the desire to have central government for all Dominican houses in the Dunedin diocese, thus endorsing the branch house system. It was during these proceedings that the Sisters first heard of the bishop's worsening health.

The Second Session of the General Chapter was held on 26 December 1894, and the Prioress, having completed her three-year term, stood for re-election. She was, by then, in her late 50s and, although not a robust person, she appeared to have the ability to recover quickly from her many illnesses. Mother Gabriel had proved herself to be an excellent administrator. During her last term of office she had established two new foundations and had handled finances amounting to £34,197, of which approximately £10,320 had been spent on buildings. She had also welcomed 28 postulants to the novitiate and 38 novices had been professed in the Dominican Order. [38] Having dominated her surroundings for so long and performed her duties so efficiently, she must have been somewhat taken-aback when those members of the community eligible to vote, elected Mother St Peter Slattery in her stead. Although she was held in high esteem by the Sisters, it was said that the control she exercised for so long over the community did not always endear her to her subjects and some members considered that it was time for a change.

One former pupil described Mother Gabriel as 'a stately, queenly lady with her head slightly bent, whose very appearance gave the keynote to her character'. [39] It was said that she had a high arched nose and dark piercing eyes and that her regal bearing was occasionally mistaken for superiority. This impression was sometimes fuelled by the fact that Mother Gabriel came from a privileged background. She was a true visionary, however, a person who had a special ability to impart knowledge and communicate her enthusiasm to others. The former Prioress was indeed a strong character and like most self-assured people, she had many facets to her personality. Inclined to be fond of authority, she was dutiful to the point of being excessively severe, determined, and often obstinate, yet she was quick to forgive and forget and was always accommodating to those in need of her time and care. Bishops Moran (New Zealand), Reynolds (South Australia) and Kelly (Western Australia) admired her immensely and each in turn appeared to support her in the majority of her undertakings. Conversely, others, including some of her own Sisters, found her somewhat demanding, impetuous and at times overbearing. [40] Like most strong-willed characters, however, she did not avoid making difficult decisions and in her lifetime achieved much in the way of progress.

Mother Gabriel Gill's loss of authority, and the 1894 demise of two foundation pioneers, Sisters Francis Sullivan and Lucy Tracy, followed by the deaths of the Sisters' lifelong friends Bishop Moran and Archbishop Kirby, were events that spelled the end of an era for the Dominicans in New Zealand. In December 1897, Mother St Peter was re-elected for a second term of office and six months later Mother Gabriel and Sister Benignus O'Connor volunteered to escort an ailing Sister Catherine Hughes to New South Wales for medical treatment. Sister Catherine was admitted to a nursing home at Ryde and the two nuns from Dunedin spent the next five months at Santa Sabina, a Dominican house at Strathfield, Sydney. Mother Gabriel's agile mind and her ability to converse intellectually with others, would no doubt have made her sojourn in Sydney interesting, for at that time in-depth discussions were taking place on the Cabra controversy, a complex subject which questioned the status of all Dominican Sisters descended from that foundation. [41]

Because of the convent's central position in Sydney, she was able to meet a wide range of religious during her visit. These included one of Australia's renowned church leaders, Cardinal Moran and from Western Australia the newly-appointed Bishop of Geraldton, William Kelly. Those months spent in New South Wales proved to be a turning point in Mother Gabriel Gill's life, for during that time she was given the space to re-assess her future and the opportunity to reach out and accept a new challenge beyond New Zealand.

Geraldton had been one of the areas suggested to the Holy See as a most likely diocese when the Plenary Council of Australian Bishops had met earlier in 1895. Considering the size of the state and the enormous responsibilities carried by Matthew Gibney, Bishop of Perth, it was seen as a move in the right direction when the new diocese was established in 1898 and William Bernard Kelly was appointed its first bishop. The son of Irish parents, he was born on 30 June 1854, at Toodyay, an early settlement in the York district, where his father John Kelly was employed in the colonial police force. Sent to Perth for an education, the youth showed great promise as a student. His ability to learn Latin impressed both Father John O'Reily (future Bishop of Adelaide) and Father Matthew Gibney (future Bishop of Perth), who recognised his suitability to study for the priesthood. The 18-year-old William Kelly enrolled at St Peter's College, Wexford, Ireland, and after completing his studies at All Hallows College was finally ordained in 1883. Appointed parish priest of his hometown Toodyay, he later served for 12 years as editor of the *Catholic Record*. This position sharpened his writing skills and gave him the opportunity to meet and make friends with a wide circle of people from every walk of life.

The new Bishop of Geraldton was once described as 'a quiet, ascetic man with a reserve of manner that might be mistaken for taciturnity'. [42] Archbishop Clune obviously shared the same opinion when he remarked, 'He [Kelly] seemed to hold the warmth and generosity of a warm heart by a cold and reserved exterior'. Bishop Kelly was a good administrator and much-admired by his flock, most of whom spoke highly of his concern for the less fortunate. It was a pity, however, that diplomacy was not a pre-requisite of his appointment, for he was often intransigent, curt and short on patience. Certainly some of the pioneer Presentation Sisters from Ireland found him difficult and his attempts to resolve the deadlock, caused by their desire to abide by the rule of enclosure*, was not the work of a skilled mediator [43]. On the other hand, the Dominican Sisters had the greatest respect for Bishop Kelly and, except for isolated incidents, found him good company, caring and understanding.

5. First Bishop of Geraldton, William Kelly
Courtesy Archdiocesan Archives, Perth

The likelihood of the Dominican Sisters in New Zealand having an Australian foundation had been raised on at least two occasions prior to the offer from the Geraldton diocese. In 1896, the Prioress at Dunedin had written to Archbishop Carr in Melbourne expressing a willingness to establish a foundation in that colony, only to find that 'most places of importance' already had convents. Later, in May 1898, when Dr Delaney, the coadjutor Bishop

*The rule of enclosure restricted the Sisters' movements to the confines of the convent, unless given dispensation

of Hobart, requested postulants, the Sisters offered to send him a small community of Dominican nuns. [44] However, this suggestion was not acted upon and shortly after his consecration on 14 August 1898, Bishop Kelly took advantage of Mother Gabriel's presence at Santa Sabina Convent in Sydney, to invite the Dominican Sisters from Dunedin to form a foundation in the newly-formed Geraldton diocese. The bishop was aware that for such a mission to succeed, he needed to recruit a religious community that would be willing to relax their rule of enclosure to suit Australian conditions.

Mother Gabriel returned to Dunedin on 3 November 1898 and reported in detail Bishop Kelly's invitation to open a mission at a small hamlet south of Geraldton, named Greenough. The encouraging response to his proposal, prompted Bishop Kelly to forward a formal request for volunteers, in early October, to the Prioress of St Dominic's Priory in Dunedin. [45] The Bishop of Dunedin and members of the Dominican Council, on the proviso that the existing schools in New Zealand were not disadvantaged, duly approved the proposition. The Prioress, Mother St Peter, wrote to all community members four days later, to inform them that Bishop Verdon 'would be quite willing for Dunedin to do for the new Foundation what Sion Hill does for foreign Branches, New Zealand and Africa, viz. to train subjects for the mission when such could be procured, further than this there would be no future connection with the Mother House at Dunedin'. [46] Because of the distance involved, it was also decided that the new foundation should later become autonomous, although it was expected that the Sisters would return to New Zealand in the case of sickness, or if perchance the mission failed. On 5 January 1899, five months before the Dominicans arrived at Geraldton, Bishop Kelly provided a frank, detailed description of their new assignment at Greenough:

*When speaking to your Sisters in Sydney I asked them to await a report from me before deciding to come to this diocese; this I considered the wiser course, because never having lived in G'ton [Geraldton] I could give them no very full, or accurate information as to the state of things in my future sphere of labour. I came to G'ton about the middle of November, and as soon as I was free I began my enquiries about the Greenough, the district which I had mentioned to your Sisters as possibly affording a fair opening for the work of your Order.*

*The information I was looking for did not come to hand very readily, owing to the frequent absences of the Greenough priest, and I was thus prevented writing to you as promptly as I could have wished. You will please accept this also as my apology for not having sooner answered your extremely kind and encouraging letter. What I have been able to learn concerning the Greenough district may be summed up as follows: There is at the Front Flats a building intended for a convent, which might afford indifferently good accommodation for six or seven nuns. The building is not yet completed, but could be in a short time at no great expense. The attendance you might expect would be twelve Catholic children and some non-Catholics making the number about thirty. – The pastor thinks the parents would be unwilling to pay any except a nominal fee, as the State Schools against which you would have to compete are practically free. They would however, contribute eggs, meat and other farm produce which would materially reduce the cost of living for you. The priest of the place will willingly say Mass for you whenever he is at his principal home, which is only quarter of a mile from the proposed convent. But he has so many places to attend to that he cannot promise you more than two Sunday Masses in each month, and an occasional week-day Mass. Should you decide to come I shall have to ask you to take charge of a second school at the Back Flats where you would have nearly as many children as at the Front Flats. With a horse and buggy you could easily cover the distance, about six miles each way, in about an hour and be always at home in your convent at night. This would I believe require a dispensation from enclosure which I am happy to do my best to obtain for you.*

*Finally WA [Western Australia] will one day I am firmly assured be the richest of the Australian provinces, its natural wealth is boundless. But the day is not yet. My diocese is so far from being rich that I find myself barely able to meet the butcher's and baker's bills. I live in a small house the rent of which is paid by some of my people. I mention these things to explain why I do not offer you pecuniary assistance in your church-like enterprise at the Greenough. Money I have none to offer you, but should the diocese develop in the future, as I am sure it will, you will share in whatever increase of wealth may come to me. I have made this as impartial a statement as I could. I am aware that I can put before you no inducement to come here, but for the love of God. If you can work for God's sake and endure hard things and wait for better times – come along. Should you think the prospects too uninviting I will not blame you.* [47]

By March the following year it was clear that Mother Gabriel Gill saw herself as part of the founding group. 'Do you know', she wrote on 6 March 1899, 'that we have promised the BVM [Blessed Virgin Mary] that our Convent at Greenough is to be named "Dominican Convent of the Holy Rosary". Pray for its success. Dr Kelly is improving the building. We do not know yet, how soon it will be finished'. [48] Towards the end of that month the sum of £300 was set aside by the Dunedin Dominican Council for the use of the new community and the names of the Western Australian founding members were announced. Mother Gabriel Gill, sub-Prioress at St Dominic's, Dunedin, was appointed head of the mission and Sister di Ricci Kirby, who had journeyed with her from Sion Hill to Dunedin, became second-in-charge. The remainder of the party consisted of Sisters Gonzales Wall, Dominica Murphy, di Pazzi Miscall, Bonaventure McEntyre and Miss Kate Murphy, a young postulant who returned some 12 months later to New Zealand.

Usually known for her self-discipline, it became obvious, as the date of departure drew nearer, that Mother Gabriel could not face the finality of saying farewell to her adopted country and many friends. She later revealed the difficulty she had in controlling her emotions:

*As far as I could, I kept my departure a secret until the week before I left. In this way I missed seeing many friends. I could not bear parting scenes. My feelings were deeper than they appeared to be and the wrench was almost beyond my strength. In the end I had to slip out by the hall door and walk up the street to the carriage alone. I did not say good-bye to any of my darling children that were all waiting in St Gabriel's Hall, nor could I turn my head towards the Convent or Cathedral as we drove away. What a meeting we shall have in Heaven – the mere thought of it brings joy'.* [49]

The group boarded the coastal steamer *Otaki* on 24 April 1899, and sailed from Dunedin at 3.15 p.m. on the first leg of a sea voyage that would take them across the Tasman Sea and into the Indian Ocean, to reach the western shores of the great Australian continent. The Sisters exchanged the more gentle and, at times awesome, beauty of the small South Island of New Zealand, for a continent of immense proportions and enormous contrasts in climate and topography. They also met the challenge of working under a new bishop in a struggling diocese, which at that stage could offer them nothing more than hardship, heat and humble beginnings.

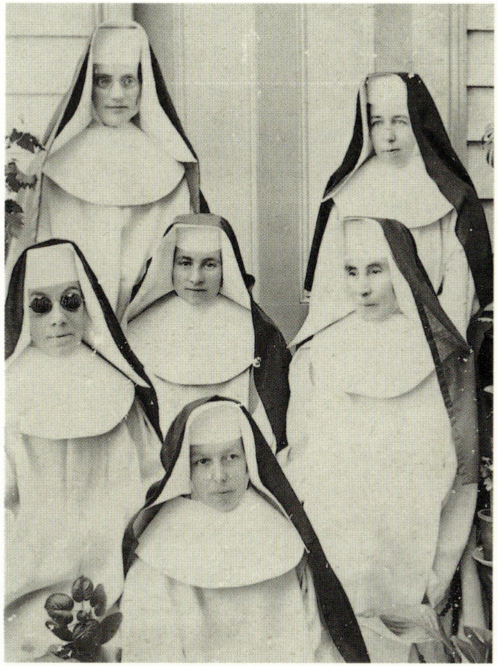

6. Pioneer group
L. to R. Back Row: Sisters Dominica Murphy, Bonaventure McEntyre
Middle: Sisters di Ricci Kirby, di Pazzi Miscall, M. Gabriel Gill
Front: Sister Gonzales Wall

CHAPTER 2

# To Sin, Sand, sorrow, sore eyes and Sardines

Of the five founding Dominican Sisters on board the steamer *Otaki*, bound for the Bluff and eventually Australia, two were originally from Ireland and the remaining three from New Zealand. The day of departure, 24 April 1899, saw a large crowd of well-wishers gather on the wharf at Dunedin to bid their last goodbyes. By afternoon the skies had become cloudy and the increasingly poor visibility disappointed the Sisters, who had hoped to catch a final glimpse of their beloved Dunedin before they sailed. At 4.00 p.m. the group sat together and said the Office (daily prayer recited from a breviary) aloud. Afterwards, Mother Gabriel Gill and Sister di Ricci Kirby recited the Rosary up on deck before settling comfortably into deck chairs to write postcards in readiness for posting at the Bluff. Despite warm and relatively calm conditions, there was a heavy swell running and by dinner time all members of the Dominican party, with the exception of Mother Gabriel and Sister Dominica

Murphy, were overtaken by seasickness. Sister Gonzales Wall was the first to succumb, followed by Sister Bonaventure McEntyre and Sister di Pazzi Miscall. Unfazed by the weather, Mother Gabriel considered the ocean far from rough and for the entire night 'slept well on a couch under open portholes'.[1] Sister di Ricci explained: 'When M.M.G. [Mother Gabriel] came to the cabin by 9.o'c. she amazed all by saying that we were only skimming the water and that the Sisters were only imagining they were ill'. [2]

The vessel entered Bluff Harbour the next morning and the passengers in transit happily went ashore. The Sisters chose to spend their final day in New Zealand with the Dominican community at St Catherine's Convent in Invercargill, where they were overwhelmed by hospitality and a constant stream of visitors. 'It was a great comfort', wrote diarist Mother Gabriel, 'to kneel in the lovely little Chapel two or three times on Tuesday and to draw near for the last time in New Zealand to the "sweet Eucharist Lord" for whose love and glory we were going through so many heart-rendings, and facing the many dangers and difficulties'. [3] At about 5.00 p.m. the travellers, loaded with gifts which included a box containing two attractive albs from the Invercargill community and a framed portrait of the Bishop of Dunedin, set off by train for the harbour. According to a diary entry made soon afterwards emotions ran high when the time came to part:

*Another set of "goodbyes" began and some of the Sisters broke down terribly, especially Mother Dominick and Srs Clare [Sr Bonaventure's sister] and Genevieve. We passed out of the convent gate in torrents of rain. When we got into the cab, M. M. Gabriel began the Litany of the Blessed Virgin in order to stifle the sobs, which were now to be heard on all sides. When we were a little calm, there was consolation in the thought that now all the hard goodbyes were over. The station was crowded, all waiting to see the last of the Nuns. A good number came on to Bluff, but on reaching the Station they had to go back to the train as it was to return in a few minutes and there was no time to go to the boat. This was a great disappointment to the poor things. The boat did not leave Bluff till about 11.30 p.m. ...We retired very merry and so ended our second day out of the dear "Alma" [Mater].* [4]

At the harbour the Sisters boarded the SS *Mokoia* and due to the rough passage through the Foveaux Strait, most of the passengers fell ill and for a brief period Mother Gabriel was left to her own devices. By then she had recognised the sincerity of her companions' condition and did her best to comfort them:

*Went round administering Count Matter's remedies to Sisters; all very prostrate. As the day was wet and the sea rough, I lay down again; not sorry to rest; the fatigue of the last week's packing and the incessant farewells and heartaches having left us greatly exhausted. Visited the Sisters several times during the day – said Office and Rosary – ship rolling and pitching, very rough weather, still making way gallantly; went on deck half an hour before dinner, sent for Fr McKillop as I did not like to be seen alone. Well it was that I had him beside me when a man like the one whom St Augustine describes, came up and became very affectionate. Dined alone at our table then undressed, being well bumped about, while seeing after the Sisters and arranging packs. Sisters all better, but weak; slept soundly.* [5]

7. SS *Mokoia* en route to Australia

Mother Gabriel had her own problems to face, however, when a couple of sand flies invaded her cabin during the night and attacked both her hands and lips. Disfigured by the bites, she must have wondered how her sensitive skin would fare on the other side of Australia where sand flies were not uncommon. Sister di Pazzi Miscall, the youngest member of the Dominican party and the first to recover from seasickness, joined Mother Gabriel on deck early the next morning. A New Zealander by birth, Mary Josephine Miscall, was the youngest daughter of Timothy and Susan Miscall of Otago and a past student of St Dominic's College in Dunedin. She was endowed with a pleasant, bright personality, and was said to be possessed of a 'glorious voice'. Her versatile skills were well-known to the Prioress and senior members of the foundation group long before she was received into the community, and they were pleased when she volunteered to join the Greenough party. It was thought that her fragile health might be at risk in the changeable climate of Dunedin and when she was professed on 16 March 1899, a decision had already been made to send her to Greenough to enjoy a warmer climate. Sister di Pazzi's delicate state of health did not deter her from working long hours as a teacher in the goldfields, and her premature death, on 22 January 1915, devastated her companions and the West Australians whose lives she had influenced for 16 years. [6]

During the crossing from New Zealand to Tasmania, the Sisters employed their waking hours by saying the Office and Rosary, writing diaries and letters and becoming a captive audience for Father Donald MacKillop SJ when he told thrilling tales about his Australian experiences. Having spent nine years ministering to Aborigines in the Northern

Territory, Fr Donald MacKillop SJ, brother of the celebrated Mother Mary MacKillop (the foundress of the Sisters of St Joseph of the Sacred Heart), could not resist passing on titbits of local information he had picked up during his travels. He also informed the Dominican Sisters that Western Australia was sometimes referred to as 'the land of the Five S's – Sin, Sand, Sorrow, Sore Eyes and Sardines, and there were two patent remedies, sulphate of quinine and sulphate of zinc'.[7] Although the priest's remarks were probably offered in a light-hearted manner, it is true that conditions, particularly in many primitive mining towns where gambling, drinking, sorrow and sore eyes were part of pioneering life, it was not uncommon to find campsites littered with empty sardine tins and broken bottles.

Sisters di Ricci, Bonaventure and Gonzales and the postulant Kate were still being treated for seasickness when their companions first sighted the coast of Tasmania on Friday, 28 April 1899. By mid-afternoon the sea could not have been calmer and as the vessel passed Port Arthur and entered the Derwent Estuary, Mother Gabriel continued to record the day's events: 'Mt Wellington stands out gloriously, its summit rising broadly above the vapouring clouds which conceal its steep side from us. At 5 [p.m.] we pass close to the Good Shepherd Convent which is beautifully situated, on the slope of a hill. Our passengers (not numerous) are all assembled on deck anxious to see Hobart in the twilight'. [8] The ship sailed at 9.30 p.m. and as usual Mother Gabriel slept effortlessly through the night, only waking when the stewardess arrived with a cup of tea. 'Why is it that I always sleep so soundly at sea?', she wrote, 'I cannot account for this fact'. [9]

The Bass Strait unfortunately lived up to its reputation for rough weather, and as dark clouds gathered a sudden squall forced the captain to run for shelter. In spite of its brief duration, the Sisters admitted that, until the vessel reached the safety of Port Melbourne, the storm caused 'much misery and invocations to St Catherine of Siena'. [10] The Dominican party retired to the Home of the Good Shepherd in South Melbourne, where they stayed until 3 May 1899. Part of the first morning was spent inspecting the convent and schools belonging to the Sisters of the Faithful Companion. Mother Gabriel, accompanied by Sisters di Ricci, Dominica, Gonzales and Father O'Malley, later went into the city to Cook's Travel Bureau to book their passages on the SS *Pilbarra*. Having made an appointment to have Sister di Ricci Kirby's troublesome eye checked the following day, the Sisters then collected a chalice that had been ordered for the Greenough mission as a presentation gift from Mother Bertrand's sisters in New Zealand. While the Dominicans were in the store Father John Ryan, an old acquaintance, appeared and kindly offered to donate a set of cruets and a large missal for the community to take to Western Australia.

Mother Gabriel's intention to travel by boat from Melbourne was thrown into chaos when, after tea and prayers at the convent, she was summoned to the telephone to answer a call from Mr McCaughan, a gentleman with whom she was acquainted in New Zealand. Despite a torrential downpour of rain and the threat of further bad weather, he insisted on visiting that evening. Mother Gabriel later explained:

*He drove up about three-quarters of an hour later and seemed more delighted to see me than he had ever been before. He made many enquiries for N.Z. friends. I introduced him to Mother Assistant and my own 5 companions. When Mr McCaughan found that we had got our luggage transhipped to the "Pilbarra", he was quite vexed and insisted on our giving up the idea of going on by coastal steamer. I pleaded that we had been booked through from Dunedin to Geraldton. He still insisted that we should go by rail to Adelaide and promised to give me £10 if I would yield, but I told him that £10 would go but a little way towards tickets for seven passengers. He then said he would make a bargain with me if I would consent to go to Adelaide by rail and take a large steamer of the German line, the rest of the way, he would double the amount.* [11]

Sister di Ricci also commented on the change of plans in her own diary of events. In an entry dated 1 May she wrote: 'Mr McCaughan called to see Mother in the evening and when he heard that she was going by the "Pillborough" [Pilbarra] he said it was a most fearful boat to travel by – very bad accommodation, bad cooking, bad ventilation and rough fellow passengers. He entreated Mother to change the boat and told her if she persisted in going by it she would regret it all her life'. [12] Taking both his advice and the offer he made, Mother Gabriel arranged to call at the shipping office the next morning. It seems that the only difficulty to arise from the late change of plans was the uncertainty involved in securing berths at the reduced rate available for missionaries. With the help of Mr McCaughan, the Sisters' earlier bookings were cancelled and new tickets were issued. Arrangements were also made to have their luggage freighted by train across to South Australia instead of being transported by ship.

After completing their business in the city, the senior Sisters joined the remainder of the group for a meal at the Sisters of Charity Convent in East Melbourne. The Dominicans enjoyed the company of their fellow religious to such an extent that they overstayed their visit and almost forgot Sister di Ricci's medical appointment at 3.00 p.m. Unable to complete all their farewells, they managed to catch a tram back into the city and arrived to find the specialist waiting. Dr Kenny successfully operated on Sr di Ricci's troubled eye and, at Mother Gabriel's request, he also supplied a lotion that might later prevent any member of the group having to suffer from the 'sore eyes, so prevalent in the West'. It is perhaps of interest to note that Dr Daniel Kenny, a wealthy property investor and church benefactor, was once a prominent member of the Catholic Church in Perth. He had arrived in the western colony in 1885 and the following year married Kathleen, the daughter of controversial Irish lawyer, John Horgan.

The train for Adelaide finally left Melbourne on Wednesday, 3 May 1899. After checking that their luggage had arrived and was safely stored on board, the Sisters discovered that the three carriages allotted to them were 'roomy and airy' and surprisingly comfortable. Mr McCaughan, who was travelling on the same train, came in to see if they were happy with the new arrangements and was most attentive. Mother Gabriel and Sister Gonzales shared one compartment, the latter taking the upper berth, and Sisters di Ricci, Bonaventure, Dominica and di Pazzi were accommodated in another. A single berth, close to the facilities, was given to the young postulant Miss Kate Murphy.

Like Sisters di Pazzi Miscall and Bonaventure McEntyre, Sister Gonzales Wall was educated and professed in New Zealand. An experienced teacher, the former Maria Wall was born in Worcester, England, on 19 July 1865 and took her final vows in the Dominican Convent at Dunedin on 16 April 1884. It was said that she had a charming and approachable manner and was well-liked by both pupils and parents. For the short time that Sr Gonzales remained in the Geraldton diocese, she worked long hours and made a great contribution to the founding of two new communities. [13] Her companion, Sister Bonaventure McEntyre, came from the beautiful Lake Hayes district; an agricultural area hemmed in by snow-capped mountains and surrounded by rolling hills and deep valleys. Her memories of crystal-clear creeks and waterfalls must have contrasted greatly with the hot, dusty and unattractive mining backgrounds of the Dominican convents at Cue, Day Dawn and Leonora. Sister Bonaventure had received her education at St Dominic's Convent in Dunedin and entered the novitiate soon after leaving school. She was professed on 27 December 1891, and it would not have been possible for her then, or at any stage during the early establishment of the Greenough foundation, to have foreseen that she was destined to follow Mother Gabriel Gill as Prioress of the Dominican Order in Western Australia. [14]

The remaining members of the group, Sisters di Ricci Kirby and Dominica Murphy, were originally from Ireland. Ellen Kirby (Sr di Ricci), born in Limerick and professed at the age of 33 on 24 February 1859, at Sion Hill, was a foundation member of two overseas communities and not a young person when she volunteered to pioneer the Greenough foundation. She was the first Superior of St Catherine's Convent in Invercargill and at various times held the position of Mistress of Novices and Mistress of Schools. Her influential uncle, Dr Kirby, Archbishop of Ephesus, and for many years, Rector of the Irish College in Rome, not only took a personal interest in Sion Hill, but also in the Dominican foundations in New Zealand and Beaumont. [15] Sister Dominica Murphy, tall, athletic and a good horsewoman in her youth, was born at Ballinamona in Cashel, County Tipperary, and educated by the Presentation and Ursuline Sisters at Thurles. Always a deeply spiritual person, she was recruited as a postulant when Mother Gabriel Gill, a close relative, visited Ireland looking for suitable young ladies to join the New Zealand foundation. Sister Dominica entered the Dominican novitiate at Dunedin in 1887 and did not hesitate to offer her services when the new mission in Australia was organised. [16]

The travellers' welcome on arrival at Adelaide, although low-key, was well organised. Archpriest Nevin had two cabs standing by and he sent the Sisters to wait in them while he helped Mother Gabriel sort out the luggage. In the meantime, she had to convince the Excise Officer on duty that the party should be exempt from Customs Duty because they were in transit and did not intend to stay in South Australia. This explanation would not have been necessary had they passed through the border one year later, for Customs Duty between the former colonies was abolished after Federation. The Sisters from Dunedin were to be guests at the Cabra Convent at Clarence Park and as they approached the grounds the Dominican Prioress, Mother Columba and all the Sisters in residence, gave them a warm, enthusiastic welcome. Mother Gabriel Gill and her companions were impressed by their surroundings. The Dominican convent, set in 20 acres of land, possessed a beautiful chapel and the grounds featured wide, gravelled walkways and parklands made colourful with several flower beds containing chrysanthemums and trumpet lilies in bloom. Healthy grapevines lined some of the paths and the visitors were informed that, in season, the nuns and children had an endless supply of fruit. [17]

In a similar incident to that on the ship from New Zealand, Mother Gabriel had the misfortune to again suffer a strong reaction from an insect bite. She described the incident under the heading Friday Morning, 5 May: 'Last night my hand was terribly bitten in two places. The inflammation is going up my wrist...The sun is bright, but the air is a little chilly. M.P. [Mother Prioress] is doctoring my hand. She thinks no mosquito could inflict such wounds'. The following day Mother Gabriel wrote:

*Lovely like summer! Hand so stiff and swollen that I cannot hold anything; cheek bitten, sore and beginning to swell.*

*Mother Prioress and Sisters say that I must have been bitten by a spider, the tarantula, very feverish, several remedies tried. In the evening after 7.o'clock the door of the community room pushed open. S. M. di Pazzi rushes in, a sweeping brush and quikup in hand and in great excitement. She is followed by S. M. Bonaventure who carries a candle in one hand and a dustpan in the other. On the dustpan there is a large tarantula – dead. S. M. di Pazzi had executed it at the door of cell for my use as she was taking a guimpe out of the box!* [18]

The Sisters remained at Clarence Park for three weeks and in that time they were very much taken with their hostesses who did their utmost to please them. On Sunday, 7 May 1899, Father Nevin arranged for two cabs to take them to Mother Mary MacKillop's former convent in Franklin Street. The building had passed into Dominican hands in 1868, after Mother Mary of the Cross transferred her community to a small, four-roomed house next door. Although Mother Gabriel still suffered from a swollen eye and face; she was determined not to be treated as an invalid and joined the other Sisters in the cab. Kneeling on the exact spot where Mary MacKillop received Dr Sheil's excommunication, Mother Gabriel was deeply affected by the visit. She later wrote: 'I could not tear myself away so that all the others had time to go all through the House before I got out of my reverie'. [19]

The Dominicans left Cabra at noon on 22 May and, after bidding a fond farewell to the Sisters who had cared for them since their arrival, they revisited the Franklin Street Convent. The Dominican Sisters living there had thoughtfully invited the travellers to share an early dinner with them before they boarded the SS *Adelaide* for the voyage to Western Australia. Before the meal was over, however, Mother Gabriel was unexpectedly interrupted with the news that the ship had not arrived as scheduled and that embarkation would unfortunately be delayed until the following day. The information that they would not sail that day was not only disappointing, but in view of the fact that there were no vacant beds available at that particular convent, the news was also inconvenient. Although the visitors offered to seek accommodation elsewhere, the Superior, Mother Xavier, would not hear of it. Instead hasty arrangements were made for the New Zealand Sisters to spend their final night in South Australia with members of the Franklin Street community.

The Sisters left the Franklin Street community by cab the next morning in time to catch the 11.30 a.m. train to the wharf. Meanwhile, Kate Murphy had gone ahead to the dock with three of the Cabra boarders. The vessel set sail at 2.00 p.m. and accompanying the Sisters part way down the Gulf were Father Hedley OP, old friends Mrs James and Adelaide Primrose and the girls from Cabra, whose tickets had been paid for by Mrs James. Gifts were exchanged and, as usual, promises were made to keep in touch. Mother Gabriel noted later:

*We had passed Larg's Bay and were nearing Semaphore where a tender came out to take off the Excise Officer, Cook's Agent and our friends. It was hard to say a last Goodbye to those who had been constantly so kind to us during those 3 weeks. We had not been treated as passers-by, but as dear and old friends who are to continue friends while life lasts. What a lovely sunset! Still in sight of land; the hills along Spencer Gulf are pretty in outline. There was one part where a view of our boat steaming across the water could be seen from the windows of the Community Room at Cabra. I wonder are our dear Sisters watching for us? To my great delight when we came on board, we found my dear old friend, Mothers Gonzaga Barry, and S. M. Aloysius and S .M. Agatha. Father O'Farrell's cousin just arrived with another Loretto* nun, S. M. Veronica, a young Sister going to Perth. I gave Mother Barry a great Irish hug to Father Hedley's amusement. It was such a pleasure to meet her again and to find that she is a fellow traveller... We have a large table to ourselves.* [20]

A number of Sisters again experienced seasickness on the journey to Western Australia and kept mostly to their cabins, only occasionally braving the fresh air on deck. Two of the Loreto group, Mothers Gonzaga and Aloysius, were on visitation to the Perth community and the former, warmly wrapped up in an opossum rug with her new ear trumpet at the ready, spent much of the first evening chatting to Mother Gabriel. The women had a lot in common and the discussions and anecdotes they shared made the journey much more interesting. Even when Mother Gabriel suffered a violent headache, due to inflamed mosquito bites and lack of sleep, the two old friends continued to enjoy each other's company and watch with interest the different sea birds and mood changes of the ocean.

By 24 May 1899, they were halfway across the Great Australian Bight. 'The ocean', wrote Mother Gabriel the following day, 'is of an intense blue, with crested waves not high but closely chasing each other. There is a sportive look about the sea that I have not noticed since we set sail'. [21] Children accompanied many of the passengers and, according to Mother Gabriel, the younger ones made 'baby music' day and night. The lack of silence, however, did not deter the pair from holding long conversations on subjects ranging from predictions about life in Western Australia to 'educational matters'. To some degree, the Australian education system differed from New Zealand and no doubt Mother Gabriel would have been keen to make comparisons. She was interested to learn, for example, that Mother Gonzaga Barry considered the Cambridge method of education superior to all others. Mother Gabriel also recorded in her diary that her travelling companion informed her

*Loreto was spelt with two t's during the 19th century and early part of the 20th century

that, 'numbers of Loretto girls go in for the various University examinations and degrees. They are not required to attend the University classes or "Keep Term" as they do in N.Z. They are fully prepared in the Convents by the Nuns and the Lay Professors. The nuns prefer sending up all their higher classes for University exams and having Diocesan Inspectors visiting their High Schools'.[22]

Unfortunately the mosquitoes continued to plague Mother Gabriel during the night and after being repeatedly attacked on her face, hands, neck, arms and throat, she decided to move out of the cabin she shared with Sister Dominica and into the single cabin occupied by Kate Murphy. The shipping company had initially allocated the private berth to the Superior, who decided, however, to hand it over to the young postulant in case one of the professed nuns might not feel comfortable sharing a cabin with a lay person. The sudden exchange of sleeping quarters was obviously an immediate success, for there was no further mention of sleepless nights, winged insects and sensitive skin for the remainder of the trip. Nevertheless there must have been a great deal of concern expressed at times during the voyage as to whether the new climate would actually suit all of the pioneers.

The vessel passed through King George Sound and anchored in the harbour shortly before midnight. Excited by the realisation that they had at last reached Western Australia, Mother Gabriel, accompanied by Sisters Bonaventure, di Pazzi and the postulant Kate, remained up on deck until almost 1.00 a.m. to get a view of the township by midnight. On reaching Albany the Sisters sent a telegram to Dunedin announcing the safe arrival of the 'Kelly Gang'. They also dispatched a wire to the Ladies of the Mission requesting hospitality should the boat be delayed at Fremantle. Another message was forwarded to Sister Dominica Murphy's cousin in Perth, Mr Quinlan, asking him to meet them at the completion of their journey.

Prior to, and after the rounding of Cape Leeuwin, the seas became rough and the heavy swell once again brought down many of the passengers only just then beginning to recover from earlier bouts of seasickness. On Friday, 27 May 1899, SS *Adelaide* was only one day out of Fremantle when strong gale-force winds began to gain momentum. The heaving vessel began to pitch and toss as it tried to negotiate the deep troughs formed by the rising seas. Suddenly, without warning, the ship's propeller screw broke and the vessel gave a sudden fearful lurch. Even the stewards had difficulty in keeping their footing. Sister di Pazzi was thrown forward towards the side of the deck and, likewise, Mother Gabriel lost her balance and was badly injured. She was carried to the saloon and placed upon cushions arranged on the floor and was in such extreme pain that she could barely move or speak. Later moved to her cabin

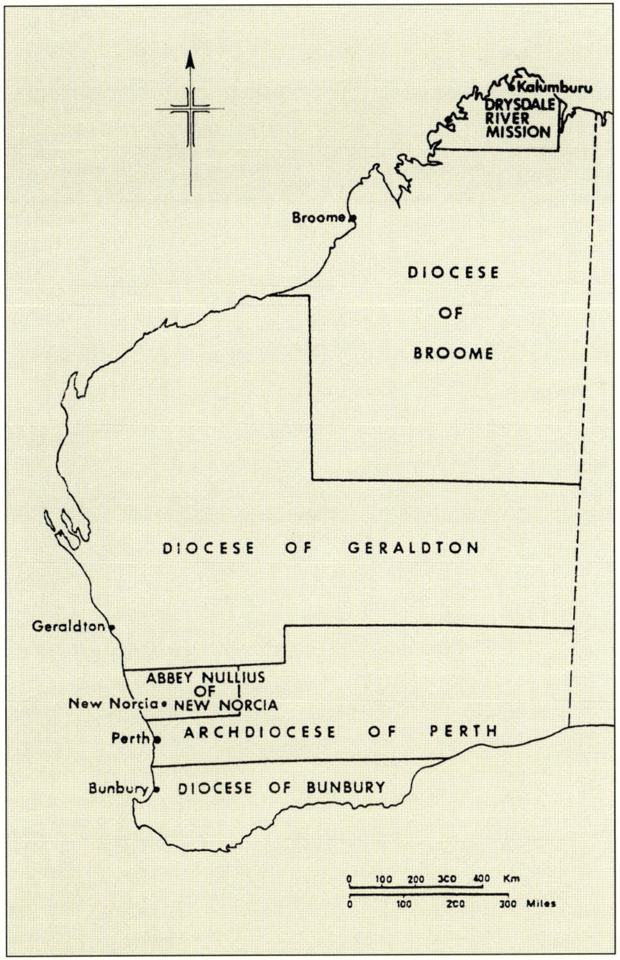


8. Western Australian Ecclesiastical Boundaries, 1969
Courtesy D.F Bourke

she spent the night in agony. At about 3.00 p.m. the following day, the pitching and rolling ceased and the seas became calm. To everyone's relief the SS *Adelaide* safely reached the port of Fremantle at 4.30 p.m. that same afternoon. [23]

As expected, Mr Quinlan was waiting to greet the Dominican Sisters, and with the exception of Mother Gabriel and Sister Dominica, who were taken to their destination by cab, the party walked to the nearby railway station where their escort purchased tickets to Perth. It was about 7.00 p.m. when they drove up to the Convent of Mercy in Victoria Square. A warm welcome awaited the weary travellers, and after Mother Gabriel had been made comfortable, a doctor was summoned to the convent to diagnose the extent of her injuries. It appears that she had sustained a slight injury under the shoulder blade and from the effects of the fall had also developed pleurisy. Acting on medical advice, the Dominican Superior spent a week recuperating in Perth. In retrospect, the enforced delay had certain advantages, for the group had been in transit since mid-April and probably needed time to adjust. During the week spent at Victoria Square, they met the Bishop of Perth, Dr Gibney, who kindly took them to visit their fellow passengers, the Loreto Sisters, as well as the Notre Dame Sisters at Highgate Hill. The Dominicans were also driven out to inspect the orphanage at Subiaco and whilst there heard the fascinating story about the building's original owners, the Benedictines, who had planted the grove of fig and olive trees. Unfortunately, Sister di Ricci was not overly impressed with Perth, which in her opinion was, 'all sand, nothing but sand', [24] a comment which must have reminded them of earlier remarks made by Father Donald MacKillop.

On 1 June 1899, Mother Gabriel was well enough to spend nearly all day on the convent balcony and three days later she was allowed to make a brief visit to the parish school where some 400 children were being instructed. The Dominicans were most impressed at the standard of education in Perth, and in particular the way the schools were conducted. Some of these observations were briefly recorded with the day's events: 'We were struck with the discipline and the nice manners of the children, free from bashfulness or forwardness. Impressed by the boarding school [Mercy] and Loreto Convent in Adelaide Terrace'. [25]

The Sisters retired early on 5 June, in preparation for the journey that would finally take them to Greenough. The day of departure was a typical winter's day with leaden skies and incessant rain. The party rose at 5.00 a.m., attended Mass at 6.00 a.m., and an hour later caught the train to Geraldton. Mother Gabriel Gill, Sisters Dominica Murphy, Gonzales Wall and di Ricci Kirby settled into one of the two carriages reserved for them and Sisters di Pazzi Miscall, Bonaventure McEntyre and postulate Kate Murphy were shown into the other. After making themselves comfortable, the Sisters dutifully said their devotions and spent the main part of the day dozing, reading and chatting.

The highlight of the train trip north was the anticipated appearance mid-way through the journey at Watheroo of the Bishop of Geraldton, William Kelly. The Dominican Sisters waited anxiously to meet him, wondering what sort of welcome they would receive now that they were under his jurisdiction. They need not have worried, for he warmly greeted Mother Gabriel and her companions and as Sister di Ricci later wrote, 'We were all taken by his cordial manner'. [26]

CHAPTER 3

# And They Came to the Greenough

It took 17 hours of train travel before the Dominican Sisters from New Zealand reached Geraldton, and considering Mother Gabriel's delicate state of health before leaving Perth, the hours spent confined in a carriage must have been rather tiring. The Sisters were met at the Geraldton railway station just after midnight on Tuesday, 6 June 1899, and, because of the lateness of the hour, they were escorted to the nearby Star of the Sea Convent, where a substantial meal was waiting for them. The original Presentation Convent, a large bungalow situated on the corner of Lewis Street and Marine Terrace, overlooked Champion Bay and the next morning the visitors would have had their first clear view of the ocean and the prominent line of white, pristine sand hills that extended along the northern coastline. The unimpressive convent building, surrounded by boxthorn and gorse rather than green grass and colourful gardens, would have contrasted greatly with New Zealand's glacial lakes and alpine beauty, all of which must have been still fresh in their minds.

The Dominican nuns, dressed in cream habits and cream scapulars, were different in appearance from the Brown Josephites and black-clad Sisters of Mercy and Presentation Sisters, who in turn had serviced the Catholic schools at Geraldton since 1883. No doubt they would have aroused the curiosity of passers-by that first morning as they left the Presentation Convent to inspect the Geraldton schools before paying a visit to the original seaside church of St Francis Xavier further along Marine Terrace. At 1.30 p.m. on Wednesday, 7 June 1899, the new arrivals set out from Geraldton on the final stage of their expedition. Mother Gabriel Gill, Sisters di Ricci Kirby, Gonzales Wall and di Pazzi Miscall occupied one carriage driven by Bishop Kelly and the remaining members of the group, Sisters Dominica Murphy, Bonaventure McEntyre and postulant Kate Murphy were taken on the 16 mile journey to the Greenough Flats by local identity Mr Englebrecht. Two priests, Fathers Ryan and Riordan, accompanied by a number of the bishop's friends, also joined the procession and, despite it being wintertime, the party left the outskirts of town and in splendid weather briskly set off through the peaceful countryside.[1]

The Sisters had previously heard mixed reports about the West Australian countryside and their spirits soared at the sight of so many green fields and again when they caught an occasional glimpse of blue sea between the dunes on their right. Despite a few anxious moments when the second buggy fell behind, while its driver extinguished a fire on one of the wheels, the drive proved to be most enjoyable. At various intervals along the route, riders on horseback and local families driving an assortment of vehicles joined the cavalcade. Some of the horsemen welcoming the newcomers rode up to join them at an alarming speed, and much to the nuns' amusement all the riders, with few exceptions, had beards and several young men had wild dandelions rakishly stuck into their hat bands. When the procession emerged from the row of low hills and entered the wide expanse of level ground known as 'the Flats', small groups of bystanders along the way began to shout, 'Three cheers for the Dominican nuns!'. It was estimated that by the time the Sisters reached the convent grounds the line of well-wishers was more than a mile long. [2]

The people from Greenough had gone to a great deal of trouble to welcome the newcomers. A lone flag fluttered high on the top of the local flour mill, and draped across numerous fence posts and roadside trees bright pennants and strips of bunting added a splash of colour to the gala occasion. A large green banner, displaying a golden harp, took up a prominent position in front of

Mr Goodwin's house and outside Mr Hackett's store a carefully prepared message, 'Welcome to Greenough', could not have failed to catch the attention of the Sisters as the carriages entered the settlement. Spanning the entrance to the convent grounds, parishioners had constructed a leafy triumphal archway from palm branches, and decorated the frame with large aloe and banksia flowers. Part of the design included a large green cross, an Australian flag and a streamer with suitable tidings. As the buggies came to a halt in the convent grounds and the Sisters approached their future home, they were finally confronted by the familiar Irish greeting *Caed Mille Failthe* on a sign attached to the schoolroom door.[3]

Representing the women of Greenough, a youthful Miss Reynolds read a carefully prepared address to the Sisters. The opening paragraph proudly announced, 'To us the wives, mothers and daughters of Greenough, is accorded the privilege of being the first to formally welcome the daughters of St Dominic to our midst. We have long prayed for this hour. From this humble little convent, the best home we can at present offer you, many blessings, we know, spiritual and temporal, will flow forth upon us and upon those dear to us'. [4]

Two Protestants, Messrs H. Hamersley and T. Clinch, then officially welcomed the new community on behalf of the local male population. Although Mother Gabriel admitted that it was not usual for nuns to speak in public,

9. Bishop Kelly and the Dominican Sisters, Greenough, 1899

10. Welcome to Greenough, June 1899
L.to R.: Bishop Kelly, (left back), Father Ryan, (centre), Father Riordan (right), Kate Murphy, M Gabriel, Sisters di Pazzi, di Ricci, Dominica, Gonzales and Bonaventure, Father Lecaille (2nd row, centre)

she responded briefly with a few well-chosen words. Thanking the people for their hospitality, she told the gathering that although the Sisters' main purpose in coming to the Geraldton diocese was to teach the children, they would also be happy at any time to instruct or counsel people of more advanced years.

During Bishop Kelly's address, he reminded those present that the Dominican Sisters had sacrificed a great deal when they accepted his invitation to Western Australia and severed ties with New Zealand. After pleading with the residents to take a personal interest in their future, he then proceeded to introduce various individuals to Mother Gabriel and her assistant, Sister di Ricci. Members of the religious community were quick to observe that the majority of people in attendance were good-natured, hard-working country folk, unsophisticated and extremely provincial with an old-fashioned habit of curtseying to people considered above their station. It was obvious that most would never aspire to higher education or be interested in studying the arts and languages, and it must have crossed Mother Gabriel's mind that a paucity of pupils would put the survival of the new foundation at risk.

A beautifully-prepared meal had been organised in the gaily-decorated schoolroom for the people in attendance.

The Sisters' rule, however, prevented them from eating in public so one of the rooms in the convent was set up for their convenience. Bishop Kelly, meanwhile, had arranged for well-known Geraldton photographer, Mr de Lucey, to record the great occasion. Fortunately several clear photographs of the historic event have survived the passage of time. One of these includes a group of residents and their children posing on the front verandah of the convent with Mother Gabriel Gill, holding a half-hidden bouquet of flowers, together with Sisters Gonzales Wall, di Ricci Kirby, di Pazzi Miscall, Dominica Murphy and Bonaventure McEntyre, Bishop Kelly and Fathers Ryan, Lecaille and Riordan. On Wednesday, 7 June 1899, the day the Dominican community took possession of the Holy Rosary Convent in Greenough, Sister di Pazzi Miscall described their new dwelling:

*We are all agreeably surprised at the appearance of the convent. It is a well built stone house containing 5 rooms besides the long school room which is attached to the Convent and a large galvanised iron kitchen which is built apart from the house. We have two good, large rooms and three small ones. A verandah runs all round the house. A corridor or passage goes right through the centre and the rooms open off this on either side. It is a very good house for a beginning but, of course, we find it very small after our own dear home. We were delighted to get into bed and have a good sleep for we were very tired. Mother di Ricci, S. M. Gonzales and Bonaventure and self all sleep in one large room and M. M. Gabriel and S. M. Dominica in another – while Kate's bed is lodged each night in the school room and carried away each morning.* [5]

Bishop Kelly remained in the hamlet for several days, offering support and giving assistance when needed. He dined at the convent, but because there was no permanent resident priest or presbytery at Greenough, he slept in a small room attached to the side of the original St Peter's Church. From the beginning, the Sisters spoke enthusiastically about their new bishop and, despite earlier warnings that they might find him stiff and lacking in warmth, they continued to be impressed by his kindness and ease of manner. After celebrating Mass the morning after the Sisters' arrival, the bishop took on the role of tradesman and as he hammered away, fitting shelves into packing cases to form cupboards, the nuns opened and sorted out the trunks brought with them from New Zealand. In the afternoon, Dr Kelly drove Mother Gabriel and Sisters di Ricci, Gonzales and Dominica out to the Back Flats to show them the tiny school they would later open at Bradley's Crossing. 'I don't see what more he could do for us than he has done', Sister di Pazzi confided in her diary.[6] The remainder of the first weekend was spent getting the house in order – unpacking, cooking and covering a number of wooden boxes with cretonne to act as seats in the parlour and music room, and making preparation for the opening of the school.

There had been two earlier attempts to establish a convent at Greenough. In 1889, a foundation stone was laid adjacent to St Thomas's chapel in the Back Flats for a proposed convent and boarding school intended for the Sisters of St Joseph of the Sacred Heart. When the building did not eventuate, the money raised towards it was transferred to central Greenough and on Sunday, 11 February 1894, the foundation stone of the present convent was laid and blessed by Father O'Reilly. For a number of reasons the building erected by Geraldton builders, Messrs Whitmore, was not fully completed for another five years and was then only finished because the Dominican Sisters were expected in June 1899. [7] On that occasion a busy-bee was organised and local volunteers handled most of the renovations. St Joseph's Dominican School, Greenough, consisted of a long schoolroom under the main roof of the convent, with stone walls 24 inches thick and an exceptionally high-raked ceiling. The door used by the pupils faced onto the road and led directly into the grounds. Later, when the Presentation Sisters took over the school and renamed it St Peter's, this well-proportioned schoolroom became a dormitory for boarders.

Although St Joseph's School opened for classes as planned on Monday, 12 June 1899, it was decided that St Thomas's, the second Dominican school, would not begin until 19 June, as it involved the Sisters travelling each day by horse and sulky to the Back Flats. [8] After saying Mass at 7.00 a.m., Bishop Kelly joined the Dominican community for breakfast, and, prior to the start of school, he assembled the Sisters and presided over the election of councillors. Sister Gonzales was appointed First Councillor and Sister Dominica was named Second Councillor and, as a result, both joined the Prioress, Mother Gabriel and the sub-Prioress, Sister di Ricci Kirby, to form the 'Mothers of Council'. The group held its first meeting eight days after the Holy Rosary Convent was established and besides appointing Sr Gonzales as the community's Procuratrix (bursar), a number of important issues were discussed during the initial proceedings.[9]

When lessons commenced at 10.00 a.m. on 12 June, the Dominican Sisters could barely curb their disappointment when only 11 children turned up for classes. The low number contrasted greatly with the enrolments made a month earlier at Northampton when, at Bishop Kelly's request, the Presentation Sisters opened a similar school in that town. In view of the constant clamouring for nuns by Greenough residents, the bishop found the situation at St Joseph's difficult to accept. 'It was extremely dull 7 of us walking about doing nothing. Bishop sat in school, greater part of the day, looking very dull', [10] wrote Sister di Pazzi after her first day at school. In the meantime, Mother Gabriel Gill, with her usual calm, presented every child with Rosary beads and each pupil in turn received the bishop's blessing. Many years later, Mr Jim Clune, a staunch supporter of the nuns, related one of the many entertaining incidents experienced by the Sisters during their first weeks in the hamlet:

*Mother Dominica, told me herself that the first days in school [Back Flats] in the West resembled a Comic Opera. She had expected to be confronted by a class of little children on her first day in school, but among the pupils she saw also old men with long beards and bare feet – strange combination – and it was a difficult business to keep serious. Above the beards were moustaches that extended like trans-Atlantic cables from one side of the room to the other, but behind the beards and moustaches were kindly faces, appreciative smiles and noble hearts.*[11]

Wednesday, 14 June, brought a slight increase in the number of enrolments at St Joseph's, and the Sisters were further encouraged by the promise of more pupils in the near future. At the same time the new community was confronted by a far more pressing problem, when one of the Sisters mentioned at breakfast the next day that the convent larder was empty.

It soon became obvious that, without some sort of providential intervention, they would have to forego dinner. The group must have been greatly relieved when Ivy Leverman presented them with some fish, nicely prepared by her married sister. The Sisters were equally delighted when Ned Goodwin delivered a piece of pork and, for the first time since their arrival, they were able to have a meal that included meat. Among the many visitors to pay their respects that day was a clergyman's wife, Mrs Wilkins, who had brought her Catholic servant to the convent for instruction. Realising that the Sisters' current financial position was a matter of some concern, she advised Mother Gabriel to hold a concert and a sale-of-work in aid of the school. When Mr Reynolds delivered a new piano later that day, the future began to look somewhat brighter, for it meant that the Dominican community was in a position to accept their first music pupil, Miss Hilda Dennison.[12]

A severe storm and high winds prevented the scheduled opening of St Thomas's School on Monday, 19 June 1899, and following the bishop's instructions, the Sisters did not venture out. Instead, Bishop Kelly and Mother Gabriel set off for the Back Flats the next morning in Mr Goodwin's buggy, while Sisters Dominica and Gonzales bravely took charge of the convent buggy. The six mile journey, however, turned into a mini-drama when the vehicle driven by the two Sisters got stuck on the road. Not only did the convent horse 'Rosie' refuse to budge, but when the bishop got out to assist, his own horse started to move off without him. Mother Gabriel, left on her own in the buggy, and obviously no horsewoman, began to panic. The amusing episode was briefly described in Sister di Pazzi's diary:

*Mother was terrified and called out, "My Lord", "Bishop", "Dr Kelly". At last they all reached The Flats in safety. Thirteen children to begin with. Mrs Silcock provided a good lunch. Bishop carried over the cups and saucers himself in a swag across his shoulders. Sr Gonzales said she would rather ride inside a horse than outside. Great fun over it. Bishop immensely amused. We three rather lonely at home.* [13]

This was the first of many daily journeys taken across the sand plains to St Thomas's. Two months after the Dominican Sisters opened the Rosary Convent in Greenough, they requested the bishop's permission to also conduct catechism classes after Sunday Mass at the North Back Flats. To provide this service at St John's Church in Bootenal, it was again necessary to drive the convent buggy over badly-formed country roads. Sometimes, when Sister di Pazzi took Mother Gabriel out to give the children instruction, the two would call on certain acquaintances and invariably ended up with gifts of farm produce to supplement the larder. Unquestionably, their greater presence in the district gradually attracted more support for their community and, as a result, parents were encouraged to enrol their children in one of the two existing Dominican schools. Sister Gonzales Wall, who eventually returned to New Zealand, later recalled her own impressions of the daily journey she took across the limestone ridge to St Thomas's:

*The weariness of the daily drive to and from the school had many compensations, the children were most responsive to the Sisters' instructions, their fresh innocent minds receiving eagerly every impression, and they were overjoyed at the coming of the Nuns among them. The scenic beauty and richness of vegetation in this fertile spot was also a great delight, the track leading as it did through beautiful native bush where bright plumaged birds and exquisite flowers abounded. In the early morning when the flowers glistened with dew, when the birds gossiped in the trees and wild turkeys came screeching by, these happy things made time pass all too quickly, and one could forgive the snail pace of good "Little Rosie" especially when a vista of the ocean came into view...Once in while, a stray camel from the goldfields would wander into these solitudes, and then the lazy pony would excel the finest racer in the country, leaving the driver no choice of roads and only stopping when a network of foliage stopped her mad career. She did not mind a stray snake or an iguana [goanna] crossing the track, but she drew the line at camels.* [14]

Towards the end of June, the State School on the opposite side of the road ceased operation, and on Monday, 31 June 1899, all the desks and benches were removed leaving the building deserted. [15] The sudden decision to

11. Holy Rosary Convent, Greenough, 1899. St Joseph's School to right

close the government school obviously worked in favour of the Dominicans for, within two months of their arrival, 38 pupils had enrolled at St Joseph's and a further 29 boys and girls at St Thomas's. Unfortunately, the Sisters had to contend with a great deal of absenteeism throughout the year and pupil numbers fluctuated, influenced by weather conditions or whether extra help was needed at home or on the farm. On 28 June, for example, only five children attended school. All arrived soaking wet and part of the Sister's duty involved drying off their shoes and stockings and making them comfortable. Among the first pupils taught by the Dominican Sisters, in 1899, were May Kemp, Esther and Walter Bishop, Gertrude Leverman, Harriet Reynolds, May Morrell, Hilda Dennison, Willie and Joseph Duplex, Dora Waldeck, Charles and Ethel Sims, Walter Bell and several children from the Bickley and Wiley families. On 30 June, two music pupils, Mr and Mrs Clinch, registered for private violin and pianoforte lessons and the tuition fees paid by them helped augment the Sisters' overhead expenses.[16]

The fact that the majority of farmers living in the once-flourishing district had their own financial problems, made the timing of the Dominican foundation inauspicious. At the height of its popularity, Greenough had a population of some 2000 persons, and although the size of the average allotment was inclined to be too small, the district had a wheat yield that was the envy of many other localities. Adverse seasons, the ruination of crops from pests and rust disease, as well as a damaging flood in 1888, had heralded a decline in prosperity and increased unemployment. The discovery of gold, therefore, enticed many of the young men working in the area to try their hand at prospecting, and a large percentage of them never returned to the hamlet. Although many parents throughout these troubled times continued to supply the convent with meat, fish, poultry, butter, eggs, vegetables, fruit, bread, milk, chaff and other provisions in lieu of school fees, the barter system was often spasmodic. Residents in a position to donate money usually did so with a specific purchase in mind, such as Mrs Rayner who gave the Sisters 12 shillings during the foundation year to buy a map for the schoolroom.

Bishop Kelly occasionally sent, or brought out, a leg of mutton, bottles of raspberry vinegar and gifts of jam or chillies, as well as plants and seeds for the garden. Nevertheless, there were times when the nuns were reduced to having one egg and no meat with which to provide a meal for themselves, let alone visiting clergy. On the occasion of Sister Bonaventure McEntyre's feast day, the first such event to be celebrated in Western Australia, the bishop came out with cherries for a pie and he stayed to share in the celebrations. Despite the many hardships the Sisters had to endure, life at Greenough was not all gloom and after completing their daily duties the group sometimes enjoyed a number of pastimes. Some of their happiest recreational activities included gathering wildflowers, teaching Bishop Kelly the art of woodcarving (which they excelled at), discussing current political topics such as the move towards Federation, creating and reciting poetry and singing in the evening, either solo or in a group, often with Mother Gabriel as accompanist. [17]

The Geraldton diocese had only been established 12 months prior to the Dominican Sisters' arrival, and the bishop was still familiarising himself with the enormous territory he had to administer. In an unusual move, he chose to make Cue his episcopal headquarters, rather than Geraldton. This decision was influenced by the fact that a large proportion of his flock at that time lived on the Murchison goldfields. Catholic education was, as always, a prime consideration and Bishop Kelly let it be known that he expected the Dominican Sisters to found a second house sooner, rather than later. At a Dominican council meeting held on 1 July 1899, it was unanimously decided that once their own foundation was better-established the Sisters would be willing to accept another mission. It was also agreed that before taking on an extra responsibility, Mother Gabriel would enquire if the Sisters at Dunedin were in a position to spare either postulants or professed Sisters for the Western Australian mission.[18]

12. Mother Gabriel Gill and Sister Philomena McGrath gathering wildflowers
Courtesy Dominican Sisters, N.Z.

Whilst visiting Greenough to celebrate Sister Bonaventure's feast day on 14 July, the bishop remained after dinner to sketch a plan of the convent he intended to build at Cue. His powers of persuasion were successful for, obviously inspired by his enthusiasm, both Sister di Pazzi and Sister Bonaventure stayed up until 1.30 a.m. improving the design and making further suggestions. During the few days he spent in Greenough, Bishop Kelly also organised minor alterations to the convent in an attempt to make life easier for members of the Dominican community. Certainly the Sisters appeared delighted when Mr Hackett completed a new laundry for them on 12 July, which they light-heartedly nicknamed 'St Edwards' after him. Six days later, Mr Englebrecht, plasterer and plumber, began work on a new stable and discussions took place regarding the possibility of extending the main building. By then, Mother Gabriel was aware that conditions in Greenough were not ideal for the type of boarding school she had envisaged. A contemporary later voiced the opinion that 'Greenough was not what Mother Gabriel and the Sisters expected. To establish a large convent and boarding school they wanted tone [class] and all they had was an acre of rocky ground and a collection of tiny rooms, no better than dog boxes'.[19]

Because the railway from Perth to Geraldton had been constructed via Walkaway and Narngulu, instead of through central Greenough as planned, stores had to be railed to Walkaway and then transported four to six miles to the convent. Travel arrangements, plus the immediate need to provide additional accommodation to attract boarders to the school at Greenough, were two of the items discussed by Mother Gabriel when she reassembled the Council on 23 July. The current layout of the convent was examined and the possibility of extending the building was raised. Due to the community's financial circumstances at the time, it was obvious that any immediate extensions would have to be produced on a moderate scale. The question of funding was, at that time, a major problem and members of the Council decided that they really had only two choices to consider. The preferred option was to approach the bishop to arrange a loan and the second, and less attractive proposition, was to request assistance from the mother house at Dunedin.[20]

Advertisements listing the wide range of subjects taught at St Joseph's, Greenough, appeared regularly in the *Catholic Record*. The course embraced all of the government school syllabus, plus elementary school book-keeping, Euclid, algebra, domestic economy and shorthand. Subjects taught in the high school were the same as in the elementary school with extra tuition in piano, violin, theory of music, harmony, singing, drawing, painting, wood carving, needlework, paper flower making, wax flower and fruit modelling, literature and languages (French, Latin, German and Italian). Pupils were also prepared for civil service, music and university examinations.[21] School concerts had become part of the way of life for religious groups trying to raise funds to establish missions in Australia, and the residents of small towns, particularly mining centres, found them a great source of family entertainment.

The Dominican Sisters had been in Greenough less than two months when they organised a concert, on 26 July 1899, in aid of the new convent. The evening's entertainment, which netted a profit of £20, drew one of the largest crowds ever seen on the Flats. A rather lengthy program was provided and among the contributors were members of several well-known pioneer families: Mesdames A. Clinch, Rowe and Whitfield, Misses Wedlow, Leverman and B. Criddle, Messrs Clinch, Cramer, Lucas, S. Maley, J. Maley and Brennan. The items were well-received and Mr Thomas Clinch JP officially closed the evening praising the participants and the 'highly qualified Sisters' responsible for the event.[22]

The original small stone St Peter's Church, begun by Father McCabe on swampy Crown land close to the Greenough cemetery, and completed by Father Lecaille on 12 May 1867, stood half a mile from the Dominican Convent along a dusty road. It was unusual for an enclosed religious community to wander along a public thoroughfare to attend a church service; however, it seems that few people in Greenough ventured out before dawn on a winter's morning and the nuns practically had the road to themselves. On returning from Mass on 4 August, the Feast of St Dominic, Mother Gabriel wrote: 'It is a strange, but real missionary experience to be walking along the middle of a lonely road with green fields stretching along both sides, in the dark, chilly morning. Sometimes we have bright moonlight, sometimes we can barely see our way'. [23]

Mass was not said every Sunday and during the weeks when the usual clergyman was not in attendance, the Sisters had to rely on visiting clergy to perform a service. Although Father Lecaille's main residence was in the Greenough hamlet, his religious duties were widespread and he was often away. Unfortunately, when he did return to the small room he used next to St Peter's Church, his sense of timing was not always reliable when it came to early morning Mass.

Reverend Adolphus Lecaille, Belgian by birth, and inclined to be unpredictable, had a lasting affinity with the Greenough district and from his base at St Peter's he played a significant role in the development of churches and religious schools in the Victoria District. This feisty, but exemplary, priest was well-known to the Dominican Sisters, who, although they admired him, rarely managed to gauge his mood swings. For example, Father Lecaille walked into the Rosary Convent early on Sunday morning, 23 July 1899, and whilst the occupants were saying their Office he announced, without warning, that he intended to say Mass and later take charge of the Blessed Sacrament which had been left in their care. One of the Sisters present recorded in her journal: 'our fears about the Blessed Sacrament were soon realized and left us without our dear Lord. At the end of Mass he turned round and gave us the most awful lecture for disrespect etc. and said he would not give us back the Blessed Sacrament. The same sermon was repeated in St Peter's public church to the people. This was our saddest day since we left Dunedin'. [24]

Two months later, the nuns walked down to St Peter's at 6.00 a.m. only to find Father Lecaille frying bacon for his breakfast. Obviously not in a gracious mood, he refused to say Mass or hear Confession at that hour and the disappointed Sisters finally turned around and retraced their steps. Within a fortnight they again set out for St Peter's, intending to attend early Mass and, although according to their own clock they had arrived on time, they were amazed to find that the priest was well and truly half-way through the liturgy. At least they received Holy Communion and the following morning Fr Lecaille made sure that he rang the church bell at twenty minutes past six, so that members of the community would know the correct time by his clock. These incidents were in contrast to the many acts of kindness he generally displayed to parishioners and the two very pleasant hours he spent with the Sisters after one disappointing encounter, when he patiently explained in detail the history of the diocese complete with dates and descriptions of the chief events. [25]

The tireless, hard-working Father Lecaille, who once expressed his feelings for the hamlet in the oft repeated quote: 'I belong to the Greenough and the Greenough belongs to me',[26] carried an enormous workload. It is therefore possible that stressful conditions caused him to become impatient and at times irascible. During Fr Lecaille's early missionary work, a fellow priest described some of his amazing achievements:

*He was insensible to fatigue, morally and physically fearless. He swam flooded rivers, walked trackless bush, was in the saddle for distances of 80 to 100 miles a day. It was customary on Christmas Day to celebrate first Mass at Northampton, a second 33 miles away at Geraldton and a third 16 miles away in Greenough. Riding through summer heat whilst necessarily fasting. Lecaille was a builder of churches, none of them impressive, but all of them functional.* [27]

During the absence of a priest, the Sisters often felt obliged to perform parish duties normally outside their sphere. The fact that they sometimes presided over public prayers on Sundays caused one local identity to raise the status of the Prioress to that of priest by informing others that 'Mother Gabriel said Mass'. Apart from giving religious instruction on weekends, the Sisters also provided comfort to parents in other devotional-type areas. On 25 June 1899, Mother Gabriel dedicated the first infant in the district to Our Blessed Lady and the following month she organised the inaugural meeting of the Children of Mary in Greenough. There were three girls present and the postulant Kate Murphy was later elected president. On 14 January 1900, the Feast of the Holy Name of Jesus, Bishop Kelly officially received foundation members, the Misses Maria and Martha Reynolds, Frances and Ivy Leverman and Nora Silcock into the Association of Mary Immaculate.

The rare occasions when the Sisters had time to spare were spent improving the convent grounds and making religious stocks and mending vestments for priests involved in the mission. On the practical side, and much to the household's delight, the convent fowls laid the first egg on 5 August 1899, and at about that time the Sisters happily announced that they would be giving their first painting lessons to Miss Grace Maley and Mrs Whitfield. In addition, Miss Criddle had also arranged to be taught singing. Besides attempting to grow a row of cherry trees, Sisters Dominica, Bonaventure and di Pazzi planted pepper trees in an effort to protect the convent from the strong south-west winds. Other improvements included the construction, by Mr Reynolds and Mr Doyle, of a fence surrounding a new paddock acquired by Bishop Kelly a few weeks earlier. [28]

The two Greenough Sisters driving daily to and from the Back Flats were aware that accidents could easily occur on the rough bush tracks. Some six weeks after the opening of St Thomas's School the convent buggy nearly overturned when 'Rosie', their horse, shied after an encounter with a stray camel. Left without the use of a vehicle whilst the broken spring was being repaired, the teachers were obliged to travel to school each day in Mr Hackett's hearse. On a less serious note, Sisters Gonzales, Dominica and di Pazzi, obviously on good terms with their superiors, decided one day to play a prank on Mother Gabriel Gill and Sister di Ricci Kirby. When the senior Sisters returned from giving catechism lessons at St John's, Bootenal, the three younger women sprang out from behind the convent door, dressed in lay clothes and armed with a revolver, axe and knife used by Bishop Kelly for hunting wild turkeys. Unfortunately the end result of the escapade was not recorded. Continuing in her role as practical joker, Sr di Pazzi one day picked up a dead snake, brought to school by Grace Maley, a pupil, and 'coiled it up on the parlor floor to frighten Mother'. [29] Perhaps by today's standards the sorts of jokes they played were not very original, but at least they showed that the Sisters were human enough to introduce a bit of light-hearted humour into their otherwise regimented lives. The occasional inter-play between the Sisters also revealed that a friendly, home-like conventual lifestyle existed within the Greenough community.

During the Sisters' first September in Western Australia, members of the community were kept busy organising a number of extra activities. On the first of the month Bishop Kelly, accompanied by Perth architect, Edgar Jerome Henderson, came out to Greenough to confirm a group of local children. Mr Henderson had arranged to stay with local identity Mr Ned Goodwin, whilst he examined practical ways to extend the convent. The confirmation ceremony was held at St Peter's on 2 September, but first the bishop said Mass for the Dominican community in St Joseph's schoolroom. Later the nuns attended to a number of young pupils who arrived to have their white veils and wreaths arranged before setting out for the church. The procession along the road to St Peter's was meant to be a special event. However, an unexpected deluge of rain practically ruined the occasion and the children and their teachers were forced to sit through the ceremony wet, bedraggled and decidedly uncomfortable. That same evening, Bishop Kelly and Mr Henderson shared tea in the parlour at the Rosary Convent and, for the first time since their arrival, the Sisters were able to participate in Benediction. After the meal, an anxious Mother Gabriel gave Mr Henderson a gentle hint that she wanted to see the bishop alone on business and, according to Sister di Pazzi's diary entry, the remainder of the evening turned out to be a mixture of business and amusement. The 22-year-old diarist appears to have been somewhat of a character and her flippant use of the word 'parliament' to describe the Dominican Council meetings was only one of many examples that revealed a keen sense of humour:

*Then Parliament sat in [the] Community room and Sr Bonaventure and I got our walking papers. We said our office in the parlor, then began to sing "All Hail Zealandia" and "God Defend New Zealand". Mother told Bishop what we were at and so Bishop sent for us when business was over. Sr Gonzales put her foot in it by telling B. [bishop] about the poetry we had composed. He insisted on seeing it and after a great fuss we sang it for him, of course leaving out certain parts. He was immensely amused and left about 10 o'clock. Asked Mother today to wash his rochet and mend his silk cassock.* [30]

At 10.00 a.m. on 3 September 1899, the combined schools of St Joseph and St Thomas held an entertainment morning at the Greenough convent. Everyone was said to be 'in a state of fuss and excitement' and according to Sister di Pazzi, 'the children all came dressed to kill'. [31] Vehicles transporting the Back Flatters to Central Greenough unfortunately became bogged in loose sand and, as a result, a number of parents and friends arrived an hour late. Despite this set-back, the program proceeded smoothly and when Bishop Kelly, followed by local identity Mr Clinch and architect Mr Henderson, later addressed the audience, each praised the Dominican Sisters and their pupils for the standard of work they had achieved in such a short space of time. The function concluded with an invitation to tea and cakes and, to the children's delight, the bishop generously distributed sweets to all the participants.

During their brief stay at Greenough, Bishop Kelly and Mr Henderson became involved in a variety of domestic tasks. These included planting the trees they had brought out with them from Geraldton and organising a number of necessary improvements to the convent property. On 7 September, the construction of a stone wall commenced and five days later two new water tanks arrived in the hamlet ready for installation. Unhappily, the earlier recommendation to build a new convent and extend the existing building for use as a boarding school had to be set aside when Mother Gabriel failed to raise a loan from Dunedin. The reasons given for the refusal were practical. The Dominican Council in New Zealand unanimously agreed that the mother house at Dunedin could not afford to take on an additional debt, particularly when they were of the opinion that any move to erect a larger boarding school at Greenough would be premature and might not be viable. Instead, Bishop Kelly approved minor alterations to the convent, as well as a new children's dormitory which was scheduled to be completed before school opened towards the end of January 1900. It seems, however, that alternative sleeping accommodation was arranged, for there is no evidence to suggest that major structural changes took place to the stone-built convent which still contains the original number of rooms. Sister Anastasia Byrne, who was received into the Dominican community at Greenough on 4 February 1901 and survived well into her 90s, later recalled that 'a house next door to the Greenough convent was used for boarders during the Dominicans stay'.[32]

There was an immediate reaction to the community's decision to provide extra boarding facilities, when two days after Bishop Kelly left Greenough Mr Morrissey, a pastoralist, arrived from Yalgoo and not only enrolled his son as a boarder, but made a 10 shilling donation to the Sisters. Many Catholics living in the Geraldton diocese, including the Dominican Sisters themselves, must have been puzzled to read an article published in the *Catholic Record* on 9 September 1899. The newspaper informed its readers: 'We understand that it is probable that a branch of the Greenough Convent will be opened in Roebourne when reinforcements of nuns arrive'. Whether the reporter made a mistake and meant Cue, or whether it was wishful thinking on the part of Bishop Kelly, is not clear. In fact, the Bishop of Geraldton returned to Cue on 15 September and continued to press ahead with plans to establish a religious foundation in that town. He was already aware that, in August, the Dominican Council in Dunedin had granted permission for Mother Gabriel to found a convent and school at Cue, provided that at least three Sisters formed the new community. [33] Totally ignoring the fact that the Dominicans were understaffed, Bishop Kelly sent a telegram to the Rosary Convent on Tuesday, 19 September, expecting to receive a speedy response. The message read: 'Cue school to open immediately. When will nuns be ready to go?'. Mother Gabriel, obviously anxious to please, did not disappoint the bishop and a wire was dispatched soon afterwards containing two words only: 'Next week!' [34] The day after he received her reply, Bishop Kelly wrote to thank 'his gang' for the small bookstand they had made for him, adding that he valued it more than a mass of diamonds because it was the handiwork of 'his own good brave little Dominicans'. [35]

The next few days passed swiftly for the close-knit group of Sisters who, although they knew a parting was inevitable in the future, were taken by surprise at the sudden decision. Certainly the thought of their beloved Mother Gabriel and Sister Gonzales leaving the Rosary Convent and living some 263 miles by railway from Geraldton was at first difficult to accept by those remaining at Greenough. At the same time, the two Sisters about to establish the first Dominican branch house in Western Australia would have been excited at the prospect of joining Bishop Kelly, for according to extant diaries they had immense admiration for him and felt comforted by his presence. With diminished expectations of a successful future at Greenough, Mother Gabriel possibly also considered that she might have a better chance of opening a larger boarding and day school in a town that was rapidly attracting a growing goldfields population.

The Sisters' final days in the convent were spent making preparations for the journey and on their last Friday together, 22 September 1899, the rule of silence was lifted at breakfast as a special privilege. That afternoon, the Sisters teaching at the Back Flats came home early to find the washerwoman ironing and packing and Mother Gabriel and Sister Gonzales completing their own private sorting. The travellers left Greenough on Sunday, 24 September, their luggage having been transported to Geraldton the day before by Mr Hackett. Mother Gabriel appeared not the slightest bit perturbed about the long journey, for Bishop Kelly had earlier wired to inform her that all arrangements had been made to meet the Sisters en route. On the morning following their departure, a lonely Sister di Pazzi recorded:

*Only four at breakfast seemed so lonely. Kate went off to B. Flats with Sr Dominica. Hilda [Dennison, a pupil] brought us her birthday presents to show us and also a tin of cakes. We tried to do up the house a bit. M. M. di Ricci moved to our dormitory and we curtained her off. Mr Hackett came and hung up the framed address in the parlour and we put an oil painting as a fire screen in the grate. Kate took possession of the music room and sleeping apartment. Mother Gabriel will have reached Cue by this time and met bishop.* [36]

A telegram sent by Mother Gabriel Gill, on 27 September, informed the Greenough community that both Sisters had arrived safely and a request was also made to have the *Teachers' Manual* forwarded by post. In the meantime, Sister di Ricci was appointed to act as local Superior at Greenough in place of Mother Gabriel and Sister Gonzales became Procuratrix and Mistress of Boarders at Cue. The extra workload shared by the Sisters still living in the hamlet gave them little time to dwell on the loss of their companions and, except for a number of minor adjustments, life continued as before. Tolerance, however, was a requirement the Sisters needed in abundance as visitors, not realising they were short-staffed, frequently called in to the convent during school hours. Unexpected interruptions often broke into their busy schedules, but, no matter how inconvenient the hindrance, the Sisters were always gracious hosts. A week after Mother Gabriel left Greenough, the Sisters were sitting down for lunch in the convent when they heard a pounding on the schoolroom door. On inspection Sister Bonaventure found Father Riordan waiting to retrieve the key to the tabernacle. Unfortunately, locating it was no easy task, and by the time he left they were forced to answer another knock on the convent door. Imagine their consternation when they found Father Ryan and an acquaintance, Mr O'Dea, standing on the doorstep expecting to be invited in for a meal. 'The thought of having to get lunch for them was too awful', wrote Sister Pazzi, 'There was nothing in the house except a bone of cold meat with hardly anything on it and only two eggs. Whilst we were in this predicament, Mr Goodwin came to the back door with a dozen eggs. We scraped the bone of the meat and together with the eggs made some kind of lunch'. [37] The men did not leave until 2.30 p.m., which meant that a good part of the day was unproductive.

Conversation at the evening meal that night would not have been difficult, for when Sister Dominica returned home from St Thomas's she was full of the 'queer experiences' she had encountered that day. She had not only feared that her horse would panic when it sighted two camels on the way to school that morning, but she was startled to discover a snake curled up beside the school door. Finally, to add more pressure to an already stressful day, two lizards (or scorpions) fell from the roof onto the middle of the floor during lunch recess. Of course such an occurrence was not unusual at that time of the year, for with the approach of warmer weather, snakes, and such like, were beginning to awaken and were on the prowl for food. For newcomers, experiencing their first Australian summer in the bush, the need to be constantly on guard must have made the settling down period so much more difficult. Unfortunately, an overactive imagination was just one of the many pitfalls to be endured. In early October, a frightened Sister Bonaventure became convinced that a snake had nestled in the corner of the convent kitchen. Helpless, she called a young local girl, Mary Buckley, to kill the intruder only to discover, to her mortification, that the so-called serpent was simply a piece of dry wood. [38]

Within a few weeks of joining Bishop Kelly on the Murchison goldfields, both Mother Gabriel and Sister Gonzales revealed that they were experiencing a certain amount of disquiet about some of the 'horrors of Cue'. In her enthusiasm to accept the bishop's invitation to establish a branch house, the Prioress had probably not anticipated his frequent absences from the gold centre and the loss of his personal support and guidance. Confronted by intense heat, dust storms and a rampant influenza epidemic, the convent near the coast at Greenough must have seemed extremely attractive by comparison. Mother Gabriel's impaired health and disappointment was reflected in the correspondence received by the Greenough Sisters throughout October. The news from Cue caused a great deal of anxiety and this was heightened on 19 October, when the new Superior of the Rosary Convent, Sister di Ricci Kirby, received a telegram suggesting that far from improving, the difficulties at the new mission were worsening. With the bishop's anticipated return to his headquarters on the camel train in mid-November the contents of the letters sent from Cue became decidedly more cheerful. It was a relieved Greenough community that learned that Mother Gabriel's health had improved to the point where an offer to send Kate Murphy to assist was no longer considered necessary.

In 1899, the Dominicans were the only religious teaching order in the Geraldton diocese working so far from the coast and their questionable health was a growing concern, particularly when it was discovered that Sister Gonzales had developed a severe eye problem. Diagnosed as a painful abscess, the affliction not only affected her ability to teach, but put her in danger of suffering permanent eye damage. Despite these complications and the brief time in which they had to prepare an entertaining program, the Sisters ended the school year by presenting a successful annual concert on 15 December. A welcome respite from the bustling mining centre to recuperate and assemble the 'Mothers of Council', more than justified the long train trip and expense involved when the two Dominican Sisters returned to Greenough for the Christmas holidays.

By the middle of November 1899, arrangements were well in hand for the first combined Dominican schools' annual concert and distribution of prizes in Greenough. On inspection, the stage at St Catherine's Hall, situated opposite the convent, was found to be too small and inclined to be rather 'rickety'. So, for obvious reasons, Sister di Ricci asked Mr Hackett and Mr Clinch to enlarge and strengthen the platform. A full dress rehearsal held on 27 November, two days before the concert, went smoothly and the Sisters were delighted to learn that the bishop would be arriving from Cue in time to attend the evening's function. Members of the Dominican community, who, because of their rule of enclosure, were not able to participate in public entertainment, had worked hard and long to make the evening a success and they were bitterly disappointed when the lead-up to the day in question was marred by a totally unrelated incident.

Though fatherly in his approach and extremely supportive of the Dominican Sisters, Bishop Kelly had his temperamental moments when matters didn't go according to plan. As with some of his confreres, the Bishop of Geraldton's behaviour was sometimes less than gracious when he dealt with members of the Presentation and Dominican religious teaching orders over which he, as bishop, had jurisdiction. The Sisters taught school as usual on the day of the concert, but allowed the pupils to leave at midday. They then scrubbed the verandah, converted the music room into a dining room for the expected arrival of Bishop Kelly and Father Ryan and spent the rest of the afternoon preparing for their guests who were expected for a meal at 5.00 p.m. Living as they were, in a rather relaxed atmosphere, the nuns, who aimed to please, were obviously unaware that they would upset the menfolk by changing conventual procedure. Sister di Pazzi later explained the commotion caused when the community disregarded one of the Dominican rules and entertained guests in a room other than the convent parlour:

*Bishop was his old self until it came to teatime and then oh! Didn't one pay for asking himself and Fr Ryan into music room for tea! A real case of "What about your rule Sister?" Would take tea nowhere except in [the] parlour and was very much displeased – sat at tea in dead silence – no one spoke for ever so long – went as soon after 6 o'c as he could possibly get away – children all began to come in for concert. We were so miserable that we hardly knew what to do or say to them. Sent them all down to the Hall at about 7.30 and then the four of us sat down in bitter disappointment and talked over the events of the evening. We could hear nothing of the concert on account of the wind, but at intervals Miss Waldeck and Miss Leverman came up and told us that they were getting on splendidly. We said Office and all night prayers. Mother went to bed and we waited up for Kate. She did not come till about 12.30; gave us very gratifying accounts of the concert. Retired at 2 a.m.* [39]

The Sisters were overjoyed to discover that the concert was also a financial success and that their efforts had raised the sum of £27. No school classes were held the following day and after Mass at 7.30 a.m. a humble Sister Dominica managed to persuade the bishop to enter the convent for an egg flip. Breakfast was to be no better than the meal the night before. It was eaten in complete silence and the concert was never mentioned. Without displaying even the slightest sign of goodwill, the bishop abruptly left the premises to inspect a building site, before harnessing the horses and leaving the hamlet. The remainder of the day proved to be no happier. 'Fr Ryan wild about everything – gave out hot and strong; vowed he would never again enter a Convent as long as he was in the Diocese. Spent a very miserable day', stated an entry written by Sister di Pazzi on 30 November. [40] Seven days later, all was forgiven. The bishop drove up to the gate, enjoyed tea in the parlour, chatted until late and made every effort to be pleasant. The following morning, after breakfast, he drove Sister Dominica and Kate Murphy out to St Thomas's and returned to the convent for dinner at 4.30 p.m. He then joined the others at recreation in the new paddock and, after having a swing, invited the Sisters to join him for a picnic at the seaside during the Christmas holidays.

The Dominicans' first introduction to a West Australian summer could not have been more trying. On Sunday, 10 December 1899, an extremely hot land breeze developed and the temperature soared to 101 degrees Fahrenheit in the shade. Accustomed to a cooler climate, the nuns found the sudden heat oppressive. 'Sr Bonaventure and I divested ourselves of every article of clothing, except one and still we were hot', penned Sister di Pazzi in the midst of the heat wave. [41] By 12 December, the thermometer had climbed another nine degrees and except for an occasional break in the weather, the high temperatures continued to plague the community for most of the summer. Sleeping was difficult and, as was evidenced by remarks made in January 1900, the Sister in charge of cooking for the community had to be flexible with her menus, 'today very hot, all the fresh meat went bad. High temperature recorded 109 degrees in the shade'. [42] Once acclimatised, the majority of the Sisters appeared to be happy and over the years quite a number of them found that they benefited from the warmer climate and open-air lifestyle.

Mother Gabriel Gill and Sister Gonzales Wall finally returned to Greenough on 20 December, where an excited and busy community awaited their arrival. Apart from preparing for the visitors and completing school commitments for 1899, members of the Greenough community were also faced with an exceptionally heavy schedule. Not only had Bishop Kelly arrived once more in the hamlet, but also a building contractor and tradesmen had commenced work on new extensions. Nothing, though, took precedence over the arrival of the Prioress and her companion. According to Sister di Pazzi, 'they drove up in great style about 2 o'clock – Mother looked terribly thin. Sr Gonzales looked grand. All took dinner together in community room, then sat on [the] verandah'. [43] The following day, Mother Gabriel assembled the members of the Council to discuss important issues involving the administration of the community. During this session the Council unanimously agreed to accept an unprofessed lay Sister and two other aspirants who had offered to join the Western Australian mission. All were accepted, but only one of these, Sister Gerard (Catherine Milligan), who eventually arrived some six months after her profession at Dunedin on 15 August 1900, appears to have remained. The possibility of staff changes was also raised and, in the light of future revelations, it is highly likely that the Dominican Sisters would have discussed the fragile situation that had begun to develop between Bishop Kelly and the Presentation Sisters about the rule of enclosure. [44]

By the end of 1899, Bishop Kelly was pleased with the number of major achievements he had managed to accomplish during his first 16 months in office. As well as establishing a new diocese and introducing the Dominican Order to Western Australia, he had sanctioned the opening of new foundations at Northampton, Greenough and Cue. With so many pressing demands from Catholic families to provide more schools in mining centres, the bishop was anxious to acquire additional religious to fulfil these obligations. He had earlier granted the Dominican Sisters permission to adopt a simpler form of enclosure which in essence meant that Mother Gabriel and members of her community could: (i) publicly attend Mass at St Peter's Church in Central Greenough; (ii) drive daily to and from St Thomas's School at the Back Flats to teach; (iii) attend the dying and also instruct, in their own homes, those Catholics who had habitually neglected Mass and the Sacraments; (iv) teach the Christine Doctrine at St John's, Bootenal, on one or two Sundays in the month. The bishop also granted the Sisters leave to hold a sale-of-work during the St Patrick's Day celebrations and also gave permission for the Sisters to accompany pupils on occasional excursions to the nearby bush or seaside.[45] The dispensation given by the bishop was renewed annually until 1941, when the status of the congregation was declared pontifical.

At the turn of the century there were eight Catholic churches, seven priests, six schools and 20 religious Sisters teaching a total of 429 pupils in the Geraldton diocese. [46] A rapid rise in population, due to increased development in the agricultural, pastoral and mining districts, continued to put further pressure on Bishop Kelly to extend Catholic education. To do this he needed more than one religious group to establish branch houses, and so he decided that during his *ad limina* visit to Rome he would clarify the canonical status of the Presentation Sisters with regard to the rule of visitation and enclosure. The bishop threatened that if the Geraldton Presentation Sisters were not prepared to accept dispensation from enclosure then, on his return, he would bring the Dominican Sisters in from Greenough to take charge of their schools. [47]

By early 1901, there were seven superior school students and 24 mixed elementary pupils (boys and girls) enrolled at St Joseph's in Greenough, 22 mixed elementary school pupils at St Thomas's on the Back Flats, and at St Gabriel's Dominican Convent in Cue there were 21 enrolled superior school students and 72 mixed elementary pupils. During the same period, the Presentation boarding and day schools at Geraldton had on their school roll 35 superior school students, 85 girls in elementary school and 52 boys in elementary school. Likewise, enrolled at their second boarding and day school at Northampton were 15 superior school students and 73 elementary mixed pupils. [48] The prospect of being placed in charge of such a promising foundation must have been an attractive proposition for the newly-established Dominicans, who, at that stage, lacked numbers, proper accommodation and the scope to extend their considerable talents.

On 3 January 1900, Bishop Kelly invited the Dominican Sisters to join him for a picnic down at the mouth of the Greenough River. The weather was perfect when they set out at about 10 in the morning. Sisters di Ricci and Bonaventure took the convent buggy and the bishop drove Mother Gabriel and Sisters Gonzaga, Dominica and di Pazzi in a larger vehicle. The party reached the picnic spot at midday and before sitting down to lunch the bishop and Ned Goodwin set the fishing nets. Part of the day was spent shooting and fishing and before leaving for home at 5.30 p.m., Mr Goodwin and a relaxed Bishop Kelly boiled the billy for tea. Sunburnt, despite being well-covered by their long habits, the nuns were delighted with the pleasant outing and were further amused by the bishop who, in a jolly mood, sang most of the way home. Reluctant to see an end to the day he joined the community for supper and left at about 10.00 p.m.

On the following morning it was a different story. Bishop Kelly said Mass at 8.00 a.m., breakfasted at 9.00 a.m., then heard confessions and chopped wood for the convent before saying his Office in the paddock down by the swing. Then, for no apparent reason, his mood changed and not only was the atmosphere at dinner unpleasant, but he refused the Sisters' request that he give them a retreat. For the next six days they were miserable. With peeling faces from their day at the river and no expectations of a retreat they were surprised when Bishop Kelly, a familiar figure in white pith helmet, drove up to the convent and informed them that he had decided to give them a retreat from 11 to 13 January. The Sisters were overjoyed with his unexpected change of mind, although the bishop's later news that he would be departing for Rome with Dr Corbett in early February came as a complete shock. Before leaving Greenough, Bishop Kelly organised a second picnic to be held on 15 January. It was to be a farewell gathering before he left Western Australia for Europe and he sent a telegram to the Presentation Sisters in Geraldton suggesting that they might like to join him and the Dominican party for a picnic lunch. [49]

When Mother Gabriel set off from Greenough on Friday, 17 January 1900, en route to Cue, she took with her Sisters Dominica Murphy and Bonaventure McEntyre. (Sister Gonzales did not return to the goldfields.) At the time, preparations were being made at the Rosary Convent to admit two boarders from Geraldton and as it happened these young ladies, the Misses Elsie Dunne and Agnes Stone, were the first Dominican students to be accommodated in the newly-completed dormitory. On Thursday, 25 January, the Sisters spent a large part of the day getting the children's sleeping quarters in order and Bishop Kelly, who proved himself useful, came out to sit with them whilst they made up the beds. They were most impressed by the fact that the Bishop of Geraldton later offered to hold the dirty candlestick for them whilst they prepared the final touches to the room. [50]

On 11 February 1900, Bishop William Kelly sailed for Rome and during his absence popular Father Joseph Ryan, a huge young man weighing every bit of 20 stone and noted for his booming voice and love of anecdotes, became co-administrator of the Geraldton diocese. Like so many St Patrick's Day celebrations held in towns where there was a preponderance of Irish Catholics, the event held at the Back Flats on Saturday, 17 March 1900, provided a day of pleasure for people of all ages, different creeds and mixed backgrounds. A large crowd gathered early in the morning to take part in a monster picnic and sports day organised by a select committee representing the whole locality. The green flag of Erin with gold harp and shamrock flew proudly overhead and practically every second person present wore a green harp or bow on their clothing. A stall in aid of the Dominican Sisters was kept constantly busy and during the morning convent pupils sang and recited selected pieces of poetry between some of the sporting events. Tiny pupils from St Thomas's School performed a charming and colourful maypole dance and loud applause broke out when residents from the Back Flats defeated the men from Central Greenough in a popular tug-of-war. Typical for those days, the tables groaned under the weight of jellies, blancmanges, dainty cakes, home-made preserves, meat (mainly fowl) and fresh fruit. [51]

The first Trinity College of London Instrumental and Vocal Music Examinations were held at the Greenough Convent on 18 August 1900, when Mr Myles Birkett Foster examined candidates: E. Dunn, E. Kelly, G. Clinch, H. Dennison, V. Fienbery, E. Hamersley, F. Hamersley, G. Maley, V. Ryan and A. Stone. Having had less than 12 months to tutor the children, who in some cases had only limited musical talent, the Sisters and parents must have been delighted by the successful results. [52] Two days after the music examinations, the West Australian Dominican Congregation suffered a serious set-back when the Superior of the Holy Rosary Convent, Mother di Ricci Kirby, often referred to by her many pupils as the 'Little Mother', and the foundation's first postulant, Miss Kate Murphy, suddenly returned to New Zealand.

At 6.00 p.m. on 20 August 1900, Mr Hackett arrived at the Greenough convent to drive the Dominican Sister and former postulant to the railway station at Walkaway. They had not gone more than a few miles when Mother di Ricci Kirby realised that they had left without money to pay for the tickets. The driver had no choice, therefore, but to return to the convent and whilst Mother di Ricci held 'Rosie', Mr Hackett was sent to the hall door to arrange for the fare. By the time they reached the station it had turned quite dark and, leaving Mother di Ricci to wait for them at the hotel, Mr Hackett and Kate continued on to the nearby ticket office. Unfortunately, they had a long wait for the train and, after their driver left to return home, local landowner Mr Hamersley, who lived in the vicinity of Walkaway, entertained the two women with amusing tales about his early life in the colony. He took his leave half an hour before the train's departure at 10.30 p.m. and before saying farewell he presented Mother di Ricci with an attractive carved sandalwood cross and gave Kate a bunch of flowers. Another gentleman, Mr McCartney, lit their way to the Post Mistress's office with lamps and eventually saw them on to the train, where they were given a reserved compartment in Second Class thanks to the Station Master. Once settled, the pair lowered the shutters and made themselves comfortable. Mother di Ricci removed her headgear, put on her night coif and wrapped a shawl and rug around her before stretching out on the seat in order to sleep. [53]

The travellers were met at the Perth railway station the following day by a Gerald and Mrs Kelly and, after cloaking their luggage, were put into a cab and driven to the Convent of Mercy at Victoria Square. By all accounts it appears that the two former members of the Greenough community had made a rather hasty departure. No tickets appeared to have been purchased in advance, which meant that not only did the two women run the risk of not getting suitable berths on the dates required, but time was wasted unnecessarily in contacting agents and arranging for tickets to be collected. Mother Dolores, who opened the door at the Victoria Square Convent in Perth, was said to be 'thunderstruck at seeing them again'. [54] Later, after a warm welcome and meal, Kate was taken across to the boarding school for the night and Mother di Ricci paid a visit to the Superior of the convent. Mother Benedict, who at the time was suffering from a cold, was apparently delighted to see the Dominican nun. Her timely arrival she explained, 'was an angel's visit to cheer the poor Sisters, who were one and all much fretted, having a few days previously got intimation from the Bishop [Gibney] that all their houses were to become independent'. [55]

They spent several hours together and during that time the Superior admitted that 'she knew all about the [enclosure] affairs at Geraldton, past and present'. [56] Although brief, Mother di Ricci's stay in Perth was both interesting and restful. Father Keogh called to see her, after first telephoning several convents to discover her whereabouts, and later Mrs Boladeras, who had connections with the Victoria District, visited. The former member of the Greenough community was also pleased to meet Dr Birkitt, personal doctor to the Sisters of Mercy, who made a special point of asking after Mother Gabriel and Sister Gonzales. Soon after their arrival arrangements were made for an agent to secure train tickets to Albany and also to provide letters for the steamship company representative in that town and in Melbourne. Before their departure Mother Dolores slipped a sovereign into the Dominican Sister's hand and thoughtfully paid the cab fare.

Following several unfortunate mishaps with the luggage and a slight fall on the staircase leading onto the Albany platform, Mother di Ricci was once again met by the Kellys, who not only escorted them to the train, but provided a basket of food to stave off hunger during the long journey south. Despite the rain, Mother di Ricci and Kate's last view of the Western Australian landscape left them with pleasant memories. 'The countryside was covered with wildflowers', wrote Mother di Ricci, 'and nearing Albany clusters of Lily of the Vale were growing wild in all directions'. The passengers boarded the SS *Orizaba* on Friday, 24 August, en route to Melbourne and according to the Sister's account in her short journal of events, the homeward trip was far from relaxing:

**Sunday 26** *Kate very ill, night rough, very little sleep, all the noise of machinery heard in cabin – not much hope of rest on "Orizaba".* **Monday, 27 August 1900** *...While travelling wear night coif and forehead band with black veil hanging over like Presentation nuns...Reached Adelaide about 5 p.m. The boat anchored some distance from wharf...The evening beautifully calm moonlight night, remained on deck until 9 o'c., then retired to Cabin to try to get some sleep while boat was still – no use, so much noise. About 11 p.m. we were off again.* **29 Wednesday** *Reached Melbourne at one – were expected by the Loretto nuns at 10.00 p.m. We drove to Albert Park; several nuns met us in the hall & gave us a warm welcome.* **6 September 1900** *Left Convent at 10.30. Drove to the "Lalune". Got selves and traps on board. We thought it so small and stuffy...Our cabins were near the screw [propeller] so the whole night the head was jumping on pillow. After one or two nights* *of this I told the Stewardess and she kindly changed our cabins...Had a splendid run to Hobart which we reached at 5.00 a.m.* **Wednesday, 12 September 1900** *After breakfast on deck first glance of New Zealand shores, fancy my feelings! All day on deck.* [57]

It is not known why Mother di Ricci returned to Dunedin. Certainly she was not young and in view of the fact that she suffered from asthma, the climate may not have suited her particular ailment. On the other hand, because Mother Gabriel, her long-time companion and head of the Dominican community, lived so far away at Cue, the altercation about the future of the Geraldton schools, which reached its peak during 1900, might have placed unwelcome pressure on Mother di Ricci as local Superior at Greenough. Later, for health reasons, Sister Gonzales Wall, who remained behind for a time with Sister di Pazzi Miscall, also returned to Dunedin and, until reinforcements arrived, the loss of yet another foundation member put the communities at Greenough and Cue at risk. Mother di Ricci Kirby, who eventually succeeded Mother Benignus O'Connor as Superior at Cromwell in Central Otago, celebrated her Golden Jubilee in New Zealand in 1909. In answer to the many kind messages sent to her by the Dominican Sisters in Western Australia she wrote: 'If I were some years under 72, how joyfully would my health and strength be spent for the precious souls in the West, but I must be content now with praying for them. What a beautiful new church in dear old Greenough. My heart turns to the old spot – our first home in the West'. [58] Mother di Ricci's death occurred in New Zealand in May 1915 and Sister Gonzales, a native of Dunedin, died in her hometown in October 1940.

By the end of 1900, the Sisters were in a slightly better position to stage a larger and more impressive annual school concert than in the year of their arrival. The evening's entertainment, which featured a 17-item program, was held at St Catherine's Hall, Greenough, on 7 November 1900. It was well-attended and long before it was scheduled to begin a large number of people began to muster in front of the hall. Seating was again a problem. Tickets had quickly sold out and by the time the doors opened some 200 people were queuing for chairs. The curtain rose on 60 youthful, smiling faces and it was soon obvious that the concert would prove a resounding success, both financially and from an entertainment point of view. A large group of girls in the opening scene wore white dresses with coloured sashes – pink to represent St Joseph's and the green for St Thomas's. The nuns, who trained the pupils and arranged the program, which included musical items, recitations and plays, had also made some of the costumes. Among the many juvenile contributors that night were the Misses Ryan, Clinch and Hamersley who gave top-class classical music performances before an appreciative audience.

Father Ryan acted as chairman throughout the evening, as Mr Hugh Hamersley, who was to be chairman, was unavoidably late. Listed among the items on the program was the overture 'Marche aux Flambeaux', by Scotsom Clark; a recitation, *Papa's Letter*, by 8-year-old May Kemp; a scene from *Macbeth* acted by the Misses Waldeck, Boladeras and Kennedy. A delightful gavotte, 'The Greenough Buds', performed by the junior pupils of St Joseph's School proved popular and a piano solo by Miss H. Hennison preceded a dramatic performance, *The Silent Woman*, involving fledgling actresses, the Misses Waldeck, Dennison and Cope. At the conclusion of a 10-minute interval the entertainment continued and during the final segment two items brought the house down. The first, 'The Lilies of Killarney', performed by pupils from the Back Flats, was a song and dance routine and the second, a comedy sketch entitled 'Exhibition Time' prepared by the boys of St Joseph, was reported to be 'equal to anything yet seen on the Greenough stage'. [59]

The Sisters also held an exhibition of the children's work on 21 December 1900, when paintings, drawings, fancy needlework, and various other fine arts were put on view in the schoolroom. Miss Waldeck revealed a more than usual talent with her panels in oils, featuring flamingoes and herons amongst grasses and reeds, and delicate wildflowers. There was little space between the artistic display of water-colour landscapes, crayon drawings of birds and fauna, cushions of many designs, including appliqué, French embroidery, Eblana and Mount Mellick, as well as examples of bead work and panels in arascene lilies and palm leaves. The main contributors, the Misses Kennedy, Maley, Waldeck, Stone, Dennison, Ryan, Leverman, Boladeras, Eakins, Kelly, Clinch, Cope, Casserly, North and Hamersley, were delighted by their parents' response and the event reinforced the local belief that at last Greenough had acquired its own cultural centre in the form of a convent school. [60]

Towards the end of 1900, Father Ryan decided not to wait for Bishop Kelly's return in February to settle the matter of enclosure and the schools. Consequently, he issued an ultimatum to the Presentation Sisters in Geraldton. They were to reconsider their stand on visitation or leave the diocese. Rather than lose the schools that they had maintained for eight years in Geraldton, the Sisters chose to divide the existing community into two groups. Those in favour of keeping enclosure established a separate foundation at Northampton and the remainder of the community, under a new Superior, accepted simple vows and retained control of their foundation in Geraldton. Having been led to believe that they might shortly assume control of Catholic education in the Victoria District, the Dominican Sisters must have felt a certain amount of disappointment at being left with just Greenough and Cue. This series of events was the catalyst that prompted the Dominican community's transfer to Dongara where they later established a fine Priory and a significant boarding and day college for young ladies.

Bishop Kelly came back to Western Australia aboard SS *Frederick der Grosse* on 11 February 1901 and soon afterwards returned to the Murchison. By then Mother Gabriel Gill had accepted life in the goldfields and continued to reside at Cue with Sister Bonaventure McEntyre, returning only to Greenough for holidays and to attend special Council meetings and important religious ceremonies. The work begun by the Dominican Sisters in the Geraldton diocese was originally undertaken on the understanding that reinforcements would be sent from Dunedin, whenever they could be spared. Unfortunately, few local girls entered the convent during the foundation years and it was far too expensive an exercise to recruit postulants from Ireland. The majority of early pioneer Sisters therefore, had some connection with the mother house in New Zealand.

The first local postulant, Miss Kate Kenny (Sr Catherine), entered the Rosary Convent, Greenough, on 27 December 1900, and was received into the community on 4 February 1901. Her father James, a Geraldton town gaoler, and his well-known brother H. E. Kenny MLA were highly-respected members of the Catholic community and loyal supporters of the Sisters. When novices entered the convent it was customary to enter the type and amount of goods and clothing they brought with them in a 'Book of Postulants' Effects'. If they left the order then these items were returned. In Miss Kenny's case she brought with her a mattress, pillow, pair of blankets, quilt, rug, four pillow cases, two pairs of sheets, four towels, four pairs of stockings, shoes, boots, slippers, three sets of collars and cuffs, underclothing, petticoats, three black aprons, two white aprons, six handkerchiefs, black dress, mackintosh, pair of gloves, writing material, work box, box of paints and a watch. Postulants then signed a form, in accordance with Article 243 of the Constitutions of the Congregation of the Dominican Sisters of Western Australia, promising that they would not claim any remuneration for services rendered during the time of probation. [61] Kate Kenny completed her novitiate training at Dongara and, in 1903, became the first professed Dominican born in Western Australia. A hard-working, earnest member of the community she taught at Dongara, Cue, Leonora, Gwalia and, for a time, was Superior at Day Dawn.

Several other postulants were received with Sister Catherine Kenny on 4 February 1901, at a ceremony performed by Father Ryan, administrator of the diocese, assisted by the future Archbishop of Perth, Father Clune CSSR, at the Rosary Convent in Greenough. Miss Annie Byrne (Sr Anastasia) came from Oamaru, New Zealand, and after taking her final vows at Dongara on 28 January 1903, she taught for the next 30 years at Cue, Day Dawn, Leonora, Meekatharra, Three Springs and Dongara. She was a talented artist in charcoal, oils and water colour and had a fine reputation as a speech, drama and music teacher. Dunedin-born, Miss Minnie Ross (Sr Anthony), was received at the same time, but left before making her profession. In 1901, Sister Philomena McGrath, who was professed at Dunedin some 10 years earlier, also joined the community. Accompanying her were Sister Gerard Milligan, a lay Sister who had been accepted the year before but waited to be professed before leaving New Zealand, and another talented artist, Sister Mary Kaveney, who sadly died in December that same year after displaying symptoms of tuberculosis. In August 1901, Sister Ceslaus Freed was also welcomed as a member and, considering that the new foundation was just then being established at Dongara, her arrival in Western Australia could not have come at a better time.

In order to make wider use of the highly-qualified skills they possessed in languages, fine arts and music, the Sisters began to plan a larger boarding school for girls in a neighbouring coastal town. The town of Dongara was considered to be an ideal choice, with easy access to railway transport for boarders and a healthy seaside atmosphere. The first move towards establishing the new Dominican foundation took place in July 1901, when a group of senior boarders were transferred from St Joseph's in Greenough to a rented house at Dongara. The first advertisement announcing the opening of St Dominick's Ladies' College appeared on 17 August 1901, and although publicity for the Dominican boarding and day school at Greenough continued until the beginning of 1902, the size of the notices became much smaller from 7 September onwards. [62]

Prior to their departure, the Sisters staged an Annual School Concert in December 1901. Held as usual in St Catherine's Hall, the event was a joint effort between the pupils of the two Dominican schools in Greenough. Some 250 persons took their seats in the hall which had been tastefully decorated with flowers and greenery by the convent boarders, some of whom returned from Dongara for the occasion. Among the participants were Maud Bishop, May Corbett, May Kemp, Vera Fienberg, Maud and Darkie Ryan, Queenie Grills, Gerty Clinch, Vera Eakins, Dick Woolhouse, Mary, Clarrie and Tony Ryan, Ivy Leverman, Ruby Miller and two members of the Hamersley family. At the conclusion of the concert, refreshments were handed out and dancing continued until the 'wee small hours of the morning'. [63]

In February 1902, the Presentation Sisters from Geraldton took possession of the Rosary Convent at Greenough as well as the two former Dominican schools, St Joseph's (renamed St Peter's) and St Thomas's. This arrangement meant that no child was inconvenienced by the changeover and that parents in the Victoria District had the choice of enrolling their children as boarders at Greenough, Dongara, Geraldton and Northampton. By the close of 1903, the number of Dominican religious in the community had increased to 17 and the Sisters had opened new schools at Day Dawn, Gwalia and Leonora. Seven Dominican Sisters lived at Dongara, five resided at Cue and another five Sisters at Leonora. At that stage the diocese had 20 churches, 10 priests, 44 nuns, five boarding schools, 10 elementary schools and there were a total of 521 children being taught in Catholic schools. [64]

The historic Greenough hamlet situated on the Front Flats, 24 kilometres south of Geraldton, has since been classified as a conservation area and restoration is gradually taking place on buildings assessed by the National Trust as being worthy of heritage listing. Today tourists can wander over the convict-built bridge and from its stone walls can trace the path of the Greenough River and visualise the extent of, and the havoc caused by, a number of disastrous floods. For a small fee, one can visit many of the places once familiar to Mother Gabriel Gill and her band of pioneers. On view is the four-roomed cottage erected on Stoney Hill by one of the nuns' chief assistants, Ned Hackett – carpenter, undertaker, general storekeeper and sometime driver for the nuns. Goodwin's cottage became St Peter's School after the Presentation Sisters took over the foundation and converted the former Dominican schoolroom into a dormitory. Still standing is St Catherine's Hall, once the mecca for many of the district's social occasions. The Rosary Convent building has remained much as it was a century ago, when Mother Gabriel Gill and Sisters di Ricci Kirby, Dominica Murphy, Gonzales Wall, Bonaventure McEntyre and di Pazzi Miscall, accompanied by the smartly dressed Miss Kate Murphy, drove into the grounds to be greeted so warmly by the people of Greenough.

Of the seven stained glass picture windows in the new St Peter's Church, opened in 1909, three were specially designed to commemorate the work and perpetuate the memory of the district's three early religious leaders. Father Adolphus Lecaille is represented by the figure of St Joseph; St Brigid, Patroness of Ireland, honours the Presentation Sisters and a third window, featuring St Dominic, the Preacher, recognises the presence in the district of the Dominican Sisters, who left a settled life in New Zealand to establish the order's first foundation in Western Australia.

CHAPTER 4

# Cue, Queen of the Murchison

By the time the Dominican Sisters arrived in September 1899, Cue was at the height of its popularity and had already earned the title of capital of the Murchison. Although small quantities of gold had earlier been discovered in the auriferous country surrounding the future town, the area did not show real promise until 1891, when Mick Fitzgerald and Tom Cue, a speculator from Melbourne, collected a number of reasonable-sized quartz specimens from a reef close to Coodardy Station. Fitzgerald, who had befriended a group of Aborigines, was quick to notice that one of them had in his possession a nugget of gold. Pointing to the east he told Fitzgerald, 'this fella slug no good, plenty big fella slugs over there'. [1] On New Year's Day 1892, after first leaving a note for Tom Cue, who had earlier left to purchase provisions, Fitzgerald rode out with two Aborigines in an easterly direction. Excited at the discovery of several small nuggets near a white quartz reef, Fitzgerald returned to the site a week later with a friend, Ned Heffernan. They were not disappointed and by the time Tom Cue appeared it was obvious that the men had found their Eldorado.

It was Tom Cue who rode into Nannine to report the find to the Mining Warden and it did not take long for the word to spread once news of the strike was broken. Within a few days there were some 500 men searching for the elusive ore in an area that later became known as Cue's Patch. Attracted by the lure of gold, and not deterred by the enteric fever that had broken out in the first four weeks, men of all ages, determined to try their luck, continued to flock in droves to the Murchison goldfields. By the end of 1892, there were at least 1000 men working almost shoulder to shoulder and the problem of providing good drinking water had been resolved with the sinking of a well. In the light of new gold discoveries, English investors soon became interested and, as a result, invested capital on a large scale. As new fields opened there was a huge leap in employment opportunities and a need for better housing and amenities became a top priority. One of the town's original pioneers later recalled 'when the gold fever really broke out and the great rush was on, there were

13. Panorama of Cue 1897
Courtesy Battye Library 6045p

thousands of people living in Cue and Day Dawn, including nationalities from all over the world'. [2] By 1893, most of the alluvial gold worth having had been removed from Cue's Patch and reef mining had become the normal practice. The town, by then, was beginning to show signs of permanent development, with a police presence, a mining warden and a progress committee. [3] Within a year 13 batteries had been erected on existing mines and a further 12 were almost completed. By 1896, to meet the demands of a growing population, a sanitary inspector had been appointed and a number of substantial commercial and public buildings had already begun to appear on the main street. The latest gold discoveries were always regular features in local newspapers and the details of the finds often appeared under the heading 'Nuggets'. On 1 January 1898, a headline in the *Murchison Times and Day Dawn Gazette* drew attention to the startling fact that, during December 1897, half a ton of gold had been produced on the Murchison fields.

Before the railway line to Cue was officially opened on 20 April 1897, the main form of transport to the Murchison goldfields was by mule team or camel train. Most goods were shipped from the eastern states to Fremantle and from there transhipped to Geraldton, where they were loaded onto wagons for cartage to the fields. As horses reacted so badly to the smell of camels, the camel drivers were barred from setting up camps close to the town and using the main street in Cue. The municipality petitioned the government to gazette a reserve nearby for the teamsters and subsequently a large Afghan camp, the headquarters of the camel drivers, was established on the outskirts of neighbouring Day Dawn. [4]

When William Kelly took up his appointment as the first bishop of Geraldton in November 1898, he was faced with a daunting task. Not only was the major part of his diocese an uninhabited tract of land, but it was also the largest and poorest in Australia. One of the reasons why Bishop Kelly was persuaded to remain in the Murchison for 10 years, instead of establishing himself at Geraldton, was the presence of a large Catholic population at Cue. In July 1899, a month after their arrival at Greenough, the Dominican Sisters had agreed to found a second mission at Cue. On the strength of this promise the parish priest, Father Stronge, decided to organise a bazaar in August, and he was later delighted to announce that £200 had been raised towards the cost of a convent school, which he hoped would open shortly. Later, on 17 September, after celebrating Mass at St Patrick's Church, Cue, Bishop Kelly addressed the congregation on the subject of Catholic education. He informed those present that two Dominican nuns, from the Rosary Convent at Greenough, were expected to open their first Western Australian branch house at Cue

14. Original convent, Cue

in October that year. The bishop also stated that a decision had been made to proceed immediately with the erection of a convent. Until such time as the new building was completed, school lessons would be given in the local church. In conclusion he added, 'The Sisters who have been appointed in charge are of the Dominican Order, which has established such a high reputation for teaching in Europe, America, New Zealand and the Eastern States. The Order has been most successful in preparing girls for the Universities and Trinity College Examinations. Their Elementary Schools also have always been ranked as first class and both courses will be taught in Cue as elsewhere'. [5]

An announcement in the *Murchison Times and Day Dawn Gazette*, on 23 September 1899, alerted readers to the fact that the Dominican Sisters would register prospective pupils on Thursday, 28 and Friday, 29 September and that classes would commence in St Patrick's Church on Monday, 2 October. School fees were listed as sixpence per week for primary school pupils and one shilling per week for students attending higher grades. In the same paper the following month, a large advertisement appeared under a bold heading calling for tenders for the erection of a convent on the corner of Marshall and Dooley Streets, Cue. The notice explained:

*It will be built of wood and iron with bungalow roof and louvre ends. A wide verandah will run all around the main building and the main entrance will be made distinctive by a handsome portico of Italian design. The main building is to consist of five rooms, a large entrance hall and cross passages. The rooms are to be used for public reception and private apartments, the whole to be neatly finished in fluted iron. The detached building will consist of a kitchen and other usual offices such as servants' bedrooms, bathrooms etc., the whole to be finished to correspond with the main building. Mr E. O'Hughes, a well-known Cue architect has the work in charge.* [6]

Two weeks later the same newspaper published the names and quotations of the builders whose tenders were being considered. Three firms submitted tenders: Little and McInnes, £379; Crooks and Bruker, £390 and E. Hadlow £407.10.0. As expected, the lowest tender was duly accepted.

On Sunday, 24 September 1899, Bishop Kelly visited Mt Magnet and the following day proceeded to Yalgoo, where, by arrangement, he met Mother Gabriel Gill and Sister Gonzales Wall and continued the journey with them to Cue. The train pulled into the station on the Monday evening and the two Dominican Sisters were taken to a rented four-room cottage, previously occupied by the late Mr G. C. Gordon. The temporary convent, which they expected to use for at least two months, had an iron roof, beaten earth floors and unlined walls roughly constructed of hessian and calico. Despite being basic, the living quarters were neatly furnished by members of the Convent School Committee who had gone to a great deal of trouble to provide the semblance of a home-like atmosphere. [7]

Three days after the nuns' arrival, a telegram sent to Greenough informed the Dominican community that Mother Gabriel and Sister Gonzales had happily settled into life at Cue. Their contentment was short-lived, for soon afterwards it seems that they had changed their minds and were less than impressed with their new surroundings. A number of reasons could be given for the sudden disappointment. Firstly, their mentor, Bishop Kelly, had to leave Cue almost immediately on diocesan business, which meant that the Sisters felt isolated for the first two weeks. Secondly, the town, despite its large population, was still in its infancy and the type of accommodation initially offered to the Sisters may have proved intolerable in the summer. Indeed, news reports reveal that within a week of the Sisters' arrival, a strong north wind blew for an entire day and later developed into a violent dust storm. Apart from the clouds of dust that enveloped the town, pebbles, pieces of tin, wood and iron flew everywhere. That evening, when the wind had abated, the majority of residents, particularly those living in houses with flimsy walls, had to spend hours removing the sand piles that had formed inside the rooms. [8] Influenza was also rife throughout the month of October, and in Cue many residents, including the Church of England minister and one of the town's prominent medical practitioners, Dr Blanchard, were hospitalised. [9] The fact that Mother Gabriel had succumbed to the disease, and that her companion had also developed eye trouble, did little to endear the strange new surroundings to either of them. Mother Gabriel must have been quite ill for the local newspaper, on 21 November, reported her recovery:

*In connection with the Convent School at Cue we regret to record that the Mother Superior has been a victim of the prevailing influenza. It is satisfactory to state that she is now on the way to recovery. During the Mother's illness the teaching staff of the school has not been allowed to deteriorate in any respect as negotiations were immediately entered into to secure the services of another Sister from Geraldton.*[10]

To add to the Sisters' discomfort, the temperatures in the mining town were rising daily. The official record registered at the post office in Cue on Saturday, 2 December 1899, was 100.8 degrees Fahrenheit. By Tuesday, the thermometer had climbed to 103 degrees and, on 19 December, the register recorded an unbearable 108 degrees in the shade. The extreme conditions continued during the ensuing weeks culminating with a debilitating 109 degrees. [11] It was no wonder that the residents of Cue left in droves to spend the Christmas holidays near the coast.

15. Original St Gabriel's School, Cue

Nineteen children had enrolled in the Dominican school at Cue when it opened on 2 October 1899. This number quickly fell during the influenza epidemic and, by 24 October, very few pupils were attending classes. Nevertheless, with an enormous amount of will-power, and no doubt, a great deal of prayer, the Mother Prioress coped with the situation without accepting assistance. By 15 December, she had fully recovered and was delighted with the success of a function held by the school that day in aid of the Cue Convent Building Fund. The Dominican pupils, who provided most of the items, had less than two months to prepare for the concert held in the Miners' Institute. Taking into account the Sisters' earlier health problems, they must have been somewhat relieved when several talented adults kindly offered to participate.

Like the majority of members attached to established religious orders, the Dominican founding Sisters in Western Australia had experienced a greater part of their community life in buildings especially designed to suit a conventual lifestyle. Women who were received and later professed in Ireland, or at St Dominic's in Dunedin, generally inhabited convents built with their own private chapels and gardens and well-defined novitiates. Although mission Sisters were aware that the work they undertook in other countries would be vastly different, one wonders if, when Mother Gabriel decided to cross the Tasman, she was actually prepared for some of the accommodation she would eventually be offered. With few shade trees, and surrounded by hard, baked earth, the convent at Cue was not designed to protect its occupants from the oppressive heat of summer and the countless dust storms that blew in from the desert regions. In addition, the complete absence of enclosed gardens or private walkways meant that the Sisters living in many of these mining towns had no opportunity to enjoy any form of exercise away from the public eye.

It was agreed at a Dominican Council meeting, held at the Rosary Convent on 9 January 1900, that separate accounts would be kept for the new foundation and for this purpose a new bank account would be opened at Cue. When Mother Gabriel Gill left Greenough to return to Murchison on 17 January, she was accompanied by two new companions, her relative, the recently appointed Procuratrix and Sacristan, Sister Dominica Murphy, and Sister Bonaventure McEntyre, Mistress of Schools. [12]

The turn of the century saw certain changes take place in the parish at Cue. Not only had ill health forced Father Riordan to leave the parish less than three months after his appointment, but there was a certain amount of reorganising before Father McMullen from Tumut, New South Wales, agreed to take his place. By this time, Bishop Kelly had left for his *ad limina* to Rome, and like her companions at Greenough and Cue, Mother Gabriel was already experiencing a great sense of loss.

During the Christmas vacation a large advertisement appeared in the local newspapers and *Catholic Record* announcing the Dominican Sisters' intention to receive boarders at Cue as well as Greenough. The new term, it stated, would commence on 23 January 1900, and boarders were expected to be in residence the day before. Members of the public were also notified that extra evening classes would, in future, be held for adults wishing to be tutored in English, Mathematics, foreign languages, singing, drawing, painting, wood-carving, art, needlework, harmony, book-keeping or shorthand.

With the exception of a few days in January, the hot weather experienced at Cue prior to Christmas 1899, had unfortunately not abated and the temperatures continued to exceed the century during the first exhausting weeks of school. Despite a cool, airy dormitory having been added to the convent to accommodate the first group of boarders, [13] the responsibility of caring for residential students during a prolonged heat wave must have placed enormous pressure on the nuns in charge. On 8 February 1900, the temperature in Cue registered 109 degrees Fahrenheit, peaking a week later, on 15 February, at 114 degrees. According to one newspaper report, the temperature taken under the iron roofs of some verandahs actually registered an unbelievable 122 degrees. Many of Cue's residents were physically and mentally affected by the stifling conditions. Tempers became frayed and, as a result of some anti-social behaviour, police reinforcements were sent in to handle any emergencies. If proof were needed to validate Kipling's observations when he wrote, 'Mad dogs and Englishmen go out in the midday sun', one would have to look no further than a local newspaper report discussing plans to hold a cricket match between Cue and Day Dawn that summer. [14]

Meanwhile, the gold industry continued to attract international attention and consequently, the sound economic situation enjoyed in the early 1900s provided Western Australia with a new-found status. By then the population had increased dramatically, and the news that Western Australia, in January 1901, had become one of the six federated States of the newly-formed Commonwealth of Australia, continued to dominate the newspapers and everyday conversation.

When Bishop Kelly returned from overseas in February 1901, one of his prime objectives was to extend the Catholic school system. That same year the Census registered the existence of approximately 7000 Catholics in the Geraldton diocese, and of this number 4000 lived either in the Murchison or Eastern Goldfields, or on outlying sheep or cattle stations. [15].

In her role as Dominican Prioress, Gabriel Gill made regular visits to Greenough to assemble and consult the Members of Council before making any decisions that might affect the community. In 1900, for instance, the Council met in January and again on 25 May and 2 June. The Sisters still had two major obstacles to overcome; firstly, the lack of ready finance to fund extensions to existing buildings, particularly with regard to boarding accommodation; and secondly, the need to resolve the scarcity of teaching staff and lay Sisters. Although community numbers increased in 1901, the Sisters were still grossly overworked and desperately short of recruits. With more than one convent to maintain, and several schools to conduct, it is little wonder that Mother Gabriel decided to break with tradition and send Sister Anastasia Byrne, one of the community's white-veiled novices, to assist at Cue. She was apparently not the only novice in those founding years to forego an orthodox religious training program, for, in January 1902, the Prioress expressed concern for other novices who 'had been scattered in our branch houses, where suitable training could not be given'. [16]

In July 1901, a special Children's Concert was held at the Workers' Hall in Cue in an effort to raise funds, and both the Sisters and pupils were delighted when the Bishop of Geraldton accepted an invitation to watch a rehearsal in the school. Prior to taking part in the performance, one of the pupils read out a poem especially written to welcome the bishop home from Europe. Bishop Kelly sat throughout the program totally engrossed by the efforts of the participants. He later thanked the children for the entertainment and their kind words of welcome and congratulated them on the progress they were making in their studies. Finally the bishop reminded his audience that children trained at convent schools were invariably good examples, and he hoped that now the Dominican Sisters had taken charge the same could be said about the children of Cue. [17]

Towards the end of October 1901, the Prioress visited the newly-formed Dominican foundation at Dongara. She no doubt had many matters to discuss, for in February the following year, the Holy Rosary Convent and Dominican schools in Greenough would be transferred to another order and the Dominican Sisters would establish a larger foundation in the Irwin District. Unable to return to Cue in time to attend a First Communion ceremony, Mother Gabriel wrote to one of her pupils from Dongara on the Feast of All Saints Day, 1 November 1901: 'You know that I take a deep interest in the children of Cue, especially in you whom I prepared for First Confession – also for Communion...How I wish I could be with you on Sunday morning. You will not forget to pray for me. I have many cares and anxieties'. [18]

By 1902, the foundation at Cue was well-established and with over 100 pupils enrolled in the day school, and 20 boarders in residence at the girls' boarding school, the community at St Gabriel's was optimistically looking forward to a successful future. In January 1900, Bishop Kelly had given the Sisters permission to teach Christian Doctrine and to visit the hospital on Sundays at nearby Day Dawn, and for quite some time the Sisters continued to travel to the neighbouring mining town to perform these duties. [19] By 1902, the visiting Dominican Sisters had become familiar figures to Catholic families living in Day Dawn, and as the population increased, the need to introduce a religious education centre in that town became a common topic of conversation. Mother Gabriel, never one to avoid a challenge, called the Council together, on 30 June, to 'discuss the expediency of opening a school at Day Dawn'. [20] The vote in favour was unanimous and it was decided to immediately seek the bishop's approval. Later, in 1903, Mother Gabriel approached Council members with a similar suggestion which resulted in another foundation being established at Leonora in the same year.

Not content with working long hours during the school year, the Sisters also took part in a Church-based proposal that enabled children living on the goldfields to spend their summer holidays on the coast. Before school commenced in February in 1903, 30 children, some of whom had never seen the ocean, were taken by the Dominican Sisters to enjoy a seaside break at Dongara. The scheme was a forerunner of the Bushies' School and quite independent of the Fresh Air League, which had similar aims. Shortly after the group's return to Cue, some of the advantages of the excursion were described in the *Murchison Times and Day Dawn Gazette*:

*The benefits they have derived from change of scene and climate are quite obvious. Perfect health has given its color to their cheeks, and its grace and vigor to their movements. It is pleasant to hear these fortunate youngsters prattle of their daily drives to the sea, of tossing waves and smooth beaches, of fishing excursions, during which strange marine creatures were drawn from their native deeps, or walks through shady valleys, and over wind-swept heights, of vineyards rich with purple and amber grapes, and orange groves where the fruit and the blossom were to be seen on the same tree.* [21]

In 1903, Bishop Kelly and a number of Dominican Sisters began to look seriously at plans to celebrate Mother Gabriel Gill's Golden Anniversary on 18 August, the following year. Ideas on how best to celebrate the important occasion were discussed, and the eventual result was that a letter was sent to the Dominican Prioress at Dunedin. The correspondence, dated 2 February 1903, was signed by Sisters Bonaventure McEntyre, Dominica Murphy, Philomena McGrath, di Pazzi Miscall, Ceslaus Freed, Anastasia Byrne and Catherine Kenny. The contents, unfortunately, dwelt more on the need to recruit postulants than the forthcoming event, the letter rather tending to present the proposed visit more as a *fait accompli* than a request:

*...Now we feel sure that you would love to have Mother with you for the celebration of that great event. Besides, circumstanced as we are here, a solemn function of this kind could not be fittingly carried out. The demand for more members is now becoming so pressing that we have been forced to take some immediate steps in the matter, and with your consent, we propose sending Mother to Dunedin for the two-fold purpose of getting postulants and celebrating her Golden Jubilee in January [actual day 18 August], as you will then be all gathered together in the dear 'Alma Mater'. Our good Bishop has willingly given his consent to these arrangements and if he can possibly manage it, will visit New Zealand for the celebration and probably accompany Mother and the numerous band of Missioners (which we feel will be the outcome of the trip) on their return to Western Australia.* [22]

The Bishop of Geraldton endorsed the arrangement: 'I am anxious that our dear Mother Gabriel should have a more splendid celebration of her approaching Jubilee than we can provide her with. I sympathise with your natural desire that she should be with you on that historic occasion. I am desirous of offering New Zealand nuns present and prospective an opportunity of taking part in the noble work of building up the Church in this progressive Golden West'. [23] It was perhaps rather naïve of Bishop Kelly not to have realised that, whilst the Bishop of Otago might happily endorse the occasional movement of volunteer missioners from New Zealand, he might not appreciate a fellow bishop's intention to poach a 'numerous band of Missioners' from his diocese. As it turned out, Mother Gabriel did not travel to her beloved Dunedin, instead, she celebrated her Jubilee at Cue and Dongara.

At 9.00 p.m. on 1 December 1903, the loud ringing of St Patrick's Church bell followed by the clanging of fire bells, brought the townsfolk running from their homes and into Austin Street to inspect the cause of the commotion. It seems that flames had quickly spread after a sudden gust of wind unexpectedly blew a curtain on top of a lamp that Father Creagh had been carrying between rooms. The combination of flaming material and the exploding lamp soon set fire to the presbytery and, fanned by strong winds, the fire soon carried the flames along to the church and into the eaves and roof. The Anglican rector, who was one of the first on the scene, thoughtfully ran into the church and rescued the Blessed Sacrament. He then passed the ciborium to the Sacristan, Sister Hyacinth Carroll, who carefully wrapped it in her scapular. Bishop Kelly was devastated, particularly when the fire began to threaten the nearby convent and school. Despite the amount of water poured onto the church building, the firemen realised that it was beyond saving. Instead, they decided to concentrate on the convent, which they managed to save from destruction after a great deal of effort. Sparks, propelled by consistent strong gusts of wind, began to shower the nuns' residence and everything, from wet bags to buckets of water and a fire hose, were used to douse the sparks.

Although St Gabriel's Convent suffered no obvious damage, it was still considered safer for the nuns to sleep elsewhere that night and Mr J. Chesson, a well-known Cue identity, kindly provided the use of his home. [24] Several members of the Chesson family have been associated with the Dominican Sisters over the years. Mary Gill, for example, the step-daughter of Arthur Chesson, was educated by the Dominican Sisters at Cue and later at their ladies' college in Dongara. An attractive, talented girl, she commenced music lessons with the nuns at the age of six and on one occasion was successful in winning a gold medal. Whilst a pupil at St Gabriel's, Cue, she won a prize for being the most popular girl in the school, although it was later hinted that the boys' votes might have influenced the outcome. In 1925, Mary married Michael Mulcahy of Milly Milly Station, a million-acre pastoral property about 150 miles north-west of Cue, and her love of music continued to play a large part in her life.

Up until such time as the ciborium containing the Blessed Sacrament could be returned to its proper place, Mother Gabriel Gill and Sisters Bonaventure McEntyre, di Pazzi Miscall and Vincent Colgan became custodians of the sacred vessel. The unexpected loss of the church and near destruction of the convent was not a happy introduction to Cue for the two new members of the Dominican community. Sister Vincent Colgan (Annie) and Sister Hyacinth Carroll (Mary), had in fact only been received into the novitiate at Dongara on 3 July 1903, and were still novices. Twenty-year-old Sister Vincent, a native of Lawrence, New Zealand, was educated at the school founded in that town by Mother Gabriel Gill. Not only did she know the Prioress before coming to Western Australia, but she also knew one of her earlier teachers, Sister Philomena McGrath. Sister Vincent later became Mother Prioress of the Congregation and although she worked in a number of country missions, she spent most of her years at Dongara. Sister Hyacinth Carroll, despite being highly-educated, chose to enter the order as a lay Sister. She was a refined lady-like person, who at first gave the impression of being rather serious, however, she had a hidden sense of humour which surfaced every now and then as she quietly went about her household chores. Preparing afternoon tea trays for visitors and answering the telephone were two of the many duties she performed with grace. Although Sr Hyacinth's death occurred in 1950, she is still remembered with affection by some of the more elderly Sisters and past pupils fondly recall her in her role as Portress at Dongara. [25]

The parish at Cue was, unfortunately, not in a position to erect a new church building until many years after the fire. In a complete reversal of the situation experienced by the Sisters when they first arrived in the mining town, church services were for some time conducted in the Dominican school. Former pupil, Mary Healey (Mrs Gray), who was born at Toodyay in 1898, accompanied her parents to Cue at an early age where her father opened a drapery store. She remained at St Gabriel's until 1910, after which she briefly attended the Dominican school at Meekatharra before being enrolled in St Dominic's College, Dongara in 1912. Mrs Gray later recollected that when she was a pupil at Cue, girls enrolled at the boarding school were given lessons in the same room as the day pupils. Two or three teachers held separate classes in a large, divided room and another Sister taught on the verandah. Sister di Pazzi took the upper classes and also gave singing lessons. The past pupil recalled that, although she was an exceptionally sweet-natured person and popular with the children, she was strict and did not hesitate to discipline the boys by wielding the cane. The former Mary Healey had happy memories of the much-admired Dominican Prioress, Mother Gabriel Gill, as well as one of the founding Sisters, Bonaventure McEntyre. Other Sisters who came to mind were – Sister Aquin Inglis, a tall Irish Sister, who was an excellent music teacher and Sister Evangelist Graham, a pleasant-natured lay Sister who loved cooking and spent a great deal of her time in the kitchen. Also remembered was Sister Baptist Hall, a true educationalist in every sense of the word. This tall New Zealand nun, of Scottish descent, was a true patriot. Never slow to extol the virtues of her beloved native land, Sr Baptist was occasionally egged on by others to raise the subject of 'God's own country'. Many of her listeners later admitted that the knowledge gained from her reminiscences often worked to their advantage when studying the history and geography of the two islands. [26]

Mother Gabriel's long-awaited Golden Jubilee was celebrated in a variety of ways. Apart from covering the events that took place at different intervals throughout the year, local and overseas newspapers recognised the stature of the woman and her numerous past and present achievements in a number of complimentary articles. After one major celebration at Cue, the *Murchison Times and Day Dawn Gazette* used typical journalese of the day to inform its readers:

*Not to many does this happen, while still in the possession of unimpaired mental vigor, and of scarcely impaired physical strength, to celebrate the completion of fifty years of hard work, and still smaller is the number of those whose Golden Jubilee is joyfully celebrated in these widely-separated quarters of the globe. Both of these distinctions have fallen to the lot of Rev. Mother Gabriel, Prioress of the Dominicanesses in West Australia, and at present Superioress of the Convent in Cue. Fifty years have elapsed, since, leaving parents and home, wealth and distinguished social position, she entered the famous Dominican House of Sion Hill and begged to be enrolled among the religious. Here her uncommon talents, her fine scholarship, and her zeal and activity marked her out as one fitted for high responsibility…It might indeed be said of her…'If you seek a monument look around you'. Eleven Convents and a still greater number of schools of all grades claim her as their foundress.*

*Three Conventual foundations, and the growth of the Community from six to twenty since her coming to Western Australia, attest to Mother Gabriel's undiminished activity, and encourage the hope that she may be spared for many years to continue her great work. Her Golden Jubilee has already been celebrated with great enthusiasm in Ireland and New Zealand, in both of which countries she possesses troops of friends and admirers – her Sisters in religion, generations of grateful past pupils and others…The pupils of the Dominican Nuns recently entertained the Prioress in the large school-hall at Cue.*

*Although no invitations had been issued, a large number of friends were present, among them Bishop Kelly and Father Baudizzone, and all thoroughly enjoyed the bright and varied programme presented.* [27]

A prepared address read during the interval by one of the pupils from the Dominican school at Cue, lauded 'the great and fruitful works' that Mother Gabriel had 'accomplished in various parts of the world'. This was followed by the presentation of a flowering shrub, which on inspection revealed 50 shining gold coins scattered among its branches, to mark the occasion of the Prioress's 50 years of service as a religious. Across the Tasman the *New Zealand Tablet*, published on 11 August 1904, acknowledged Mother Gabriel's contribution as a member of the Dominican Order and to the cause of Catholic education in their nation. Members of the Association of the Children of Mary in Dunedin, Oamaru, Invercargill, Queenstown, Cromwell and Lawrence each sent their own congratulations to the organisation's 'First Directress'. 'We regret', they wrote, 'that the labours of your difficult Mission in Westralia prevent your presence amongst us. What a *Caed Mille Failthe* you would receive from Catholics, and not a few non-Catholics of Dunedin were you once more to appear in our midst'. [28] In view of Mother Gabriel's premature death the following year, her contemporaries and former companions must have later experienced a tinge of regret that she had not been able to celebrate at least part of her Jubilee in New Zealand.

The Dominican Sisters in Dunedin had earlier commissioned a beautifully-crafted wall panel to be completed in time for the foundress's Golden Jubilee. Fashioned from native woods by J. J. Marlow of Dunedin, the 'Jubilee Wreath' consisted of two photographs, one of St Dominic's Priory, the other of the chapel, and on the principal panel a reproduction of a painting of St Catherine of Siena. This was bordered with lettering 'elegantly printed on white satin, beautifully decorated in water colours by the eminent New Zealand artist, R. Hawcridge'. [29] A feature of the gift was the appropriate commemorative wording, including a list of the foundations established by Mother Gabriel and a poem, entitled *The Mother of the Missions*, especially written for the occasion by Sister Alphonsus Owens. In addition to the presentation gift, a sum of £50 was forwarded to Western Australia.

The actual day of the Golden Jubilee, on 18 August 1904, was celebrated at the Priory in Dongara with the remaining members of the community. As a memento of the special day, a photograph of the Prioress, taken in the grotto that afternoon, was sent to Dunedin in September with an accompanying inscription written by Mother Gabriel: 'My Golden Jubilee. I stood close to the little statue of our sweet Immaculate Mother, and held in

16. Mother Gabriel's Golden Jubilee portrait, 1904

my hand the Sion copy of our Holy Rule & Constitutions which was placed in my hand on 8th December 1858, four years after my Holy Profession and 4 days before my eldest brother died'. [30]

For some time, there had been talk of building a new convent at Cue and, to help turn that dream into a reality, Mother Gabriel, after her return from Dongara, made arrangements to hold a bazaar on 3 October 1904, followed by a concert on 9 November. The events must have been a financial success, for, in January the following year, the Shire of Cue received a letter from architect, Mr E. Hughes, seeking permission to build a new residence for the Dominican Sisters. The Shire had no hesitation in approving the application and subsequently a new, more commodious convent was erected and ready for occupation in March 1905. The community at that time consisted of the Prioress, Mother Gabriel Gill, Sisters di Pazzi Miscall and Gerard Milligan and two novices, Sisters Baptist Hall and Evangelist Graham. Changes had also taken place that year in relation to the day school at Day Dawn, earlier established in the parish church. One month after the opening of the new St Gabriel's Convent at Cue, Sister Philomena McGrath and two novices took up residence in the newly-erected St Hyacinth's Convent at Day Dawn. The completion of this building meant that Sisters staffing the neighbouring church-school no longer had to commute each day from Cue.

It was on Saturday, 22 April 1905, whilst she was staying at the convent opened in Day Dawn just two weeks earlier, that the intrepid Mother Gabriel Gill met her untimely death at the age of 68. Foundation Sister, di Pazzi Miscall, who in her own words was 'completely crushed' by her Superior's death, later wrote an account of the events that preceded her demise:

*She was in her usual health up to the end; no one had any idea that she was so near death. We used to laugh and joke with her about being so bony, and she always said that the worms would have nothing to feed on when we went. Only a day or two before she went out to Day Dawn, I was in her room doing something for her and we were laughing over our both being such walking advertisements for Holy Poverty. She was so merry and had no thought of dying. She was always planning and had spoken to me of plans for the next ten years.* [31]

Instead of leaving Cue on Friday, as she usually did when she conducted weekend classes at Day Dawn, Mother Gabriel decided to make the journey on Wednesday, 19 April, during Holy Week. At 1.20 p.m. that same day, the Prioress and Sister di Pazzi said Vespers together at St Gabriel's and later, after the younger Sister returned from school, she went straight to the refectory to join the Mother Prioress. Sister di Pazzi was surprised to find her lying down, looking very tired, and complaining of a bad headache. Although her Superior sometimes suffered from head pains, bouts of extreme exhaustion and the occasional slight attack of angina, she always recovered quickly and rarely took to her bed unless forced to do so. Spy Wednesday in Holy Week was a day of abstinence and for that reason Mother Gabriel refused to eat meat when her companion offered to bring her a cooked dinner before setting out to Day Dawn. It was only through persistent coaxing and a reminder that, for medical reasons, Bishop Kelly had earlier absolved her from fasting, that Sr di Pazzi was able to persuade her Superior to eat a grilled chop and some fruit. No amount of persuasion, however, would change her mind about cancelling the fancywork lesson she had arranged to give that afternoon at St Hyacinth's Convent.

When Sister di Pazzi checked later, she was not overly surprised to find Mother Gabriel already robed in her travelling cloak, seated at the piano giving a lesson to a pupil before she left Cue. On the suggestion that the bumpy coach-trip to Day Dawn be left until the next day, Mother Gabriel reminded Sr di Pazzi that she had already neglected her duties that day by breaking her fast and in which case she would not contribute again by cancelling a lesson. As she left the convent in Cue she called out, 'I'll be home Saturday without fail, and we shall have a very happy Easter Sunday, please God'. [32]

Sister di Pazzi and the two novices had arranged to come out to Day Dawn the next day with a group of school children to attend Mass, and it was during this ceremony that Mother Gabriel became faint. This in itself was not considered a matter of great concern, for she had often taken a turn when sitting too long in a confined area. Although Mother Gabriel rested intermittently on her return to St Hyacinth's Convent, unfortunately a number of visitors interrupted what rest she might have had. Still determined to fulfil her duties, Mother Gabriel refused to hand over a pupil due for a music lesson, and then, defying all common sense, decided to interview a prospective student wishing to take singing lessons. She was most enthusiastic about the quality of the person's voice and for a time seemed to improve.

By evening, however, the Dominican foundress was not well enough to attend Tenebrae and she slept fitfully during the night. Sister di Pazzi and the novices travelled back to Day Dawn on Good Friday and were surprised to find the patient looking pale and thin. The Cue Sister later wrote, 'I went over to her bedside and knelt down besides her asking what was the matter. She said, "I don't know, but I think I must have either pneumonia or fever"'. [33] By the time the community had returned from Mass they found that her condition had worsened. Yet, despite the Sisters' pleas, Mother Gabriel remained resolute and refused to see a doctor, adding that she would be all right if she were only home at Cue.

Realising that she would shortly have to end her visit and return to St Gabriel's Convent, a worried Sister di Pazzi took it upon herself to arrange for a doctor to call on Mother Gabriel at St Hyacinth's in Day Dawn. Unfortunately Dr Frost, a Catholic neighbour, was not immediately available, which meant that Bishop Kelly and the Dominican Sisters had to leave for Cue without knowing the result of the doctor's diagnosis. During the short cab journey home, the bishop, a long-time friend and admirer of Mother Gabriel, expressed his concern about her appearance. He was surprised how quickly she had deteriorated and recalled that when they had met a week earlier he 'had never seen her looking so fresh and young'. [34] As the group drove away none of them was aware that the fond goodbyes they had given before leaving that day, would in fact be their final farewell.

Tenebrae was held as usual during the last three days of Holy Week and Bishop Kelly was expected to return to Day Dawn that evening to attend the service. Although members of the Cue community were reminded that they had witnessed Mother Prioress in similar situations in the past, they continued to feel uneasy. In her eagerness to discover the latest information about the invalid's condition, Sister di Pazzi asked the bishop if he would mind making further enquiries at St Hyacinth's Convent and if possible to let them know that night.

It was well after 11.00 p.m. when Bishop Kelly arrived back in Cue to find an anxious group of Sisters waiting for news. The report he delivered was far from favourable. Not only had Dr Frost ascertained that Mother Gabriel was suffering from an acute attack of pneumonia, but he also inferred that there was a possibility that she might not pull through. A dejected Bishop Kelly informed the equally depressed community that he had heard the patient's confession and anointed her and had also promised to bring the Blessed Sacrament to Day Dawn the next morning. In the meantime, Sisters Philomena McGrath and Josephine Kenny kept a constant vigile over Mother Gabriel throughout the night. When Sister di Pazzi requested the bishop's permission to walk back to Day Dawn with Sister Gerard, the last cab having gone, Bishop Kelly was quick to point out that her proposal, although well-intentioned, was not practical. Having been assured by the doctor that there was no immediate danger, he suggested instead that all should retire and return with him in the morning.

An early morning attempt to hire a horse and buggy failed and it was 7.00 a.m. before the party set out for Day Dawn. The vehicle had almost reached its destination when a rider approached and sensitively broke the news that, sadly, the Dominican Prioress had just passed away. The nuns were devastated and Bishop Kelly, still clutching the Blessed Sacrament, remained for some time in a state of disbelief. It appears that although Mother Gabriel suffered greatly, she was conscious to the end. About 6.30 a.m. on Easter Saturday she asked for Bishop Kelly and on being told that he was back in Cue, she asked instead to see Father O'Malley. The parish priest had barely left when Mother Gabriel, with the help of Sister Josephine, was gently raised and propped up with pillows. The priest was fetched a second time and, as Sister Philomena McGrath later explained, 'Mother fixed her eyes on him when he entered and never changed her position. The prayers for the dying were scarcely begun when Mother breathed her last at 7.00 a.m. on Holy Saturday'. [35]

Later that day, the white and silver coffin containing her remains was taken to Cue, followed by two carriages carrying Bishop Kelly and the Dominican Sisters. Still dazed by the turn of events, Sister di Pazzi Miscall described Mother Gabriel Gill's unexpected return to St Gabriel's Convent when writing to the Prioress's former community at Sion Hill in Ireland:

*This was Saturday afternoon. Yes the day she promised to be back! She kept her promise, but, oh, what a homecoming! I shall never forget it. The Convent bell tolled as we were coming up, and there were crowds of people waiting at the Convent; nothing but sobs could be heard on all sides, and the little children were heartbroken. Oh, it was a most pitiful sight. The coffin was carried up the carriage drive. This was the first time Mother had ever come up it, as the Bishop had got it made as a surprise for her. The body was laid in our own little oratory in the new Convent, the first time that this room had ever been used; also we were not a month in the new house...All night until 11 o'clock crowds kept coming to take a last look at dear old Mother. Everyone loved and respected her. It was wonderful to see the crowds of Protestants who had perhaps only spoken to her once, but who were deeply afflicted by her death.* [36]

The unexpected death of the Dominican Prioress stunned a great many people around the world, and for some time wide-spread messages of regret began to flow in from those whose life she had touched in Ireland, New Zealand and Australia. The funeral was large by any standards. In fact it was said that nearly the whole population of both Cue and Day Dawn were present. Bishop Kelly, in a soutane and rochet accompanied by two acolytes, preceded the hearse followed by members of the Hibernian Society in full regalia. Instead of proceeding straight to the cemetery, the procession of some 300 persons slowly wended its way through the town. Included were Dominican pupils, dressed in white with black bands, and residents from the Central Murchison District. A large number of mourners also attended in an assortment of vehicles. The Rule of Enclosure prevented members of the Dominican community from attending, but they were able to view part of the activity leading up to the funeral.

17. Graves of Mother Gabriel Gill and Sister Felicitas Plunkett, Cue

'The crowds were so great', wrote one of the Dominican diarists, 'that everything seemed just a moving mass. Then we saw people coming back and we knew that all was over. It seemed so strange that Mother, who did everything for the mission in New Zealand and here too, should have such a lonely desolate looking grave'. [37]

Indeed, it seems incongruous that this refined, highly-educated, elegant woman who, until her arrival at Greenough, had been surrounded by so much natural beauty, would be laid to rest in a patch of barren, inhospitable ground, denuded of trees and exposed to a relentless sun. Mother Gabriel's remains lay buried in the Cue cemetery for over nine years until December 1914, when Father James O'Neill of Milton, New Zealand, supervised the transfer of the coffin to the nuns' private cemetery at Dongara. According to Sister Vincent Colgan, the late Prioress had often expressed a desire to establish 15 Dominican foundations in honour of the Holy Rosary before she died. Ironically, this ambition was achieved when St Hyacinth's Convent at Day Dawn, her fifth and final house in Western Australia, was founded a few weeks before her demise.

At the time of her death, Mother Gabriel had been absent from New Zealand for six years, and instead of residing, as one would have expected, in the Priory at Dongara, she had obviously adjusted to life in the goldfields. Sister Gonzales Wall, who returned to Dunedin soon after Cue was established recalled: 'At Cue, the Sisters found a true-hearted progressive people, mostly miners and their families who had come from the Eastern States'. [38]

It is obvious that Mother Gabriel Gill, a tireless worker who loved a challenge, admired the pioneering spirit of people living in the Murchison, most of whom had a reputation for being honest, hard-working and generous to a fault. It was the former Mother Prioress's boundless energy and propensity for forward-thinking that made her quickly recognise and seize an opportunity. This was evidenced by the optimism she displayed when she organised a Dominican novitiate in Ireland, and later when she agreed to form a new foundation at Greenough, despite Bishop Kelly's admission that he could not offer any pecuniary assistance. Fortunately for the many Dominican foundations she established, it was Mother Gabriel Gill's missionary zeal, determination and sense of duty that made her a survivor.

At Leonora, on 14 July 1905, the sub-Prioress Bonaventure McEntyre received news of her appointment as Prioress and, on 31 December that year, she assembled her first Council meeting. By then the number of Councillors had been increased from three to five. These included Sisters Dominica Murphy, di Pazzi Miscall, Ceslaus Freed and Philomena McGrath (Secretary). During the meeting it was agreed that Sisters Hyacinth Carroll, Vincent Colgan and Patrick Doyle, having completed their term as novices, would be accepted for profession. A second Council meeting held 10 days later resulted in a unanimous decision to send Sister Dominica Murphy to Ireland. The purpose of which was two-fold. The Council hoped that the voyage would improve her health and that during her visit she might secure some well-educated girls as postulants. The move, directed towards seeking new recruits was of the utmost importance for, at that time, the community lacked a sufficient number of professed Sisters to sustain the foundation at Dongara and the branch houses at Cue, Day Dawn and Leonora, and a day school at Gwalia. Most of these convents were considered too far apart for easy government and the new Prioress must have been relieved when at least one of her problems was partly resolved by the arrival of three postulants from Ireland and the profession of five novices between the years 1905 and 1907.

Many Sisters were musicians of high calibre, and although it was never their intention to train pupils for the public stage, it seems that the early lessons they gave, and the talents they shared, often inspired certain pupils to reach their full potential and become performers of some standing. Lulu Benstead, a former Dominican boarder at Cue, was a prime example. During her years as a pupil she took part in several concerts at both Cue and Day Dawn and, despite her being a mere child, it was said that her voice enthralled the audiences, including many a hardened miner. In 1908, when Miss Benstead left Western Australia to study singing with one of Europe's top masters, she was happy to give credit for the early training she had received to the Dominican Sisters at St Gabriel's Convent in Cue. [39] Among the candidates from Cue who successfully passed the Trinity College of London Music Examinations that year were:

**Intermediate:** Irene Smith, Mary and Katie Toohey and Mary Troy.

**Junior:** Kath Chesson, Pat Troy, Fred Smith, Alice Toohey and Gladys Wilmot.

**Preparatory:** Lyndon Rogers, Ruby Rebecchi, Bernard Smith, Annie Cook, Reg Johnston, Berti Gray, Alice and Eileen Chesson, Jack Myssonski, Tom Oates, Peter McInnes, Isabel Rodgers, Rosie Troy and Florrie Easton.

Several convent students also gained certificates from the Associated Board of the Royal Academy and Royal College of Music for various grades of examination in musical knowledge, instrumental performance and singing. [40]

On 28 December 1908, Sister di Pazzi Miscall was appointed Superior of St Gabriel's Convent at Cue and Sister Baptist Hall became both Procuratrix and Sacristan. Unfortunately, the Sisters were no sooner back in the goldfields after the Christmas holidays, than they were subjected to a violent windstorm that swept through the town and carried away the verandah and part of the roof of the boarders' wing. Anxious to repair the damage before the start of the new school year in February, Cue's parish priest, Father Verlin, swiftly gathered together a group of men willing to restore the building. The Sisters were pleased to note that despite a growing slump in the mining industry, in 1909, St Gabriel's Convent School in Cue commenced classes with a roll call of some 80 pupils. [41]

Deportment, callisthenics, sports days and a variety of extraneous activities such as Empire and Arbor Day were an integral part of school life. The Dominican School

18. Deportment class, St Gabriel's Convent, Cue

Sports Day, held at the Cue recreation ground on Empire Day 1909, was in stark contrast to today's competitive events. It was a happy, carefree day, spent in a picnic-like atmosphere with parents and friends cheering the children on to victory. Both boys and girls were awarded championship prizes for running, skipping, throwing, and for participating in novelty races, such as threading-the-needle. On Monday, 21 June that year, the Dominican Sisters held a special Arbor Day ceremony in the school grounds that had only recently been enclosed by a high picket fence. The Sisters had long looked forward to planting shade trees and they were delighted when a large crowd arrived at 4.00 p.m. to witness the tree-planting ceremony. Among those present were Bishop Kelly, the mayor and mayoress and town councillors of Cue and many parents and friends. The Bishop of Geraldton, who was given the honour of planting the first tree, was followed by a group of children selected to plant the remaining 14 trees. During the speeches Mr J. Chesson was thanked for his generosity in providing a quantity of soil and Mr W. Grey for arranging free cartage of plant manure. The Mayor of Cue offered to donate a guinea to the child who produced the best flower garden by October, and to further encourage interest in the playground, several other prizes were also announced. [42]

A disastrous storm of cyclonic proportions hit the town of Cue on Sunday, 9 January 1910. The streets were littered with twisted sheets of iron and debris, all communication services with outside centres were severed and large buildings and houses were demolished within minutes. During the morning, the weather had been oppressively hot, then by 3.00 p.m. the sky had become overcast and vivid chain lightning and thunder preceded a violent dust storm. By 4.30 p.m., the town was enveloped in dense, blinding clouds of dust, then followed by heavy rain with large hailstones. The winds were so powerful that many of the buildings, including the Cue Hotel, rattled and swayed precariously and were in danger of collapsing. As the velocity of the wind increased, sheets of iron torn from the roofs were carried through the air and deposited a considerable distance away. The storm was brief, and although there were no personal injuries, damage to property was extensive and there were few buildings left standing at the end of the day.

The Dominican school was destroyed and the partially-built Catholic Church, being erected by Mr G. McInnes, was completely levelled. The same gust of wind also unroofed the dormitories in the convent occupied by the Sisters. This was a great blow to the nuns, who only a few months earlier had paid off a long-standing debt on the building. Among the many places to suffer damage that day were the Australian Workers' Association Hall, the Oddfellows Hall, the Cue Brewery and the Cue One battery. Mr Lee Steere's large store in Railway Terrace was totally wrecked with much of the timber being reduced to matchwood. Alf Chesson's Cremorne Hotel, situated between Cue and Day Dawn, was another well-known landmark exposed to the full force of the cyclone and totally destroyed. [43]

Since 1903, when the original Catholic Church was burnt down, the school had continued to be used as a place of worship. In view of the latest disaster, Catholic parishioners realised that there was a sense of urgency about the need to re-erect the school building. In the meantime, the Dominican Sisters were given permission to hold classes in the Australian Workers' Association Hall. A meeting was called a week after the storm had taken its toll and a crowd gathered in the Catholic presbytery to discuss the damage and to suggest ways of raising funds to rebuild the two buildings destroyed. Father Flahavan took the chair and, after he informed those present that it would cost in the vicinity of £250 to rebuild the school, it was unanimously agreed that work should begin as soon as possible. It was decided that the Dominican community should not have to bear the burden of re-financing another building, and that on completion of the new St Gabriel's School, construction would commence also on a new church building. Before the meeting closed, a sum of £35 was donated towards the cost of the buildings and the following men were appointed to form a fund-raising committee: Warden Troy, Messrs J. Chesson, J. Meaney, T. Healey, J. Hickey, T. Cant, J. Murphy, F. Connaughton (Meekatharra), J. Toohey (Nannine), C. Drew (Mt Magnet) and C. Rodin (Yalgoo).

19. Convent school pupils, Cue, 1903

The new school was more sturdily constructed than the first, with extra timber being used and the inclusion of 'three cables thrown across the building, fastened at either side to iron bolts embedded in cement'. [44] The school was completed at the end of February 1910, and later that year a number of new changes were made with regard to the refurbishment of the classrooms. For example, dual desks of the latest design were installed in the senior classroom, and the walls in the lower classes were made more interesting with the introduction of bright new Bible history charts and suitable kindergarten pictures. A new school library was also opened to encourage children to read more widely. By paying a penny to borrow a book of their choice, pupils could take their favourite reading matter home, knowing that the subscription paid would go towards the purchase of new books. It appears that Dominican School concerts were also popular in two other Murchison towns, Nannine and Meekatharra, for, in July 1910, 18 pupils from Cue travelled to Meekatharra to present a concert in aid of the school extension fund. [45]

After administering the diocese from Cue for many years, Bishop Kelly returned to Geraldton in February 1910, and finally took up residence in the fine episcopal 'palace' completed for him in 1901. By then there were 10,377 Catholics in the Geraldton diocese, which amounted to 30 per cent of the population [46], and the successful development of pastoral and agricultural industries in wide-spread areas meant that the port town of Geraldton was really booming. Bishop Kelly had occasion to revisit

Cue in June that year, when he officially opened and blessed the new, well-ventilated, wood and iron Gothic-style church, which also included a nuns' chapel. Father Graber, who was later appointed Dean of the West Murchison, and the parish priest of Sandstone, Father Ryan, both assisted at the ceremony. Father Joseph Ryan, the same young priest who had been closely associated with the Dominican Sisters at Greenough and Dongara, died suddenly soon afterwards and his passing would have been keenly felt by the foundation Sisters who from their arrival had befriended him. [47]

St Patrick's Day, regardless of whether the participants were Irish or not, was always regarded as a major event on the year's social calendar. This was particularly so when the town boasted the presence of a Catholic community and school, for the Sisters and pupils were nearly always happy to organise or take part in some form of entertainment or display. So popular was 'Paddy's Day' in Cue that at one meeting, held in 1911 by Dean Graber to organise the event, it was mooted that all business people in Cue and Day Dawn should be asked to close their premises on 17 March. [48]

20. St Patrick's Church, Cue

In 1911, the Sisters opened yet another school at Meekatharra and with only scant resources to draw upon, they must have been concerned by further requests from Bishop Kelly to establish more foundations. While on a visit to the branch houses in June, the Dominican Prioress, Mother Bonaventure, was asked by the bishop to establish a new convent and school at Mt Magnet from Cue. The request was placed before Council and despite concerns being aired about the difficulty of sparing staff, the Dominicans reluctantly agreed to give the proposal a fair trial. On 19 August, the bishop visited Mt Magnet to discuss the opening of a new Dominican convent and school. Whilst there he gave the Church Committee permission to build a verandah on the side of the church and he also suggested that they obtain an estimate on the cost of building a convent. The Dominican Sisters arrived at Mt Magnet in September 1911, and after settling into temporary accommodation near the railway station they opened school on the Monday after their arrival. [49] An advertisement appeared in the *Mt Magnet Miner* on Saturday, 30 September and continued to appear until November 1911:

***CONVENT DAY SCHOOL, MT. MAGNET.*** *Conducted by the Dominican Nuns. Pupils prepared for Adelaide University Examinations. Also for Theoretical and Practical in connection with Trinity College of Music, London, and the Associated Board of R.A.M. and R.C.M., London. Tuition given in the following subjects: Music (piano, violin etc), Singing, Painting, Woodcarving, Art, Needlework, Book-keeping and Typewriting. For terms apply to Mother Superior, St Joseph's Convent, Mt Magnet.* [50]

Catholic parents in Mt Magnet were excited about the establishment of the new foundation and at a special meeting held at the church on 17 November 1911, Mrs O'Brien read an address to Bishop Kelly on behalf of the Ladies of St Brigid's Congregation. 'It is with feelings of unbounded pleasure that we have assembled here this evening to meet Your Lordship that thereby we may testify our deep gratitude to you for having placed the good Sisters in our midst, and assure you that we shall ever put forth our greatest efforts to ensure their comfort and well-being'. [51] In an effort to provide financial assistance for the newly-established St Joseph's Dominican Convent at Mt Magnet, it was decided that pupils attending St Gabriel's School, Cue and St Hyacinth's School, Day Dawn, would present a concert on 28 November. The Sisters left Mt Magnet on Wednesday, 6 December 1911, to spend the Christmas holidays at Dongara. It was their intention to re-open the school on the first Monday of February, when it was anticipated that there would be a marked increase in enrolments. According to local newspaper reports it appears that a serious outbreak of measles and mumps had been raging in the Murchison for some time. By December, there were signs that the epidemic was beginning to abate and life on the fields was beginning to return to normal. There was an air of optimism in one report written in January 1912: 'Many convalescents had left for the seaside and there was every likelihood that after the holidays there would be renewed activity in mining matters and that many of the old prospectors would return'. [52] Whether through illness, a lack of staff or pupils, or for financial reasons, it appears that the Sisters withdrew from Mt Magnet in December 1911 and St Joseph's Convent School did not re-open as planned in 1912.

In the meantime, the annual Dominican School concert, held at Cue on 14 December 1911, was described in the *Sower* as an 'unqualified success not withstanding inclemency of weather'. The Workers' Hall was illuminated with numerous electric lights and because variety concerts were still a popular form of entertainment, tickets were in

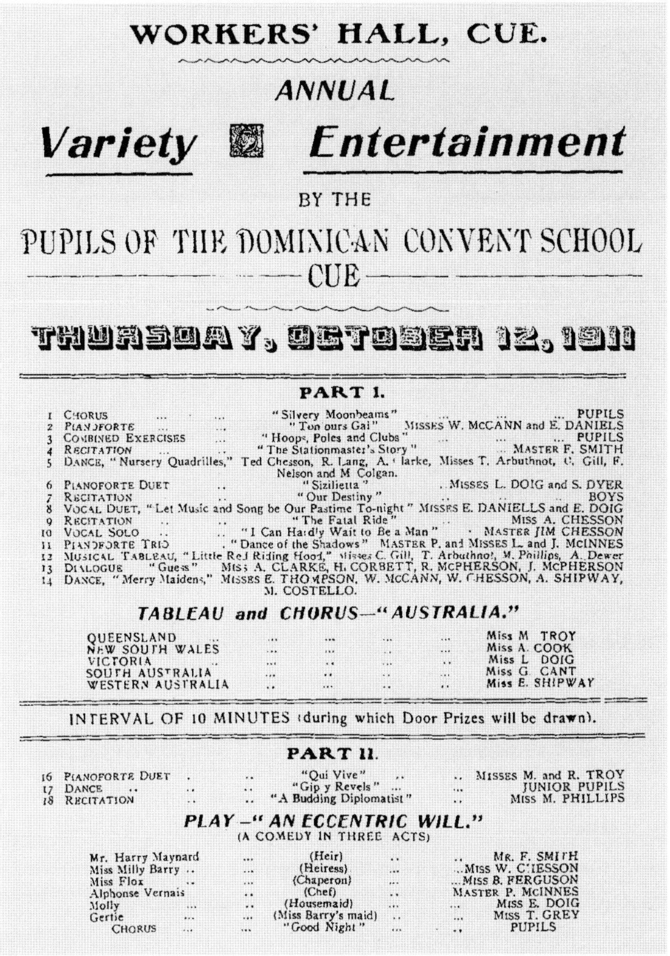

WORKERS' HALL, CUE.

ANNUAL

Variety Entertainment

BY THE

PUPILS OF THE DOMINICAN CONVENT SCHOOL

CUE

THURSDAY, OCTOBER 12, 1911

PART I.

| | | | |
|---|---|---|---|
| 1 | CHORUS | "Silvery Moonbeams" | PUPILS |
| 2 | PIANOFORTE | "Toujours Gai" | MISSES W. McCANN and E. DANIELS |
| 3 | COMBINED EXERCISES | "Hoops, Poles and Clubs" | PUPILS |
| 4 | RECITATION | "The Stationmaster's Story" | MASTER F. SMITH |
| 5 | DANCE, "Nursery Quadrilles," | | Ted Chesson, R. Lang, A. Clarke, Misses T. Arbuthnot, C. Gill, F. Nelson and M. Colgan. |
| 6 | PIANOFORTE DUET | "Sizilietta" | MISSES L. DOIG and S. DYER |
| 7 | RECITATION | "Our Destiny" | BOYS |
| 8 | VOCAL DUET, | "Let Music and Song be Our Pastime To-night" | MISSES E. DANIELLS and E. DOIG |
| 9 | RECITATION | "The Fatal Ride" | MISS A. CHESSON |
| 10 | VOCAL SOLO | "I Can Hardly Wait to Be a Man" | MASTER JIM CHESSON |
| 11 | PIANOFORTE TRIO | "Dance of the Shadows" | MASTER P. and MISSES L. and J. McINNES |
| 12 | MUSICAL TABLEAU, | "Little Red Riding Hood," | Misses C. Gill, T. Arbuthnot, M. Phillips, A. Dewer |
| 13 | DIALOGUE | "Guess" | MISS A. CLARKE, H. CORBETT, R. McPHERSON, J. McPHERSON |
| 14 | DANCE, | "Merry Maidens," | MISSES E. THOMPSON, W. McCANN, W. CHESSON, A. SHIPWAY, M. COSTELLO. |

TABLEAU and CHORUS—"AUSTRALIA."

| | |
|---|---|
| QUEENSLAND | Miss M. TROY |
| NEW SOUTH WALES | Miss A. COOK |
| VICTORIA | Miss L. DOIG |
| SOUTH AUSTRALIA | Miss G. CANT |
| WESTERN AUSTRALIA | Miss E. SHIPWAY |

INTERVAL OF 10 MINUTES (during which Door Prizes will be drawn).

PART II.

| | | | |
|---|---|---|---|
| 16 | PIANOFORTE DUET | "Qui Vive" | MISSES M. and R. TROY |
| 17 | DANCE | "Gipsy Revels" | JUNIOR PUPILS |
| 18 | RECITATION | "A Budding Diplomatist" | MISS M. PHILLIPS |

PLAY—"AN ECCENTRIC WILL."

(A COMEDY IN THREE ACTS)

| | | |
|---|---|---|
| Mr. Harry Maynard | (Heir) | MR. F. SMITH |
| Miss Milly Barry | (Heiress) | MISS W. CHESSON |
| Miss Flox | (Chaperon) | MISS B. FERGUSON |
| Alphonse Vernais | (Chef) | MASTER P. McINNES |
| Molly | (Housemaid) | MISS E. DOIG |
| Gertie | (Miss Barry's maid) | MISS T. GREY |
| CHORUS | "Good Night" | PUPILS |

21. Dominican concert, 1911

demand from people of all denominations. About 90 pupils appeared on stage to sing the opening chorus 'Starlight on the Quiet River', followed by pianoforte duets performed by Misses Toohey and Troy, and Master and Miss L. McGinnis. The nuns and parents had put a great deal of effort and thought into the evening's program, which included the usual violin and vocal solos, recitations and operettas. Before Dean Graber presented the prizes and complimented the Sisters and performers on the evening's 'intellectual treat', the curtain came down on a colourful finale consisting of four tableaux featuring the seasons. The fact that the themes did not conform to climatic conditions in Australia revealed the wide-spread nostalgia that still existed for the 'Old Country'. Spring was represented by a May Day festival, Summer by a picnic, Autumn by a harvest, and Winter by a distribution of Christmas gifts.

The unexpected loss of yet another valued member of the community occurred on Monday, 10 June 1912, when Sister Felicitas Plunkett died at Cue at the age of 29. Born in Dunedin and educated at St Dominic's College in that town, she entered the Dominican Order in New Zealand in 1902 and was professed three years later. Shortly after her religious profession, she volunteered to join the West Australia mission. Described as petite and charming, she was a popular teacher at both the Leonora and Cue convent schools.

Sister Felicitas, it seems, enjoyed excellent health until she suddenly fell victim to typhoid fever, a common cause of serious illness and death on the early goldfields. Within three weeks, despite careful nursing and the best medical attention available, the young nun died after a great deal of suffering. Because her death occurred within the Octave of Corpus Christi, a Requiem Mass was not possible, according to the liturgical convention of the day. Her body, therefore, was quietly interred the next day in the cemetery at Cue alongside that of Mother Gabriel Gill and it was not until the following month, on the Feast of the Seven Martyred Sons of St Felicitas, that the usual liturgy took place in the parish church.

Before leaving for his *ad limina* visit to Rome in 1913, Bishop Kelly proudly informed his parishioners that since the establishment of the diocese 15 years earlier, no fewer than 80 buildings had been dedicated and erected for diocesan purposes. A great number of these structures, which included 28 churches, 18 convents, 14 schools and 25 presbyteries, were of a simple design, but nevertheless very important to the people who frequented them. [53] The period prior to, and after World War I, was a time of financial uncertainty in the Murchison. Unfortunately, a number of prominent gold mines were only rich on the surface and for some time had been showing signs of petering out. As a result, the growing decline in gold production eventually saw the closure of a number of long-established mines and the relocation of many families to other towns. By 1915, immigration had almost been brought to a halt and manpower was further affected by large numbers of young men joining the Armed Forces. Author, Mr P. Heydon, summed up the situation when he wrote:

*During 1916, there was little local news of interest being printed. World War I was of vital interest, and most of the news concerned the fighting in Europe. There were casualty lists regularly printed. Some of the wounded men returned to Cue, Day Dawn, Meekatharra and Mt Magnet. There was very little mining being carried out in Cue. The Great Fingall at Day Dawn was slowly grinding to a halt, and there was gloom all round.* [54]

Whilst visiting Cue in October 1916, Bishop Kelly wrote to the local Church Committee to formally thank members for the kind offer they had made to continue in their efforts to reduce the overdraft on the church. He suggested that 'some of the priests of Cue have not evinced much interest in the matter, and others, for various reasons, have remained too short a time in the parish to deal effectively with it'. In answer to queries raised about pieces of school furniture having allegedly been sent to the Dominican school at Three Springs, the bishop pointed out that this information was incorrect. It was true that certain

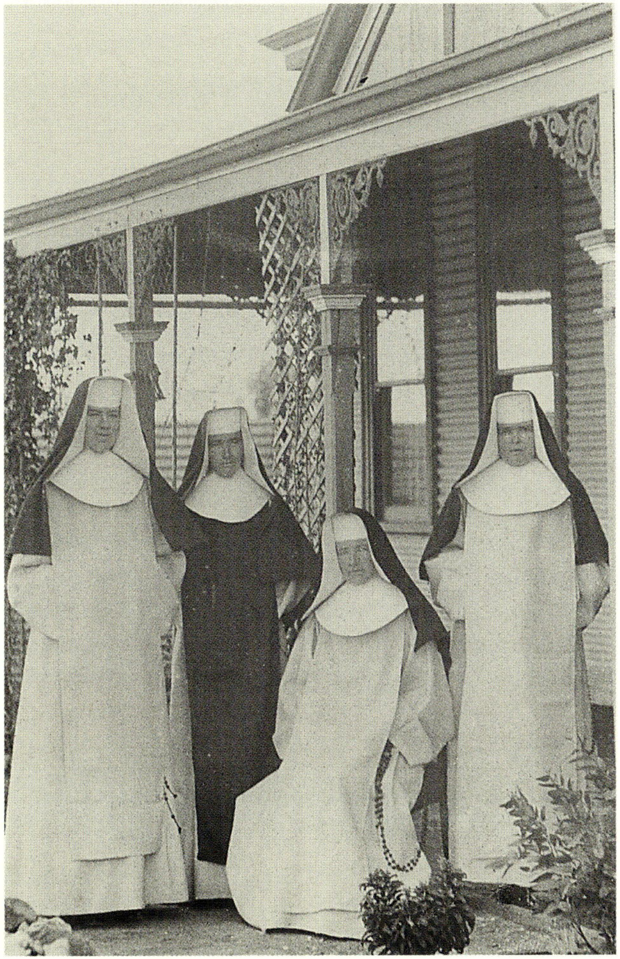

22. Second Convent, Cue, 1911
L. to R.: Sisters Aquin Inglis, Imelda Buckley, Benignus O'Connor, Teresa McQuillan

household items had been donated by the Sisters, but they were entitled to do what they wanted with these as they had been purchased with their own money. He admitted that the community at Cue had given the convent at Meekatharra five small, spare desks on the understanding that they would be returned on demand. Addressing a number of questions asked in relation to church and convent finances, Bishop Kelly took the opportunity to clarify some misconceptions about contributions sent to Dongara. Quoting from figures supplied to him by Sister Teresa McQuillan, the Dominican accountant during the previous two years, he informed the honorary secretary that in 1915 a £10 donation was received from the Cue Church Committee, £26 from the Meekatharra Convent and £5 from the Dongara Convent. It was also noted that the Cue Convent had sent £5.9.9 to Dongara in August 1915. In the following year, £6.12.6 was collected by Mrs Brophy, the Cue Church Committee donated £28, the Day Dawn Church Committee £3, the Meekatharra Convent £4 and the Dongara Convent £5. The bishop also reminded the committee that the mother house was the property of the whole community and its purpose was to provide the nuns with a home during sickness, school holidays, annual spiritual exercises and finally, in their old age. As all Sisters owned the property it followed that all were expected to help pay for its purchase and also for its upkeep.

The bishop concluded by stating: 'To say that this burden should fall upon the small staff that may be stationed there during any one year shows a failure to appreciate the situation'. [55]

The closure of the once-profitable Great Fingall Mine on 12 April 1918, was a major set-back to the towns of Day Dawn and Cue, and following weeks of uncertainty and depression, there was a mass exodus of people from the fields. The year was not all doom and gloom, however, for when the communication came through late on Monday night, 11 November 1918, that Germany had signed the Armistice, tears of joy overtook people's fears for the future. The welcome news quickly swept through Cue getting everyone out of bed. The clang of the fire bell mingled with the joyous peel of church bells while a train whistle continuously pierced the night. As people thronged the main street in high spirits, patriotic songs and hearty cheers filled the air and kept up the momentum until well after midnight. [56]

Following the closure of the Cue One battery, a new State battery which opened on 19 September 1919, temporarily gave the town a new lease of life. The establishment of a government battery gave miners, who still had crushings, the opportunity to get their gold processed. The presence of these prospectors in the district, together with a number of pastoralists and their employees, contributed to the survival of at least some of Cue's remaining domestic and commercial suppliers. Between the two World Wars the mining industry continued to be dogged by a series of highs and lows. The country had no sooner recovered from its involvement in World War I, than it was subjected to a world-wide depression. Although the mid-1930s saw the birth of two successful mining towns in the Murchison, Reedy and Big Bell, both were short-lived. The outbreak of the World War II also put further pressures on the mining industry when large numbers of local men enlisted and authorities were forced to intern all un-naturalised Italians, thus creating a shortage of labour in the district. Somehow, St Gabriel's Convent School managed to survive each crisis and although class numbers fluctuated, the Dominican Sisters continued to live up to the high reputation they had gained in education circles since their arrival at Cue in 1899.

The question of the Dominican Rule of Enclosure once more came to the fore in May 1943, when the parish priest of Cue, Father O'Connor, wrote to Bishop A. Gummer of Geraldton. In his letter, the priest rightly pointed out some of the inconveniences suffered by the Dominican Sisters working in his parish. These problems had arisen, he explained, because of the 'new regulations promulgated, or rather the revocation of old regulations, at their annual Retreat last year'. The priest queried the fact that most of the dispensations, earlier agreed to by Bishop Kelly, had been withdrawn. The Sisters, he stated:

*...are not permitted to go outside the convent grounds, which I might add, except for their back yards, are non-existent. Take Reedy for example, the grounds there are very small & only two blocks for church and convent. Accordingly when a Sister wants to have a walk, she has to keep going around in circles in the convent back yard. Should the Sisters wish to take the children for a walk – which is practical here, seeing they have some Boarders – they cannot do so. I cannot take the children for a Picnic during the year, because the Sisters cannot accompany them, and I would not take the responsibility of looking after the young children. Again the Sisters here have run a concert here during the past few years. Such concerts, apart from being a great source of Revenue towards the support of the Sisters here, raised the standard of Catholic Education in the estimation of the people of this town. The Sisters can no longer hold such concerts since they cannot accompany the children to the Public Hall.* [57]

Father O'Connor was also concerned that the Sisters could no longer visit people in their own homes, and that hospital visitation was only allowed when he was not in Cue. He felt that sick people would welcome a visit and likewise parents living at Big Bell, who were anxious to have their children attend religious instruction, would be delighted if he could take the Sisters with him when he offered Mass in that town. The Sisters, he wrote, 'work very hard, they are going from dark to dark, between spiritual exercises, school, music and other lessons'. [58] He also reminded Bishop Gummer that the late Bishop Kelly knew from first-hand experience the needs of his people, which is why he gave permission for the Dominicans to relax their rules whilst working in country parishes. As a result of Fr O'Connor's letter, a circular was sent to each branch house explaining that perhaps too rigorous an interpretation had been placed on the rules when they were amended.

When Sister Dominic Galvin was first appointed to Cue in 1945, she found the area 'dry, dusty and barren'. [59] She recalled that in common with many goldfields buildings, the church, convent and school were all constructed of corrugated iron. The oblong-shaped church, which was situated some distance from the convent, had a steep roof tied down with strong wire cables to protect it from the high winds. Sister Dominic could, in her mind's eye, still clearly see the wooden altar 'delicately carved and displaying exquisite traceries' and

23. New St Patrick's School, Cue, 1949

remembered that the intense heat during summer played havoc with the wood, causing cracks to appear. One of the Sisters' duties was to prepare St Patrick's Church in readiness for services on Sunday. There were times when, after having completed the work to their satisfaction, the occurrence of a sudden dust storm would leave them disheartened and with no alternative than to begin again.

Sister Dominic recalls that during the war years, Cue's parish priest, Father O'Flaherty, dug a large slit trench in the ground between the convent and the school to safeguard the parishioners, pupils, Sisters and sacred church vessels in case of a Japanese bomb attack. The priest also planted tamarisk trees along the path to the presbytery and 20 years later these hardy shrubs were still thriving. The Sisters did not make public visits in those years and always ate their meals in silence in the room designated as the refectory. In keeping with their rule, visitors to the convent were entertained in the parlour and when the priest came to dine he was always served in that particular room. In the 1940s, the Sisters from Cue usually joined members of the Meekatharra community for the term holidays, only returning to Dongara for Christmas. [60]

In 1953, Sister Dominic was re-appointed to Cue and with Sister Pius Nolan formed the teaching staff at the Dominican day school, the boarding section having been closed that same year. She was pleased to note that, although the corrugated iron church, convent and presbytery (originally Bishop Kelly's headquarters), remained unaltered, the former school building had been replaced by a modern well-designed two-room structure. The old-style desks no longer existed, instead the classrooms were pleasantly furnished with smart tubular furniture, each desk with individual seating. In July 1954, Superintendent A. H. Trotman's general report to the Education Department stated: 'this is a very pleasing little school where standards are high and methodology thorough. The children are friendly and keen to give of their best – verbal definitions generally are marked by refreshing spontaneity. To Sr Raymund [Creed] must be given credit for her conscientious efforts on behalf of this little group. It is to be hoped that numbers will not grow any smaller'. [61] Unfortunately, his wish about class numbers was not realised, for, in 1965, the school had only 22 children enrolled. Two years later, when one of the parents died and her young family of four was sent to Perth, the number of pupils attending classes was sadly reduced to 18.

For a further three years, despite numerous setbacks, the Sisters stoically continued to operate the school. One of these, Sister Benvenuta Brophy, also remained committed to the task of providing religious instruction to anyone requiring lessons and it was due to her efforts that seven small children received their First

Holy Communion on the Feast of Christ the King in 1967 at St Patrick's Church, Cue. Three of the children taking part were pupils from St Gabriel's Convent School and four were residential students at the Kyarra Native Hostel. During the early 1960s, Sisters Michael Ryan and Pius Nolan had also taken religious classes on Saturdays for Aboriginal children living at the hostel and on occasions had as many as 20 children in attendance. [62] The summer of 1968 was particularly hot, and the temperature on the day that St Gabriel's Convent School opened for the last time was comparable to that experienced by the two foundation Sisters from Greenough 69 years earlier. Although two new names were added to the school roll call at the beginning of that year to maintain the total of 18 pupils, only 10 of these children remained when St Gabriel's re-opened for the second term. By then, it had become obvious that, as with the demise of the once busy gold mining centre, the Dominican Sisters' time at Cue also had come to an end.

24. First Communion group, 1966
Sisters Joseph O'Connor and Paul O'Connor

News of the Sisters' departure was not unexpected, but nevertheless there were many who felt the loss keenly once their withdrawal was finally announced. When the Shire of Cue met in November 1968, members resolved that when the convent closed the Shire Clerk should ask if he could inspect two of the pianos belonging to the Dominican community. It was agreed that if the instruments were offered for sale, and were considered suitable, then he would enquire about purchasing one of them for the Shire Hall. Consequently, just prior to the departure of the two remaining members of the Cue community, Sister Benvenuta Brophy (now Sr Catherine) and Sister Norbert Burke (Sr Pauline) in December 1968, one of the convent pianos was purchased for the sum of $70.

While numerous changes occurred during the years in which the Sisters were in residence, the constants were there too; the prayers and dedication of the Sisters and priests and the generosity of the people which each successive Dominican community experienced to the end. Members still remember the many friends who supported them, among them the Price, Doyle, Morrissey, Muscardini, Elder and Murphy families. One of the memories of all the Sisters who travelled by train to Cue and beyond, is the kindness of people along the way – the Seaman family at Wurarga, the Coyne and Nevill families at Yalgoo, all of whom, over many years, supplied food and drink to refresh them at these stops. The Seaman's daughters, Margaret and Pam, became boarders at the Dominican

Ladies' College and in December 1952, Margaret was accepted into the novitiate at Dongara. Later, as Sister Gemma, she proved to be an excellent teacher at both primary and secondary levels and was also Sister-in-Charge at the Santa Clara Convent and school at Bentley (1966-1968) and at Morawa (1975). When ill-health necessitated her leaving the field of teaching, she became a member of the community at St Catherine's, Doubleview, where her kindness and attention to the needs of others have been valued highly by both visitors and residents.

The once heavily-populated gold centre is no longer significant. Modern prospectors with lightweight gold detectors, have since superseded old-fashioned fossickers. Tourists, rather than miners, wander the main street past the mellow-toned public buildings and central rotunda which marks the site of the first water well. When, in 1978, the last train pulled out of the former busy station, it appeared to those present that the last act had been played and the final curtain brought down on the grand old frontier town of Cue – no longer Queen of the Murchison.

25. Centenary celebration, Cue, 1991
L. to R. Back Row: Sisters Emmanuel Lynch, Bernadette Punch, Michael Ryan, Margaret Scharf
Front: Sister Eileen Leahy, Mrs Mary Grey (ex-pupil), Sister Xavier Ryan

# On the Banks of the Irwin

CHAPTER 5

Six months in advance of their withdrawal from Greenough in 1902, the Dominican Sisters transferred all of their senior boarders to Dongara, leaving sufficient staff at the Rosary Convent to continue teaching the younger pupils attending St Joseph's and St Thomas's.

From the middle of July 1901, until December that year, these boarders were accommodated in a rented stone house next door to the flour mill at Dongara. Francis Pearse built the Royal Steam Roller Flour Mill, situated close to the railway line, in 1894, and the dwelling, originally known as Mill House and later as the Bungalow, was originally used to accommodate the miller employed there. After the mill had ceased operations, these premises were periodically rented out. It is believed that two of the front rooms were also used briefly by the Misses Nairn, three sisters who, prior to 1901, conducted a private ladies' school. The building, which was later purchased by Mr Joe Clarkson, was considered by the Sisters to be ideal for the short-term accommodation needed to form the nucleus of the future Dominican Ladies' College. [1]

Classes for high school students commenced at Dongara on 22 July 1901, with four foundation boarders, May Maxted, Una Pearce, Rachel Cohen and Beatrice Boladeras. Two weeks later, four young ladies, Edith and Janet Nairn and Ida and Beatrice Criddle, were enrolled as day pupils and towards the end of that year the name of Vera Adams, the local policeman's daughter, was added to the roll. Unfortunately, Dominican annals do not record the name of the first Sisters to take up residence at Dongara. However, it stands to reason that as Mother Gabriel Gill and Sister Bonaventure McEntyre were then still teaching at Cue, the Sisters heading the new foundation would have been drawn from the community at Greenough. The occupants of the Rosary Convent at that time were three professed Sisters Dominica Murphy, Philomena McGrath and di Pazzi Miscall and three young novices, who had only been received into the novitiate on 4 February 1901 – Sisters Anastasia Byrne, Catherine Kenny and Anthony Ross.

Sister Ceslaus Freed, who was professed at the Dominican Priory, Dunedin, New Zealand, on 11 July 1901, and appears to have left for Geraldton almost immediately, would also have been available to teach at the new foundation in Dongara. [2] This diminutive woman, who later became Mother Prioress General, remained on the staff of the Dominican Ladies' College at Dongara for some 47 years, with the exception of three months spent at Day Dawn. It has been said that many of the musical successes gained by the college during those years were largely attributed to Sr Ceslaus's expertise. However, when reminiscing about their former teacher and colleague, most people identify Sr Ceslaus with her lifelong passion for gardening and promoting the classics. It appears that she set an extremely high standard in the teaching of English and poetry and past pupils, some now in their 80s, can still recite from beginning to end Gray's *Elegy Written in a Country Churchyard*, *The Boy Stood on the Burning Deck*, *The Slave's Dream*, and *The Deserted Village*. Sister Ceslaus obviously had a keen sense of humour. In his memoirs, Cyril Penny recalled how on one occasion, when he was cutting lucerne for the milking cows and calves in the paddock next to the Priory at Dongara, he was attracted by a noise coming from the senior classroom. Intrigued, he peeked through the window only to see a group of students in gymnastic tunics doing their exercises. One girl predictably screamed when she spied him, but discreetly said nothing when reprimanded. Cyril, who admitted that he was 'a bit of a devil', could not resist borrowing a piece of white chalk and on a large blackboard outside he sketched Sister putting the girls through their exercises. He cheekily captioned the drawing, 'Sister Ceslaus tore her drawers', and gallantly owned up when one of the girls was later blamed. Fully expecting to be dismissed over the incident, he was taken completely by surprise by Sr Ceslaus's reaction. 'Well', said Sister, without the hint of a smile, 'I didn't know I was so ugly!' [3]

The few foundation Sisters at Dongara must have been highly-organised for, despite the inconvenience of moving house in the middle of a school year and caring for boarders, they still found time to arrange a variety of school activities and prepare students for the examinations held on 14 November 1901. The inaugural presentation of prizes took place at Dongara on 17 December 1901, and top student Janet Nairn, having achieved the highest marks in the examination, became the new foundation's first recorded dux. In the absence of the parish priest, Father Benson, Father Joseph Ryan distributed prizes to a number of successful pupils including Mary Maxted, who had received 93 marks in the Trinity College of London Examinations (Intermediate Harmony Grade) held in June. During the evening Ida Criddle won a prize for general improvement and Rachel Cohen for regular attendance, while Edith Nairn was awarded the much-coveted school Wreath after being judged by her fellow students as the most amiable and obedient girl in the school. [4]

When the Dominican Sisters founded their new school at Dongara in July 1901, they clearly had no intention of withdrawing from Greenough the following year. Indeed, prior to returning to Cue to begin the first term in 1902, Mother Gabriel listed, as late as January, the number of Dominican foundations she was responsible for, including Greenough. On 25 January, she recorded: 'Nearly half our present Community is unprofessed and we have three Convents [Greenough, Cue and Dongara] with four schools attached [St Joseph's, St Thomas's, St Gabriel's, and St Dominick's, Dongara] to provide with teachers'. [5] Her report was followed by an advertisement, announcing the re-opening of the Dominican boarding and day school at Greenough, which continued to be published in the *Catholic Record* until as late as 22 February 1902. [6] It would appear that as well as retaining the foundation at Greenough, the Dominican Sisters planned to establish the head house and novitiate at Dongara and develop a significant boarding school and college that offered a wider range of academic subjects and opportunities.

Looking at the size of the Dominican community at that time, it is obvious that without further reinforcements the Sisters did not have enough members to operate their existing schools and convents in the Victoria and Murchison Districts, let alone a new foundation. It is possibly for that reason that Bishop Kelly withdrew the Dominicans from Greenough and arranged to bring the Presentation Sisters in from Geraldton, thereby allowing the Sisters to concentrate on Dongara. On 21 February, *The Geraldton Express* described the Dominican Sisters' departure by train for Dongara, and also their future plans:

*In Dongarra the Dominicans have established their Priory in a commodious and charmingly situated residence purchased but a short time since. Here they will devote themselves entirely to the training of novices, carrying on for the present no schools but those which they have at Dongarra and at Cue. Their place has been taken by the Presentation Nuns, a community of whom took possession of the convent at the end of last week and opened the schools both at Greenough and the Back Flats on Monday, so that there has been no interruption of scholastic work.* [7]

Another notice also appeared regularly in the *Catholic Record* from as early as 2 November 1901. This advertisement, which gradually increased in size, alerted readers to the benefits of having their daughters educated at the new Dominican High school for Girls established at 'a convenient and salubrious centre' in Dongara. 'The Convent', it stated, 'stands among beautiful surroundings, close to the Railway Station. The course includes all the branches and accomplishments of a young lady's higher education, in imparting which the Dominican Nuns have everywhere met with notable success. Apply Reverend Mother, St Dominick's Convent Dongara'. It is interesting to note that from the beginning, the Saint's name was included in the title of the new school and that for many years the spelling included the letter 'k'. [8]

A larger notice of the curriculum later appeared informing prospective parents that the newly-established educational centre, conducted by the Dominican nuns at Dongara, offered students a course that 'embraced all the subjects prescribed by the State School Syllabus; as well as Book-keeping, Euclid, Algebra, Domestic Economy, and Shorthand'. The high school curriculum, besides offering all the usual core subjects, also listed piano, violin, theory of music, harmony, singing, drawing, painting, wood-carving, art, needlework, paper flower making, wax flower and fruit modelling, literature and tuition in French, German, Italian and Latin languages. The prospectus once again emphasised the town's picturesque and healthy position and its close proximity to the railway and the sea.

By 1902, the Dominican Sisters' reputation as teachers at Cue and Greenough had spread, and residents, long-associated with the Irwin and Murchison districts, began to enrol their children in the new St Dominick's College at Dongara. Among the earliest names recorded were those of Ida Criddle, Millie Pollock, Edith and Janet Nairn, Kitty Fitzgerald, Ruby Millar, Lella and Reeta Newton, Bessie Broadhurst, Vera Adams, Nellie Botta, Dolly McIntyre, Tottie Ross, Vera Fienberg, Muriel Wilson, the Chesson twins and their sister Mary, Norah and Lupeta (Louie)

Driscoll and May Corbett who became the first past pupil to enter the Dominican Order. [9]

After leaving the former Mill House in December 1901, the Dominican Sisters moved into larger rented premises on the Irwin Road (Brand Highway), commonly referred to as 'Six Chimneys' or the 'House of Many Chimneys'. Early 1860s settler Samuel Fortesque Moore, who built a house, a blacksmith shop and a store on the opposite side of the road, originally owned and leased the site in question. Various tenant farmers made use of the property over the years, until Mr J. McKnight, a squatter, eventually built the long stone building noted for its chimneys. Apart from acting as a temporary convent and boarding school for a brief time in 1902, the house was used for a multitude of purposes until it was sold in the early 1920s. [10] Foundation boarder, Janet Nairn, later recalled attending classes at 'Six Chimneys' and also some of the events that occurred prior to the opening of the new Dominican buildings overlooking the Irwin River at Dongara:

26. House of Six Chimneys, Dongara
Courtesy Nigel Aldridge

*When we returned after the Christmas holidays, the whole community was at home – Mission Sisters and boarders from the goldfields had come down for holidays. The twin Chessons and Mary were among the number – so there had been a lively time and they were all living now on the Irwin Road, in the long stone house of many chimneys. That house holds precious memories for me, for there some of the pupils, and nearly all the Dongara notables of those days, were invited to the first "Reception" (Sr Josephine RIP). It was a gala day for all and an eye-opener for the locals. If I remember rightly, Mrs Bartlett, wife of the one and only doctor, helped to cut the Reception cake. Near the convent was a small cottage where several priests spent the summer holidays.*

*Bishop Kelly was a great favourite with the children and in the early days before he bought his first car, he used to drive a two-seated buggy and many a joy ride he gave us. Then there was big Father Ryan, nearly 20 stone, who used to come out from Geraldton; when he preached, his voice would resound far and wide. He was a great man – God rest him. Of course Father Creagh played a big part in Dongara in those days. Then came dear old Father O'Hare.*

*Later the Convent was transferred to the present site, then only one storey. Originally an hotel, the horse railings remained for some little while outside the front of the building and 'The students' – for Mother Gabriel would not allow us to be called anything else – had a marvellous time on these when*

27-30. Progressive stages of St Dominic's Priory and College, Dongara

*there were no nuns about, needless to say. In those faraway days, it was considered most unladylike to raise one's feet more than six inches off the ground, let alone to climb, do balancing tricks in mid-air, and to try and turn oneself inside out... I can remember Ruby Millar, later Mrs French, she hailed from Carnarvon; Vera Fienberg, now Mrs Phillips of Geraldton, a lovely Italian girl, Nellie Botta, from Day Dawn – she died young, May Corbett was destined to be the first ex-student to enter the Novitiate in a few years. Ida Criddle came about that time and wee Dolly McIntyre, whom Mother M. Gabriel insisted upon our calling Daphne – Dolly was too babyish! Milly Pollock came later and so did Essie O'Connor and Renee Smith.* [11]

In December 1901, Mother Gabriel Gill and Sister Bonaventure McEntyre came down from Cue to spend the Christmas holidays at Dongara with Sisters di Pazzi Miscall, Dominica Murphy and Philomena McGrath. The latter, a professed Sister, had arrived earlier from New Zealand to assist and, in 1902, became Sacristan and Mistress of the primary school at Dongara. For some time, the community had been keen to acquire a permanent building at Dongara and, on 8 January, Mother Gabriel called members of the Dominican Council together to examine an interesting offer she had received regarding the purchase of the former Dongarra Hotel. The property, which had an asking price of £1000, included a large building surrounded by four acres of land, a portion of which had been fenced-in for fruit and vegetable gardens. Members of Council were impressed with the building's potential and, after taking a secret vote, a decision was made to purchase the old hotel if Bishop Kelly could arrange the necessary finance. [12]

The single-storey construction, built as a hotel by William Criddle Jnr in 1881, was situated on a rise on the south bank of the Irwin River, close to the original track and lower ford that once led to Port Irwin (Port Denison). The owner's family had a long association with the Victoria and Irwin Districts. In 1852, the birth of Mary, daughter of William Criddle Snr and his wife Elizabeth, was the first to be registered in the Champion Bay book of births. Dongara, was originally known as Dhungarra (Aboriginal for 'meeting place of seals'), and until the 1940s most people continued to use two r's in the spelling of the name. By 1871, the Irwin Roads Board had been and formed and a school, police station, courthouse and post office had been established in the tiny township. William Criddle Jnr's main object in building the hotel was to provide comfortable accommodation for teamsters travelling between Mt Magnet and the port. The hotel appeared to prosper up until the Dongara-Denison bridge was completed in 1889 and the track became obsolete.

On 25 January, a delighted Mother Gabriel informed the Sisters that Bishop Kelly had agreed to arrange a loan to purchase the property from Mr Criddle. The news meant that, for the first time since their arrival, the Dominican Sisters could look forward to the prospect of establishing a larger, more permanent boarding school and Priory. The jubilation that followed the announcement was short-lived however, when the Prioress drew the Council's attention to other more pressing matters. A cablegram, sent earlier to Dunedin requesting reinforcements, had been answered in the negative, thus dashing Mother Gabriel's hopes for an increased membership to share the workload and putting out of reach her desire to establish a suitable novitiate. Disappointed, the Prioress expressed concern about the injustice being currently done to Dominican novices who had completed the first year of their probation. It worried her that, instead of receiving training in a proper novitiate under the guidance of a Novice Mistress, the young ladies who had entered the order were being scattered throughout the branch houses. Under those circumstances, Mother Gabriel felt that it was impossible to offer future postulants a normal religious training while community numbers were so low. [13] Several young ladies had been accepted at Greenough as choir and lay postulants between the years 1899 and 1901. Understandably, some of these applicants were found to be unsuitable for religious life and others chose not to continue after their probation period.

Mother Gabriel raised two questions with Council members before returning to Cue. Firstly, would it be advisable to admit novices to profession status if in another year the same state of affairs continued? Secondly, could dispensation from the novitiate be obtained, and if so would the novices be competent afterwards to instruct others in the Rule (Constitution), customs and spirit of the Dominican Order? As a result, the Council unanimously decided that all novices and postulants should remain in the new mother house at Dongara to receive their training according to the Dominican Rule. It was also agreed that an exception should be made in cases of extreme necessity, provided that the novice in question had at least one year's training to her credit. The Council came to the conclusion that, unless they closed one of their three schools, the possibility of carrying out some of these decisions could prove extremely difficult. Finally, it was decided that Mother Gabriel should discuss all of the difficulties raised with Bishop Kelly and seek his advice. [14]

On Monday, 27 January 1902, Sister Catherine's sister, Ellen Kenny, who had completed a short period of postulancy, was received as a novice at a ceremony held at the 'Six Chimneys' convent at Dongara. Suitably dressed in white, with two small bridesmaids and a basket bearer in attendance, Miss Kenny was clothed in the cream religious habit of the Dominicans and the white veil of a novice during the formalities and given the religious name of Sister Mary Josephine. [15] At this point the postulant was considered to have entered the novitiate. Postulants normally spent six months in the convent before being received and given the white veil. The first 12 months was a spiritual year and a further year in the novitiate prepared them for making their first profession. The community's ability to carry out this routine, at that time, was of course still debatable.

Thankfully by April 1902, the staffing situation at Dongara was beginning to show signs of improvement. Shortly after accepting one prospective choir Sister into the novitiate, Mother Gabriel received word from Dunedin that five young ladies would more than likely join the community in the near future. Only one of these, Annie Colgan (Sr Vincent), reached profession. The New Zealand Sisters also indicated that Sister Magdalen might eventually become part of the Dongara community, as her doctor had suggested that a warmer climate might benefit her health. [16]

A significant, but not unexpected, change took place in 1902 when, after an agreed two-year period of trial, the Dunedin community put into effect arrangements that would see the Western Australian foundation become independent of New Zealand. The establishment of an autonomous Dominican community in the Geraldton diocese was officially declared at a Council meeting held at Dunedin on 16 May 1902, and, subject to the Bishop of Dunedin's approval, Mother Gabriel was appointed Prioress, Sister Bonaventure, sub-Prioress, and Sister Dominica, Mistress of Novices. At the same time the Dunedin Prioress in New Zealand, Mother Raymond, added the following rider to a copy of the Council minutes sent to Bishop Verdon on 15 June: 'The appointment of Mother Gabriel as Prioress, does not preclude the possibility of her returning to St Dominic's should she at any time wish to do so'. [17] In his reply to Mother Raymond the Bishop of Otago stated:

*When the General Chapter of the Dominican Nuns of Otago, assembled in St Dominic's Priory, Dunedin, in the early part of the year 1899, applied for permission to send a Foundation of Dominican Nuns to West Australia, I gave unwilling consent and laid down the following conditions... Mother Gabriel petitioned to be allowed to go to Australia with the new Foundation, but I only gave her temporary leave of absence for a time not extending as far as two years. As, however, Mother Gabriel has manifested a strong desire to settle down permanently in Australia, I hereby resign all claim to her future services and as far as I can, I allow her to transfer to the Bishop of Geraldton the obedience which she heretofore owed to the Bishop of Dunedin.* [18]

Bishop Verdon's statement was slightly confusing, for, according to the minutes of a Council meeting he had attended at Dunedin in October 1898, the bishop had willingly given his consent and suggested that, due to distance, Greenough should become independent after a year. Furthermore he had also given full permission for novices to be trained at Dunedin for the Western Australian Dominican Convent. The Bishop of Dunedin then proceeded to confirm the Western Australian appointments and at the same time he issued the following instructions. 'I require that Mother and her community acknowledge in writing that St Dominic's Priory, Dunedin, is now entirely free of any obligation to assist or support in any way the foundation of West Australia or any member of that foundation'. Mother Gabriel signed the official renunciation at Dongara on 24 August 1902, and soon afterwards returned the document to New Zealand. [19] She was obviously touched by the open invitation she had received to return to Dunedin if she wished in the future and she added: 'personally I, M. M. [Mother Mary] Gabriel, thank Mother Prioress and her Council for their kind consideration in my regard. It is quite possible that I may some day avail myself of the privilege granted to me'. [20]

Earlier in the year, Mother Gabriel had suggested that a number of local residents might care to oversee the promotion and proceedings of a Grand Art Union being organised in aid of the Dominican school. It was a most successful campaign and, on 13 June 1902, the event came to a conclusion when a small, but representative, group of ladies and gentlemen gathered at the school in Dongara to draw the prizes that were on display in the study hall.

Dr Bartlett, one of the town's leading citizens, congratulated Mother Gabriel and those involved with the success of the extremely well-organised proceedings. [21] On Wednesday, 29 October 1902, the Dominican students entertained the residents of Mingenew for nearly three hours at a concert held in conjunction with a bazaar. Both events were repeated at Strawberry two days later. How the girls travelled from Dongara, or why they were invited is not clear, but it is obvious from the program that the performance required enormous input on the part of both teachers and pupils. The many items presented by the students consisted of songs, both choruses and solos, piano solos and duets, recitations, Indian clubs, dance routines and musical exercises. The travelling concert must have been a great success for it was reported that the finale, which took the form of a farce, provoked wholesale laughter and a great deal of applause from an appreciative audience. [22]

During Mass, on the morning of Wednesday, 28 January 1903, the Dominican Sisters celebrated their first ceremony of profession in Western Australia. The formalities, which involved a local girl, Sister Catherine (Miss Catherine Kenny), and Sister Anastasia (Miss Annie

Byrne) of Oamaru, New Zealand, were conducted by Bishop Kelly at Dongara, with assistance from Reverend Fathers Hunt and Creagh. The ceremony of profession, in keeping with those days, was an impressive event to witness. At 10.00 a.m. the celebrant commenced the Veni Creator, the choir joined in as the novices, holding a crucifix in their right hand and a lighted taper in their left, knelt between two professed Sisters. After first confirming their intentions to join the order of St Dominic, the Bishop of Geraldton impressed on the young ladies the need to practise self-denial, mortification and penance. He reminded them that their religious life would be based on the vows of poverty, chastity and obedience. The Sisters making their profession then received the black veil, a symbol of penance, from the Prioress in exchange for the white veil and whilst the choir intoned an appropriate psalm, the newly professed Sisters lay prostrate before the altar. That particular morning's ceremony concluded with the appropriate and beautiful benediction service.

Whilst the former hotel at Dongara was being renovated, use was made of a brick building across the road on the site of the future school playground. One window of the 'study hall', which only seniors attended, looked out over the path from the convent and the girls worked at their lessons seated around a large polished table. The floors were also highly-polished and it was a rule that no student dare cross over the boards unless she was wearing a pair of slippers. For convenience, a small 'slipper room' was located nearby. Attached to the building was a kindergarten that accommodated younger children from Infants to Grade IV. The Dominican boarders, who were still accommodated at 'Six Chimneys', used to walk along the river bed to attend classes and to the annoyance of a farmer and his wife, some girls could not resist helping themselves to a fig or two from an old orchard along the way. [23] This was a common practice in the past and few children walking along lanes, or cutting across the countryside to reach their destination, could pass a mulberry or fig tree, or an unattended grapevine, without sampling the fruit.

Despite being more than satisfied with the transfer of the school from Greenough to Dongara, Mother Gabriel still held concerns about the lack of space for boarders. Consequently, on 28 January 1903, during the annual school holidays, she assembled members of her Council to discuss the feasibility of adding a single-storey wing to the original building. She informed the Sisters that the proposed extension would provide three well-ventilated rooms, consisting of a spacious dormitory, a small clothes room and an extra lavatory. Although a proper estimate was not available in time for the meeting, it was expected that the tender would come in at approximately £500. The proposal was unanimously agreed to by the Council and a decision was made to seek the bishop's approval without delay. At the same time, it was intended to petition Bishop Kelly for the following three exemptions: 'that the sub-Prioress should go to a branch house as local Superior, acting also as Procuratrix (bursar) and accountant; that no assistant at present be appointed to that house and that two novices join the Cue staff as teachers'. [24] By August Mother Gabriel and Sister Philomena McGrath had opened a new foundation at Leonora, a flourishing gold mining town in the Eastern Goldfields approximately some 400 miles from Geraldton and 370 miles from Cue.

According to a document held in the Geraldton diocesan archives, William Criddle sold the remaining piece of land at Dongara to the Dominican Sisters in 1903. It appears that Dr Kelly, the Bishop of Geraldton, entered into, and signed, a memorandum of agreement on 14 April that year to purchase from Mr Criddle Location Block No. 1057, consisting of 100 acres, less about 10 acres which had been sold in small blocks since the original survey. The price agreed upon was £400, of which £200 was to be paid in cash upon completion of the transfer. The document also stated that the vendor reserved the right to remove the engine room, all machinery, fixings, timber, wool press, wooden trough, sheep race and sheep dip from the property. [25]

Dongara, one of the earliest settled areas in the Irwin district, attracted its fair share of holiday-makers during the early1900s. The location, which enjoyed the benefits of both a country and seaside environment, was close to rail transport and an ideal site for people wanting respite from the hot weather conditions experienced in Western Australia's inland during the summer months. A description of the area, written in 1903, suggests an agreeable town, removed from the hustle and bustle of a city, yet situated within reasonable distance of both Geraldton and Perth:

*Two miles of a pleasant drive, along an excellent road brought the party to the old fashioned village – which straggles amid trees – and has so struggled for nigh on 40 years – around the hilly margin of the celebrated Dongara Flat. Solid homesteads suggestive of prosperity, creeper covered and flanked with apple and orange trees, dot the winding roadside; while each upon its own eminence, stands the post office, the schoolhouse, the Agricultural Hall and Literary Institute, the Anglican and the Wesleyan churches. Further along the road at the limit of the townsite, rises an imposing four-storeyed stone building, a flour mill, the property of Mr F. Pearse, constructed of local material some eight or nine years ago. The plant which is from the works of H. Simons of Manchester is said to be one of the best and the most up-to-date in the State and has a capacity of five sacks per hour…Unhappily so much magnificent wheat land in this syndicate-owned district is so locked up that settlement is completely checked and production in consequence retarded. And should that happy time arrive when the river flats could be thrown open to the people their known richness would rapidly attract an immense agricultural community. A proof of the fertility of this region is found in the fact that Dongara Flat, consisting of some three thousand acres of rich, black, loamy soil, though regularly cultivated for five and thirty years, has never been artificially fertilised; yet the wheat continues to average about twenty bushels to the acre, and the hay a ton and a half. There is, of course, a good and constant market for the product of the Dongara mill, which is largely marketed in handy fifty-pound bags, and finds ready sale among the stations and the pearling luggers of the North-west. Dongara has many features of natural beauty and it is easily understood why it has become a sanatorium for the Cue goldfields. During the past summer all the hotel and other available accommodation was overtaxed by visitors from those arid regions. Here about eighteen months ago the Sisters of the Dominican Order opened a school, in a commanding position of course, and in premises formerly occupied as an hotel. The known excellence of their educational methods has attracted a large proportion of local children, as well as a number from the goldfields. In addition to their own pupils, the Sisters received some forty goldfields children during the summer holidays; for Dongara is happy in the possession of a capital beach, varied surroundings and a breeze that blows cool in the dog-days.* [26]

In January 1904, the Sisters at Dongara began to think of ways to utilise part of their extensive property and at the same time supplement some of their living expenses. A decision was made by members of the Dominican Council to establish a poultry farm in connection with the Priory. It was to be known as the 'Kiwi Poultry Farm'. The Dominican community agreed to contribute £16, while Miss McDowell, who was to have charge of the farm, was expected to contribute a one-third part of the capital and be entitled to a sum equalling one-third of the profits. [27] Apart from the business side of the project, the Sisters and boarders were always assured of a good supply of fresh farm eggs. On 2 July 1904, Mother Gabriel wrote to a Mr Herbert. The contents of the letter were in the form of a statement, which leads one to believe that the recipient had an interest in the financial affairs of the community:

*I have just handed Mr Criddle a cheque for £200, the balance of the £400 for the extra ninety-six acres adjoining the Priory. This brings our account close to the margin of our overdraft, but there is not, I think, any reasonable cause for uneasiness. Since your last visit to Dongara we have made valuable additions to our property – a new Study Hall and Kindergarten have been built and enclosed with a fence at the opposite side of the road where Mr Criddle's stables and sheds formerly stood – value at least £200. A new refectory has been built for the Boarders at the back of the kitchen – £50 –*

*a verandah has been erected along the eastern gable – £15. The land has been under cultivation. The return in wheat and vegetables has been about £45 to £60. We have 50 sheep and lambs on our run and we are beginning a poultry farm. Already the latter has yielded us £14. I trust this statement is satisfactory to you.* [28]

Unfortunately, Mother Gabriel Gill was not destined not to see the single-storey convent at Dongara transformed into an impressive two-storey Priory; nor was she able to share in the success of what later became a separate college and prominent boarding school for girls. Two months later, on 14 July 1905, the Dominican sub-Prioress, Sister Bonaventure McEntyre, received notification from Bishop Kelly that she had been appointed Prioress. With a change in leadership it was inevitable that new ideas would be introduced and that, in keeping with the times, the community would consider a number of new directions. Shortly after the arrival of two Sisters from New Zealand, Sister Benignus O'Connor and Sister Felicitas Plunkett, the bishop further announced the appointment of Sister di Pazzi Miscall as sub-Prioress and Sister Ceslaus Freed as Mistress of Novices. [29]

Despite the shortage of Sisters, members of the community, with some assistance from the postulants, continued to maintain the four convents and three boarding and five day schools established at Cue, Dongara, Day Dawn, Leonora and Gwalia. The subject of recruiting new members was again raised on 10 January 1906, with the result that a decision was made to send Sister Dominica Murphy to Ireland to recuperate from an illness, and, if possible, to seek suitable volunteers for the Western Australian mission. During her absence Sister Benignus O'Connor replaced her as a Member of Council. Born in London, of Irish parents, in 1863, Sr Benignus, was taken as an infant to Newcastle West, County Limerick, where she spent her childhood. She was educated by the Sisters of Mercy and for a short time became a postulant at the Mercy novitiate in Bagot Street, Dublin. In her 20s, she decided to enter the Dominican novitiate at Beaumont when Mother Gabriel was preparing recruits for her mission in New Zealand. In 1906, she left Dunedin to join the community at Dongara and during the years spent in Western Australian served as Superior at Day Dawn, Cue, Yalgoo, Leonora and Three Springs. On Sr Dominica's return from Ireland in April the following year, she happily announced that three choir postulants from Dublin, the Misses Rose Inglis (Sr Aquin), Kathleen Rice (Sr Reginald) and lay postulant, Mary Buckley (Sr Imelda), had volunteered to serve in Western Australia.

In 1906, the Church of the Holy Family, a practical but unimpressive building, was built on the same side

31. Church of the Holy Family, Dongara

of the road as the Dominican Priory at Dongara. The new place of worship became the focal point of parish activities and a number of improvements were made over the years, including a wide flight of steps that led to the church on top of the hill. The small parish church, which had replaced an earlier timber and clay chapel with a straw-thatched roof, remained in use until 1977, when Bishop Francis Xavier Thomas dedicated the present new brick building to Our Lady Star of the Sea.

The encouraging results of the Trinity College Theoretical Music Examinations, held in December 1907, proved to be a fine advertisement for the school when they were published at the beginning of the following year. All Dominican candidates who sat for the examination at Dongara passed with flying colours, the majority of them with honours (80 marks or better). The successful students were as follows:

**Senior Division:** Lily Lawson (14 years) 80 marks, May Corbett 80 marks, Millie Pollock 60 marks.

**Junior Division:** Nora Nairn (13 years) 96 marks, Vera Adams (13 years) 95 marks, Eileen Jones (10 years) 95 marks, Mary Kavanagh 93 marks, Minnie Linthorne 83 marks, Louie Driscoll 80 marks and Leslie Fitzgerald 71 marks.

32. Boarders, Dongara, c 1906
L. to R. Back Row: May Corbett, Minnie Linthorne, Essie O'Connor,
Front : Eileen Jones, Rose Lawson, Vera Adams, Lily Lawson, Mary Chesson,

Special praise was given to Miss Lily Lawson, who, apart from being awarded a medal as dux of the college, achieved her fourth success in public examinations that year. Besides gaining honours in the senior division, she was also successful in the Adelaide University Primary Examinations, as well as in the Intermediate Pianoforte and Intermediate Theory (honours) in the Trinity College, London, Examinations. [30]

During the January holidays in 1908, Mother Prioress, Sister Bonaventure, assembled the members of Council and, as usual, raised a number of major issues. High on her list of priorities was a strong recommendation to increase the size of the Dominican Convent by providing new cells (bedrooms) for the Sisters and a long-overdue novitiate. With further extensions in mind, Mother Bonaventure also informed the group that it had recently been brought to her attention that the roof of the Priory needed to be renewed. She had ascertained that the cost of adding a second storey over the main portion of the convent would amount to £410 and she was convinced that such a move would prove to be a practical solution to both the immediate problem of space and the replacement of the roof. During the meeting, the Sisters unanimously agreed that if the bishop's approval were granted the community should immediately proceed with the project.

After a second storey was added to the central section of the building, the older girls' classes were transferred to the convent and junior students moved into the former senior 'study hall' across the road. Good manners and etiquette were always important issues in a Ladies' College and when Mother Gabriel was in charge, she expected each girl to make a deep curtsey on entering a room. To improve their deportment, the older students used to regularly lie flat on the floor for a 10-minute period during study time to complete a series of exercises. Callisthenics, and the use of rods and dumbbells were also typical forms of exercise in convent schools, particularly during the Victorian and Edwardian eras when a straight back and correct stance were considered significant additions to the appearance of any refined young lady. At that time, the Sisters were the proud owners of two horses, 'Nobby' and 'Chance'. Although a sulky was initially the popular choice of transport for members of the community, they later progressed to a much more elegant and comfortable phaeton. The students, meanwhile, made use of the sulky and two retired horses, 'Madge' and 'Dolly'. Most girls later admitted that the spring dray, which was occasionally brought out to cope with an overflow of passengers, was much more fun to drive. [31]

An annual school concert was held on Friday, 11 December 1908, and on Tuesday, 15 December, a large crowd gathered in the college study hall to witness Father O'Hare present the following prizes:

**Kindergarten Preparatory Grade Class Prize:** Zoe Walgreen. **Arithmetic:** Ettie Welfare. **Needlework:** Josephine Watson.

**Kindergarten Work:** Annie Driscoll, Minnie Rowland, May Driscoll. **Study Hall** Class Medal: Ist place – Kath Cullinan, 2nd place – Irene Smart. **Intermediate Grades** Class Medal: 1st place – Gracie Quinlan, 2nd place – Vera Adams and Eileen Jones. **Senior Class Medal:** Dux – Lily Lawson. **Religious Knowledge:** Louie Driscoll, Reg Fitzgerald. **Music:** Eileen Jones, Gracie Quinlan, Rebecca Sampson. **Politeness:** Leslie Fitzgerald. **Deportment:** Vera Adams. **Order and Industry:** Vera Quinlan. [32]

As part of Arbor Day celebrations during the early 1900s, Dominican students planted the majority of the trees along the front of the building facing the river. The original grounds were then very different in appearance from those of the future Priory. There were no wide steps leading down to green lawns and instead of the terraces, built later, a slight bank or slope lay directly below the long front verandah. Indeed, except for a large old gum tree and the river beyond, there was little to link the foreground with the future well-ordered shady convent and college gardens. In March 1909, the Prioress consulted Council members about the possibility of building a new dining room to accommodate the increased number of boarders. She also suggested replacing the flimsy wooden rails above the slope in front of the original building with a substantial form of balustrade, and providing new stone steps in lieu of the old wooden ones. The Sisters were obviously determined to make the exterior of the school attractive, for the Council was again consulted, on 20 September, about the advisability of having the grounds in front of the building landscaped. As a result, a decision was made to form substantial terraces to the slopes and to level the remaining section in order to plant a section of grass. The lawn was to be negotiated by a winding path leading from the front steps down to the main gate and the estimated total cost of the improvements was expected to be between £20 and £40. [33]

The old hotel building assumed a grand appearance when the second storey was completed in 1909. The carefully laid out grounds, with a series of structured stone walls, formed the nucleus of what would later become the Dominican Priory's much-admired formal gardens. Evelyn Gildea of Kalgoorlie, after an absence of some years, visited Dongara in 1909 and noted with interest the new buildings and roads in the 'pretty little coastal town' which was rapidly claiming attention as a popular Western Australian summer resort. She was also amazed at the way the Dominican Sisters had taken an ordinary colonial building and turned it into an impressive convent and school.

*First we visited the convent chapel (a perfect little gem, breathing peace and sanctity); next the classrooms, fitted with the latest educational appliances: the large, airy dormitory, with its curtained alcoves; the dressing rooms, recreation hall, and lastly a magnificent dining hall, which the Prioress told me had been completed only a short time ago. It is a spacious and lofty room, 30 ft. by 20 ft., with plastered walls and ceiling, jarrah dado and polished jarrah floor. This room, like the rest of the building is lighted with acetylene gas. The upper storey consists of novitiate, infirmary and cells, but being a secular these rooms were forbidden to me, as the Dominican rule is one of strict enclosure...From the refectory we were taken to the orchard, where rows upon rows of grape-vines were bursting into leaf, and orange and lemon trees were weighed down with their load of golden fruit...From the orchard we passed to the vegetable garden, where many varieties of vegetables were growing in abundance, and I thought what a boon was this educational establishment to parents with delicate girls or to those on the Fields, offering as it does every home comfort. It should prove a perfect sanatorium for delicate girls. I was about to inquire as to the number of pupils, when we entered another field, where a band of 25 to 30 girls were engaged in an exciting game of rounders. Their happy laughter rang out upon the air, and the Mother Prioress informed me that these were the boarders, enjoying their afternoon recreation...How different, I thought, was this from our city schools, where it would be impossible to enjoy such freedom in the fields and such peaceful seclusion for study. At first I was inclined to wonder at the large number of boarders in this apparently little known paradise, but when I considered the home-like conditions, the beautiful fields, the possession of cows which provide abundant supplies of fresh milk, cream etc., and the horses for riding and driving, the wonder was, not that the number was so large, but that it is not three times as large. The grounds were being tastefully laid out in couch lawns, and terraces 8ft. wide with a drop of 18 in. from one to the other, and a flight of stone steps with a stone balustrading along the front terrace had just been completed.* [34]

33. Study Hall, St Dominic's College, Dongara

The continuing success of the convent schools depended very much on the number of novices being professed and although several girls, including Miss May Corbett (Sr Augustine), eldest daughter of James Corbett (Town Treasurer), Perth, and Miss Rose McQuillan (Sr Teresa) entered between February and August 1909, few local postulants were attracted in the early years of foundation. At that time, the Western Australian Dominican community consisted of Sisters Bonaventure McEntyre, Dominica Murphy, di Pazzi Miscall, Philomena McGrath, Anastasia Byrne, Ceslaus Freed, Catherine and Josephine Kenny, Vincent Colgan, Felicitas Plunkett, Hyacinth Carroll, Bernard Rogers, Peter Geeson, Reginald Rice, Patrick Doyle, Benignus O'Connor, Aquin Inglis, Baptist Hall, Patrick Doyle, Evangelist Graham, Imelda Buckley and Paul Hutton.

Unfortunately, the excessive demands being made on the Dominican community were difficult to meet and so, at the beginning of January 1910, Mother Prioress met with Council to consider what means should be undertaken to secure additional members. Subsequently, a decision was made to send Sr Dominica Murphy and Sr di Pazzi Miscall to the eastern states the following year to recruit new members for the mission. In what proved to be a successful venture, the two Dominican Sisters returned to Western Australia on 30 June 1910, accompanied by a group of nine postulants. The new arrivals included the Misses Mary McCusker (Sr Rose), Ellen Hughes (Sr Clement) and eight others who shortly afterwards 'returned to the world'. [35]

In April 1910, the Prioress consulted the Dongara members of Council about the possibility of further enlarging the Priory. The outcome of this meeting was a decision to press ahead with arrangements to convert the choir and adjoining front room into a dormitory and to turn the rooms directly behind them into one large area to form more spacious facilities for younger children. It was intended to build another wing over these rooms to provide a senior dormitory with similar amenities. The extensions, which also included replastering the existing dormitory for use as a classroom and building a new choir above it, were expected to cost some £1600. At the same time it was suggested that the construction of a tennis court might prove to be an attractive and practical addition to the college. [36] Work on the additions commenced in May 1910 and was not completed until the end of that year.

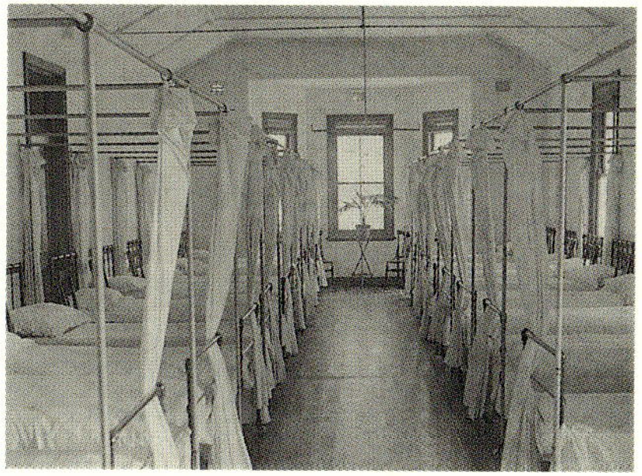

34. Dormitory, St Dominic's College, Dongara

With 36 boarders in residence in 1911, the sum of money spent on the new additions was considered to be a sound investment. Completion of the new additions, which according the *Sower*, published in January 1911, provided space to accommodate from 50 to 60 senior and junior students, meant that the Dominican community could also put in place long-held plans to introduce a spiritual retreat for ladies. The retreat, to be held over a period of three days during the school vacation in January 1911, offered applicants 'peaceful surroundings, extensive shady grounds for calm meditation, airy comfortable rooms and a spacious devotional chapel'. Conducted by Father Goodman of the Sacred Heart Monastery in Randwick, New South Wales, it was the first retreat of its kind in the diocese and the nuns were delighted when 24 ladies, including some from as far away as Perth, attended. The annual event arranged by the Dominican Sisters was still attracting women at the end of the First World War in 1918. [37]

The domestic side of life was made easier for the lay Sisters when a large laundry with the latest fittings was added to the Priory in the middle of 1911. At the same time a tennis court, under construction opposite St Dominic's, created a great deal of interest. Indeed, one newspaper correspondent went so far as to suggest that on completion the court would not only be an additional source of amusement to pupils attending the College, but that it would also prove to be 'another aid to the acquirement of womanly grace and ease'. [38] As with most missions, members of the Dominican Congregation found it impossible to keep within budget while trying to establish new branches and maintain the properties they owned. In order to raise the finance needed for general improvements, building programs and household expenditure, it was often necessary for the Sisters to work long hours behind the scenes to make special functions a financial success. This meant that as well as performing their teaching and religious duties, the nuns were kept busy during the year preparing for various concerts, bazaars, exhibitions and field events. Using their many talents, they generously contributed artwork, sewing and woodcarvings for Sales of Work and raffles, as well as sewing costumes, painting backdrops and arranging the choreography for entertainments.

In January 1911, the Council unanimously agreed to accept Miss Elizabeth Leddin (Sr Jordan) as a lay postulant. The following year, her elder sister Catherine (Sr Agnes) and Miss Catherine Pickerd (Sr Aloysius) joined her. The Leddin sisters, who came from Port Fairy, a coastal town much admired by tourists on the south coast of Victoria, were young when they arrived at Dongara. Both women proved to be great workers and, in keeping with other lay sisters, made a point of dedicating their busy lives to the well-being of others in the community. Sister Jordan later suffered from a skin allergy and it suited her to work mainly indoors where she could generally be found either at the ironing table or maintaining a perfect shine on the already highly-polished jarrah boards. Sister Agnes on the other hand, was noted for her cooking and skills in handling the laundry. She would rise very early every morning to light the wood stove and on Mondays to light the copper for washing, both fires having been set the previous night. According to those who shared their lives, both sisters willingly and cheerfully carried out the daily chores that were part of their chosen lifestyle. Despite the hardships, there was always someone with a keen sense of humour who inspired others to laugh. The corridor connecting the lay Sisters' rooms on the floor above the kitchen, for example, was light-heartedly and aptly labelled, 'Stokers Alley'. [39]

The constant demand for more postulants continued to plague the community and when, in January 1911, Bishop Kelly asked the Sisters if they would consider establishing another Dominican foundation at Meekatharra, the request must have raised a certain amount of uncertainty about staffing. In June the bishop made a similar request to found a convent and school at Mt Magnet. By May, the Sisters had opened a convent and school at Meekatharra and by September another convent and school at Mt Magnet. Unfortunately, for a number of reasons, the foundation at Mt Magnet was closed two months later.

St Dominic's Feast Day, celebrated as usual on 4 August, was made even more special in 1913, when Father Fenelon from Cue and Father Roulier from Leonora marked the occasion by composing a collection of poems based on the Saint's life. The new works entitled 'St Dominick', were beautifully recited by students from the college whilst other pupils took part in a series of nine tableaux representing various aspects of the storyline. The following verse illustrates the continuity of Dominic's work:

*Since then seven hundred years have flown*
*Adown the hill of time,*
*Yet over the world his name is known,*
*And all his work sublime.*
*That glorious work still doing,*
*His footsteps still pursuing,*
*Behold, in every clime*
*The mystic and the teacher,*
*Soothing the woes of man –*
*The noble friar – preacher,*
*The Nun Dominican.* [40]

Before giving the children permission to spend the remainder of the holiday at the beach, the Bishop of Geraldton, Dr Kelly, reminded them that 'being as they were, under the training of the Dominican nuns, they shared in a special way in the benefits which the great Founder [St Dominic] had conferred on the world'. [41]

On 3 January 1913, the 'Mothers of Council' assembled once more at the Priory. According to the Prioress, Mother Dominica Murphy, the meeting was primarily held to consider what could be done to relieve the strain of keeping up the four branch convents with the community's limited staff of teachers. As a result, it was agreed to unite the Sisters teaching at Cue and Day Dawn under one Superior in Cue. The Sisters would then live under one roof and travel each day to Day Dawn. Meanwhile, the female boarders from St Gabriel's would be transferred to Dongara and the few boys boarding at Day Dawn would be taken to Cue. The community's workforce was further depleted on 13 July 1913, when Sister Imelda Buckley died after a short illness. The Prioress must have been extremely pleased when, on 16 October that year, she received a letter from her counterpart in Dunedin inviting two Sisters to visit New Zealand. Even more heartening was the news that Bishop Verdon had given permission for the visitors to seek postulants during their stay in the South Island. It was therefore agreed that Mother Bonaventure and Sister di Pazzi should leave Western Australia before the end of December.

Plans were changed when Sister di Pazzi became ill on 9 December and the doctor advised her not to travel for at least two months. Rather than postpone the trip, it was decided to replace Sr di Pazzi with Sister Ceslaus. Their recruiting mission completed, the Sisters returned to Dongara on 15 April 1914, with five young ladies, the Misses Mary McDonough (Sr Stanislaus), Jean Wilson (Sr Berchmans), Nellie Houlahan (Sr Antoninus), Mary Culhane (Sr Alacoque) and Mary Heavey. Miss Julia Grennell had arrived a month earlier and it was suggested that Miss Heavey continue her education at the college, as she was considered too young at the time to enter the novitiate.

It was in 1914 that the Sisters were granted permission to use part of their property as a private cemetery. Further works carried out at Dongara in September that year included the erection of a windmill and tank to service two cottages adjoining the Priory. These houses had been transferred to the Dominican community a year or two earlier. The total cost of the windmill, water pipes and labour amounted to £39 and two years later consideration was given to various ways of providing extra water for farm purposes. A well near the convent kitchen, over which a locally purchased oil engine had been installed, unfortunately proved useless, due to an inadequate water flow. This left the community with no choice but to accept the advice given to them regarding an alternative supply and towards the end of February 1916, the Sisters had the added expense of paying workmen to sink a new well.

In June 1917, builders began to erect a full-length balcony along the western side of the convent to protect the building from seasonal rains and strong winds. As the project was going to prove expensive (approximately £250), a committee had earlier been formed to raise funds towards some of the building costs. One of the events organised by the committee to raise money was a special St Patrick's Day sporting event held at the beach on 17 March 1917. Catholic and non-Catholic children, accompanied by their parents, took part in an active program that included horse racing and numerous novelty events. Cool drink and ice-cream stalls were popular with people of all ages and afternoon teas, served by the parish ladies in Mr Moore's shed, did a brisk trade throughout the day. That same night a well-attended supper dance was held in the specially decorated hall and local residents merrily danced the hours away to music provided by Miss Hackett and the Misses Healy. [42]

By then the final chapters of the 1914-1918 Great War were being played out, and although outwardly the schools and convents continued to operate as before, the common loss of family members and friends affected the lives of students and Sisters alike. A serious breach of rule on the part of three boarders occurred in August 1915, when they left the dormitory after lights out to sneak down to the railway station to see the soldiers pass through on the way to the Front. The young ladies concerned were given no second chance. Instead they were expelled and sent home. It seems that despite the loss of school fees, rules were rules and discipline was strictly adhered to by the Sisters. Of the 417,000 Australians who had volunteered to serve overseas, 32,000 were from Western Australia and when one considers that 6000 of these young West Australian men lost their lives and another 12,000 were seriously wounded, it is not difficult to understand the impact their absence made on the social fabric and economy of the state. During the war years, 24 young men from Dongara lost their lives and, like most students in Australia, the girls from the Dominican College contributed in various ways to the War Effort. Throughout the hostilities 'penny bazaars' in aid of the Belgians were popular and countless socks and scarves were knitted for the 'Boys at the Front'. Above all the girls prayed for their safe return and a peaceful end to the war.

World War I was not the only catastrophe to occupy the Sisters' minds in 1917, for in that particular year the Sisters experienced the usual traumas and difficulties associated with living too close to a river that periodically burst its banks. In 1917 the Priory became temporarily isolated when floodwaters from the Irwin River came perilously close to the main building. By 8.00 p.m. a decision was made to move the fowls to safety and, by 11.30 p.m., the Sisters were still keeping a watchful eye on the fast flowing water which had risen as high as the kindergarten door. Three-and-a-half hours later the river had passed the garden gate and, by 5.00 a.m., one corner of the terrace was completely covered with a sheet of water.

Despite the short duration of the flood it was later agreed that, because of water damage, the kindergarten would unfortunately have to remain unoccupied for some time. [43]

35. Dominican Sisters, St Dominic's Priory, Dongara, 1919

In 1919, nine years before a separate college was erected next door to the Priory, the Dominican building, used as both a convent and school, was a prominent, two-storeyed structure with spacious verandahs, balcony and deep-set windows. From the front gate a path, leading to the terraces and eventually the steps, passed through colourful flowerbeds and grassed areas, made shady by the overhanging branches of well-established pepper trees. The *Sower*, published that year, described the upstairs chapel as having a fibrous plaster ceiling, white walls and a polished jarrah floor. The warm golden glow of highly-polished wooden stalls, reserved for the Dominican Sisters, and long rows of honey-coloured benches for boarders and the occasional visitor, was enhanced by the rich red carpets and matching curtains. Tinted statues of the Sacred Heart, Our Lady, St Dominic and St Catherine of Siena added a feeling of sanctity to the chapel as did the magnificent marble altar brought from Italy at the start of World War I in 1914. Today, this altar, a gift from Father O'Hare, has pride of place in the beautifully-designed chapel attached to St Catherine's Convent in Doubleview, Perth.

The interior of the Priory, at that stage, featured a wide staircase and a cheery dining room with bright wall pictures and long tables covered with white cloths. The dormitory, with a large front window overlooking the gardens, was described as 'a long, white, airy room with polished floor and bright linoleum containing twenty curtained-off

36. Dr Bartlett in front of Priory extensions, c 1919

37. Dining room, St Dominic's College, Dongara

beds'. In July 1919, a new roof was erected over the balcony on the eastern side of the Priory to provide extra sleeping accommodation and also to protect the lathe and plaster wall from the weather. From the enclosed verandah the boarders had sweeping views across a large section of the convent grounds, including an open paddock with shady native trees, under which a few cows and horses happily mingled with moor-hens in a rural setting.

Towards the end of 1919, Mr Irwin Moore offered to sell 100 acres of land at Nargo to the Dominican Sisters. The property, which had a well and was also fenced, was situated about five miles from the Priory and the cash purchase price at £50 was considered to be more than reasonable. On 20 December, members of the Council discussed the proposal and decided to accept Mr Moore's offer. The land which was mostly leased by the Sisters was sold in 1947 to Mr Patrick O'Brien, who had offered to buy it for £60 or £65 cash. During the 1920s, other properties in the vicinity of the Dominican building were also purchased. These included 'blocks comprising in all 15 acres, adjoining the Priory property on the south-west'. After Mother Bonaventure McEntyre consulted members of the Council on 12 April 1921, it was decided to purchase the blocks of land at the valuation price of £60. Two years later, on 25 September, the Sisters also agreed to buy 44 acres of fenced land close to the Priory for £300 from local identity Mr Hughes. [44]

When Bishop William Kelly died on 26 December 1921, the Sisters lost a long-time friend and mentor, and as with other religious in the diocese, they found themselves in a position of having to get acquainted with a new leader. Time was against this happening, as Richard Ryan CM, was not appointed Bishop of Geraldton until 1923, and then holding that office only until March 1926, before returning to Victoria. By the 1920s, St Dominic's College at Dongara was beginning to gain a reputation for quality teaching outside of the Geraldton diocese and also with non-Catholic parents. The school buildings, although not large, were well-equipped and already the Priory gardens with its tiered grass terraces, huge date palms and shady trees were beginning to take on the appearance of a cool oasis. The Lourdes Grotto, a much-photographed inviting bower constructed of stone, was a familiar landmark. Built in the early 1920s, it was a favourite retreat for Dominican students and Sisters. Two years later, the familiar statue of St Dominic, carefully wrapped in canvas,

38. Statue of St Dominic in Priory garden

was lowered by means of a block and tackle and positioned on a marble plinth set in the grounds. That same statue now occupies a special place in the foreground of St Catherine's Dominican Convent at Doubleview in Perth.

The demand for music tuition continued to increase and in October 1922, the Sisters were in a quandary as to whether they should spend £35 on having an old piano completely serviced, or whether money should be put down as part payment on a new one. Despite making a decision to have the instrument repaired, the Prioress, Mother Bonaventure, was more than delighted when two months later Father Hart of Three Springs offered for sale a piano for £80. The community had quite a number of on-going expenses to contend with at the time. These included giving approval, on 11 December 1922, for the Priory to be re-painted at an estimated cost of £100, and in May the following year, £700 was set aside to build a number of new music rooms. In March 1924, it was decided to spend £80 to irrigate another acre of farmland for the production of lucerne, and in May that same year the question of choosing the best lighting for the new music rooms and dining room was discussed. Surprisingly, it was discovered that the entire building could be lit by electric light for £230, including the purchase of a plant. In view of such a reasonable estimate, members of the Council had no difficulty in agreeing to make the changeover to electricity. [45]

A decision, made on 13 September 1926, to consult an architect, with a view to erecting an additional building on land west of the study hall and music rooms, marked the beginning of a new and exciting era in Dominican history. The estimate to erect a separate college wing was in the vicinity of some £7000 to £8000 and to secure a loan from the bank it was first necessary to obtain permission from Archbishop Clune, who at that time was Apostolic Administrator of the Geraldton diocese. Unfortunately, the Archbishop of Perth insisted that the current interest rates were too high and advised the then Prioress, Dominica Murphy, that she would be wise to consider only half of the overall project. [46]

Disappointed that they may not be able to proceed with their dream of completing a new college building, the new Dominican Prioress, Mother Vincent Colgan, assembled the Council on 13 January 1927, to consider other matters that needed immediate attention. She first sought the members' approval to accept an offer of £800 on a house at Invercargill, New Zealand, which had been signed over to the Sisters by Sister Concepta Waterson at the time of her profession. The prospective buyer, it appeared, was prepared to pay yearly instalments with interest set at six per cent on the unpaid purchase money, until such time as a loan could be secured. A second pressing decision was also needed on whether to purchase a second-hand Sunshine harvester for the property. Both propositions were readily agreed to without further discussion.

Council members again assembled, on 31 January, to discuss arrangements for the erection of the new college and were informed that the Union Bank was quite prepared to advance the sum of £4000. Although a decision was made to press ahead with plans to build a portion of the building, the Sisters were obviously not convinced about the wisdom of such a move and the day before the contractors were to commence work on the site, the Council was reconvened for further discussions. By that stage, boarding school enrolments had noticeably increased and the Sisters were convinced that it would be short-sighted on their part not to build the college in its entirety. The Archbishop was again approached and, on this occasion, acceded to the Sisters' request, with the proviso that the bank be willing to advance the extra money. A new loan of £6000 made the contract price of £8233 more affordable and without further delay the builder, Mr E. Coombe of Perth, commenced building on 18 May 1927. It was soon discovered that a number of items had been omitted from the contract. These included terracing the slope in front of the new building in concrete, providing a front fence of the same material with iron gates, erecting a covered walkway between the school and Priory, grading the ground at the back and sides of the new building and providing some furnishings. The Council unanimously decided that they would seek permission to borrow a further £1600 and, to offset any shortfall of funds, they would sell some blocks of land they owned near the beach. [47]

The completion of the two-storeyed college and boarding school in 1928, designed by Edgar Le Blond Henderson FRIBA of St George's Terrace, Perth (son of the Sisters' original architect in Greenough, Edgar Jerome Henderson), meant that for the first time in 29 years, the Dominican Sisters in Western Australia were able to separate boarding accommodation from the convent. The new St Dominic's College, which ultimately cost some

39. Group of Boarders on front steps of Priory, 1922

£10,000 to erect, had its own entity and was only connected to the original building by means of a covered passage way. The building's solid walls were constructed of concrete blocks made from local river gravel and cement, and in accordance with health requirements, a comprehensive septic system was installed. Access to the upper level was gained by means of a staircase from a hall in the centre of the building. The rooms were well-ventilated and provided with every modern comfort available to students in the late 1920s. A wide verandah, or sleep-out, measuring over 200 feet long by 12 feet wide, contained evenly-placed rows of snow-white quilted beds, which were protected from the wind and rain by sliding windows. These windows, which had louvres above them for all-year ventilation, caught their fair share of cool sea breezes when opened during summer. The colonial-style college had 40 boarders enrolled at the time of opening and according to a description written soon afterwards, there was ample space left to accommodate at least another 20 residential students:

*On the lower floor are the classrooms, five in number, one of which is an art room. Four of these measure about 18 ft. by 16 ft., the other being 28 ft., by 16 ft. A reception room and office are also provided on this floor. Upstairs is a large dormitory, two Sisters' rooms, cloak room, bathrooms and lavatories, the remainder of the floor space being divided into 62 dressing cubicles, one of which is allotted to each pupil. Cupboards and other conveniences have been provided in plenty.* [48]

40. St Dominic's Ladies' College, Dongara; tennis courts in foreground.

Before the opening ceremony, a foundation stone, inscribed in Latin *Laudare, Benedicere, Praedicare* (to praise, to bless, to preach), was laid by Archbishop Clune who also performed a pontifical High Mass with assistance from Father Lynch of Three Springs, Father Prendiville of Perth and Father O'Hare of Dongara. Two of these priests were closely related to two of the Dominican Sisters – Father Michael Lynch (later Dean Lynch) was the brother of Sister Emmanuel and Father Redmond Prendiville (later Archbishop of Perth) was the younger brother of Sister Laurence. The official opening and blessing, on 6 May 1928, took place before a large crowd gathered in front of a wooden dais set up on the lawn. Besides the Archbishop, three well-known politicians, Senator Lynch, Hon. J. Hickey MLC and Hon G. Kempton MLC, paid tribute to the Sisters' achievements and endorsed the launch of an appeal towards the cost of the new wing. Mr Kempton told the audience that he had visited the convent over a period of many years and had 'always been struck with the wonderful affinity between pupils and teachers'. He also added that the Sisters set a high standard and no matter where he travelled he had heard nothing but praise for the Sisters and their work. [49] By then the West Australian Dominican Sisters had earned a fine reputation throughout the state as progressive educationalists and talented teachers of the arts, music and languages.

No doubt inspired by the progress taking place in the construction of the new college building, the Dominican Sisters realised that, for the first time since their arrival in 1899, they were in a strong position to establish a first-class residential college and high-level academic centre for girls. Not only did the new curriculum offer a basic education, but it also reflected the growing trend for women to recognise that entry to university was now acceptable and well within their reach. In January 1928, Mother Vincent Colgan suggested that a two-year scholarship, valued at £48, be given to the top student in the Junior Certificate Examination, provided that six candidates were involved and no less than eight subjects passed. [50] The scholarship was later extended to students in other schools within the Geraldton diocese.

Members of the Dominican Order have always been conscious of their rich inheritance and every foundation has consistently maintained strong links with their founder, St Dominic. Not only has the traditional motto *Veritas* (Truth), been used in every Dominican college, but the black and white school uniforms introduced at St Dominic's College in February 1928, were symbolic of the colours chosen by St Dominic for the order he founded seven centuries earlier. The combination of the two shades, worn by nuns and pupils alike – black representing penance and white for innocence – was instantly recognisable, as was the Dominican motto *Veritas*. Used as part of the school crest and featured throughout the college and on special occasions, the Latin dictum, familiar through the words of a school hymn, served to remind all those involved with the teachings of St Dominic to strive for 'Truth':

*Guard us ever sainted Father,*
*As through life's dark night we pass,*
*Keep thy children ever faithful*
*To their motto, 'Veritas'*

Ellen (Nell) Mason was typical of the young country boarders enrolled at the college during the 1920s. As she had earlier attended the Dominican Convent at Meekatharra, the decision to continue her education with the Dominican Sisters at Dongara was not unexpected. Chaperoned by her mother and in the company of Nancy Peterkin, another girl from Meekatharra, 11-year-old Nell, dressed in her new black and white uniform, set off by train on the long journey to Dongara. The trip necessitated changing trains at Geraldton and it was not unusual for other boarders, such as Marjorie Campbell from Mt Seabrook Station, to be picked up en route. Most new boarders quickly adapted to the college routine after a short settling-in period. This included attending daily Mass at 7.00 a.m., studying before breakfast, and again at night, listening attentively to 'pep talks' and having to wash and dry one's hair on Saturday mornings. Junior students were given the privilege of having hot cocoa at night and avoiding the main staircase, which was out of bounds, was a rule not to be ignored.

In those days, lay Sisters did the cooking, cleaning and washing and, in keeping with the times, food at the college was simple and wholesome. On one point at least, St Dominic's College had an advantage over most other boarding schools, for crayfish and salmon were not considered a delicacy in Dongara and in season their appearance on the school menu was a weekly occurrence. Nell Mason (Mrs Marshall) still clearly recalls many of her past teachers, all of them long since gone: Sister Ceslaus, who felt 'closer to God's heart in a garden'; Sister Aquin, who taught music; Sister Laurence, intensely proud of her brother Archbishop Prendiville and Sister Augustine, who delighted in taking her students on practical botany excursions along the banks of the river and on occasions as far as the river mouth. [51]

After a long period of time without novices, a number of Sisters were either received or professed during the 1920s and early 1930s. Sister Pius Nolan, described as 'gentle, prayerful and unassuming', became interested in the Dominican Convent at Dongara after meeting Father Michael Lynch, a fellow passenger on board a ship sailing from Ireland in 1922. She was received as a choir novice in July 1923, and, among other centres, served at Cue for many years. A month later, Sister Alphonsus O'Connor, formerly a nurse on the staff of a large Sydney hospital, was professed in the chapel at Dongara. Her medical background proved to be an invaluable asset when she was ministering to the needs of both boarders and Sisters, and doctors often complimented her on the correctness of her diagnosis as well as her nursing skills. Sister Alphonsus was also an accomplished dressmaker and, apart from conducting sewing classes with the students, she made most of the Sisters' religious habits.

Gertrude Wood (Sr Raphael) entered the convent at Dongara in 1928 with Kathleen Dowdall (Sr Paschal) after spending a brief time as a postulant at Dunedin. A Jewess by birth, Gertrude Wood was orphaned at an early age and for a time was sent to live with a wealthy aunt in New Zealand. Gertrude's guardian had taken the unusual step of converting from Judaism to Christianity and by the time her young charge returned to relatives in Sydney her interest in the Catholic religion had strengthened. Sister Raphael is remembered not only for her musical talents, but also for her special love of birds. Sister Concepta Flattery, who was present at the time of Sr Raphael's death, tells the story of a kookaburra landing on the narrow sill of her fourth floor hospital room and remaining there until she died. This occurrence both amused and gave comfort to those who knew her well.

Sister Pascal, who travelled with Sister Raphael from New Zealand, was highly-regarded as a music and singing teacher and over the years higher grade students achieved excellent results under her tuition. Sister Joseph O'Connor, a contemporary once wrote: 'I think Sr Paschal's second love was carpentry and handyman jobs. As the years went by she accumulated and used with great expertise nearly every tool in a handyman's kit. Even in her eighties she went around looking for jobs and items to repair. One Prioress was heard to say, "I tremble when I see Kathleen going around with that electric drill in her hand"'. [52]

Sister Concepta Waterson was not a young person when she arrived from New Zealand to enter the Dongara novitiate. The daughter of a ship's captain, she had lost her mother as a child and with her father often away she was said to have led a rather lonely life. Sister Concepta brought with her some beautiful china and silver cutlery which she kindly donated to the community. Florence Teresa Keeley (Sr Carmel), the daughter of William and Susan Keeley, was born in Geraldton in 1897 and after her profession taught at Meekatharra and Yalgoo. Never a robust person, her failing health did not allow her to continue teaching and she returned to Dongara where she will be remembered by many as the Procuratrix. As well as being responsible for ordering provisions for the pantry she later took charge of boarders studying at night. A dedicated, meticulous worker she took pride in keeping a well-stocked pantry to cater for the needs of both Sisters and boarders and with careful planning she rarely exceeded her budget. Many a novice setting out on a picnic had reason to be grateful for her thoughtfulness when they peeked inside the hamper she had quietly provided. [53]

Sister Imelda Heron, who came to Western Australia from Pettigo, Ireland, in 1926, and joined the Dominican Sisters five years later, was one of the many dedicated lay Sisters who contributed to the well-being of the community. After two of her brothers died, she assumed the role of the eldest child in a large family and was therefore the only member in a position to assist her father, James, on the family's mixed farm. Familiar with hard work, she had little education and was totally at ease with

41. Sister Benedict Lyons tending calves, 1922

42. Senior students, Dongara, 1928
L. to R. Back Row: I. Bingham, S. Watson, J. Rogers, M. Power, M. Punch, N. Mason
Front: J. Punch, J. Rigby, A. Clarkson, M. Lynch

outdoor life. Sister Imelda was received on 4 August 1932, and during the 10 years that she remained at Dongara, part of her duty involved milking the cows. It has been said that when not in the cow-yard with her favourite cow, 'Susie', she was in the dining room, preparing and tidying up for boarders. Later Sister Imelda transferred to Three Springs and Bedford Park and returned to the country for a brief period before finally leaving for the metropolitan area to live in Dominican convents at Scarborough and Doubleview. [54]

Among several local girls who joined the Dominican community during that period were past pupils Mary O'Connor (Sr Joseph), Anne Ryan (Sr Xavier), Mary Lynch (Sr Emmanuel), Mary Punch (Sr Philomena) and Joan Punch (Sr Bernadette). After successfully gaining her Leaving

Certificate at the college in Dongara, Mary Punch, or 'Molly', as she was called, completed her diploma at the Claremont Teachers' Training College before taking a position for three years in government schools with the Education Department. Sister Philomena was widely recognised and appreciated for her organisational and academic skills. She was also known for her ability to impart her knowledge and during her lengthy service at Dongara took great pains to ensure that every student understood what she was teaching.

With the exception of the Great Depression years (1929-1932), the Dominican boarding school continued to expand, and not only were enquiries received from the Murchison and Eastern Goldfields, but also from as far afield as Bunbury in the south-west to Derby in the north-west. Initially, girls from Grade I to Leaving Certificate were admitted as boarders, although, in future years for practical reasons, only senior primary and secondary residential students were enrolled at the college. Each year in the Public Junior and Leaving Certificate Examinations, conducted by The University of Western Australia, Dominican students achieved some excellent results. The Sisters were exceptionally pleased when they were notified on 7 May 1931, that St Dominic's College at Dongara was registered as a secondary school by both the Education Department and University.

As earlier suggested, the teaching of physical education was regarded as an important part of college life. Originally, classes consisted of daily exercises, dancing and club swinging and although many of these activities continued well into the 1930s, the gradual development of courts and playing fields meant that more competitive

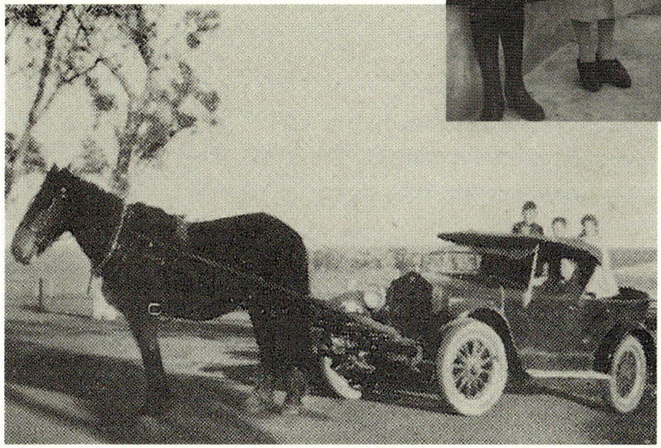

43-45 1 Children of Mary
2 G. Broadhurst, Mde de Mouncey, P. McGinness
3 War-time petrol restrictions

sports such as tennis, basketball and hockey became more popular. If expert instruction were seen to be of benefit to the students the Dominican Sisters never hesitated to provide tutors. The very capable Madame de Mouncey, despite her unlikely appearance as a sportswoman, was regularly employed as a swimming coach during the 1930s and 1940s by a number of Perth private schools. The Sisters, recognising the importance of taking swimming and lifesaving lessons in a country like Australia, decided in April 1938 to engage her services as an instructor. For a number of years Madame de Mouncey travelled to Dongara to teach swimming and to prepare some of the more experienced swimmers for examination. Madame de Mouncey, who, in 1939, became the first woman in the state to obtain the Sea Water Diploma from the Royal Life Saving Society, generally remained for a fortnight and it was due to her expertise that many of the girls gained certificates in a various grades and were awarded the bronze and silver medallions for achievement in swimming, diving and lifesaving.

Apart from reasons of comfort and convenience, the style of the school uniform worn by pupils attending St Dominic's College did not alter a great deal over the years. Some minor changes, however, took place in 1934 when pullovers were introduced as part of the winter outfit and more serviceable berets replaced college hats. In line with current fashions, smart new dresses were also designed for the college graduation ceremony, held in December 1935. The soft white crêpe de Chine outfits, worn with tan stockings, featured turned-down collars and sky blue bows of silk at the neck. When assembled in a group, the elegantly dressed young ladies made an enormous impression on the audience which did not fail to show their appreciation. [55]

In 1936, after answering to the name of St Dominic's for many years, the names of the college and Priory were suddenly changed. For some time the Sisters had expressed concern that the titles could be confusing and when the Council met, on 7 January, to discuss the matter, it was unanimously agreed that henceforth the convent would be known as the Dominican Priory, instead of St Dominic's Priory and that the title of St Dominic's College – a Boarding and Day School for Young Ladies, would be changed to the Dominican Ladies' College. Advertisements, listing the advantages a student might expect if she enrolled at the college, appeared regularly in the *Catholic Record*, the *Sower* and the *Geraldton Express* throughout the 1930s. Prospective parents were informed:

*The College is situated on a hill open to the play of healthy breezes, and commanding a magnificent prospect, yet quite secluded – an inviting retreat for study. It is surrounded by extensive grounds – 100 acres – and is within easy reach of the sea. No more charming or healthy situation could have been chosen in which to combine physical and mental culture...The Recreation grounds are furnished with Tennis and Basket Ball Courts, and other means of healthful amusement and exercise.*

*The system of Moral Training adopted in the College is a happy blending of heart and mind culture, with its external expression of lady-like Modesty and Gentleness. The Health and Physical Development of the students are maternally watched and tended. Long walks into the country and to the seaside, excursions and picnics on free days and outdoor amusements obviate the too great strain of study, and avert the physical ills which are sometimes found to attend the rather sedentary habits inseparable from a Student's Life. Young Ladies of all Denominations are received* [56].

Verse Speaking lessons were introduced to all pupils in 1939 and throughout the year students were encouraged to test their skills by sitting for music, theory, elocution and French examinations set by the Trinity College of London, the Western Australian University Board, the Australian Music Board and Alliance Française. Prizes were also given at the end of each year for Christian doctrine, plain and fancy needlework, mending, swimming, lifesaving and sport, with special awards presented under the titles of Order and General Proficiency, the Lady Baron's Gold Challenge Medal, the Good Conduct Prize (nuns' choice) and the Wreath for Amiability and Unselfishness (awarded by pupils' votes).

In June 1936, the Prioress, Mother Laurence Prendiville, discussed with the Council the possibility of building a cottage at the beach. Plans were duly submitted and in October a tender of £437.10.0 was accepted from Mr Crothers of Northampton. The cottage, still in use today, has over the years been a boon to many overworked Sisters in need of respite. Three years later the same builder was asked to erect a dairy, a new kitchen, a store-room and more bedrooms for the Sisters at a cost of £1352.

The first Bushies' School in the Geraldton diocese was held in January 1938, when the Dominican and Presentation Sisters spent two weeks of their well-earned holidays providing religious instruction for children attending non-Catholic schools in inland areas. For the Dominican Sisters this involved hosting children from the Morawa, Perenjori and Carnamah areas. The schools, initially organised by Father M. Lynch, were held at the Dominican Ladies' College, Dongara and the Stella Maris Presentation in Geraldton. Each morning after breakfast, the young guests attended Christian Doctrine lessons, interspersed with hymn singing practice. During this period they were prepared for the Sacraments of Confession and First Holy Communion, which they received on the last day in the presence of the bishop and their parents.

The afternoon was spent in swimming, sight-seeing, picnicking and playing games. Father Keith Spain was in charge of the Bushies' School in the Geraldton diocese for 35 years and during that time he was assisted by fellow priests, members of the two women's teaching orders, groups of lay volunteers and later by the lay missionaries of St Joseph. When the venue was later transferred to Geraldton, St Patrick's Christian Brothers' College replaced the Dominican College at Dongara, and a second outreach commenced with Bushies' Schools held during the May and August holidays at Leonora, Port Hedland and Shark Bay. [57]

Mr Lionel Criddle, long-time resident of Dongara and the grandson of the original owner of the Dongarra Hotel, has many happy memories of his lifetime association with the Dominican Sisters. He remembers with pride how he taught Sister Vincent Colgan to drive, in a 10 h.p. Hillman Standard and recalls that even though she was the first member of the Dominican community to obtain a driving licence, Sr Vincent never took advantage of the lessons. The first convent car was originally owned and later donated to the community by Sister Immaculate Ashleigh who taught in country schools before entering the convent. At the time, there was no resident doctor at Dongara and with two licensed drivers in the community, Sisters Immaculate and Marie Therese Sharman, the small car was a godsend when the Sisters and boarders needed to seek medical or dental treatment in Geraldton. Several generations of boarders identify with Mr Criddle for, in his role as local carrier from 1942 until the early 1970s, he used to transport the boarders and Sisters to picnics and outings. During the holiday periods he was also employed to ferry the girls and their luggage to and from the college to the station. There were two railway lines, one leading north, the other south, and most boarders had to travel long distances to reach their homes during the holiday breaks. On break-up day, Mr Criddle would be up at 5.00 a.m. to cart the luggage to the station, returning in time to convey a carload of laughing, chattering schoolgirls in his specially fitted-out charabanc.

46. Mr Lionel Criddle's charabanc

From the establishment of the first small boarding school near the flour mill at Dongara in 1901, until the closure of the large residential, built in 1928, the Dominican Ladies' College was 'home' to countless girls. As boarders, they spent the best part of each year together in a family situation, but because the college was also associated with school, the rules, by necessity, were more rigid than in a home environment. The Sisters were aware of this situation and throughout the year arranged as many outings as possible away from the college buildings. True to a promise made earlier, the Sisters held a mammoth boarders' picnic on 10 April 1937, to commemorate the enrolment of the school's sixtieth boarder. Although beach visits were common practice during the hot summer months, coping with the entire boarding school for a whole day down at the seaside required a great deal of organisation. According to an article written by one of the parents, the Sisters contacted Mr Criddle and shortly afterwards 30 excited students, in the care of two Sisters, climbed aboard his waiting bus for the journey to nearby Port Denison. Depositing his first load of passengers at a shed, placed at the Sisters' disposal by the local beach committee, the driver then returned to pick up the remaining 30 girls. A fire was lit from wood gathered on-site and at noon some of the contents of a huge hamper were handed out by senior students, an exercise which was repeated at afternoon tea time and again before their departure for Dongara at sunset. The day was spent indulging in simple pleasures such as swimming, beach walking, gathering shells and examining strange sea-creatures, and as the day progressed many of the boarders took part in organised community singing. It was a happy occasion that was successfully duplicated some six months later when the college went beyond its projected target of 70 girls and enrolled its seventy-third boarder. [58]

In 1942, during World War II, the growing threat of a Japanese invasion became a grim reality when Singapore fell. With an unprotected coastline and a large proportion of Australia's Armed Forces already fighting overseas, Western Australia was totally unprepared when enemy Zeros attacked Darwin in February 1942 and proceeded further south to bomb Port Hedland, Broome and Kalamburu. As the situation became more serious, many women and children living close to northern ports were evacuated, and the majority of students boarding in coastal schools were relocated inland. On 23 March 1942, senior boarders from the Dominican Ladies' College at Dongara were evacuated to 'Parakalia', a farm on the outskirts of Three Springs owned by Mrs Sarah Maley. According to one of the evacuees, Ida Edwards (Mrs Gallop), the day the Sisters and pupils were to leave Dongara, the Irwin River burst its banks and flooded the convent road. It was several days before the water subsided enough to allow traffic to cross the bridge and the party to reach Three Springs. Mrs Gallop recalled that Mrs Ethel Shute and Joe, a farm assistant, resided on the property where they were billeted and several local children joined them in their studies. Among the visitors was future Dominican Sister, Suzanne Vandeleur. [59] Too young to be affected by the war, the girls' brief break in the country proved to be a happy interlude with days spent in quiet, uninterrupted study. In their leisure hours the girls explored the property, using a so-called 'Roman chariot', or alternatively a cart painted green and appropriately nicknamed 'Eire'. Both of the horses used to pull the vehicle were borrowed from their kindly host family. The evacuees remained in the wheatbelt, savouring country life, until recalled to Dongara, on 22 July, to resume their normal studies.

Despite the war years, the annual Bushies' School, organised by the Sisters, continued to operate during the Christmas holidays. On Saturday, 10 January 1942, just prior to the Japanese bombing of Darwin, the fifth Summer School was held at the Dominican Ladies' College in Dongara. Although numbers were down on previous years because of war-time petrol restrictions, a crowd of some 40 young people from as far away as Big Bell, Carnamah and Winchester, took advantage of the Dominican community's kindness. Father Lynch provided daily transport to and from the beach where, accompanied by their hostesses, the children enjoyed an afternoon of recreation. Despite the fun times, the spiritual side of their stay was not neglected. On Friday, 9 January 1942, 10 members of the Bushies' School received their first Holy Communion and the following morning Bishop O'Collins confirmed another 19 children in the convent chapel. [60]

A special Midnight Mass, held in the Priory gardens on Christmas Eve 1942, to cater for a contingent of soldiers camped in the district, was an occasion not easily forgotten. An altar, decorated with delicate pink flowers from the Priory gardens, was erected on the top terrace for better viewing. During the ceremony, a canopy, softly draped in satin and ornamented with scattered asparagus fern and golden leaves, was bathed in muted light from two strategically placed floodlights arranged by the soldiers. A second terrace in front of the Priory acted as a prie-dieu for those participating in communion. As the Army trucks arrived and more than 700 men gathered in the grounds, they could not help but be impressed with the cathedral-like scene before them. The softly lit grotto, fernery and palms formed an ideal backdrop for the Christmas Crib and there must have been many a moist eye in the audience when the band's joyous rendition of 'Adeste Fidelis' and 'Silent Night' broke the stillness of the night.

Before the military chaplain, Father Lyons MSC, celebrated Mass, he gave a comforting message to those away from their homes and their loved ones. He also thanked the Colonel for giving the servicemen leave, the electricians for the beauty they had created,

47. Gypsy scene from "Zurika"
L. to R. Back Row: H. Collins, P. Reynolds, A. McDonald, M. Kitsche, M. Smith, P. Money, M.Davidson
Middle: M. Slattery, V. McDonald, M. Seaman, H. Raffan, J. Munckton
Front: J. Nairn, P. Collinson, A. Willmott, V. Elsworthy

the Priory chaplain, Father Cullen, for his assistance and finally the Mother Prioress General Vincent Colgan for preparing and making the grounds available. During the Mass, the Army band played several hymns and, for the half hour it took two priests to give Holy Communion, there was a complete hush over the garden as the nuns' choir beautifully sang several well-known numbers, including Schubert's 'Ave Maria'. [61] It was not unusual for the college to use the garden setting for school performances and on one memorable occasion, in December 1949, the Sisters successfully staged two colourful operettas. *The Broken Statue* and *Zurika* were performed before a large audience, which included the Bishop of Geraldton, A. J. Gummer, the Member for the District, the Hon. David Brand (later Sir David, Premier of Western Australia) and Mrs Brand, as well as parents and past pupils of the Dominican Ladies' College.

On Thursday, 8 December 1949, the Dominican community's Golden Jubilee was commemorated with a Solemn Pontifical High Mass celebrated at Dongara by Bishop Gummer. Sharing the event were Fathers Gallagher, Moffatt, O'Sullivan, Stinson, O'Connor, Wellems, Dean Michael Lynch, Dom William Gimenez OSB and Dom Michael Cave OSB (who later became chaplain to the Doubleview community). The Sisters had come a long way since their arrival in 1899, and although by 1949 some of their foundations no longer existed, there were still schools operating at Cue, Leonora, Gwalia, Meekatharra, Three Springs, Yalgoo, Mingenew and also a successful convent and school established nine years earlier in the Perth diocese at Bedford Park.

Apart from educating girls, the Sisters also taught a number of local boys at primary school level. During the 1930s, Sisters Catherine Kenny and Dominic Galvin conducted classes in a former workman's cottage in the playground area, commonly referred to as the Infant of Prague Classroom. Later, between 1947 and 1950, local identity John Rowland was one of a small group of boys who attended mixed primary school classes at the college and, although not of the Catholic faith, he has the greatest respect and admiration for his former teachers. When describing that part of his life he wrote:

*The contribution to the community throughout the Mid-West region cannot be underestimated. The Sisters not only taught scholastic classes, but also music, sport and manual skills. They operated the kitchens, huge laundry, aviaries, vegetable gardens, a dairy herd and large poultry run, conceding only to hire farm hands to sow, cut and cart hay. Depending on the time of day, the Convent and School could be awash with a myriad of sights and sounds. The strains of violins, piano or vocal arpeggios, the chanting of arithmetic tables, the lowing of cows being herded into the dairy, or the screams and shouts from Sisters and students in the playgrounds.*

*With habits tucked up into that wide leather belt, flowing scapular tossed back over the shoulder, and long wooden beads rattling, the young Sisters taught the girls how to swing a tennis racquet, bounce and pot basketballs or heave heavy medicine balls down long lines of spread legs in team relays. Meanwhile the boys were taught the fine points of marking and kicking a football or how to face a cricket bat to the fastest of underarm throws. Those same Sisters ran between sewing classes for girls, providing all the necessary skills to overcome the idiosyncrasies of treadle sewing machines, and groups of 5 to 11-year-old boys learnt how to manage fretwork hand saws, hammers and nails, and still have ten fingers at the end of it.* [62]

48. Sisters at recreation.
L. to R.: Sisters Assumpta Moriarty, Ambrose Bernet, Perpetua Gill, Francis Huntsman.

Drama, speech, music, perception and theory were taught in all grades. The study of elocution (Art of Speech) was always a popular subject at Catholic girls' schools and it was not unusual for convent-trained candidates to gain top honours in speech examinations. In 1955, Lesley Allnutt of Mingenew, a student at the Dominican Ladies' College in Dongara, gained 90 marks in Second Grade Art of Speech and received a letter from her University examiners commending her for her excellent work. That same year the Dominican Ladies' College announced that all students who sat for the Junior and Leaving Certificates had gained 100 per cent passes and several members of the Dominican community had either completed their training at the Teachers' Training College or gained further subjects towards their University Arts Degrees. Later in 1963, all 54 Dominican Ladies' College candidates who sat for speech examinations were successful, many of the students gaining honours and credits. In March 1963, the Dominican Sisters reminded parents that the college was registered as a secondary school and that scholarships were available to students who met the criteria. Courses of study covered the majority of subjects generally taught in secondary schools and girls were also prepared for nursing, commercial, teaching and university courses.

49. Tennis Group, 1949
L. to R. 4th Row: P. Jones, J. Starkey, N. Nevill, R. Burge, M. Donegan, M.Campbell, E. Robinson, M. Smith, M. Gee, M. Hill, P. Broadhurst
3rd Row: M. Barnard, P. Vandeleur, J. Munckton, M. Donovan, M. Seaman, B. Seaborne, H. Collins, V. Vincent, B. Priddis, G. Lynch, A. Willmott, L. Maund, G. Cunningham, B. Bodycoat, M. Nevill
2nd Row: Max Bonner (coach), L. Buckley, R. Bromby, F. Schloithe, V. Elsworthy, P. Seaman, P. Alvertani, L. Allnutt, D. Starkey, J. Bradley, G. Young
1st Row: D. Knuckey, A. Starkey, D. Young, J. Kerr, P. Starkey, F. Knuckey, D. Harris, R. Jensen

A new curriculum was introduced state-wide in the 1960s and, in line with that period, students became involved in a wider exchange of ideas and extra-curricular activities. On 24 September 1961, the Dominican Ladies' College took part for the first time in the Inter-Dominican School Sports held at Lathlain Park in Perth. The event was later transferred to Perry Lakes and the girls continued to travel from Dongara to Perth to participate. The college still held its own faction sports, with the four college houses, Siena (green), Aquino (gold), Ferrer (blue) and Penafort (red), competing against each other. The titles of each house, taken from the names of Dominican Saints have been traditionally used in other Dominican schools over the years. During the 1960s, well-known tennis coach, Mr Max Bonner, provided his customary week of intensive tennis coaching. His arrival was always eagerly anticipated and as an added incentive the top players competed each year for a tennis racquet on the final day. Miss Dawson gave dancing lessons and trained the girls in deportment, and, in 1965, Mrs Neilson joined the staff as a teacher of physical education.

An article published in the *Cathedral Chronicle* in 1965, revealed that the Sisters were quick to recognise the changes taking place: 'A Dominican Sister is guided by her Constitution. The Dominican makes every effort to train girls to realise that to cultivate liberty does not mean to allow licence, but rather having developed self-control as they advance through to the senior classes this self discipline should make supervision less necessary'. [63] This observation was endorsed by comments made by Monsignor Bryan VG at the College Speech Night in 1965, when he reminded the audience that during the time they cared for the students the Sisters had been intent on building their character and teaching them to become good citizens. Apart from overseeing the girls' academic studies, the Dominicans had also prepared the students to accept success and failure, bearing in mind that the secret of success for each person was having confidence in oneself. The Monsignor urged the girls not to lose contact with the Sisters 'who had seen them grow up, watched their characteristics develop and shown such an interest in them individually'. [64]

50. Welcoming Miss Australia, 1961
L. to R.: P. Cousins, M. Mazzuchelli, J. Lyons, Miss Tanya Verstak, (Miss Australia, later Miss Universe), P. Stirling, M. Shute, S. Bavoillat, A. Burge

The Geraldton diocese, in the period from 1962 up until 1968, was blessed with the presence of a number of men and women lay missionaries who came from the eastern states in answer to an advertised plea from Father Keith Spain. Hard-working Fr Spain, parish priest at Dongara and a firm supporter of the Dominican Sisters, had initially called for volunteers to assist with religious instruction by correspondence for children living in isolated areas. His scheme had merit for whilst he did his utmost to answer everyone's needs, he realised that with so few religious on hand some people's requirements could not be met without outside assistance. The first five lay missionaries, Helen Fisher, Cathy Walsh, Lila Hulme, Bill Sullivan, Bob Menner and Brian Cathie arrived in Perth in February 1962, where they were met by Fr Spain and Bishop Thomas. Lila Hulme went first to Stella Maris, and later to Dongara, and Brian Cathie went to Nazareth House on the Chapman River. The others remained at Dongara and were joined a month later by Laurie Lister, Terry Bruisamarello, Jennifer Madden, Kerry Hall and Flora Riccupero (who served at Bluff Point and later entered the Presentation Convent in Geraldton). Bill Sullivan recalls that in the middle of the year, Vince Loughlan arrived in his Land Rover and together with Terry Bruisamarello spent some time with Father Moffat in Three Springs demolishing the old St Joseph's Church. The building was re-erected the following year by Laurie Lister and Vince Loughlan at Dongara. Meanwhile, the group living at Dongara was accommodated in

51. Senior students, 1963-1964
L. to R.: H. Weston, M. Valentine, M. Markey, M. Campbell, P. Lane

buildings adjacent to the Priory and, as well as helping Father Spain, the volunteers also assisted the Sisters with work at the convent and college. [65]

Speech Night, held at the college in early November 1969, was as usual a well-organised event. The lower Secondary Choir, prepared by Sister Anthony Sachse (Prioress), chose excerpts from the *Mikado*, Miss Dawson's dancing class performed the colourful Japanese Awa Dance ...dents from Sister de Montfort Evan's French classes ...election of songs in French. Thanks were extended ... the evening to all teachers including several lay ...ors: Miss Dawson (dancing teacher), Mrs Clinch ... coach), Mr Murray (athletics and swimming ... and Mr White (tennis coach). Parents were ...d that the prefect system had been replaced that ... a Student Council and mention was also made ...ange student, Lexie Rossiter, who with Miss ...rdon, had been chosen by the Lions Club to be ...epresentative in Japan during the Christmas .... In her 1969 annual report the principal, Sister de Montfort endorsed Monsignor Bryan's earlier statement when she spoke convincingly about, 'the aims of the college to prepare the girls for the life ahead of them, to develop the full potential of their minds and to make them good Christian leaders, ready to share the responsibility of the modern community'. [66]



The arrival of 55 boarders, just prior to the commencement of classes on 5 February 1970, coincided with an uncomfortable week of extremely hot humid weather. On Sunday, 15 February, heavy rain developed and continued to lash the coast from a south-easterly direction. By Tuesday morning, the situation had worsened and, in view of the rapidly rising river, the Shire office contacted the Sisters warning them that a flood was imminent and likely to cut off the school and convent from the town. It was decided that day scholars would be sent home and with the water expected to overflow the banks by midday, the Dominican household had no choice but to play a waiting game. At 2.30 p.m. Sister Pierre Ross (Sr Diane) from the Dominican Convent at Mingenew rang to inform the Sisters at Dongara that the Strawberry bridge was under water and the railway bridge had been washed away. The section of river near them was already half-a-mile wide and rising fast and, according to the locals, the floods were far worse than anything seen in living memory.

The floodwaters by then were over the banks of the Irwin River and slowly seeping past the swings into the college playground. Sandbags were sent for, and it was decided to build a levee at each of the gates leading from the road into the college and convent grounds. To assist Sister Jordana and the Priory's handyman, Mr Canny, a group of fourth and fifth year students started to remove the sand from the playground jumping-pits and barrow it to where the bags were being filled and placed in position. By late afternoon the water had extended along the road in both directions and the tennis courts were awash. The force of the water soon breached the sandbags and the level of the river continued to rise. By 10.00 p.m., the water had covered the lily pond, reached the convent steps and two terraces in the Priory garden and submerged the drive to the triangular garden bed. The playground was completely covered with at least four-and-a-half feet of water and it was well over the top of the convent wall before it eventually began to subside. At the same time Cyclone Ingrid caused a great deal of havoc throughout the district when the Greenough River also flooded resulting in the Geraldton Road being cut and Walkaway being marooned. [67]

A second more damaging flood, caused by Cyclone Mavis in 1971, was the catalyst that finally saw the closure of the Dominican Priory at Dongara and the termination of the boarding school and college. Having experienced the expense and inconvenience of a similar disaster only 12 months earlier, it must have been difficult for the Sisters to accept the devastation caused by yet another flood. At 2.00 p.m. on Sunday, 28 March 1971, the bed of the river was dry; yet by 2.40 p.m. the level of the water had risen enough to reach the top of the terrace. Twenty minutes later the water had encroached as far as the east side of the convent forcing its way through fowl yards and over a paddock until it surrounded the laundry and convent. It was at this point that the Sisters decided, with the help of Father Spain and Bill Sullivan, to move some of their more valuable possessions to safety. Not only did the muddy water enter the house to a depth of two feet, but also it also completely submerged the playground and demolished the sports shed. By 5.00 p.m., the head of St Dominic's statue in the garden was under water and the telephone, power and water services were out of action. About 7.00 p.m., for a brief period of time, optimism ran high when the level of the river began to subside. The relief, however, was short-lived for, by 11.30 p.m., the floodwaters continued to spread through the ground floor of the convent. Fortunately, the flood peaked in the early hours of Monday morning and, because it was thought that the worst was over, the students were given permission to visit Fr Spain's presbytery after breakfast to view the damage. They were amazed to discover that the road to the bridge had been washed away and an old cottage, locally referred to as 'Simpson's house', had collapsed like a pack of cards.

During the morning, five elderly Sisters, later transferred to Perth, were evacuated by jeep and taken to safety by means of the back route across paddocks and sand dunes to the Sisters' beach cottage. Meanwhile, after contacting some of the children's parents through a local radio station, the Sisters arranged for all remaining boarders to be temporarily billeted out to families living at Denison. Although power had been restored to the convent by 4.00 p.m., the building was once again left in darkness when, half-an-hour later, two more light poles fell. With no lights and a large section of the convent awash, the Sisters wisely decided to sleep at the college. By Tuesday, 30 March, plans were set in motion to send the boarders home, or to stay with friends, until they received further information regarding the re-opening of the school.

After some of the visiting Sisters had dispersed, the Prioress Provincial Sister de Sales Patterson and Sister Assumpta Moriarty, both of whom had come from Perth to assess the situation, returned south, accompanied by Sister Philomena Punch. Left behind at Dongara were four Sisters – Suzanne Vandeleur, Kath Levitzke, Bernardine Hanafin and Josephine Hanafin. The sight that greeted them following the flood was one of utter devastation. The windmill had collapsed, part of the grounds, the terrace walls and some trees had been washed away and large sections of the gardens denuded. Furthermore, the subsiding waters had left an ugly trail of dark squelching mud. By the weekend, a temporary road was in place and carloads of enthusiastic helpers had arrived to offer assistance, among them Father Barden, who had thoughtfully organised a group from the Christian Brothers College in Geraldton to help clear some of the layers of mud deposited inside the convent. A party of Presentation Sisters, also from Geraldton, drove out to the Priory with afternoon tea and kindly offered to take any laundry back with them and if necessary arrange to accommodate the Dominican boarders.

It was estimated that it would take at least two weeks to put the kitchen back in working order; a decision was therefore made not to recall the boarders until 26 April. In the meantime, fires were lit in all the rooms to dry out the walls and floorboards and locally formed busy-bees descended upon the ruined gardens in an attempt to put them back into some semblance of order. Later, 29 prisoners from the Geraldton Regional Gaol, were sent out with three officers and a warden to clear the grounds and to participate in a general clean up prior to the return of the boarders. The response from everywhere was incredible. Ladies from Geraldton and Dongara swept floors, cleaned cupboards and washed up endless piles of crockery. Among the many to offer their services were ex-pupil Ida Edwards, Mrs Fitzpatrick and Mrs MacDonnell from Geraldton, Mr Finkelstein and his daughter, Kerry from Yuna, Eric and Margaret Weller and the Sisters from Morawa. Not to be left out, a group of crayfishermen volunteered to shift the furniture. One of the earlier lay missionaries, who had returned about the time of the flood, became a 'Jack of all Trades' which prompted one of the Sisters to later remark, 'Bill Sullivan was a great help in getting the college ready for the return of the boarders and for helping to keep the Sisters both sane and happy'. [68] School re-opened on 25 April, after a closure of some four weeks, and with the return of the boarders, day scholars and staff, life returned to some sort of normality.

Yet, the Dominican Sisters had other more pressing problems to face. Disheartened by two floods within two years and deeply concerned that the bad seasons recently experienced by farmers would continue to affect the enrolment of boarders, members of the Provincial Council were forced to review an earlier suggestion, made in 1969, to close the Dominican Ladies' College at Dongara. At that time, despite decreasing numbers, the decision to withdraw was deferred indefinitely. In 1971, there were only 15 day scholars and 34 boarders on the roll. Apart from the constant flooding, the Sisters also realised that with the greater opportunity for at least lower secondary education in country areas and the introduction of buses to transport students into larger centres, the prospect of attracting a viable number of boarders in the future was minimal.

On 16 June 1971, the Prioress Provincial, Mother de Sales, informed the Sisters at Dongara that the Provincial Council had decided that the Dominican Ladies' College was now redundant and would cease to operate after the end of that year. Letters were to be sent to the boarders' parents asking them to make alternative arrangements for their daughters, and it was intended that the property and buildings, apart from the beach cottage, would be put up for sale. [69] On 25 September, Kathy Healy became the first and last ex-student to be married in the convent chapel. Because of the Dominican Sisters long association with the district and the building's historic significance, an Australian Broadcasting Commission team from Perth arrived at Dongara on 30 November to make a film featuring the Priory, the Dominican Ladies' College and the associated grounds.

The last Mass and final graduation ceremony held at the Dominican Ladies' College took place on 3 December 1971. For everyone it was a special and emotional occasion. Bishop Thomas presented the graduates with gold crosses and chains and expressed his gratitude for the 70-year commitment made by the Dominican Sisters to the Geraldton diocese. He reminded those present that although Dongara had closed, the Sisters still had a strong presence in the diocese with the schools they continued to operate at Mingenew, Three Springs and Morawa. With the money raised earlier by the Parents' and Friends'

Association, currently defunct, the Sisters organised a farewell party. Each girl received a small souvenir to remind them of their Alma Mater and, in turn, the students presented the community with a silver tray.

Records reveal that the last Dominican students to depart from the college on 8 December 1971, were: (First Year High) Merrilee Brennand, Catherine Campbell, Monica Lynch, Angelina Marsh, Cheryle Meanwell, Beverley Russ, Jennifer Shields, Michelle Buckley, Elizabeth Dempster, Deanie Drummond, Amanda Powell, Susan Welby, Tracey Yelverton, Janne Cousins, Jenny Colero; (Second and Third Year) Joanne and Kerry Finklestein, Theresa Lynch, Rhonda Matsen, Gaye Miguel, Keryl Murphy, Joynie McGagh, Joanne Pugsley, Anthea Roach, Veronica Clinch, Christine Davis, Dale Hayward, Susan McCartney, Catherine Nowers; (Fourth and Fifth Year) Rita Bowtell, Anne Cox, Sue Downie, Sue Norrish, Sue Porteus, Patricia Coffey, Christine Cox, Lynette Councillor, Sonia Fitzpatrick, Margaret Harris, Frances Lynch, Lorraine Matsen, Jan McNaboe, Sari Meyer, Lynda Morrow and Vickie Norrish. On 11 December 1971, Mrs Vera Phillips (née Fienburg), an 84-year-old foundation pupil, wrote:

*Dear Mother Superior,*

*We heard on TV and also read in the paper that the Dominican Priory was closing its doors. I received a great shock. I was one of the first pupils. In fact I was also one of the first pupils to enrol at Cue when the nuns came there to open a school in 1899. After six months in Cue I went down to Greenough for Music and Theory exams and stayed there as a boarder, until the school was taken over by the Presentation nuns from Geraldton.*

*We went to Dongara. I think there were about six girls. We were housed in different cottages. Then the nuns bought the old hotel and renovated it to a certain degree to make it suitable for the purpose for which it was bought. I was there until I was about 15 years old. I do not know the nuns at the Priory now, as all the originals have passed on (God rest their souls) and are buried in the little cemetery at the Priory. I am sure it is heart-breaking for all the Nuns to leave the priory as such a lovely building has risen from the humble hotel and the first Priory. God bless you all and may you continue to succeed in your work.* [70]

About 30 Sisters gathered to celebrate their final Christmas at the Priory and on Christmas Eve friends and parishioners joined them in the convent chapel for Midnight Mass. Before making their final departure on 28 January, the Sisters invited Bishop Thomas and the diocesan priests to dinner. Not wishing to see the contribution they had made towards external religious instruction diminish, the Sisters announced their intentions to inaugurate a Motor Mission in 1972. It was expected that the Sisters attached to the new mission would live at the Three Springs and Morawa convents and visit Catholic children in government schools in those parishes. Cartons of books, pieces of furniture and other useful items from the convent and college, including the stained glass panel that once graced the front door, were gradually packed during the Christmas holidays. These were then stored in the refectory and recreation hall at Dongara, awaiting the completion of a new Provincial house which was being built at Doubleview in Perth. The marble altar in the former convent chapel was subsequently dismantled by an Italian stone mason for removal to the metropolitan area, where it was eventually installed in the new St Catherine's chapel. In the interim the Dominican Sisters employed a caretaker and his family to look after the former Priory and college buildings.

A number of former Dominican Ladies' College students entered the novitiate at Dongara over the years. These young ladies not only added a lifetime of local knowledge to the Sisters from New Zealand, but also lessened the need to seek more members from overseas. Past pupils who became Dominican Sisters included: Teresa Barden (Sr Gabriel), May Corbett (Sr Augustine), Bernice Gill (Sr Perpetua), Frances Haddock (Sr Francesca), Mary Lynch (Sr Emmanuel), Andrea Lane (Sr Augustine), Sally Leeson (Sr Agnes), Kath Levitzke (Sr di Ricci), Inez Lloyd (Sr Dolores), Gladys O'Connor (Sr Bertrand), Mary O'Connor (Sr Joseph), Anne Ryan (Sr Xavier), Patricia Ryan (Sr Michael), Margaret Seaman (Sr Gemma), Mary Punch (Sr Philomena), Joan Punch (Sr Bernadette), Patricia Sachse (Sr Anthony), Pauline Sachse (Sr Christopher), Suzanne Vandeleur (Sr Julian) and Anita Willmott (Sr Margaret Mary).

The twin towns of Dongara and Denison, 360 kilometres north of Perth, are today still noted for their peaceful surroundings, protected beaches and calm, clear waters. Both areas are popular holiday resorts and high on the list of preferred places for retirees. Fishing and an endless supply of crayfish, delivered fresh from the cray boats that operate out of the port, also attract numerous visitors. As a result of increased tourism, the main street at Dongara, renowned for its shady Moreton Bay fig trees, is rapidly showing signs of modern development. Since the Sisters' departure in 1971, the former Priory and Dominican Ladies' College have had a somewhat chequered history. Sometime after the closure of the college the buildings were converted into bed and breakfast style accommodation and given the name Priory Lodge. The first proprietors made a number of alterations and added a swimming pool, but, by the 1990s, the buildings were badly in need of repair and refurbishment. The once lush gardens had become forlorn and overgrown and, except for several distinctive palm trees, little of the former glory of the grounds remained. The property has recently been purchased by Terry O'Meara and his wife Connie who are presently restoring the buildings with an eye to retaining much of the original design and past history. The major staircases, balustrading, steps and jarrah floorboards in the hallways and many rooms have been stripped and restored with high gloss finish. They hope to breathe new life back into the gardens, establish the chapel area as a wedding reception centre and offer dining facilities and reasonably-priced accommodation.

The peaceful Dominican cemetery, approached by a shady lane adjacent to the old Priory, sits in isolation on top of a slight rise. The first Dominican Sister to be interred in the private burial ground was Sister Imelda Buckley, a lay Sister, who had arrived from Ireland only six years prior to her death on 13 July 1913. She was described as a quiet, prayerful person, and a valued member of the community. A Requiem Mass held in the nuns' chapel at the Priory, was followed by a graveside service, conducted by Father Scanlon on Tuesday 15 July. Later, when 17-year-old student Clare Punch died of tuberculosis in 1927, her parents gratefully accepted the Sisters' offer to arrange for her to be buried in the convent cemetery. Clare was one of five children born to Matthew and Rose Punch of Leonora. Two other daughters, Mary (Sr Philomena) and Joan (Sr Bernadette) later joined the

52-54. Former Priory and college gardens, Dongara

Dominican Order. The Punch family was close-knit and generously supportive of the Dominican community. Clare initially attended the Dominican school at Leonora and, in 1922, went to board at Dongara where one of her sisters was already enrolled at St Dominic's College. In 1923, Mr and Mrs Punch and the younger members of the family, Margaret and Joan, moved to Dongara. It was four years later that Clare fell seriously ill. After lengthy specialist treatment in Perth she showed no signs of improvement and Dr McAleer finally diagnosed her condition as advanced tuberculosis. Clare died on 21 October 1927. Mourned by her family, teachers and fellow students, she was dressed in the full regalia of a Child of Mary and buried in the Priory cemetery. It was only a month or two later, after returning to her home in Kalgoorlie, that another student, Stella Saligari, also died of the same complaint. [71]

The tiny hillside cemetery, overshadowed and almost hidden by oleanders and pepper trees, continued to be used as a place of burial for the Sisters until 1971. It was a hallowed place to which the other Sisters retreated in search of solitude and to pray in peace. The secluded burial ground was also used by the younger novices to practise for speech examinations, or to memorise lines for the occasional community concert performance, and it was said by those who frequented the site, that they felt 'at home with the joyous spirit of those who had gone before them and were happy in the knowledge that they would not disturb or be disturbed'. After the Priory and Dominican College closed, it became increasingly more difficult to maintain the cemetery at Dongara. The time and loving care previously given to keeping the graveyard in perfect order were no longer possible and the knowledge that from time to time it was the target of vandals distressed the present community. Efforts were made by successive administrations to safeguard the sacred spot, but when these failed, and only after much soul searching, the decision was taken, in 1996, to exhume and re-inter the remains of all of the Sisters in the Karrakatta Cemetery, Perth.

55. Dominican Priory cemetery, Dongara

In September 1996, the Dominican Sisters, accompanied by a group of friends and ex-students, gathered at the former Priory's cemetery to share in a Mass offered by Father Brian Ahearn, parish priest of Dongara, in gratitude for the outstanding contribution made to the Geraldton diocese by the 35 pioneer Sisters resting there. Among the remains about to be re-interred were the Dominican foundress Mother Gabriel Gill, three of the five foundation members, Sister Bonaventure McEntyre, Sister Dominica Murphy and Sister di Pazzi Miscall and the last member to be buried at Dongara, Sister Stanislaus McDonough. It was a sad, but precious and peaceful experience for those privileged to be there. Father O'Hare, who had a presentiment about his death and had earlier expressed a wish to be buried in the nuns' small cemetery at Dongara, had been laid to rest in the Dominican cemetery after he died suddenly in the Priory chapel on 9 November 1928. The priest's remains were also exhumed at the same time as those of the Dominican Sisters.

On the eve of All Souls Day, 1 November 1996, members of the Dominican congregation and families and friends came together at the Karrakatta cemetery to witness the laying of a commemorative stone inscribed with the names of each re-interred Sister, as well as that of Clare Punch. Five days later, a Requiem Mass was concelebrated by Bishop Justin Bianchini and Father O'Flaherty in the Chapel of the Holy Spirit in the Utakarra cemetery at Geraldton. The ceremony marked the occasion of the re-interment of the last remains taken from Dongara, those of Father O'Hare.

56. Dominican Priory chapel, Dongara

For over 72 years the Dominican Sisters devoted their lives to teaching in the Irwin District and during those years they influenced the lives of thousands of students. Despite having transferred their activities to the Archdiocese, the Sisters have kept their holiday home at Port Denison and so retain close links with Dongara. An Old Girls' Association was formed in 1941 and ties between the Sisters and past pupils of the former Dominican Ladies' College have remained strong. Although the ex-students are now widely scattered, many still meet at re-unions in Dongara or for casual gatherings at St Catherine's Convent in Doubleview, to share their present lives with old school friends and the teachers who guided them in their youth.

CHAPTER 6

# Footprints in the ...ds of Time

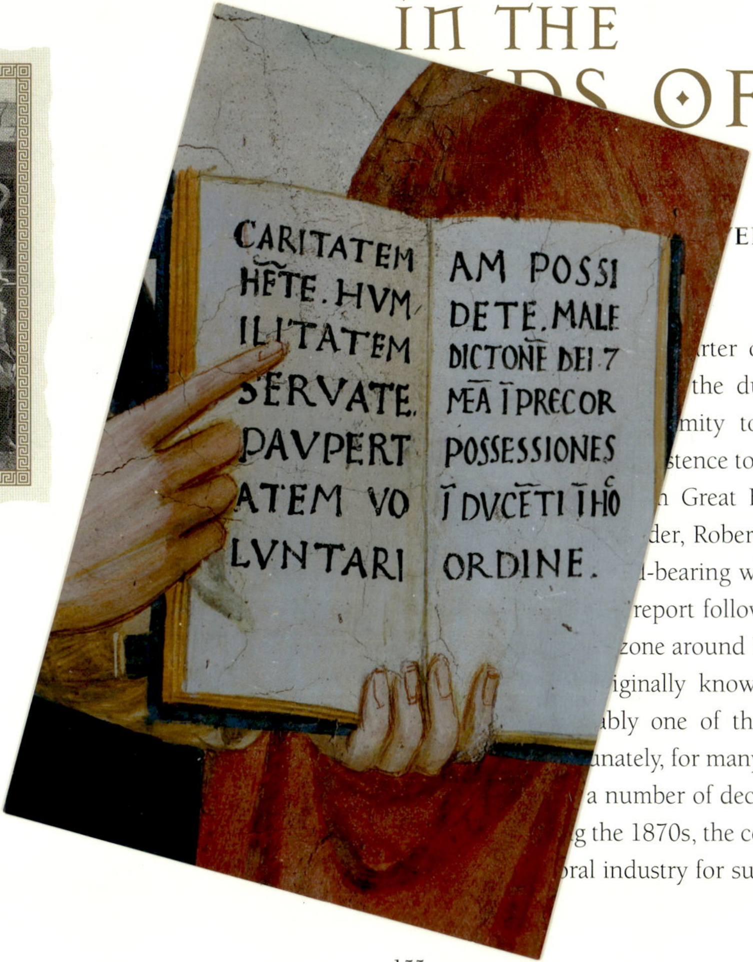


...ENT AND SCHOOL,

...rter of a century Dame Fortune
... the dual towns of Cue and Day
...mity to each other, both mining
...stence to the discovery of gold and in
...n Great Fingall Mine at Day Dawn.
...der, Robert Austin, had suspected that
...d-bearing when he explored the area in
... report following the expedition referred
...zone around Mt Kenneth, Mt Magnet and
...iginally known as the Great Salt Lakes)
...ably one of the greatest goldfields in the
...unately, for many reasons, his prediction was
... a number of decades.

...g the 1870s, the colony was heavily dependent
...oral industry for survival and there was a move

to establish more sheep stations in various directions beyond the Darling Scarp. Between 1870 and 1884, the number of sheep in the colony increased from 600,000 to 1,500,000 and, to satisfy the demands of the English market, pastoralists successfully developed station properties in isolated regions. [1] Access to water remained a major problem and the wells sunk by pastoralists were crucial, not only to the success of their stations, but often to the survival of prospectors exploring likely areas. Ned Heffernan, after his involvement in the discovery of gold at Cue's Patch, later found a promising reef of quartz not quite four miles south of Cue. Realising that he was without the means to develop the find, beyond extracting a certain amount of gold from the surface, Heffernan decided to approach a mining company with a view to their commencing mining operations on a larger scale. Author P. Heydon, commenting on various gold discoveries in the Murchison, wrote: 'In later years, this dark blue reef was to be responsible for the establishment of the well-known Great Fingall gold mine – one of the most famous mines in West Australian history. After the discovery of the reef at Day Dawn, other miners flocked to this area'. [2]

The Great Fingall Consolidated Limited Gold Mining Company at Day Dawn, which had its headquarters in London, was originally considered one of the major mines operating outside Kalgoorlie and

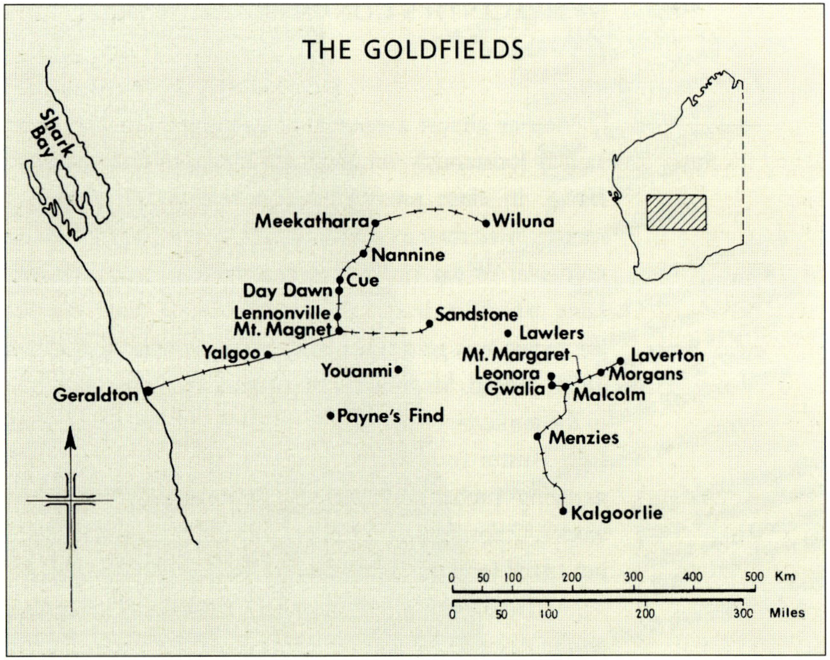


57. The Western Australian Goldfields.
Courtesy D. F. Bourke.

Coolgardie and one of the richest in Australia. An impressive administration building, constructed by Italian stonemasons from local limestone in 1902, dominated the harsh landscape and was an integral part of the mining operation for many years. Large mining companies continued to employ a huge workforce and until the gradual diminution in the production of gold, Day Dawn was considered a lively and progressive town.

Amongst several versions of the way the town acquired its name, it has been suggested that the choice of the title, Day Dawn, was given to the area by pioneer prospector, Ned Heffernan, after whom the town's main street was later named. The popular legend suggests that Ned, accompanied by an Aboriginal woman, was taken to a rocky outcrop in his quest for gold. As daylight broke he discovered signs of the precious base metal and decided that at long last his day had dawned. The site, when developed, became the Great Fingall Mine. A second tale has a shepherd as the central character. He allegedly caught sight of the glint of gold while sitting on top of a bluff in the early hours of the morning and, like Heffernan, was convinced that his day had dawned. Former Cue identity, Phillip Heydon, states that the town had originally been gazetted Bunda Wadra, but a request from the local community to Sir John Forrest put the name to popular vote. Three names were put forward for consideration, first St Albans, in honour of the owner of the Big Gold Mine, secondly Heffernan after the prospector who discovered the reef, and finally Day Dawn after the mine. [3]

The gold boom during the 'Roaring Nineties' had an enormous impact on the western colony. New discoveries not only brought great wealth to the state, but were also indirectly responsible for the development of large towns, fine buildings and the rapid extension of the railway and road systems. By the time the Murchison goldfields were proclaimed in 1891, the pastoral and mining industries had learned to co-exist. Gradually, shanty towns and makeshift 'tent cities' were replaced by townships, boasting laid out streets, business houses, public buildings, churches and schools. Altogether the Murchison District produced a record 239,788 ounces of gold in 1902 and from the turn of the century onwards employment opportunities for migrants were boundless. A considerable proportion of the population, before World War I, was either Austrian or Italian and, therefore, largely Catholic. In fact, one newspaper article, published on 26 April 1900, calculated that at least one-third of the population in Day Dawn was Italian, which gives some veracity to the story that, at one stage, the town's Italian Club had 2000 financial members on its books. In view of the increasing number of Catholic families living in the area, Bishop Kelly became concerned about the children's spiritual welfare and so, in January 1900, he granted the Dominican Sisters at Cue permission to teach Christian Doctrine and to visit the hospital at Day Dawn on Sundays. [4]

Residential buildings on the goldfields were generally of a small cottage-style and, except for the concession of verandahs, were not designed to combat the severe summer heat. Cartage to the fields was expensive and not always reliable, which, in 1902, prompted some builders to complain that their businesses in Day Dawn were being disadvantaged by the shortage of railway trucks in the Railway Department. The deficiency made it almost impossible for them to obtain timber from the mills and, in desperation, some contractors were forced to have materials sent directly from Geraldton. [5] The lack of a good supply of water to both Cue and Day Dawn was another serious situation facing the authorities. A new water scheme, introduced to Cue in July 1901, had not proved satisfactory and, one year later, people in nearby Day Dawn were still waiting patiently for the Municipal Council to pipe water into the town. Thankfully, the formation of the Cue and Day Dawn Water Board, three years later, overcame most of the major concerns associated with this problem. [6]

On 30 June 1902, the Dominican Council assembled in the Priory at Dongara to 'discuss the expediency of opening a school at Day Dawn with the approbation of the Bishop'. Until then, the decision to establish a Catholic school in the rapidly-expanding mining township had not been a top priority. The nuns from Cue had been happy to continue giving religious instruction during the weekends, knowing that the teacher at the Day Dawn State School was a practising Catholic. The situation changed when the Education Department appointed a new male, non-Catholic, to the government school in 1902. Mother Gabriel felt that the transfer of teachers was an appropriate time to raise the possibility of opening a new Dominican day school in the old church at Day Dawn.

In 1902, Messrs Allen and Grey, the proprietors of livery stables and a coaching firm, approached the Cue Council for permission to introduce a tramway system between Cue and Day Dawn. It was suggested that the venture should be a joint project between the two councils and that if the application were acceptable they might consider adopting the Caillet monorail system, which was operated by animal power. The business partners offered to enter into a bond of £500 to complete the line within one year. Day Dawn, however, refused to consider the proposal and the meeting held to discuss the subject finished in some confusion. [7] It appears that a certain amount of rivalry existed between the twin towns, for although

Day Dawn possessed the larger, more successful mines, Cue boasted finer buildings, a mayor and a mining warden in residence. At that time, a similar transport system existed between Cossack and Roebourne and had the plan been accepted in Day Dawn and Cue, when first proposed, it would have been of great benefit to people living in both towns. The Sisters from Cue, in the meantime, travelled to and from Day Dawn each day by gig.

The church-school at Day Dawn opened in July 1902, and the two Sisters involved in the new foundation were encouraged to find that, within a very short space of time, their enrolments had increased. Catholic parishioners, although trying to establish their own lives in the still primitive mining town, were most supportive of the Sisters and very active in raising funds. On Wednesday, 20 August, an enthusiastic group of ladies and gents met at the Day Dawn Hotel for the purpose of selecting a social and dance committee to raise funds for a new Catholic Church. Mrs Meehan was elected president and Miss McCarthy honorary secretary, and the nuns were overjoyed at the prospect of getting new premises in which to hold their classes. [8] In the same month, the Dominican community severed its ties with the mother-house in New Zealand and the West Australian order was constituted into an autonomous foundation.

58. Dominican Convent School, Day Dawn, c 1905

The climate at Day Dawn was one of extremes. As in many towns bordering desert regions, the weather was extremely hot in summer and freezing cold in winter. Either way, the four mile journey from Cue every day was a tiring and unattractive proposition. It came as no surprise, therefore, that in 1905, three years after opening the church-school, a practical decision was made by the Dominican Council to erect a convent for the Sisters teaching at Day Dawn. By then, the combined population of Cue and Day Dawn was said to be between 7000 and 8000 persons and, with 1900 men employed at the Great Fingall Mine, the Sisters seemed assured of full classes for some years to come.

At 4.00 p.m. on Sunday, 9 April 1905, St Hyacinth's Dominican Convent at Day Dawn was blessed and officially opened, followed by Benediction. Foundation members of the new community were Mother Philomena McGrath (Superior), Sister Josephine Kenny (professed novice) and Sister Peter Geeson who had only recently been given the white veil. The new foundation was governed from St Gabriel's Convent in Cue, where Mother Gabriel Gill remained with Sister di Pazzi Miscall, Sister Gerard Milligan and novices, Sister Baptist Hall and Sister Evangelist Graham. The Prioress kept in touch when she made the short journey to Day Dawn each Friday afternoon to prepare for the private music and embroidery lessons she gave the following day to a growing group of pupils.

Despite its impressive name, the new St Hyacinth's Convent was no more than a simple cottage, constructed of wood and galvanised iron and comprising two rooms, a kitchen and a wide verandah built to ward off the sun. Sister Philomena was the only person in the Day Dawn community from New Zealand, the other two members being West Australians and better acclimatised to the dry conditions. Sister Josephine was a member of a well-known Geraldton family and Sister Peter Geeson (Margaret) was born at Dongara in 1881. Described as an excellent exponent of needlework, as well as teacher, Margaret Geeson received her education in Perth with the Sisters of Mercy at Victoria Square and later commenced her teaching career at a Mercy Convent. It was after hearing Bishop Kelly's appeal for teaching staff for his diocese, that she was persuaded, in 1906, to make her profession with the Dominicans at Dongara.

Ruby Herbert (Mrs Hutchison MLC), with her sister and three brothers were among the first pupils to enrol at St Hyacinth's Dominican School when it opened in 1902. Pleasant memories of her schooldays on the Murchison goldfields included seeing in her 'mind's eye' the dainty figure of Sister di Piazzi in her cream Dominican habit, waiting patiently at the schoolroom door to welcome the first small group of foundation pupils. She recalled that the tiny nun was smiling gently as she re-assured the children and invited them to 'come in out of the sun'. The admiration Ruby held for the serene, but determined, Mother Gabriel, never diminished. She was reminded of the time when she took her infant brother to the convent to be baptised and Mother Gabriel presented a shawl as a gift. Ruby admitted that it was on her suggestion that the child be christened Albert Gabriel, after the community's much-loved Prioress, and she recalled that her mother, who had a fine voice and acted as the church organist at Day Dawn, was thoroughly delighted with the choice. [9]

St Hyacinth's Dominican Convent had been open for less than three weeks when the shock announcement of

Mother Gabriel Gill's unexpected death began to circulate. The news stunned the towns of Day Dawn, Cue, Leonora, Gwalia, Greenough and Dongara where she had established foundations, and for a time members of the Dominican Order in Western Australia found it difficult to recognise fact that she would no longer be part of their long-term plans. The fact that the foundress had died whilst on a visit to Day Dawn placed extra stress on the Sisters working there. With almost 100 pupils in attendance at the school, they were particularly anxious that classes would continue to operate as normal. By July 1905, Bishop Kelly had confirmed the appointment of Sister Bonaventure McEntyre as Prioress, and ever-resourceful, the Dominican Sisters began to reassess their current situation and consolidate plans for the future.

In 1908, the community at Day Dawn opened St Thomas's Academy, a small boarding school for boys. The new venture was the result of a request made earlier by parents living in distant areas who felt that their sons' educational needs were better met by enrolling them at the convent as boarders. An advertisement appeared regularly in local newspapers including the *Sower*, a small informative Catholic diocesan paper established in 1903 by Bishop Kelly, a former editor of the *West Australian Catholic Record*:

*ST THOMAS' ACADEMY, BOARDING SCHOOL FOR BOYS AT DAY DAWN.*
*The Dominican Sisters admit to the Academy as boarders only boys to the age of 12 years. There is also a Day School for Boys and Girls conducted by an efficient staff of teachers of the same order and private lessons in Art or any branch of study are given to ladies not pupils at the school. For terms etc., apply to Mother Superior.* [10]

On 12 January 1909, Mother Philomena McGrath was re-appointed Superior of Day Dawn and Sister Peter Geeson became Sacristan and Mistress of Schools. The third member of the community at that time was Sister Catherine Kenny, the natural sister of Sister Josephine, who in 1905, was one of the original group of Sisters to take up residence in the new St Hyacinth's Convent. By 1909, the majority of people at Day Dawn were becoming somewhat apprehensive as the Great Fingall Mine began to show signs of a decline in the quantity of gold being produced. As the downturn in gold production became more noticeable a feeling of despondency swept through the mining centre and residents slowly began to consider their futures.

When the Dominican school at Day Dawn re-opened in February 1909 after the Christmas holidays, the Sisters were disappointed to find that enrolments had already been affected by the periodic shutting down of the mine's battery. Whereas the number of pupils attending the convent at Cue, in 1909, had risen to 80, St Hyacinth's attendance had fallen from 100 pupils to 70. [11] Regardless of the uncertain times, the Catholic Ladies' Committee organised a social evening in Clifford's Hall to lower the debt on the convent building. Although only £30 was raised, the people who attended the function enjoyed the social gathering and appeared to forget their immediate problems.

The same devastating cyclone that hit Cue early in 1910 swept Day Dawn, and although the damage was minimal compared to that in the larger mining centre, the town experienced high winds and torrential rains. It was a time of great excitement for many of the town's children, particularly for the boys, who revelled in the unusually large puddles on the ground. The Sisters did not share the boys' sense of adventure, for the aftermath of the storm entailed much extra work for the nuns who were left to clean up the mess. Despite growing concerns about future employment and a serious strike on the woodline, which resulted in 40 men being retrenched, the Sisters were determined that Catholic children living at Cue and Day Dawn would never be deprived of a religious education.

A centre for the Adelaide University Examinations was established at St Hyacinth's in 1910 and, from 23 to 25 August, the candidates sitting for the entrance examination to the South Australian University took their allotted places in the convent schoolroom. The supervision of all candidates was entrusted to the mayor of Day Dawn, Mr A. J. Blight, and the Reverend Dr Graber, who had earlier been appointed the local secretary for the Examination Board. Among the successful entrants that year was Miss Ruby Rebecchi, a Dominican pupil from St Hyacinth's who did credit to her teachers by passing all of her subjects with top marks – English Literature, Arithmetic, Algebra, History and Geography. [12]

For some time, there had been no significant gold discoveries announced in the Murchison fields and a number of the more affluent mines were beginning to show signs of winding down. In certain cases, the companies were financially troubled. At the end of 1910, a well-attended public meeting was held to discuss the precarious future of the mining industry. By then the Cue One Mine, which was important to the survival of nearby Cue, was idle and the owners were looking for new methods to increase the production of gold. To further add to the year's woes, Day Dawn suffered a loss of jobs when the Great Fingall was again forced to reduce its workforce. Life, however, was not entirely cheerless, for people living in the Murchison goldfields still enjoyed a full and varied social life. The parish ladies at Day Dawn, ever mindful of the existing debt on the convent, continued to hold monthly functions in the schoolroom to raise funds. Euchre parties, dances, exhibitions and sports events were commonplace throughout the year and concerts were always regarded as the highlight of the town's social calendar.

Annual school concerts were not only popular forms of entertainment, but they also served to raise funds for specific projects and to display the work achieved by pupils during the school year. In December 1910, a large group of children from the Day Dawn Convent School participated in an evening of entertainment in Chesson's Hall. The lengthy program included items such as the 'Irish Peasants' Dance' by the two Misses Moncrieff and Masters Parnell and Robinson, as well as piano and violin items, along with exhibitions of club swinging and callisthenics. The Misses Blight, Moncrieff, Jeffry and Hoppe with Masters Chesson and Curtis, as well as two members of the Stevens family, received a burst of applause when they performed the colourful Lilliputian Quadrilles. [13] Tugs-of-war were also very popular on the goldfields during the early 1900s and on 17 March 1911, two contesting teams representing different nationalities took part in the St Patrick's Day celebrations. The Austrian tug-of-war team, captained by Mr Canaletich, competed against Mr Boland's team from Cue and amid rousing cheers of encouragement the pull lasted for 10 minutes. Despite the contrast to living conditions experienced in their homeland, most European migrants appeared to enter into the spirit of the community and readily adapt to life in the outback. Members of the Italian and Austrian communities were very supportive of many parish activities; in particular card nights and dances.[14]

In August 1911, the Dominican Prioress, Mother Bonaventure McEntyre, accompanied by Sister Ceslaus Freed, arrived from Dongara and with the Superior of Cue, Sister Benignus O'Connor, made her usual visitation to all Dominican branch houses. At that time Sister Catherine Kenny was the Superior of St Hyacinth's Convent in Day Dawn, Sister Peter Geeson was the Procuratrix and Mistress of Schools, and Sister Reginald Rice served as sacristan. The visit of the Prioress was considered a great occasion and under the direction of Mother Catherine, the children attending the Day Dawn convent arranged an impromptu concert in honour of her visit. There was great jubilation on the part of the pupils when the Prioress granted the school a half-holiday for their efforts. [15]

By 1911, it was obvious that Day Dawn was not going to live up to its early expectations and, although the news of an occasional gold strike lifted the people's spirits, it was clear that the towns of Cue and Day Dawn were gradually winding down. Health conditions were also of great concern and, with no vaccination available, contagious diseases spread like wildfire through the close-knit communities. During the last term of school an epidemic of measles and mumps gained momentum and several schools in the Murchison District, including the convent school at Day Dawn, were obliged to close down temporarily. [16] These were difficult times for the Sisters who had the added responsibility of caring for young male boarders whilst trying to make ends meet.

A number of local changes took place in 1912, among the most significant being the amalgamation of the two municipal governing bodies in Cue and Day Dawn. Finally, after years of negotiations, it was decided, for practical reasons, to form a combined Cue-Day Dawn Roads Board, with a newly-elected board, and meetings to take place in Cue. By then only two Dominican Sisters, Sister Anastasia Byrne and Sister Bernard Rogers, staffed the foundation at Day Dawn. Both of these teachers had an excellent rapport with their pupils and long after their deaths were spoken of with fondness. Sister Anastasia, a native of New Zealand, was, according to some of her companions, a born actress. As one of the artistic members of the Dominican community, her talents were in constant demand as a teacher of music, singing, speech and oil painting. She was never happier than when she was preparing for a concert or had a group of five to eight-year-old boarders in tow. Sister Bernard, the daughter of Andrew Rogers, a farmer, and his wife Elisha (née Mullany), was born on 25 April 1871, at Roscommon in Ireland, and apart from her teaching and administrative talents is remembered for her soft Irish brogue. She liked to share with others her great faith in the 'Saircred Hearrt' (Sacred Heart of Jesus) and Australians, listening to her read aloud *The Family Rosary*, taken from *Around the Boree Log*, were enthralled by her Irish lilt, particularly when she came to the words 'Glory Dadda Glory' and he 'gloried like a shot'. [17]

It had been common knowledge for some time that the accommodation used at Day Dawn was no longer suitable for either the nuns or boarders. Finally a decision was made to close the boys' boarding section at the end of 1912 and when the Dominican Council met on 3 January 1913, the main subjects raised were the problems involving maintenance and limited staff. The Council, which consisted of the Prioress, Mother Dominica Murphy, the sub-Prioress, Sister Bonaventure McEntyre and Sisters Benignus O'Connor, Philomena McGrath, di Pazzi Miscall and the Council secretary, Sister Ceslaus Freed, quickly came to the conclusion that, under the present circumstances, there was little likelihood of improvements being made to the building. After talking the matter over, and making various suggestions as to how best to relieve the situation, it was agreed that the most sensible solution would be to unite the Cue and Day Dawn school staffs under one Superior at Cue. The community would then live together at St Gabriel's Convent and, as travel conditions between the twin towns had improved, the Sisters teaching at St Hyacinth's would drive to Day Dawn on a daily basis. It was further decided that female boarders enrolled at Cue would be transferred to the Dominican College at Dongara, and the boys, formerly accommodated at St Hyacinth's, would be kept in Cue. [18]

The internment of certain nationalities, the lack of migrant workers from Europe at the commencement of World War I, as well as the enlistment of many young Australian men for war service, had a noticeable effect on the district. In 1915, the Great Fingall Mine, which had been steadily declining for some time, registered a substantial loss which resulted in the dismissal of many miners. By April of that year, the mine's management let it be known that they were struggling to continue, and that there was every likelihood that the operation might cease within a week. Although the Great Fingall Mine remained open for a few more years, its eventual closure could not be delayed beyond 1918. The announcement that the mine would finally close sounded the death knell for the once-prosperous mining centre. Almost overnight wood and iron buildings were dismantled and reassembled in other localities and there was a great deal of sadness as people gradually bid each other farewell and moved on. Within weeks the main street, formerly the scene of much activity, had already taken on the appearance of a deserted thoroughfare.[19]

At the beginning of 1917, the Dominican Sisters still had over 50 pupils enrolled at their day school in Day Dawn. [20] These numbers gradually decreased as the population dwindled and when St Hyacinth's finally closed its doors, parents, still seeking a religious education for their children, transferred them to the Dominican school at Cue. After Bishop Kelly approved the closure of the school, the building was dismantled and moved to Dongara, leaving the almost deserted town at Day Dawn with no tangible reminder of the 15 years of service given to the mining centre by the Dominican community.

The last Sisters to serve at Day Dawn were Sisters Bonaventure McEntyre and Teresa McQuillan. Sister Teresa had been in Day Dawn earlier as a postulant and a delightful tale is told about her introduction to the mining centre. Fresh from New Zealand, it seems that 16-year-old Rose McQuillan was sent into the town to post letters at the post office. It never occurred to her that the building might not be a structure of some importance, easily identified by a large sign on the window or above the door. Confused, the young postulant, demure and soberly dressed in black, headed for one of the larger buildings in the hope that it might prove to be the post office. A kind gentleman seeing her bewilderment, directed her to a most unlikely-looking iron shed. It was sometime later that she discovered that, had she continued in the direction she was taking, she would have been seen entering questionable premises with which no respectable woman, let alone a postulant, would have been associated. [21]

Two well-known West Australian female politicians were among the many children educated by the Dominican Sisters in the goldfields. Mary Alice (May) Holman, the Member for the Forrest electorate from 1925 to 1939, became the first Labor woman to achieve parliamentary status in Australia. Her father, John Holman, a miner, was elected the Member for Murchison in 1901, and three years later was appointed the Minister for Railways and Labour in the first Western Australian government. May's two great passions, politics and music, were no doubt influenced by her father's interests and the Dominican nuns who taught her at St Hyacinth's. The second pupil, the Hon. Ruby Florence Hutchison MLC (née Herbert), made history in 1954 when she became the first woman ever elected to the Legislative Council. She was one of the first pupils to enrol at St Hyacinth's school in Day Dawn and, throughout her busy lifetime, never forgot the Sisters who educated her and encouraged her thirst for knowledge. On returning to the scene of her early childhood she later confided to one her former teachers that she had had a rude awakening. Like most deserted mining towns, by 1960 there was little left that was recognisable in Day Dawn and, sadly touched by the experience, she felt moved enough to describe the scene to one of the Dominican Sisters:

*There is nothing quite so stark as the ghost of the past confronting one in the picture of an untidy, deserted mine-scattered piece of country, wind blown and barren of any beauty, where once a thriving township of some thousands of souls hustled and bustled in the busy life of surrounding rich gold mines. The Roman Catholic Church was the only red brick building in the town and I found a line of broken bricks still in the ground and so traced the spot near a large surviving pepper tree where our convent and school once stood.* [22]

59. Day Dawn foundation pupil, Ruby Hutchison, MLC (née Herbert), 1960

## ST CATHERINE'S CONVENT AND SCHOOL, LEONORA AND DOMINICAN SCHOOL, GWALIA

Leonora was once the centre of the north-eastern goldfields and, like many of the frontier towns that rose to significance in the 1890s, it has a colourful and exciting history. First explored in 1860, the area was visited nine years later by noted explorer, future premier and first Australian-born baron, John Forrest, who, with his party, had set out to find the missing members of the Leichardt expedition. It was from his camp nearby, that Forrest sighted and named Mt Leonora, in honour of Mrs Leonora Venn, wife of H. W. Venn, a minister in Forrest's cabinet.

In 1892, gold was discovered at Coolgardie and, prior to the precious metal being found at Kalgoorlie the following year, a number of prospectors were fossicking in the area around Mt Margaret and Mt Leonora. Several rich strikes were made during that time and within two years other gold-seekers were rushing to the Leonora and Mt Malcolm districts praying that they also had the 'Midas touch'. By February 1896, Edward 'Doodah' Sullivan had pegged the Johannesburg, near Leonora. The registering of other well-known leases, such as the Trump, Tower Hill and Leonora Gem followed in close order. Shortly afterwards, there was great interest shown in the neighbouring town of Gwalia. Prospecting in that area led to major gold discoveries, culminating in the establishment of the Sons of Gwalia Mine west of Mt Leonora. In time, this development was recognised as the second largest underground mine next to the fabulous Golden Mile at Boulder. Herbert Clark Hoover, a young American graduate of Stamford University, who later became president of the United States, was appointed the mine's first manager in May 1898. He left Western Australia soon afterwards but the company with which he had been associated provided continuous employment for some 65 years. [1]

The Leonora district was also noted for its pastoral development and, as early as 1896, James Willis introduced the first consignment of cattle and sheep to the area. The taking up of mining leases resulted in an increase in population and in 1898, to cope with the influx of travellers, a Cobb & Co. coach ran directly from Coolgardie to Leonora. Goods were transported by donkey and mule teams in competition with Afghan camel trains. Later, as routes to the town improved, horse teams were introduced and teamsters not only hauled essential supplies the long distance between Menzies and Leonora, but also much of the machinery needed to operate the mines. The town was originally positioned at the base of Mt Leonora, but it was not until after three locations had been considered that the present town-site was officially declared in April 1898.

The following year, to facilitate mining procedure, a public battery was established on the site of Doodah Sullivan's former mine. [2] From the turn of the century onwards, the district continued to show rapid progress. In July 1900, the Sons of Gwalia Mine shareholders were paid their first dividends, and two months later Leonora was declared a municipality. A report furnished by Warden Burt the following year appeared optimistic about the future of the town:

*Leonora is the centre of a very important mining district and gives every promise of becoming a very large town. Its population is about 316. The railway should reach there next year, and it will then become the distributing centre for the whole of the East Murchison Goldfield. Many new and permanent looking buildings were added during the year, footpaths formed, and altogether the place has a business-like and substantial appearance about it.* [3]

60. Catholic Church, Leonora

A large proportion of miners working in the area were either Italian or Yugoslav and because many were practising Catholics, there was an immediate call to service their spiritual needs. The quality of life improved for many of these New Australians when the first Catholic Church, erected by Father O'Malley in Gwalia Street, was officially opened on 28 July 1901. Improvements were constantly being made to make Leonora more attractive and in October that year, a decision was made to remove all primitive hessian buildings from the main thoroughfare and extend the town boundaries. Later, in an effort to keep the dust down to a minimum, the streets were watered daily. By 1902, the first water scheme was completed, and a new public school was opened halfway between Gwalia and Leonora. On 20 June 1902, when the extension of the railway from Kalgoorlie was opened, the mining centre welcomed its first train. A further increase in population saw the township quickly expand to include, among other businesses, a major corporation, seven hotels, several general stores, chemist shops, bakeries, tailors' premises, a post office, police and fire stations. The majority of Leonora's main buildings were constructed of brick or adobe and some of the designs were architecturally pleasing.

Bishop Kelly lost no time in asking the Dominican Sisters to establish a foundation in the fast-growing mining centre, and when the Prioress wrote to Father O'Malley on

11 February 1903, she did not fail to stress the urgency of the bishop's request. By then, Mother Gabriel Gill was concerned that no firm arrangements had been made before the commencement of the school year and she was determined to seek answers to a number of questions, 'Would you let me know some particulars as to what your good people can do for us, what accommodation and furniture they will provide?', she wrote, 'Would you be able to collect sufficient money to pay the fare of four nuns to Leonora? We have very few pupils and Cue is not promising well, so that the Dominican common purse is almost empty at present'.[4] She also informed Leonora's parish priest that Bishop Kelly wanted the convent to have boarding accommodation from the beginning. In light of this, the Prioress suggested that she should be present when building began, for although the Sisters had Papal sanction to carry out missionary work in Western Australia, the Dominican Rule was strict with regard to buildings and enclosure.

By January 1903, the railway extension from Kalgoorlie and Menzies had reached Leonora, establishing a 780 mile link to Geraldton which made the lengthy five-day coach ride from Kalgoorlie no longer obligatory. On 4 August, the Dominican foundress, accompanied by Sister Philomena McGrath, embarked on the exceptionally long rail journey from Cue to Perth, and then via the new service to Leonora, to open the new foundation. [5] The two Sisters were some 800 miles by rail from their mother house at Dongara and, as was to be expected in the Eastern Goldfields, the heat in summer was unbearable. In common with the type of housing on the goldfields during that era, the original St Catherine's Convent was built of corrugated iron with the walls and ceilings lined with hessian. Approximately 100 pupils enrolled for classes at the new Dominican school, which for the first eight years was conducted in the Catholic church.

61. Leonora plains with Gwalia in the distance
Courtesy F. Indirisie

The size of the class numbers called for extra staff and a month after their arrival, they were joined by Sisters Anastasia Byrne, Catherine Kenny and a novice, who travelled overland by horse and buggy to Leonora, via Sandstone.

Many residents continued to live on the leases at Gwalia, a reasonable distance from Leonora, a situation which persuaded the authorities to form a sister link between the two towns. The majority of people made the journey between the towns by cab until a popular steam tram was introduced on 10 October 1903.

62. Opening of Leonora electric tram, 1908

The tram, connecting the two mining centres, was once described as the most isolated public transport in Western Australia and when the line was officially opened, being a gala occasion, the Municipal Council at Leonora declared a public holiday. Hundreds of people lined the gaily-decorated route that day to watch the new steam tram as, amid colourful bunting, it pulled two double decker carriages along Tower Street. This cheap, rather jolly form of transport, was much appreciated by the residents and the carriages were rarely empty. School children were carried free of charge and people living at Gwalia often shopped at Leonora, which was fast developing into the district's commercial centre. Likewise, the residents of Leonora conducting business in, or visiting Gwalia, where the Sons of Gwalia Mine was situated, used the service regularly. It was said that on occasions both the passengers and tram driver gave in to temptation and on the way stopped to quench their thirst at one of Leonora's seven hotels, wherein the cost of a pot of beer was sixpence. It is most unlikely that these unscheduled stopovers took place when the Dominican nuns later travelled each day to teach at Gwalia. [6]

By 1906, it was estimated that 61,600 passengers had taken advantage of the service. The steam tram was eventually replaced by a more modern electric version after a powerhouse was installed at Leonora in 1907.

The upper deck of the original tram was then dismantled and the carriages painted maroon and gold to suit the change-over. The new service, which commenced in October 1908, continued to operate until a fire put the powerhouse out of action in 1915. To avoid disappointment to the tram's regular patrons, an Overland truck was converted to run on rails. In turn, taxis were introduced in 1921 and later a bus service provided transport between the twin towns. [7]

Some months after the nuns' arrival at Leonora, a second Dominican day school was opened at nearby Gwalia. Sister Anastasia Byrne and Sister Catherine Kenny travelled daily the few miles that separated Leonora from Gwalia. In 1904, the Dominican community at St Catherine's, Leonora, consisted of Sisters Bonaventure McEntyre, Philomena McGrath, Anastasia Byrne and Catherine Kenny. The following year Sister Bernard Rogers joined the group and taught at Gwalia. One former resident later recalled, 'the Sisters did splendid work, and shared wholeheartedly in the hardships and trials endured by all pioneers'. [8]

Both Dominican schools proved popular, for they offered a high standard of education, including private tuition in music, languages and the arts, as well as preparation for examinations for entry to the Public Service and the University of Adelaide, which at that time catered

63. Pupils, St Catherine's Convent, Leonora, 1909

for students from Western Australia wishing to obtain a degree. To advertise their presence in the town, and to inform parents that accommodation would be provided at the Dominican Boarding and Day School, Leonora, for boy boarders under the age of 12, a notice appeared at various times in the *Sower*, the *Catholic Record* and local newspapers. Each advertisement stated: 'The course embraces a thorough English Education, French, Latin, Mathematics, Bookkeeping, Shorthand, Typewriting, Music (Piano and Violin), Singing, Drawing, Painting, Art, Needlework and Harmony...At Gwalia, where the

Dominican Nuns have a day school, arrangements can be made by ladies for receiving tuition in any of the above subjects'. [9] It did not take long for the Sisters in Leonora to gain a reputation as quality teachers, and the parents of the Dominican candidates who achieved high marks in the 1908 Trinity College of London Music Examinations were more than pleased with the results when they were published in January the following year:

**Junior Grade**: Edith Lovelace (97 Honours), Lily Williams (91Honours), Tom Creed (91 Honours).

**Preparatory Grade**: Lily Prisk (100 Credit), Earl Creed (98 Credit), Hilda Collie (95 Credit), Dorothy Lovelace (93 Credit), Edward Morris (74), Vera Scott (74), Charles Dunkley (66) and Violet Williams (66). [10]

On 1 January 1909, the *Sower* reported that a successful bazaar was held at Leonora which resulted in £240 being raised to help finance additions and alterations to the church. The extensions, which were officially opened and blessed in March, included the lengthening of the church by 18 feet 6 inches, adding a nuns' chapel and a sacristy. The wood and iron building was lined with stamped metal, which featured three ecclesiastical patterns painted in graduated colours that ranged from 'biscuit to oak buff '. A dado of small fluted sheets of iron, painted in dark salmon, ran around the lower portion of the church. A coved ceiling featured three rose centres highlighted in

64. Rehearsing for a concert, Leonora, 1915. L. to R.: N. Hamilton, - Hamilton, S. Vincent, M. Powell,

gold. Ruby and green glass windows lighted the sanctuary and the nuns' chapel and sacristy blended in with the remainder of the church. Ten electric tantalum lights, with fancy white shades tipped with gold, took pride of place together with the gyrating electric fan attached to the centrepiece. [11]

Following the pattern set by most country towns, St Patrick's Day at Leonora in 1909 was an unqualified success. About 400 adults paid for admission to the recreation ground to attend a full day of sports events. One mile and two mile bicycle races were contested with prize money of 10 and 15 guineas on offer for the respective events. Running races were also held with the winner of the main event being the recipient of a gold bracelet. Special transport was arranged to bring people in from Gwalia and at various intervals during the day the local brass band set the atmosphere by playing Irish tunes. The last event finished about 6.00 p.m., but 70 couples, who wished to prolong the celebrations, came back later to the Federal Theatre where they spent an enjoyable night dancing to the music of a piano, violin and cornet trio. [12]

Minor improvements were also made to the convent during 1909. Members of the Hibernian Society erected a long-awaited iron fence to the front of the property to provide more privacy for members of the community and Messrs Looney and Deery of the Central Hotel presented the Sisters with an invaluable acetylene gas plant for use in the convent. Towards the end of the year an All Seasons Carnival featuring artistically prepared stalls representing Spring, Summer, Autumn, Winter, as well as Day and Night, proved popular and was considered a financial success. The proceeds were divided between the church and the convent and with the amount given to the Dominican Sisters it was hoped to erect additional sleeping accommodation for the six members of the community then living at St Catherine's Convent. [13]

As well as achieving excellent music results each year, the Sisters were noted for their expertise in sewing and fancywork and they generally organised an annual exhibition of children's work in the classroom at Gwalia. On display were delicately worked practical items such as night-dress bags, sachets, brush and comb bags, cushions, table centres, napkins and daintily trimmed pillow shams, made from various attractive fabrics. On the last Wednesday before school closed for the Christmas holidays in 1909, St Catherine's School held its final function for the year in the Federal Theatre at Leonora. A newspaper account reported: 'the entertainment was of a very enjoyable nature. The dressing and grouping of the children in the various items presented was artistically thought out and showed careful training on the part of the ladies responsible'. Among the performers that evening were pupil Seddon Vincent, 'a tiny tot' dressed in a green satin coat and white breeches, who sang a verse of 'Kathleen Mavourneen', accompanied on the piano by his equally pint-sized sister, and the Misses Essie Hobart and Hilda Collie who also received a good reaction from the audience for their interpretation of a popular comedietta, *A Pair of Lunatics*. [14]

The Leonora and Gwalia convent schools often held their end of the year concert and distribution of prizes within a few weeks of each other, which meant that the two commitments must have placed the Sisters under a great deal of pressure, for not only did they have to diversify the program and costumes, but also the scenery. Apart from training the students, arranging the choreography and preparing items, the Sisters had to organise the venues and rehearsals, and, at times, even paint the backdrops and sew costumes. The fact that they had many other duties to perform and that the events were held during the heat of summer, showed just how dedicated the members were in their desire to provide their pupils with an all-round education.

Catholic schools were also popular with Protestant families, not only because of the extra courses offered, but because of the emphasis placed on refinement and good manners. To most parents discipline was an important issue and they were convinced that the practical lessons given by the Sisters on acceptable social behaviour nearly always bore fruit. Respect and unselfishness were promoted from an early age and at every opportunity the clergy reinforced the example set by nuns. When the Dominican pupils at Leonora broke up for the Christmas holidays in December 1910, a visiting priest reminded the children that they had certain obligations to fulfil even though they were on vacation. He impressed on the class the necessity of doing their part to add to the happiness of the home by being helpful, loving and respectful to their parents. [15]

On Wednesday, 19 January 1910, Dr Graber, Leonora's parish priest for the past six years, was given a pleasant send-off in the church-school and was presented with a purse of gold sovereigns. The priest, when thanking his well-wishers during the proceedings, proudly announced that the original parish debt of £2250, which included improvements to the church and convent buildings, at the time of his departure amounted to only £28. [16] The lowering of the parish debt made it a great deal easier for the newly-appointed priest, Father O'Hare, to plan ahead – a top priority, at that stage, being the building of a new school to accommodate the large number of children attending St Catherine's that year. Although plans and specifications had been approved by the Local Board of Health, the Superior was advised, in July 1910, that it would be wiser to apply for a more suitable block of land on the south side, as the proposed site near the convent was considered to be too low-lying. [17] The decision to build a larger school was timely, for the population in Leonora had risen from 314 persons in 1901 to 1154 in 1911. Over the same period of time the population at Gwalia increased from 884 to 1114 persons.

A large crowd gathered on Wednesday, 8 February 1911, when the Mayor of Leonora, Mr W. Price, performed the official opening of the new St Catherine's School in Hoover Street. Built by Messrs Gamel and Trim at an estimated cost of £800, the wood and galvanised iron building was described as being well-equipped and capable of accommodating 250 children. The ceilings were lofty, with good lighting and plenty of ventilation, and, unlike many constructions on the goldfields, the walls were lined. The dimensions of the main schoolroom were 48 feet x 24 feet and if necessary there was ample area in the spacious lobby and large cloakroom to provide extra classes. Considering the sweltering temperatures during the long summer months, the installation of four large rainwater tanks, each with the capacity to hold 1000 gallons, was a particularly welcome improvement. [18]

In 1912, Leonora suffered considerable damage as a result of two severe storms. The first impact occurred on Sunday, 4 February, following a day of oppressive heat and consistent bursts of thunder and lightning, which locals insisted were more severe than anything witnessed in the past. Not only were the power station and tramcars severely affected, but almost all the electric lighting and telephone systems were in disarray. At Station Creek the Water Board machinery was also damaged and for a time it was feared that there might be a prolonged shortage of water. A second and more damaging storm took place the following day when hurricane-force winds struck Gwalia and Leonora. The wind struck with such velocity that campsites were flattened, and twisted sheets of iron and wreckage were scattered for miles throughout the bush. [19] The Catholic Church at Gwalia was completely destroyed by the cyclone and arrangements were immediately made to establish a collection to finance the erection of a new church building. Father Tyler called a general meeting at the Gwalia Workers' Hall on Monday, 12 February 1912, to organise contributions, and in the true spirit of the Australian outback, people, regardless of creed, quickly showed their generosity. In the meantime, the children, previously taught in the Gwalia church, travelled daily into Leonora to attend lessons at St Catherine's School.

65. Taken at Leonora convent during opening of new school, 1911

66. Physical Education instructor, Mr Jimmy Hill, Leonora, 1918
Pupils include: S. Vincent, J. Punch, T. Morris, A. Kirk

As with many mining centres during the Great War (1914-1918), the population of Leonora soon showed signs of decreasing. The reason for the sudden decline was generally attributed to both the loss of men leaving the district to enlist for war service and the gradual petering out of large deposits of gold in the principal company mines. In 1917, the Mother Superior of St Catherine's Convent made representation to the mayor with a request to lease a tram car for the use of the children travelling from Gwalia to attend the Dominican school at Leonora. The matter, which was referred to the directors of the Leonora-Gwalia Tramway Syndicate, resulted in an arrangement being made to transport the children from Gwalia into Leonora for the sum of one penny a trip. [20] That same year the Dominican community established yet another foundation at Three Springs and by 1922 convents and schools founded by the order existed at Dongara, Cue, Leonora, Meekatharra, Three Springs and Yalgoo.

A lack of priests, and the absence of a bishop in Geraldton between March 1926 and February 1930, meant that the diocese was temporarily administered from the Perth Archdiocese. Consequently, the Dominican Sisters were withdrawn from Leonora at the end of 1925 in favour of another religious group. The last two Sisters to serve at St Catherine's, Augustine Corbett and Peter Geeson, were replaced in February 1926 by the Sisters of Mercy from Perth who went there at the request of Archbishop Clune. For the next 14 years Sisters from that community took up residence in the galvanised iron convent, which in goldfields style, still had the original internal walls made of hessian. For the first few years, five Sisters of Mercy successfully conducted classes in the former St Catherine's School with an enrolment of some 70 pupils. These numbers did not last, however, and in 1935, due to uncertain times, the names on the roll diminished to 48.

By 1939, Archbishop Prendiville had made arrangements for the four Sisters of Mercy living at Leonora to staff a new school and convent about to be built at Norseman. At that stage, the parish of Leonora was expected to return to the jurisdiction of the Bishop of Geraldton and both the Archbishop and Bishop O'Collins were keen to see the goldfields foundation pass once again into Dominican hands. [21] On 18 July 1939, Sister Vincent Colgan contacted the Bishop of Geraldton, Bishop O'Collins, from St Dominic's Priory in Dongara. She informed him that, although Father J. Halpin had written to say that the roads were still in 'a bad way', she would be hopefully setting out from Mt Magnet for Leonora, with Sister Anastasia Byrne, to inspect the convent and school before making a decision about returning permanently to the mining town. She expected to be away for over a week and promised upon her return to give the bishop a definite answer about reopening the convent. [22]

Sister Augustine Corbett, accompanied by Sisters St Anne Graham, Pius Nolan and Antoninus Houlahan, were appointed to the staff of the Leonora school in 1940. A large Italian population still existed and the fact that the station master, postmaster, bank manager, mining registrar, chemist, baker, two hotel-keepers and two policemen were all of the Catholic faith meant that the Sisters had instant support from a variety of areas. Besides having a roll call of 60 pupils during the first term, the Sisters had a satisfactory number of private pupils enrolled for music and commercial classes. At that time a Catholic school did not exist at Gwalia and nearly three-quarters of the children came in by taxi to Leonora, for which the Church provided from its funds £60 per annum for two trips each day. [23]

The school building contained two classrooms. One Sister taught Infants and Grades I and II in the smaller room, and two Sisters shared the larger room to teach Grades III, IV, V and VI. A fourth Sister cooked the meals and attended to the laundry and other household chores for the busy teaching staff. Part of the lay Sister's domestic duties included preparing meals for the parish priest, a routine that sometimes involved him making six visits to the convent a day to receive breakfast, morning and afternoon tea, dinner, tea and supper. Despite being fully occupied with teaching, carrying out their religious duties and caring for the house and boarders, members of the community still found time to mend the priest's clothes, make vestments, act as sacristans, visit the hospital and even perform a baptism if the priest was absent and the child's life was threatened by illness. Behind the scenes, to help raise money, the Sisters made an endless supply of aprons for sale and supervised some of the young boys who made fret-work dolls' cots from 3-ply wooden sheets taken from the sides of old tea chests. The girls were then shown how to make miniature bedding and sew sheets to match.

Sister Xavier Ryan, who taught at Leonora from 1942 until 1943, and again between 1955 and 1960, recalls that on one occasion she dressed 40 dolls for a fête. [24]

Four young boarders were waiting when the Dominicans returned to Leonora. Under the circumstances the Sisters felt obliged to accept the children, who lived mainly on sheep stations, too far away to attend day school. The Sisters were concerned that the only sleeping accommodation available at that time was a section of the convent verandah, that not only had a clay floor, but also a less than desirable roof structure. The dust storms, which according to Sister Augustine Corbett were worse than on the Murchison, caused havoc and she was up 'night after night' trying to protect the boarders. Finally, in desperation, the Superior approached the manager of the Sons of Gwalia Mine and asked if he would consider giving the Sisters some lattice and timber at a reduced rate. Sister Augustine's request was successful and shortly afterwards lattice, paint, nails, cement for the floor and a smart new door were delivered to the convent. With assistance supplied by a generous group of parishioners, the original space was converted into a comfortable sleep-out. The main wall was painted pale green, the lattice dark green, and the doors and window frames light brown. The end result was pleasing to the eye and the Sisters were delighted when the willing band of helpers offered to return at a future date to mend the fences and carry out any necessary whitewashing. [25]

67. Sports Day, Leonora, 1959

68. St Catherine's School, Leonora

Apart from his numerous parish duties, Father Michael Lynch (later Dean), whilst living at Leonora, was also active in other areas. A popular priest and keen sportsman, he trained the Dominican pupils to take part in the annual inter-school sports, held alternately at Leonora and Gwalia. Competing in the events were Leonora, Gwalia, Menzies and the Mt Margaret Native Mission School which was in the vicinity of Laverton. It was a great thrill when, on the second occasion in the mid-1940s, St Catherine's, Leonora, carried off the shield. In 1947, all the championship cups except one, were awarded to the convent school, and the shield was lost by only half a point. Again in 1948, Leonora pupils won the shield and four of the eight sporting cups. [26] Later, when Father Keith Spain became parish priest, he continued to encourage sporting activities and hastened to organise the construction of a new tennis court and cricket pitch to further increase the pupils' opportunities to develop sporting skills.

Father Spain was also principally responsible for the erection of a third classroom in Leonora to accommodate the overflow of pupils from Gwalia. It was built in memory of two district pioneers, Mr and Mrs Peter Hill Snr, after their daughter May provided the bulk of the finance needed for the new addition. Later, when a large number of New Australians arrived to work at the Sons of Gwalia Mine, they found it difficult to arrange transport for their children to Leonora. As a result Fr Spain arranged, in 1950, to have two of the three classrooms from St Catherine's transported by jinker to Gwalia, and he also volunteered to drive two Dominican teachers out each morning, and to pick them up again in the afternoon. The two rooms re-erected in Gwalia were used to house children in Infants to Grade VI, whilst pupils in higher grades continued to attend St Catherine's, often cycling in to Leonora.

Sister Bernadette Punch was Superior of St Catherine's Convent, Leonora, from 1950 until 1953 and assisting her for one year from 1950, was Sister Michael Ryan. Teaching at Gwalia in 1951 were Sister Bertrand O'Connor and Sister di Ricci Levitzke (Sr Kath). According to an Education Department report, written in September 1953, Leonora, by then a one teacher school, had 24 pupils with an average age of 9 to 10 years. The Superintendent's remarks regarding Sr Bernadette's efforts were most complimentary: 'There is an excellent tone in the school; the control is very good, and the children exhibit a delightful spontaneity. A number of children are not particularly strong mentally, but they are anxious to give of their best. It has been a pleasure to examine this well-organised little school'. [27] Meanwhile, in 1953, the day school at Gwalia had two teachers and a total of 39 pupils. Sister Michael taught 16 children in Grades I and II and Sr Bertand had charge of 23 pupils in Grades from III to VI. After inspecting the lower classes at Gwalia Superintendent Deacon stated: 'This is not an easy group of children, and in the circumstances the teacher [Sr Michael] is doing good work. The children are happy and co-operative, and are receiving excellent training in social habits. The classroom is adorned with a number of useful teaching aids'. [28] The same report also provided a general assessment of the work completed that year by Sr Bertrand: 'The classes have been very well organized, and the curriculum provided is properly balanced. Control is very good, and children are working to capacity. The classroom is a model of neatness and care'.

Although most parents contributed to their children's education by paying school fees, there was an obligation on the part of religious to accept all needy Catholic children free of charge. The Dominican community at Leonora, therefore, was never financially well-off and the many acts of kindness rendered to them by the townsfolk had always been greatly appreciated. On one occasion, a station owner who admired the Sisters' efforts and realised that they often found it difficult to make ends meet, donated a small sum of money for each member. Sister Xavier Ryan, who was a member of the Leonora community between 1942 and 1943 and again from 1955 to 1960, recalled teaching 25 pupils in the 1950s and receiving only £1 in school fees for a week. It astounded her that one young male pupil managed to earn the princely sum of £2 week by working in a butcher's shop after school. Fortunately people were generous with their time and assistance and over the years the Sisters gained many supporters and established lasting friendships, among them the Hill, Hadfield, Cogan, Patroni, Bell, Boladeras, Mazza, Paseri, Pianto and Ainsley families. [29] Several well-known priests and religious had early connections with Leonora. For example, the fathers of both Archbishop Barry Hickey and Father Russell Hardiman were mining registrars in that town and former Dominican students Peter Hill and Bill Ainslie later entered the Marist Brothers. Two sisters, Margaret and Joan Punch, the daughters of the former Mayor of Leonora, Matt Punch, also entered the Dominican Order.

69. Leonora community, 1960
L to R. Back Row: Sisters Anne Graham, Mercedes Clune, Michael Ryan. Front: Sisters Xavier Ryan, Clement Hughes.

Sister Joseph O'Connor, who was assigned with Sisters Clement Hughes and Michael Ryan to Leonora in January 1954, found the car journey to St Catherine's extremely tedious, particularly when on one occasion the car broke down and the occupants were stranded in a treeless area on a hot day. In those days the bitumen ran only as far as Kalgoorlie and to reach the more distant goldfields the driver had to negotiate a dirt track for the remainder of the way. Once she had settled down at Leonora, Sr Joseph loved the place and would have willingly returned had the school not ceased to operate.

In 1963, after 70 years of continuous production, the Sons of Gwalia Mine, which during its lifetime yielded some 2,500,000 ounces of gold, finally shut down. More than 800 people, two-thirds of the population, deserted the town, leaving many houses empty. After the mass exodus of people from the fields, many corrugated iron and hessian dwellings were permanently neglected and left to decay, whilst more substantial buildings were jacked up and carted away for use elsewhere. That same year, the Dominican Sisters closed their foundation at Leonora and the last members to serve in the Eastern Goldfields, Sisters St Anne Graham, Eymard Regan and Declan Callaly returned to Dongara shortly afterwards.

A year after the town's demise, Bishop Thomas had no choice but to announce that the parish of Leonora-Gwalia would shortly be closed and the parish priests, Fathers Moffatt and Tobin, recalled for other duties. He also informed the pastoralists, prospectors and others remaining in the district, that Mass would be celebrated whenever priests were available from Kalgoorlie. By 1964, Gwalia had taken on the appearance of a forlorn ghost town and even though the street-lights still burned brightly, row upon row of houses were lifeless and dark. Only the shell remained of a once-lively hotel and, although still filled with water, the deserted swimming pool, on the hill overlooking the mine, looked desolate behind bolted gates.

After the closure of their foundation at Leonora, the Sisters fulfilled a commitment to Catholic families still living at Leonora by travelling from Perth in the second term holidays to give Christian doctrine lessons and to prepare a group of children for the sacraments. For some 10 or 11 years after they left St Catherine's Convent, the Sisters continued to operate the Bushies' School during the August holidays. Accommodation was usually provided for the Sisters and girls at the Hadfield family's old homestead, whilst the boys were supervised by Father Keith Spain in Jack Bell's shearing shed. [30] Sister Declan, who returned later with Sister Vianney O'Brien, wrote: 'Each time there was little less standing of convent and school but contacts between past pupils and "old" teachers assure us, that while the material signs of our presence are gone, the spiritual heritage which we endeavoured to pass on remains in the hearts and lives of the people'.

70. Final Year 7 Class, Leonora, 1963
L. to R.: C. Smith, A. Angelucci, E. Parravicini, M. Sbizzirri, E. Mazza

Surprisingly, the nickel boom that took place in the late 1960s and 1970s, including the rich strike at Poseidon, breathed new life into Leonora. In 1984, the area experienced another high in gold production when Sons of Gwalia Mine resumed its working life with open-cut mining and the Tower Hill and Harbour Lights mines recommenced operations. A bitumen road, constructed through arid countryside, eventually provided easier access for those involved in the mining and pastoral industries, and also for the many tourists who visit in the spring when the harsh grounds are literally carpeted with a colourful explosion of wildflowers.

In 1996, Leonora celebrated its centenary, and among the many invited guests were the Dominican and Mercy Sisters, Father Hardiman and the former Bishop of Geraldton, Archbishop Hickey. Reflecting on the visit, Archbishop Hickey recounted memories of his boyhood in the mining town:

*Mining towns have their ups and downs, but they have a spirit that endures. The pioneering spirit of the people of Leonora and Gwalia still thrives in the hearts and memories of the hundreds that turned up for the centenary, and in the hard-working people who keep the town going today. In 1984 when I became Bishop of Geraldton, the "Record" said that I was returning to my "Spirit Land". I have returned there again, so have so many other people to their lasting delight.* [31]

Today, Gwalia remains a ghost town, but not forgotten. A favourite place for history buffs, the former mining centre has recently stirred the interest of heritage conservationists and with foresight the owners of the Sons of Gwalia have since committed the sum of $250,000 towards its restoration. Meanwhile, 230 kilometres from Kalgoorlie, Leonora is thriving, and in 1998, still retains its title as the centre of the north-eastern goldfields. Strengthened by the success of mining companies, in particular the Sons of Gwalia Ltd, confidence in the future continues among those presently living and working in the Leonora-Laverton area.

## HOLY ROSARY CONVENT AND SCHOOL, MEEKATHARRA

Meekatharra, described by the wife of former Prime Minister Malcolm Fraser in 1977 as 'the end of the earth', in 1911 became the site of the Dominican Sisters' sixth foundation in Western Australia. Mrs Tammy Fraser's much-quoted view is contrary to that of elderly Sister St Anne Graham who speaks excitedly about Meekatharra and recalls how, when the assignation list was posted at the beginning of a new year, the Sisters assigned to that foundation were usually delighted. The town, situated in promising pastoral country some 80 miles north of Cue, was in fact, said to be a popular place with most members of the Dominican community.

Its name, alleged to be the Aboriginal word for 'place of little water', was first recorded in 1885, when the title Meekatharra Spring was used to identify the boundary of a pastoral lease. The town, which was gazetted on

30 August 1901, served for many years as the centre for a number of rich gold mines and, for a time, Meekatharra continued to live up to its promise of a bright future. [1] By 1909, although there were many worthwhile mines still operating in the Murchison, a number of once-prosperous towns were on the decline as a result of a downturn in the production of gold. The shutting down of Lennonville's one major mine during that period, and the sudden dispersal of the town's population, meant that only 12 Catholic parishioners remained out of a congregation of some 100 persons. At that time, Meekatharra, then at the height of its popularity, had a growing number of Catholics and no proper place of worship. Consequently, when the Catholic Church at Lennonville, described as 'the finest in the diocese', became available in 1909, the parish priest of Meekatharra, Father Corcoran, immediately began negotiations to purchase the building.

Arrangements were made to dismantle the church and transport it by jinker to Meekatharra where Mr Harry Pidgeon had agreed to re-erect the building on the corner of High and Regan Streets. So delighted were the town's Catholics at the prospect of having their own church, that even Father Corcoran's reminder about the £500 debt incurred by the purchase and removal, failed to dampen their enthusiasm. As it turned out, by August 1909, mainly through the generosity of Mr Fred Connaughton, the outstanding amount owed by the parish had almost been re-paid. [2]

On 9 May 1909, a good cross-section of society from as a far away as Cue, Paddy's Flat, Yaloginda, Twelve-Mile, Nannine and Garden Gully came into town to witness the opening, blessing and dedication of the new Church of the Most Holy Redeemer by Bishop Kelly. Mrs George Herbert accompanied the choir on the organ and, after Mass, Mr Thomas Ryan, representing the remainder of the parishioners, read a welcoming address to the bishop, which had been signed by leading members of the congregation. In his response Bishop Kelly stated with some conviction that 'inter alia, he hoped to see soon a Catholic school flourishing in their midst'. [3]

A second public event celebrated in Meekatharra that year also proved to be a red-letter day. The agenda for St Patrick's Day 1909, included a lengthy program of horse-racing followed by an evening ball, held in the Country Women's Association Hall. One article published later explained: 'The Catholics of Meekatharra celebrated the day in real Irish style. Those who failed to sport the "dear little plant" wore "the immortal green" and one felt, with their Catholic and enthusiastic spirit, that one was once again in the land of saints and scholars. The races, which recalled for many the balmy days of Galway,

Baldoyle and Leopardstown, were the chief attraction'. [4] Apart from the fun-loving activities, there was the business side to the celebration, and no-one was surprised at the end of the day when it was announced that a handsome sum of money had been raised towards the Church Building Fund.

The completion of the railway extension from Nannine to Meekatharra in 1910, not only reduced the length of time spent in travelling, but it opened up new work opportunities for local residents when the town became the railhead for the transportation of stock from northern cattle and sheep stations. On 18 July 1910, Catholic parishioners at Meekatharra gave a warm welcome to 18 Dominican pupils who had travelled by train from Cue to present a two-night concert in the Australian Workers' Association Hall in aid of school extension funds. The events were listed as the first of their kind in the town and on both occasions the venue was overcrowded. Unfortunately, the continuous demand for encores, whilst encouraging, had to be disregarded in view of the length of the program. On the return trip to Cue, the performers broke their journey at Nannine where they repeated the concert before another large audience. Whilst it is true that the purpose of the visit to Meekatharra was primarily to raise funds, it also served to acquaint the parents of future pupils that the Dominican schools offered a wide range of artistic activities as well as studies. [5]

When Lot 184, Meekatharra, adjoining the Catholic Church on one side and the school reserve on the other, was put up for auction on Thursday, 12 January 1911, it was purchased by Father Flavahan on the understanding that it would be utilised as a future site on which to build a convent and school. Once having acquired the site, the parish priest lost no time in calling tenders for the erection of a suitable convent. The new building was estimated to cost in the vicinity of £500 and an appeal was quickly launched to raise the necessary funds. Before volunteers had an opportunity to canvass the district, however, some of the men in attendance at the meeting immediately subscribed £128 to bolster the proposed campaign. A contract for £479 was finally let to Messrs Crooks and Brooker and it was suggested that the building be completed by May so that the Dominican Sisters could occupy the convent prior to opening the new school. [6]

The Dominican foundation at Meekatharra was established on Tuesday, 16 May 1911, when two professed choir Sisters and a lay Sister arrived from Dongara to take up residence in the new convent. On the Sunday following the nuns' appearance, Bishop Kelly took part in several ceremonies that attracted not only parishioners, but also visitors from out of town. In the morning he celebrated Mass at 10.00 a.m. and confirmed a combined group of 30 children and adults who lived either in the township or

71. Group of Meekatharra pupils, 1911

outlying districts. After lunch the bishop officially welcomed the Dominican community before blessing the new convent and dedicating it to Our Lady of the Holy Rosary. The building, designed in a cottage or villa style, was constructed as usual in corrugated iron. Running through the full length of the residence was a passage, or breezeway, 10 feet wide, with lattice strategically placed at either end to allow the air to circulate. The convent, which was practical and thoughtfully planned, consisted of a reception and music room on either side of a wide entrance hall and separated from the public rooms were the Sisters' community room, refectory, three bedrooms, bathroom and kitchen. The Bishop of Geraldton, after thanking Meekatharra's parishioners and non-Catholic residents for their contributions, announced that, apart from the sum of £200 outstanding on the building and furnishings, the convent was remarkably free of debt. Before leaving Meekatharra, Bishop Kelly, always keen to promote sport in Catholic schools, promised to supply the boys with a football and the girls with tennis balls and racquets. [7]

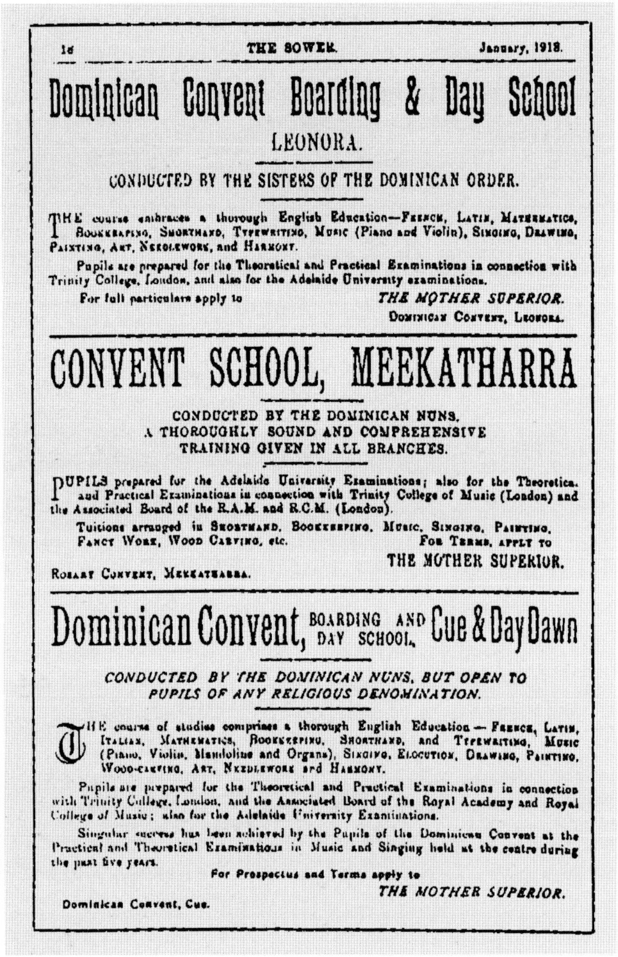

16 THE SOWER. January, 1918.

Dominican Convent Boarding & Day School

LEONORA.

CONDUCTED BY THE SISTERS OF THE DOMINICAN ORDER.

THE course embraces a thorough English Education—French, Latin, Mathematics, Bookkeeping, Shorthand, Typewriting, Music (Piano and Violin), Singing, Drawing, Painting, Art, Needlework, and Harmony.

Pupils are prepared for the Theoretical and Practical Examinations in connection with Trinity College, London, and also for the Adelaide University examinations.

For full particulars apply to THE MOTHER SUPERIOR.

Dominican Convent, Leonora.

CONVENT SCHOOL, MEEKATHARRA

CONDUCTED BY THE DOMINICAN NUNS.
A THOROUGHLY SOUND AND COMPREHENSIVE
TRAINING GIVEN IN ALL BRANCHES.

PUPILS prepared for the Adelaide University Examinations; also for the Theoretical and Practical Examinations in connection with Trinity College of Music (London) and the Associated Board of the R.A.M. and R.C.M. (London).

Tuitions arranged in Shorthand, Bookkeeping, Music, Singing, Painting, Fancy Work, Wood Carving, etc.

For Terms, apply to THE MOTHER SUPERIOR.

Rosary Convent, Meekatharra.

Dominican Convent, BOARDING AND DAY SCHOOL, Cue & Day Dawn

CONDUCTED BY THE DOMINICAN NUNS, BUT OPEN TO PUPILS OF ANY RELIGIOUS DENOMINATION.

THE course of studies comprises a thorough English Education — French, Latin, Italian, Mathematics, Bookkeeping, Shorthand, and Typewriting, Music (Piano, Violin, Mandoline and Organs), Singing, Elocution, Drawing, Painting, Wood-carving, Art, Needlework and Harmony.

Pupils are prepared for the Theoretical and Practical Examinations in connection with Trinity College, London, and the Associated Board of the Royal Academy and Royal College of Music; also for the Adelaide University Examinations.

Singular success has been achieved by the Pupils of the Dominican Convent at the Practical and Theoretical Examinations in Music and Singing held at the centre during the past five years.

For Prospectus and Terms apply to

THE MOTHER SUPERIOR.

Dominican Convent, Cue.

72. Advertisement for Dominican schools, 1918

The Holy Rosary Dominican Convent School opened on Monday, 22 May 1911, with 40 pupils in attendance. Within weeks, class numbers rapidly rose to 60, eventually peaking with an enrolment of 100 pupils. Classes were held in the parish church and, as with all church-schools, desks and blackboards were removed on Fridays for weekend services and returned on Monday mornings. The school curriculum advertising the benefits of a Dominican education appeared regularly in the *Sower* and occasionally in the local papers and *Catholic Record*. Judging by the number of subjects available to Dominican pupils attending the Holy Rosary Convent at Meekatharra, it would seem that children living in the outback in those early days suffered few educational disadvantages. The main inconvenience associated with the town's isolation was the fact that candidates from Meekatharra sitting for the Associated Board of Music Examinations had no alternative but to travel some 80 miles to the examination centre at Cue. Whilst the excursion would have entailed a great deal of planning by the nuns, and additional expense for parents, undoubtedly the train journey was an exciting event for the children.

On 26 June 1911, the Dominican Prioress, Mother Bonaventure McEntyre, paid her first visit to the new foundation. On arrival she was warmly greeted by Sister di Pazzi Miscall (Superior) and Sister Bernard Rogers and, before inspecting the convent and school, was given an enthusiastic welcome by the 70 pupils enrolled at that time. [8] On 27 April the following year, Bishop Kelly, accompanied by the Dean Graber, pastor of Cue, revisited Meekatharra. Arriving at Nannine, by the morning train, the priests were joined by Father Flavahan, who accompanied them on the two-hour drive to Meekatharra. Before blessing the new presbytery, near the Church of the Most Holy Redeemer, the bishop examined a group of children who had been prepared for confirmation by Sisters di Pazzi Miscall and Baptist Hall. Impressed by the standards set at the Holy Rosary School, he congratulated the Sisters on the progress they had made since their arrival.

The new Catholic presbytery, completed by builder G. McInnes in 1912, was constructed of wood and iron and lined with stamped metal, a popular material used for ceilings and interior walls during that period. The building, which consisted of four rooms and a latticed annexe at the back, cost approximately £375 and the people generously contributed to the furnishing. Among the many gifts received before the residence was occupied were window treatments donated by Mrs Baker, door mats, linoleum and a patterned hall carpet, and from the Dominican Sisters, a beautifully carved table fashioned by them from local wood. Bishop Kelly, pleased with the efforts made by the Catholic community in Meekatharra, remarked that most of the visits he had made during the last few years had involved the establishment of new church buildings. He recalled that, since 1909, he had blessed and opened a church, convent, school and presbytery in the town.

According to the *Sower*, published in May 1913, the March input of the Fenian Mine at Meekatharra was 2624 tons of ore for 2200 ounces of gold and it was predicted that production would continue to improve with double the number of stamps working in 1914. There was added excitement and a feeling of buoyancy among the Meekatharra residents that year, when a reef allegedly carrying rich veins of gold was discovered in stony ground, about three miles south of Garden Gully. [9] As interest in the mining industry continued to increase, the population rose accordingly and in turn generated new businesses and further employment in the town. It was soon obvious that the church-school was no longer suitable for the number of pupils being taught there and a new building was badly needed.

The Dominican Sisters, who had been teaching for the past six years under trying conditions, were greatly relieved when the construction of a new convent school commenced in December 1916, and was completed in the New Year. The building, which occupied a site between the

73. Holy Rosary Convent, Meekatharra

church and convent, was constructed at a cost of £600 by well-known local builder, Mr A. E. Douglas. The three outside walls of the school were protected from the weather by verandahs and, in touch with more modern practices in country schools, an acetylene plant was installed for lighting purposes and water had been laid on as part of the building program. The school, which measured 60 feet by 25 feet, was lined throughout with V-jointed jarrah and featured jarrah flooring. On completion it was possible for the Sisters to introduce a range of new activities for the main schoolroom, which was both spacious and functional and separated from the lower classes by a set of folding doors. [10]

In contrast to many other mining towns which had collapsed prior to, and during World War I, Meekatharra still had nine mines operating, four licensed hotels and reasonable employment opportunities as late as 1918. On Monday, 18 March that year, the Australian Workers' Association Hall in Meekatharra was filled to capacity when Dominican pupils from the Holy Rosary School presented a 'Grand Juvenile Entertainment'. The program, which was presented in two parts, not only gave the Sisters an opportunity to display their teaching skills, but gave the children a chance to perform in public before parents, relatives and friends. Musical items included a cornet solo entitled 'Selection of Irish Airs' by Master A. Taylor; a pianoforte trio, 'Silver Trumpets', by the Misses Williams, Burnside and Gerrans and a violin solo, 'The Broken Melody', by Miss Buggentheim. In addition, there were also combined and solo exhibitions of club swinging, an action song by the infant and junior classes, a musical monologue, 'The Game of Life', by Miss E. Bourgoin, and a chorus which concluded with an emotive, but popular wartime song, 'Somewhere in France'. The concert, which commenced at 8.00 p.m. and did not finish until late, was followed by a dance for adults which lasted until the small hours of the morning. [11]

Shortly after the closure of the principal mine at Day Dawn in 1918, Sister Aloysius Pickerd was transferred to the Holy Rosary Convent at Meekatharra to assist with the increased enrolments at the school in that year. The shortage of Dominican Sisters in the community at that time, meant that her place in the school at Cue was temporarily filled by a lay teacher. Towards the end of May 1920, additional strain was placed on the community when ill-health forced Sr Aloysius to return to the Priory at Dongara and Sister Josephine Kenny was assigned to take her place. By August she had also taken ill and arrangements were made to send Sister Hyacinth Carroll to replace her in the school. In 1921, the following new community members were appointed to Meekatharra: Sisters Vincent Colgan (Superior), Reginald Rice and Berchmans Wilson. [12]

Sister Joseph O'Connor has happy memories of her years at Meekatharra in the 1930s and although, on reflection, she admits that she found the weather extremely hot, she grew to love the town and its people, particularly the children living in that isolated part of the world. Sister Joseph, a former Dominican pupil, made her final profession at Dongara on 2 February 1933, and was only 22 years of age when she arrived at Meekatharra to join the Superior of the Holy Rosary Convent, Sister Teresa McQuillan, and her companion, Sister Brigid Kelly. Unlike her former novitiate companions, Sisters Paschal Dowdall (Sr Kathleen), Raphael Woods, Philomena Punch and St Anne Graham (Sr Mary Anne), who remained at Dongara after their profession, the young Sr Joseph was immediately assigned to the distant Dominican branch house at Meekatharra. It must have been daunting to find that her first class consisted of 44 pupils in classes ranging from Infants to Standards I, II and III. In those days religious Sisters rarely left the convent and apart from teaching, studying and giving private lessons before and after school in music, shorthand and typing, Sr Joseph still had to perform her daily religious duties.

An intelligent, determined woman, with a keen sense of humour, Sister Joseph O'Connor was one of the Dominican Sisters chosen by the newly-appointed Prioress, Mother Laurence Prendiville, to study and sit for the Teachers' Certificate Examination. This exercise was a new experience for members of religious communities, for until 1930, when it was agreed to accept external students, students intending to teach only in Catholic schools were not accepted at the Teachers' Training College in Claremont. With 13 units to complete, spare time was at a premium for Sr Joseph. The new teacher was quickly recognised for her English skills and also for her ability to quietly control a class of lively pupils, which is no doubt why, on occasions, she was asked to supervise boys in the upper classes who had proved boisterous.

74. Catholic Church, Meekatharra, school to left.

A stony, barren terrain dominated the landscape at Meekatharra and sudden dust storms at times made domestic life difficult. The cream serge habits and starched headgear worn by the Dominicans were a constant source of concern and frequent washing was necessary to remove the marks made by the red dust. To make matters worse, the water that ran hot from the taps in summer was often brown in colour. Fortunately the Sisters shared the ironing which, because of the intense heat, proved to be a tiresome and exhausting chore. Sister Joseph recalls that in the early 1930s, during the Great Depression years, tramps who were hungry and looking for work, often found their way to the convent door and despite the community's own lean situation, the Sisters never failed to supply them with a meal and enough food to reach the next stop. Sister Evangelist Graham, who at that time was in charge of the household duties, was nervous of the itinerants, particularly if they were unkempt and she was alone in the convent. One evening, at about 5.00 p.m., when the remaining members of the community were giving lessons in the school, she was confronted by an exceptionally scruffy man. Anxiously playing for time, she suggested that he take a seat on a bench on the front verandah while she got him something to eat. Neglecting to close the door properly she retreated indoors, intending to run out the back to fetch one of the other Sisters. To her complete surprise she found the stranger hard on her heels. Shaking with fear, Sr Evangelist mustered enough courage to angrily inform the intruder that if he didn't remove himself from the premises he could go hungry. Imagine her consternation when she thought she recognised his eyes. 'Are you the bishop?', she gasped in awe, to which he replied in the affirmative, adding, 'and what a nice way to greet me. If you had been lying under a car to fix it, while that terrible dust storm was blowing, you'd be scruffy too'. A good laugh and an apology from both sides saw Bishop O'Collins retreat to the presbytery for a shower and Sr Evangelist to the kitchen to prepare a welcome meal. Of course, Sr Evangelist never lived the incident down and when she met with the bishop on future occasions he would tease, 'A nice way the Dominicans treat their bishop – and the poor old hoboes!' [13]

In 1936, Mother Bonaventure McEntyre became Superior at Meekatharra. Serving with her in the community were Sisters Berchmans Wilson, Evangelist Graham and Joseph O'Connor. Sister Bertrand O'Connor, who taught at the Meekatharra Convent between 1945 and 1949, recalled that the convent then boasted four bedrooms, a spare room, a parlour, a refectory, a kitchen and a small disused bathroom which was mainly used for storing odds and ends, including bottles of home-made ginger beer. The ceilings were high and still consisted of the original pressed or stamped steel, and although electricity had been connected to the building, for some time candles were still used in the bedrooms. In summer, the bedrooms were extremely hot and, in order to catch the breeze through the lattice, the Sisters sometimes placed their mattresses in the long central passage. A mining battery, which operated not far from the convent, made a great deal of noise day and night, however, as with most consistent sounds, the Sisters soon became accustomed to the monotonous pounding of machinery. [14] There were other discomforts to contend with, and those Sisters accustomed to colder climates must have longed at times for leafy trees and verdant surrounds when, clad in heavy robes and uncomfortable guimpes and veils, they faced a day's teaching in a hot galvanised iron schoolroom. Many benefits flowed from the Sisters' work. As some members of the community later recalled, the many friends they made, the pupils they taught and the sight of Aboriginal and white children happily studying and playing together made it all worthwhile.

During the mid-1940s, both Sister Bertrand, who taught Grades from I to III in one classroom, and Sister di Ricci Levitzke (Sr Kath), who had charge of Grades IV to VII, also privately tutored some of the government school children in music, typing and shorthand. The Superior of the Convent, Sister Aquin Inglis, taught music and assisted Sr Bertrand with some of the younger pupils. On the domestic scene, all Sisters

75. Catholic school, Meekatharra

helped with the washing and Sister Evangelist cooked the meals while Sr Bertrand was responsible for looking after the church and she recalls that there was always a lot of brass to polish. The Sisters rarely complained, and it was obvious to those who knew them, that the missionary spirit, inherited from the founding Sisters, had a great influence on their daily lives.

Between 1945 and 1949, Meekatharra was served by four different priests, Fathers Bede Lazaro (a Benedictine from New Norcia), Thomas Naughton, Michael Moffatt and John Brennan, and the Dominican Convent hosted three Superiors, Sisters Aquin Inglis, Augustine Corbett and Baptist Robson (Sr Margaret). [15] Sister Baptist was to spend another five years in the town, between 1958 and 1963, as principal of the Holy Rosary School. She still has fond memories of the Meekatharra children and of their parents, who showed the Sisters so many acts of kindness, by bringing them gifts of food, carrying out repairs and making it easy to call on them for help. Later, Sister Margaret Robson was appointed congregational bursar, a position she held for many years and which she fulfilled competently for the benefit of all the Sisters.

Sister Dominic Galvin, who went to Meekatharra in 1951, spent two years at the Holy Rosary Convent. Her companions during that time were Sisters Aquin Inglis (Superior), Augustine Corbett, Brigid Kelly and Evangelist Graham and she recalls that the community's one luxury was a Kelvinator refrigerator. As well as teaching music after school hours, Sr Dominic took the lower primary classes and also privately coached adults in commercial subjects until they had attained a high enough standard of proficiency to sit for a commercial college examination. Each family paid the Sisters a small, set weekly tuition fee, regardless of how many children in the family were enrolled. The fee, which was not compulsory for people in poor circumstances, was little more than a token and sometimes when funds were low Sr Aquin made home-made toffees and sold them after school. [16] Fortunately, the Sisters had many caring friends and without their consistent support the small community could not have continued to exist. The number of families involved with the Dominican Sisters, since they established their foundation at Meekatharra in 1911, is too numerous to list, but no record would be complete without the names of Gran Touhey, Tottie Ross, and Annie Williams and the Ryan, MacDonald, Healey, Trenaman, Campbell and Hovell families, as well as two unrelated couples with the same surname of Hayes. One of the couples, Colin and Mary Hayes, now live in Doubleview, Perth, and continue to assist the Dominican Sisters in a variety of ways.

By 1970, the Holy Rosary School had an enrolment of 30 pupils in Grades I to VIII and the Dominican Sisters, influenced by the closure of the mines and lack of teaching staff, made a practical decision to close the school on 16 December 1970. The last community comprised Sisters Bernadette Punch, Paschal Dowdall (Sr Kathleen) and Norbert Burke (Sr Pauline), and when Sr Bernadette was granted extended holiday leave in November 1970, Sister Lidwina de Groot (Sr Sophie) arrived to assist the remaining two Sisters with the closure of the school. During the final weeks all the necessary formalities were finalised and parents were consulted about the possibility of transferring their children to the local government school or to nearby boarding schools. After 60 years' residence in the locality, it was an emotional occasion for the Sisters, particularly as the Holy Rosary school at Meekatharra was also the last of the Dominican foundations on the Murchison goldfields to close its doors, St Gabriel's Convent at Cue having closed two years earlier. The 60-year-old school register, located in 1970, reveals that a total of 1400 children had attended classes at the Meekatharra convent. According to the then parish priest, Father Closs, the Dominican Sisters had provided more than a primary school education, for the Holy Rosary Convent was the only centre in the area to offer music, typing and book-keeping instruction. Among the many parents affected by the Sisters' departure, was Mr Phil Gerick, proprietor of the town's general store, who had had seven of his eight children at the school and another about to begin. The feeling that swept through the town when the news of the Sisters' departure was announced, was summed up by Mr Gerick when he stated, 'It's not only the Catholic side of the community that will be sorry to see the school go. Children of all religions have been taught at the school since the early 1900s and the nuns seem to have a way with young children. The whole town is upset and will be sad'. [17]

## SACRED HEART CONVENT, ST PAUL'S SCHOOL, THREE SPRINGS

Three Springs, a small country town, 315 kilometres north of Perth and 108 kilometres east of Dongara, received its first settlers in 1906. Three years later, the parish priest at Dongara, Father O'Hare, celebrated the first Mass in the area for three local Catholic families. On that occasion the ceremony was held in a private residence, that later became a presbytery and in turn the home of Mr and Mrs A. Saggers. By April, there were signs of increased settlement and the Midland Railway Company's intention to shortly release for sale some 60,000 acres of the finest agricultural land created a great deal of interest. As a result, pioneers had selected almost every acre of land along the length of the Midland railway line from Mingenew to Carnamah by the close of 1909 and clearing had begun in earnest. [1]

For at least seven years, prior to establishing a convent and school at Three Springs, the Dominican Sisters from Dongara regularly visited several towns situated along the railway line to provide religious instruction to children attending government schools. Occasionally, the Sisters also gave private lessons in music and fancywork. Sister Dominica Murphy, accompanied by either Sister Bonaventure McEntyre or Sister Peter Geeson, usually caught the early Saturday morning train and travelled to Strawberry, Mingenew and Three Springs. After completing their many duties, the travellers usually caught the night train back to Dongara and did not reach the Priory until well after 9.00 p.m. Before the Sisters' involvement, catechism had been taught by a number of devout Catholics who lived in the area. Among the early supporters, before a parish was formed in Three Springs, were members of the Berrigan, Thomas, Lynch, Brown, O'Shannessey, Maley, Oliver, Brown, Ahearn, Sheridan and Turner families. [2]

In 1911, to meet the demands of Catholic families living in and around Three Springs, discussions were held between Messrs Brown, Sheridan, Ryan and Lynch regarding the possibility of erecting a local church. A major step towards achieving that objective was taken when the Lynch brothers offered to donate a piece of ground on the outskirts of the town. [3] The first Catholic Church at Three Springs, a corrugated iron and timber building, erected in 1911 by Father Scanlan for £400, was, when not in use, rented out for meetings, dances and picture shows to bring in extra revenue. That arrangement ceased, however, after a town hall was officially opened on 20 June 1912, and the larger building became the main social venue for local residents. The parish, in the meantime, continued to raise funds for a more permanent church building and hopefully towards the erection of a convent and school. In 1913, members of the Catholic Church Committee held a successful three-day bazaar in the town hall and the following year a similar event raised the sum of £300.[4]

In 1916, the Dominican Sisters at Dongara accepted an invitation from Father Scanlan to establish a new foundation at Three Springs. Subsequently, arrangements were made through Bishop Kelly to transport a disused presbytery from Mt Morgans for use as a convent. The building, once the residence of Bishop Kelly's former co-administrator, the late Father Joseph Ryan, had become obsolete when the principal mine in that town collapsed and the people moved on to seek new employment. Excited at the prospect of a religious teaching order opening a school at Three Springs, the Church Committee willingly accepted the cost of dismantling, transporting and re-erecting the new convent.

In January 1917, three Sisters took possession of the Sacred Heart Convent at Three Springs. Accompanying Sister Philomena McGrath, the Superior of the new community, were lay Sister Rose McCusker and the newly-appointed Procuratrix and Mistress of Schools, Sister Peter Geeson. Classes commenced on 30 January and until a new school was erected more than half a century later, the Sisters continued to teach in the corrugated iron building that doubled as a church. Most of the children living on outlying properties either rode or drove to school and, as was the custom in those days, they often raced each other along the way for a lark. During school hours, the horses were usually confined opposite the convent in Glyde's paddock, where they were tethered in the shade afforded by several tall gum trees. [5]

The first year of school ended on a highly successful note when well-wishers and parents were invited to view the children's work on 20 December 1917. Not only were the guests visibly appreciative of the nuns' efforts during the first 12 months, but they were also impressed by the high standard of work and surprised by the number of articles on display. Before the presentation of prizes took place, the audience was given the opportunity to assess some of the pupils' artistic talents. A short program, carefully arranged by the Sisters, consisted of vocal and violin solos and duets, recitations and a well-prepared cantata, 'Soot and the Fairies'. After praising the work done by the nuns and thanking the children for the entertainment they had provided throughout the evening, Father Scanlan announced the names of the students who had won class prizes:

**Infant School**: Ethel Maley, Teddy Duffy. Grade I: Edna Hopkins. Grade III: Mervyn Klopper. Grade IV: Lily Brown. Grade V: James Lynch. Grade VII: Lily Berrigan. **Christian Doctrine**: Junior Division, Mervyn Klopper, Mary Honner (equal). Senior Division, Clara Berrigan. **Needlework**: Alma Thomas. **Good Conduct**: Madge Rooke. **Shorthand and Book-keeping**: Cetie Honner. **Certificates for the Royal Academy of Music**: Primary Division (piano), Madge Rook, Clement Honner, Forrest Honner; (violin), Annie Burn. Elementary Division (piano), Clara Berrigan. Lower Division (violin), Richard Honner. [6]

Dominican pupil, Master Cetie Honner, was also successful in winning a Narrogin Farm School Scholarship valued at £44. It is little wonder that a newspaper report summarising the Dominican community's first year in Three Springs stated, 'it is most consoling to see the telling effects the presence of the good Sisters have had upon the children'. [7]

In 1920, Sister Philomena McGrath was re-appointed Superior and Sacristan of the Three Springs community and Sister Baptist Hall, who was considered by her contemporaries to be an 'able and distinguished member' of the Dominican teaching order, became the Procuratrix and Mistress of Schools. Unfortunately, Sr Philomena's second term of office was brief and sickness unexpectedly forced her to return to the Priory at Dongara where she died on 27 February 1920. In the meantime, Sr Baptist Hall, with assistance from Sister Concepta Waterson, took charge of the Sacred Heart community.

The Three Springs parish, created in 1921, extended from Coorow to Mingenew and included the districts of Morawa and Perenjori. Father Hart was appointed the first parish priest and succeeding him were Fathers Timmins, Flavahan and Lynch. Before such time as a second-hand 'T' model Ford became part of the parish scene, local priests visited the various centres in a sulky or buggy and pair. Their journeys often took them along uneven, roughly-formed bush tracks, which is probably why, after a motor car was introduced, some parishioners jokingly suggested that, despite the vehicle being faster, it was not always as reliable as a horse. [8] Later, in 1933, the size of the area administered by the priest diminished when Morawa and Perenjori became separate parishes.

76. Group of boarders, Three Springs, 1951

Almost from the beginning, the Sisters agreed to accept a few young male boarders, as well as girls, to assist a number of parents living on outlying farms. Enrolment for male boarders was spasmodic however, and accommodation was offered on a small scale only until the end of the 1930s. This situation changed after the Superior was approached by a group of parents concerned about the distance their children had to travel to receive a Catholic education. The Sisters' decision to accept more boarders resulted in additions being made at the rear of the convent and an advertisement being placed in local newspapers announcing the opening of a Dominican boarding school for boys in Three Springs:

**BOARDING SCHOOL FOR BOYS UNDER TWELVE YEARS OF AGE:** *The Course of Instruction covers the requirements of the Primary School Syllabus of the Education Department with special attention to morals and religious training of Catholic boys. The school Year is divided into three terms of 13 weeks each, commencing on or about 8th February, 27th May and 9th September. Fees are payable in advance at the beginning of each term.* ***Board and tuition****, £17 per term.* ***Laundry****, £1/10/0.* ***Music*** *– piano or violin £3 per term.* ***Elocution****, £1/10/0 per term.* [9]

The enquiries from parents, wishing to enrol their sons at the Sacred Heart Convent School, mainly came from the Arrino, Perenjori, Morawa and Winchester areas. Most children were enrolled as weekly boarders and on acceptance the following list of requirements was provided for each applicant:

*1 Best Suit and Cap (grey melange), 1 Pair best Shoes (brown), 2 Pairs Grey Pants and 2 Grey Pullovers (for winter wear), 3 Pairs Field Grey Pants and 3 Field Grey Sports Shirts (for school wear in summer), 3 pairs of Pyjamas, 4 Singlets, 2 Light Blue Shirts (for best), 3 Pairs Grey Socks, 2 Pairs Sandals, 2 Pairs School Shoes (for winter), 1 Pair Sand Shoes, 1 Pair House Slippers, 1 Dozen Handkerchiefs, 4 Serviettes, 4 Towels (one for Bath), Toilet Requisites, Tie (to be had at school), Dressing Gown, Travelling Rug. All Clothing to be clearly marked.*[10]

In 1941, when Sister Dominic Galvin was transferred to Three Springs to teach the junior primary class, she joined other members of the Sacred Heart community, Sisters Concepta Waterson, Stanislaus McDonough and Alocoque Culhane. The corrugated iron convent and the church-school were situated on the same side of the road in close proximity to each other and Sr Dominic later recalled that both buildings attracted the heat in summer and the cold in winter. At one end of the school building, which was still used as a church on Sundays, were two small rooms. One of these doubled as a sacristy and sleeping quarters for the priest until a presbytery was built. The other area served as an extra classroom.

Parish priest, Father Michael Lynch, the brother of Sister Emmanuel OP and nephew of well-known Senator Patrick Lynch, originally came from the Three Springs area and many past students will remember the enthralling ghost stories he told, and the practical jokes he enjoyed playing on them. The future Dean had an approachable manner and was a popular figure with the parishioners and children and much-admired by the Dominican Sisters who appreciated his support. When the Three Springs basketball team defeated the Dominican boarders from Dongara, Fr Lynch was one of the first to congratulate the players and among the first to join in the victory celebrations. As well as study, boarders at the school were often involved in a variety of outdoor activities. On Sundays, it was not uncommon for two Sisters to take a group of boarders for a walk to a popular spot known as the 'Ten-Acre Block'. The boys looked forward to these outings, which they regarded as a cross between a nature study walk and an adventure. For the Sisters it was a rare opportunity to explore the surrounding countryside, especially during the wildflower season when donkey orchids and sun-dews brightened the bush and the fields were awash with colourful everlastings. [11]

By 1943, partly due to the influx of war-time evacuees, there were 43 boys boarding with the Dominican Sisters at the Sacred Heart Convent in Three Springs. To cope with the extra numbers, the former Sheehan residence, on the opposite side of the road, was purchased, re-named St Joseph's, and used as a separate boys' boarding wing detached from the convent. The last of the female boarders residing at the convent left in approximately 1951, and, in 1960, the residential section of the school ceased to operate altogether when the male boarders were transferred to other schools. The building, known as St Joseph's, was eventually removed and taken to Dongara, where it became the administration centre for the lay missionaries working in the area at that time. Three years later a new brick Dominican Convent was erected on the site of the boarding wing section.

77. Original parish church, Three Springs, first convent in background

Several parish improvements also took place at Three Springs during the 1940s. Father Brian Gallagher, who later became the Bishop of Port Pirie, South Australia, was then in charge of the parish and during his term of office, not only was a new brick presbytery completed in 1946, but early in 1947, the new St Paul's School was blessed and officially opened by Bishop A. J. Gummer. After 30 years of painstakingly arranging and re-arranging classrooms before and after Mass, the Sisters could not hide their delight at the prospect of teaching in a modern brick building with spacious playgrounds. Finally, on 21 September 1958, the Three Springs parish reached new heights when, due to the efforts of Father Michael Moffat, the new St Paul's Church in Touche Street was officially opened by Bishop Gummer. The fine, new building, designed and built by Mr Stan Costello of Kalamunda, at a cost of approximately £18,000, was greatly admired by the large crowd who assembled that day despite inclement weather. [12] It is said that Fr Gallagher changed the name of the original church, the Sacred Heart, to St Paul's, because the title of the Western Australian

78. St Paul's School, Three Springs

79. Sacred Heart Convent, Three Springs, original boarding wing to right

town reminded him of St Paul's, near Tre Fontane outside Rome, the site of three springs, or fountains, where according to tradition, St Paul was beheaded.

On 22 February 1964, Bishop F. X. Thomas officiated at the opening of a new Dominican Convent at Three Springs. Built on the opposite side of the road to the original convent, the building, adjacent to the new Catholic church and school, contained a chapel with a sacristy, five bedrooms, a kitchen, pantry, a community room, a refectory, a parlour, an enclosed sleep-out, bathrooms, a laundry and a long corridor which ran down the centre of the building. The total cost of the convent, including an exterior brick wall and concrete paths, amounted to approximately £14,000, a cost shared by the Dominican community and the Three Springs parish. The altar in the chapel, fashioned from black and white terrazzo by Mr Boschetti of Wonthella, was designed by Father Moffatt and donated by Mr Barney Ryan, the brother of Sisters Xavier and Michael Ryan, in memory of their parents, Thomas and Charlotte Ryan of Meekatharra. [13]

After retirement, Sister Xavier Ryan spent three years in the Three Springs Convent and during that time was devoted to visiting the sick, lonely and elderly in that town. Anne Ryan, the eldest of seven children, was born at Mt Magnet, where her father was employed on one of the mines. A gifted seamstress as well as a serious student, she was capable of making dresses for the rest of the family by the time she was 14. As a young girl, Sister Xavier did not realise how useful this gift would be when, during the 1950s, she would be called on to make habits for the large group of novices who entered the order during that period. In 1928, whilst still a pupil at the Meekatharra Dominican Convent, Anne Ryan won a scholarship to St Dominic's College at Dongara and later, at the age of 19, she joined the order and entered the Dominican novitiate at the Priory. In 1939, Sr Xavier Ryan obtained her Bachelor of Arts degree from The University of Western Australia and during her religious life taught numerous children in Dominican schools at

80. St Paul's Church and presbytery, Three Springs

Dongara, Mingenew, Reedy, Cue, Leonora, Three Springs, Scarborough, Doubleview and Bentley. [14] When asked to describe her memories of Sr Xavier, Sister Perpetua Gill stated:

*One cannot think of Sister M. Xavier without recalling her apostolate of keeping in touch with ex-students, family members, friends, acquaintances and priests she had worked with or whose work on the missions she had helped. She prayed for them all, wrote to them and always enclosed holy pictures, badges, medals or kits that she had made or crocheted. Hundreds, possibly thousands, were distributed throughout her life. Sister M. Xavier saw this hobby as a means of nurturing the faith of the recipients or of bringing a blessing on those who wore or carried them.* [15]

Sister Xavier Ryan's younger sister Patricia (Sr Michael), also a former Dominican student, was born at Meekatharra, and after her profession at Dongara in 1945, she was assigned to country schools at Dongara, Mingenew, Yalgoo, Leonora, Cue and Three Springs and at Scarborough in the metropolitan area. A humble, generous-natured person, Sister Michael later studied for the Nursing Aide Certificate and in 1975, after practical experience in several government hospitals, obtained a certificate that qualified her for work in geriatric nursing. This new turn in Sr Michael's career enabled her to devote her time to elderly Sisters in need of care at St Catherine's in Doubleview.

In the same year that the convent was officially opened, new school uniforms were introduced and girls attending St Paul's Convent School were quickly recognised by the green plaid skirts and matching green pullovers they wore in winter and in summer by their neat, green check dresses. Likewise, the boys looked smart in grey shirts and trousers, topped by green pullovers. Fortunately, St Paul's School had a strong Parents' and Friends' Association and as usual with such organisations, members were ever mindful of the need to upgrade the buildings and grounds and replace equipment. The Sisters were extremely grateful when members of the association took the time, during the 1966 August holidays, to repaint the classrooms in pleasant pastel shades of green and mauve. On their return to classes after the mid-year break, the pupils were pleasantly surprised and, for at least a time, set about their lessons with renewed interest.[16]

The Golden Jubilee heralding the arrival of the first Dominican Sisters in Three Springs was marked by celebrations which took place in August 1967. On this occasion Dean Lynch spoke of the Sisters' earlier hardships and he reminded those present that in 1917, when the Sisters were invited to form a foundation in Three Springs, they were deprived of daily Mass, had few, if any, comforts and experienced many hardships. At the conclusion of the ceremony, former pupils presented the

Sisters with a suitably inscribed golden chalice on behalf of grateful parishioners. Included among the many other gifts received by them in appreciation of their past services was a much-appreciated radiogram and a television set, still a rarity in many Western Australian homes.[17]

By the 1970s, despite St Paul's school being well-established, it was obvious to those involved that the foundation's days were numbered. The introduction to country towns of a regular bus service providing easier access to larger centres, falling pupil numbers, as well as a down-turn in religious vocations, persuaded the Provincial Council that they could no longer maintain the school at Three Springs. It caused deep regret in the community at that time when Sisters Francis Huntsman and Pauline Burke, closed St Paul's in December 1974. It has been estimated that since 1917, nearly 900 pupils had been educated by the Dominican Sisters at Three Springs. For the wheatbelt town and surrounding areas, the closure of St Paul's School meant the end of an important era in local history.

The school building was later used for parish purposes, and although they were no longer associated with Catholic education in Three Springs, over the ensuing years the Dominican Sisters continued to maintain an involvement in the district. As well as preparing children for the sacraments, they extended their ministry to include visits to the local hospital, the Lady Brand Lodge and to residents in their own homes. The Motor Mission, which had been founded at Morawa in 1972, to serve mid-west towns where no Catholic school existed, was revised in 1975 and from a second base at Three Springs Sister Bernadette Punch and Sister Francis Huntsman taught religion to Catholic children in that town, as well as at Coorow, Carnamah and Eneabba. For the next few years, until 1981, other Sisters including Paul O'Connor, Vianney O'Brien and Xavier Ryan continued the Motor Mission State School apostolate to Carnamah and Coorow and the visitation of homes and the hospital in Three Springs. From 1982 until 1993, when Sister Xavier shared the work with Sister Bernadette, they were assisted at different times by Sisters Emmanuel Lynch, Michael Ryan and Bertrand O'Connor.

81. Nativity play, St. Paul's School, Three Springs, 1962
L. to R.: ...., A. Taylor, K. McDonnell, P. McCagh, H. Sears, J. McAuley (Kneeling): B. Shute, A. Louzenski

After the closure of the Dominican school at Three Springs, although other members of her community were later transferred to Perth, Sister Bernadette Punch, who

82. Three Jubilarians, Three Springs, 1986
L. to R.: Sisters Emmanuel Lynch, Xavier Ryan, Bernadette Punch

admitted to 'living and breathing Three Springs', chose to remain in the town among people she knew and loved. Sister Bernadette immersed herself in pastoral and parish activities until 1998, when she felt the time had come for her to move on to yet another stage in her busy life. Her departure put an end to the Sisters' presence in town after more than 80 years – the longest continuing involvement of the Dominican Sisters in any of their foundations.

## ST HYACINTH'S CONVENT AND SCHOOL, YALGOO

St Hyacinth's Convent, established at Yalgoo in 1922, became the Dominican Sisters' ninth foundation in Western Australia. Although explored by A. C. Gregory in 1846, and later in 1854 by R. Austin, the area which became the scene of Dominican activity for over 28 years was not pioneered until the early 1890s, when pastoralists began to develop what later became a thriving sheep industry.[1] The Yalgoo goldfields, which were never as lucrative or well-known as some of the other rich gold-bearing centres in the Murchison, were declared open in January 1895. By then, the Gold Rush, activated by the proclamation of the Murchison goldfields in 1891, was in full swing and prospectors were searching likely ground for that elusive 'pot of gold'.

The mining industry at Yalgoo mainly owed its existence to the discovery of the wealthy Emerald Reward Mine in 1892 and to its continued contribution to the district over the next 16 years. Apart from economic and employment opportunities, one of the most significant benefits gained from the gold boom years in the Murchison was the expansion of the railway system. In 1894, a line was constructed from Geraldton as far as Mullewa, and two years later the track was extended to Yalgoo. In 1898, the line reached Cue and in 1903, the railway terminated at Nannine. As a result, the arid hinterland became more accessible, transport was made easier and towns mushroomed in what was previously inhospitable country, miles from anywhere. By the turn of the century, it was estimated that Yalgoo's population amounted to 200 residents in the township and 1300 in the district. Many of these people were involved in the mining industry until a continuing decline in the production of gold became more evident from 1903 onwards. [2] The demise of the former rich Emerald Reward Mine in 1908 and the advent of the First World War brought about many changes and the post-war years proved to be a turning point in the district's pastoral industry. Not only was there an enormous demand for sheep and wool at that time, but it so happened that the Yalgoo area experienced excellent rainfall between 1917 and 1919.[3]

Although Yalgoo had no resident priest for many years, a Catholic church had been erected in 1909, to cater to the needs of a growing population. St Saviour's Church, built in timber and iron and lined with fluted iron, had a neatly-furnished priest's room attached for visiting clergy. Although the building was of simple design, the parishioners involved had gone to a great deal of trouble in furnishing the interior. A fine-toned organ, with 12 stops, had been purchased for the use of the parish organist, Miss Estie O'Connor, and Mr Maurice Ahearn, whose work later included the baptismal font in the Geraldton cathedral, had been commissioned to fashion a Gothic-style confessional. By October 1909, the building was completely free of debt, mainly due to the efforts of Father Flavahan, who had earlier organised a successful fund-raising event in the form of a sports day. His successor, Father Roggero, generally celebrated Mass on the first and second Sundays of each month and during his absence, Mrs C. Williamson kindly provided religious instruction to those preparing for Confirmation or their First Communion. [4] Years later, when the celebrated Father Hawes was in charge of Yalgoo, he described St Saviour's Church as 'certainly the prettiest little building of corrugated iron he had ever seen – white walls and red roof, with a stately altar and spacious sanctuary, as long as the nave, even an apse with leaded stain-glass windows'. Likewise he was impressed with the presbytery provided for him at Yalgoo which he explained was 'a very comfortable little bungalow with a verandah all around, a sitting room, bedroom, kitchen and bathroom'. [5]

Architect-priest, Monsignor John Cyril Hawes, widely recognised for his contribution to the state's heritage, is without doubt the best-known priest to have served in Yalgoo. This was not only because of his personal involvement with the design and building of the

83. St Saviour's Church and presbytery, Yalgoo, 1908

heritage-listed former Dominican Convent Chapel of St Hyacinth, but also because of his interesting background and lifestyle. John Hawes, a qualified English architect and one-time Anglican Benedictine monk, converted to Catholicism in March 1911 and later took Holy Orders in Rome. In November 1915, at the invitation of Bishop Kelly, he arrived in the Geraldton diocese and was not only a competent stonemason and builder, but a fine horseman. Indeed, in 1926, much to the delight of his parishioners, his horse 'Babs' took part in, and won, the Maiden Hack Race at the Yalgoo Races. [6]

Father Hawes was the priest in charge of Mullewa and Yalgoo when, in 1921, the Dominican Sisters finally accepted an invitation to establish a foundation at Yalgoo. He had been aware for some time that parishioners in that town were anxious to provide a religious education for their children, such as was available at Mullewa. Feeling the mounting pressure, Fr Hawes wrote to the Prioress of the Dominican Order at Dongara on 12 October 1919. He informed her that he had been in touch with the Bishop of Geraldton to suggest that a convent at Yalgoo might make a convenient halfway house between the Sisters' foundations at Dongara and Cue. Likewise, he had also pointed out that the Dominican Sisters would be ideally suited to found such a mission, for they already had a school at Cue and a number of novices nearing profession at Dongara. In stating his case, Fr Hawes frankly admitted that Yalgoo was only a very small town with approximately 40 pupils attending the government school. Only 17 of these children, excluding those under six years of age, were Catholics, however, it was also anticipated that many non-Catholic parents would seize the opportunity to enrol their children in a convent school that offered extra subjects and encouraged the arts. As an added incentive, the priest reminded the Prioress that a number of pastoralists living some distance from the town had young children who might be regarded as potential boarders. [7]

The priest also raised the possibility of the Church Committee being able to acquire the former Warden's house at Yalgoo for a convent. This well-constructed and spacious residence was situated well back from the main street and was only a couple of minutes' walk from the church. Built on the summit of a hill, it was exposed to cool breezes in summer and had a fine view across the lakes and distant hills. Father Hawes suggested that, if additions were provided to the back of the residence, the building would make an ideal convent and school. The availability of the building at that stage seemed to be more of a problem than funding, since Catholic station owners in the district had already displayed a willingness to assist financially and also to provide on-going support to any religious community which might care to accept the invitation to Yalgoo.

When writing to Mother Bonaventure McEntyre, the priest let it be known that he was not prepared to bind the Dominicans to a commitment until he had secured 'the house in question, or got a new building put up for a convent'. [8] In some ways this consideration on their behalf must have come as a surprise, for in those days the Sisters were very often given short notice and expected to accept so-called 'temporary' accommodation which often lasted for a long period of time.

Initially, Mother Bonaventure was reluctant to commit her community to a foundation at Yalgoo, because she was under the impression that the Presentation Sisters in Geraldton had already accepted an offer to serve in that town. The priest later explained that the confusion originated a few years earlier when, during his absence, two Presentation Sisters visited Yalgoo and the subject of a Catholic school was discussed. It appears that the visiting Sisters agreed to establish a foundation on the condition that the priest move into the sacristy, thus allowing the presbytery to be used for a convent and the church for a school. According to Father Hawes, these suggestions were not acceptable, the main objections being that the sacristy was only 'three steps from the presbytery, with no really separate premises or privacy for anyone' and that most of St Saviour's parishioners did not wish to have their church used for any other purpose than for worship. [9]

Father Hawes, in October 1919, also informed Mother Bonaventure that he had leave from Bishop Kelly to return to England the following year. The priest confided that he hoped, afterwards, to remain in charge of the Yalgoo and Mullewa parishes and 'dreaded terribly the possibility of being sent somewhere else'. Under the present circumstances, he felt that he would prefer to see the opening of the new Dominican foundation deferred until a later date as he wanted first to complete the stone church at Mullewa and then, if re-appointed, concentrate on the convent at Yalgoo. 'Should the Bishop ask you to take up the Rosella Hospital in Geraldton', he wrote on 26 October 1919, 'I hope you won't forget the prior claim of Yalgoo and your offer to work here'. [10]

On 22 July 1921, Father Hawes again contacted the Dominican Sisters and explained that, although he had earlier offered to purchase the Warden's house in Yalgoo, the government had refused to sell the property. It is interesting to note that shortly afterwards, the same building was wrecked in a gale and an unsuccessful attempt was made by the priest to purchase some of the roofing iron, timbers and other materials from the ruins. At this stage, other options were discussed with leading members of the congregation and it was decided to form a fund-raising committee and in the meantime to look for a suitable site on which to build a convent and school.

Father Hawes's main concern was, however, that in the interim the Dominican Sisters might be persuaded to open another foundation rather than one at Yalgoo. [11]

By 1921, although the production of gold at nearby Payne's Find continued to remain steady, the opening of a promising new gold mine at Gnow's Nest, some 20 miles out of Yalgoo, and the prospect of yet another mine opening at Field's Find, breathed new life into the town. It was anticipated that at least 70 men would eventually be employed on the mine and, in view of the expected rise in population, building a convent and school once again became a top priority. Determined not to waste more time than was necessary, Father Hawes again contacted the Dongara community on 7 August. 'For the sake of the children here', he wrote, 'I am anxious for a Catholic school and should you consider it wise & prudent to start & see your way clear to make a foundation from Dongara, I should give my energetic support to it'. [12]

84. Dominican Chapel during construction, 1921.
Courtesy Geraldton Diocesan Archives

Teams were already busily carting machinery to Gnow's Nest mine when, on 22 August 1921, he received confirmation that the Dominican Sisters were still willing to form a foundation at Yalgoo. Parishioners were immediately stirred into action when they heard the news and promptly responded by raising £40 after Mass for the proposed foundation. Subscription lists were later distributed and committee members began to organise a Popular Girl Competition in conjunction with a bazaar to be held during Race Week at the end of September. A great deal of social activity surrounded the competition and residents were showered with invitations to attend various functions in aid of the candidates. [13]

On 11 September, the Prioress was notified that a request for a grant of land had been sent to the Commissioner of Lands, Mr Troy. She also learnt that, in anticipation of the commissioner's approval, Father Hawes had not only secured the services of a first-rate young carpenter, Harry Jermy, but he had also tentatively made arrangements to have the redundant former Dominican Convent at Day Dawn transported to Yalgoo. When it arrived, it was intended to re-erect the building on an elevated site and enlarge it for use as a school. Space was to be left for a new stone convent with verandahs protecting the front elevation. It was planned also to construct a small convent chapel of local stone on the west end of the building. Father Hawes enclosed a rough sketch plan in his letter and asked the Sisters to examine his proposals and to comment on any improvements or alterations they might wish to make. [14] Three days later, another note was sent asking Mother Bonaventure, 'whether the School Rooms should be connected with, or adjoining the Boarders' House – or separated by a fence & put 20 yards or so apart – to keep the day-scholars out of the boarding quarters?'. [15]

Towards the end of September, Father Hawes wrote to thank the Mother Prioress for the painting she had donated and sent down for the bazaar and at the same time informed her that he had received notification that the Land's Department had granted the Catholic Church an acre of land in Henty Street. The block, which was once part of the Emerald Reward Gold Mine and not included in the original town survey, overlooked the township. Keen to begin, Fr Hawes decided he would delay the completion of the church he was building at Mullewa, and sent a letter to Sister Bernard Rogers at Cue, asking her to advise Mr Kelly to send the disused building down from Day Dawn as soon as possible. [16]

The materials arrived from Day Dawn on 20 October 1921, and within a week the foundation and posts had been put in position and the framework of the schoolroom walls had been erected. The project's carpenter, Hendry (Harry) Cutton Jermy, described by Father Hawes as 'a man whose heart is all in his work', [17] had arrived in Australia from England about the same time as Yalgoo's priest, although it appears that he did not settle in the area until after the war. It is evident that Jermy and the architect priest had enormous respect for each other's talents and during the early 1920s they worked well as a team on both the Dominican Convent and chapel in Yalgoo and the church and Presentation Convent in Mullewa.

According to information sent by Father Hawes to the Sisters at Dongara, the whole building was to have a frontage of 110 feet, inclusive of the schoolroom. In an effort to improve the former Day Dawn convent, Fr Hawes decided to make various alterations such as raising the height of the walls and widening the east wing from 10 feet 2 inches to 11 feet 6 inches. He also changed the kitchen, adding a little dining room with serving hatch beside it for boarders. The building, when completed, was to have stone fireplaces and chimneys and the priest expressed the wish that, until the stone extensions in the front were completed, the Sisters would temporarily take their meals in the kitchen. He later proposed to erect a small trellised summerhouse on the north-west corner of the building away from the kitchen, the heat and the flies. Father Hawes finally suggested that the nuns might consider either Tuesday, 1 February 1922, or the following Monday, 7 February, as the possible opening date for the new Dominican school. Either day, he stressed, would be well in advance of the opening of the State School. He was cautious, however, about promising to have the water scheme ready and indicated that in the meantime the Sisters might have to make do with rain water tanks and carting a certain amount of water. [18]

The six candidates in the successful Popular Girl Competition, the Misses Mollie Clark, Grace Rodan, Thelma Hazeldene, Nellie Flanagan, Kathleen O'Donohue and Phoebe Buckingham (who married Hendry Jermy on 26 May 1923), raised £312 and it was hoped that the bazaar, to be held on 7 December 1921, would be just as profitable. In the meantime, the new building was making steady progress. By November, the framework of the convent had been completed, and the schoolroom where Harry Jermy camped and had his workbench was already floored and roofed. Because it was considered that the old Day Dawn building could suffer badly in the first strong gust of wind, a decision was made to strengthen the framework by using new heavier timber (jarrah). Although the extra work meant a certain amount of delay, it was considered a sensible move in view of the district's unpredictable weather.[19]

At the time of his death, on 26 December 1921, Bishop William Kelly had been in charge of his Episcopal See for 23 years, and until his successor, Father Richard Ryan CM, was appointed in 1923, Father Hawes continued to work on the buildings earlier approved by his close friend the Bishop of Geraldton. The news of the bishop's death could not have come at a worse time for the architect-priest, who at that stage was not only trying to complete the Dominican buildings at Yalgoo, but also the stone church at Mullewa. His attendance at the impressive interment ceremony, held in the cathedral he had earlier designed for Bishop Kelly, along with other related matters, meant that he was absent from Yalgoo at a crucial stage. On 3 January 1922, Fr Hawes apologised to the Dominican Sisters for not having finished the building before the community took up residence. He admitted that unless he could find a second reliable carpenter to assist in speeding up the process, he could not hope to get the project completed by the end of the month. He indicated that his experience, so far, led him to believe that 'only incapable men who wanted a pound a day, for ten shillings worth of work' were willing to apply.

Father Hawes planned to finish off the main building of the convent by the end of the month, leaving the external painting and final details involving the verandahs, bathroom and schoolroom until later. It was his intention to open the school temporarily in the two dormitories, which unfortunately meant that the Sisters could not accept boarders for the first month. These included the two children belonging to Mr and Mrs Halligan, who occupied the manager's house at the State Battery, Payne's Find, as well as the children of another married couple living at Gnow's Nest mine. The workmen generally appeared on the site at 8.00 a.m. and remained until 5.00 p.m. and the priest assured the Sisters that noise would be kept to a minimum so as not to interrupt lessons. [20] Three weeks later, Fr Hawes once more provided an up-to-date report on the situation. He informed the Prioress that the building would not be ready the following week, despite Mr Jermy doing his utmost to finish the job, working in temperatures which sometimes reached 118 degrees Fahrenheit (48 degrees Celsius). He enquired if the Sisters could arrive on Friday, 10 February, and open school on the following Monday or Tuesday, when he guaranteed that the building, with the exception of the schoolroom, would be ready. The priest also mentioned that the parish ladies had held a meeting to consider two estimates for the purchase of a piano from either Nicholson's or Thompson's Stores in Perth. The latter appeared to offer a better reduction on a Beale piano and it was decided to get Mrs McKenna, who was in the city, to select a suitable instrument. [21]

By way of apology, Father Hawes explained that there had been several reasons for the unexpected delays on the school. A powerful 'willy willy' had not only blown down a number of buildings in the town, which necessitated the carpenters leaving their work on the convent to make urgent repairs, but one of the labourers had suffered a bout of influenza and another had been delayed for a week. The priest's own work on the small chapel also had to be set aside when he spent a fortnight in Geraldton to attend Bishop Kelly's funeral. Indeed Fr Hawes admitted that it would be at least another week before he got back to Yalgoo as he had to return first to Mullewa. He added, 'I am engaged on plastering the chapel now – I want the Sisters to have a comfortable, cool place to say their prayers in – as cool as can be up here in the summer time! Thick stone walls, good roof & plenty of ventilators etc help that way'. [22]

The Dominican Convent Chapel of St Hyacinth, designed and built by Father Hawes, was constructed of local stone, the medium most-loved by the architect-priest. Described by heritage architect, John Taylor, as 'an Inter-War Romanesque style masonry chapel with terra cotta tiled roof',' it was, Taylor stated, 'the smallest of Hawes' church designs world-wide'. [23] Access to the chapel was originally through the attached convent, which has since been demolished. The 70-foot high bell tower had a set of four chiming bells with an attached rope used by the bell-ringer. For many years the Sisters continued to ring the Angelus on the chapel bells and the daily chimes became a familiar part of life in Yalgoo until the Dominican foundation closed.

85. St Hyacinth's Dominican Chapel and Convent, Yalgoo, c 1922

During the absence of a bishop in Geraldton, the administrator of the diocese, Father John Graber, appointed Mother Dominica Murphy as Superior and Sacristan of St Hyacinth's Convent in Yalgoo, and Sister Reginald Rice as Procuratrix and Mistress of Schools. It was agreed that Sister Evangelist Graham was to accompany them as the third member of the foundation. Her time at Yalgoo was brief and shortly afterwards her place was taken by Sister Aloysius Pickerd. As usual, Father Hawes kept the community at Dongara informed about proceedings. He explained that the Sisters would be met on the evening of their arrival by Mrs Clarke, a parishioner who had arranged to have a fish meal served to the Sisters in a private room at the railway refreshment rooms. Bedsteads, bedding, a dozen chairs, kitchen utensils and a set of crockery had been supplied from a list provided by Mrs Rodan and, after being driven to their new home in Henty Street, the Sisters would find that most of the essential furnishings were already in place. The priest hoped that they would be willing to wait patiently for their chests of drawers and wash stands until Mr Jermy found the time to make them. 'The wood', he wrote, 'was already on site and it was expected to work out much cheaper if the carpenter crafted them, for apart from the purchase price there were freight expenses to be considered'. Finally, Fr Hawes suggested that the official opening ceremony for St Hyacinth's Convent could be held over until later in the year, in which case he thought the Prioress might care to travel up for the occasion and at the same time inspect the completed works. [24]

The front entrance gate, set halfway along the picket fence, was constantly opened and closed during the Sisters' first week in residence as parishioners and parents alike pushed past the lintel displaying the title 'St Hyacinth's Convent', either to welcome the newcomers or to enrol their children. The convent school finally opened for classes on 24 February 1922, with 23 pupils in attendance. It appears that by the end of the following month, the dormitories, built for prospective boarders, were still being used for classrooms. Nine-year-old Kathleen O'Connor (Sr Joseph O'Connor's sister), was one of three O'Connor girls educated by the Dominicans. When writing on 21 March 1922, to 'Aunt Bessie', who conducted the Children's Page in the *West Australian Catholic Record*, she stated:

*The Sisters are very nice. We had Mass in the chapel the day after the Sisters came up. The chapel is lovely. The roof outside is tiled. The tower is very large and has four bells in it. Carmel is learning the piano, Mollie the banjo and I am going to learn the violin later on. The schoolroom is not finished yet. There are 23 children going to school and they expect more after Easter.* [25]

The foundress of St Hyacinth's, Sister Dominica Murphy, a tall, short-sighted Irish woman with piercing blue eyes, was one of the six foundresses of the Dominican Order in Western Australia. During her years as a religious in the Geraldton diocese, Sr Dominica served not only as local Superior in branch houses, but also as Dominican Prioress at Dongara. She taught religion in Yalgoo and gave music lessons after school to a number of children and adults. The artistic side of her nature came to the fore during the lead up to concert time and nothing delighted Sr Dominica more than when a pastoralist showed interest in a performance, or when a lonely old prospector eagerly asked, 'When is the next convent kids' concert coming up?'. According to one of her former pupils, Mary O'Connor (who later joined the Dominican community), Sr Dominica had a great sense of humour which was particularly evident when the elderly nun recounted amusing tales about the early pioneering days. Recalling some of the stories earlier told to her, Mary O'Connor, now Sr Joseph, wrote:

*One I remember was about a horse called Rosy which was given to them to travel between Cue and Day Dawn. Mother [Dominica] was a great horsewoman and loved to drive. Rosy was temperamental and did not like to be driven, so one day she just sat down on the road and refused to budge. All Mother's cajoling and threats couldn't shift her, so Mother (in full stiff headdress, habit and cloak) got out of the sulky and sat on Rosy's head! She said that it was the only way to shift a stubborn horse. Rosy objecting to this form of humiliation, rose swiftly and tipped Mother off. Luckily she was able to get back on the seat and take the reins before Rosy took off at a great pace and... they got to school on time. When I told some of the senior Sisters they said, "Don't believe it, Mother often draws the long bow when she gets a good listener"'.* [26]

St Hyacynth's second foundation teacher, Sister Reginald Rice, is remembered by most of her past pupils for her sense of fun and large brown eyes that could not hide a hint of laughter. A prayerful person, she taught the upper primary classes at Yalgoo and on Wednesdays gave sewing lessons for which the pupils paid a small amount and supplied the materials. By the end of the year

86. St Hyacinth's Convent pupils, 1925
L. to R. Back Row: Peter Coyne, Tom O'Connor, Peter Moore, George Sheldon, Reg Clarke, Luke Bunter, Joe Elder, Pat O'Connor, Georgie Pearce, Allan Powell,
Middle: Gwen Clarke, May Coyne, Grace Powell, Kath O'Connor, Carmel O'Connor, Mollie O'Connor, Rene Nielson, Edie Powell, Nellie Powell
Front: Ethel Moore, Alma Clarke, Johnny Coyne, Annie Moore, Jane Bunter

Sr Reginald's sewing classes presented a fine display of doileys, supper cloths and duchess sets, all beautifully completed in fancywork and finished with crocheted edges. Pupils who reached a certain standard were thrilled when Sister took them aside and showed them how to do shadow-work on delicate organdie pillow shams. Sister Evangelist Graham, hardworking and loyal, took care of the convent's household chores, including the cooking, and spent the few moments of leisure she had by knitting or doing crochet work.

Although there had been a noticeable winding down of gold mining operations since World War I, a considerable number of prospectors continued to work on small leases throughout the 1920s and 1930s, often bringing ore into the battery for crushing. To meet the needs of increased enrolments an extra classroom was added in 1926 and, two years later, Mr Wally Holmes successfully bored for water and later erected a windmill. Further improvements embraced new playground areas, which were enclosed with a completely different style of fencing from the picket fence used elsewhere on the property. The closure of the Gnow's Nest mine in 1929 and the frightening effects of a world-wide depression, saw many pastoralists suffering financially and country areas inundated by an influx of city people searching for work. According to author Alex Palmer, Yalgoo, because it was the first gold town on the Geraldton-Meekatharra railway line, received more than its share of unemployed men, fossickers and down-and-outs during the early 1930s recession. By 1942, all mining operations had wound down and Yalgoo's population had fallen to such a level that the government school had to close its doors for several years, leaving the few pupils they had left to enrol at the convent. At that stage, the whole of Australia was deeply embroiled in a Second World War and faced an extremely uncertain future.

Sister Dominic Galvin, who taught at Yalgoo during the late 1940s, with Sisters Michael Ryan and Raymund Creed (Superior), described the area as being generally barren, dry, hot and prone to frequent summer dust storms. The town, which at that time was showing signs of being run-down, consisted of one hotel and two stores, Coyne's and Nevill's. The highly-respected owners of these stores were both extremely generous to the Sisters and the Church, as were Yalgoo's Town Clerk and Justice of the Peace, Mr Jack O'Connor and his wife and daughters. The number of boarders enrolled at St Hyacinth's after the war was never extensive and very often they included members of the same family. Sister Dominic recalled that in one particular year, eight female boarders and one small boy were enrolled, two of the girls and the boy coming from one family. 'All the boarders', she wrote, 'played happily with one another, regardless of race'. [27] Some railway employees lived in a row of houses near the railway station and several of their children attended the convent school, including the stationmaster Mr Smythe's two sons. The younger boy was enrolled in primary school classes and, because the parents were reluctant to send the older brother away to boarding school for higher education, Sr Dominic was asked to tutor him in addition to teaching the junior primary school classes. Both the parents and Dominican Sisters were jubilant when the student successfully gained his Junior Certificate. Music lessons were conducted in a small room next to the sacristy and Sr Dominic recalls that two of the most talented music pupils at that time were Colleen and Michael McDonald. Yalgoo's annual fancy dress ball was always a major event and pupils from St Hyacinth's Convent looked forward to participating each year. Mrs Nevill, the mother of Gloria, one of St Hyacinth's pupils, was a keen supporter of the Sisters and she not only assisted with the costumes, but also instructed the children in marching and dancing.

The school building during the late 1940s, was described as a long, galvanised iron structure, with a schoolroom that ran the length of the building. One Sister taught the upper primary classes at one end of the room, while another was responsible for the lower primary school children at the other end. No partition existed between the classes and occasionally for a change, Sister Dominic took the younger pupils outside where they received their lessons al fresco in an open bough shed. For a special holiday treat, St Hyacinth's boarders were sometimes taken for a picnic in the bush. Everyone contributed to the event by carrying the food and other essentials. This included a large kerosene tin of water that had a long, stout stick threaded through the handle for easier cartage and to minimise spillage. For relaxation, the Sisters, not wishing to break their rule of enclosure by appearing in public, often walked in the nearby bush on Sundays, enjoying both the peaceful surroundings and the exercise.

Because of the shortage of priests, the liturgy was only occasionally celebrated on the Sabbath and when this happened one of the Sisters, accompanied by one or two boarders, would walk down to the church at the bottom of the hill to make preparations. Decorating the altar was not always an easy task because, with the exception of the wildflower season, there was a limited choice of flowers or foliage surrounding the convent and church. [28] A grotto, said to be a replica of the Holy Sepulchre, had earlier been fashioned from an old open cut at the rear of the convent. In all probability, Father Hawes's original intention was to utilise the stone-lined excavation as a cooler, for he had used that description when he marked the spot on one his early sketch plans. The Francis children, Dorne and Hilary, boarded at Yalgoo during the 1940s and both recall playing in the grotto, more commonly referred to by the children as the Sepulchre. Stonework formed the top section of the hollow, which featured a large cross surmounted on a cairn or boulder. A circular stairwell led down to a subterranean chamber of stone which had sufficient ceiling height to allow a person to stand comfortably and a ledge on which lay an effigy of Jesus in bas-relief. Years later, those who remembered the peace and tranquillity of the little 'quiet room', were devastated to discover that the cross had disappeared and the grotto had been filled with rubbish. [29] Fond memories also remain of the now demolished school and convent featuring, among other things, a fireplace in the convent parlour, which, in typical Hawes fashion, displayed a niche. In this particular case the recess was used to hold a statue of the Immaculate Virgin and a fitting Latin inscription carved by the priest on the wall above clearly read, *Beati immaculata in via qui ambulant in lege Domini*. The quotation, taken from Psalm 119, translated reads, 'How blessed are those whose way is blameless, who walk in the law of the Lord'.

Apart from the three foundation members, the following Sisters were assigned to the convent at Yalgoo, between 1923 and 1949: Anastasia Byrne, Baptist Hall, Benignus O'Connor, Teresa McQuillan, Brigid Kelly, Berchmans Wilson, Alocoque Culhane, Carmel Keeley, Raphael Wood, Dolores Lloyd, Jordan Leddin, Hyacinth Carroll, Peter Geeson, Pius Nolan,

Bertrand O'Connor, Michael Ryan, Magdalen Lewis, Dominic Galvin, Gabriel Barden and Raymund Creed. Sister Raymund, an outgoing personality, gifted needle-woman and dedicated teacher was fondly known as 'Aunty Ray' to many of her friends. Sister Raymund who arrived in Western Australia from New Zealand in 1927, was appointed local Superior of the convent and principal of St Hyacinth's school in 1946, and became the last Dominican to serve in that capacity before the foundation finally closed in 1950.

Education Inspector Alex Dineen commenced his half-yearly report on St Hyacinth's, Yalgoo, in June 1950, by stating, 'This is undoubtedly one of the most charming and efficient little schools I have yet seen'. Unfortunately, a decline in the district's mining activities and the accompanying loss of population was gradually reflected in the number of pupils attending the school and the Dominican community had no choice but to withdraw. The buildings, at first rented out to various local families, were eventually sold to members of the Nevill family who dismantled the structures and re-used the material to erect a shearing shed on their station property.

Today, Monsignor Hawes has earned his place in history. Once described by Bishop Kelly as 'priest, architect, painter, decorator, poet, horseman and horse-breaker', he was a man of many talents who has left behind an architectural heritage trail that surpasses any single contribution made throughout Australia. In 1980, following a 10 year consideration, a decision was made to restore the former Dominican Convent Chapel. After the Sisters' departure from the district the buildings slowly began to deteriorate, until only the ruins of St Hyacinth's Chapel and the convent chimneys remained. Over the years, concern was expressed for the loss of the heritage chapel. In 1977, despite tenders having been called, an expected grant was not forthcoming and the project did not proceed. The Shire, recognising the building's significance and its potential as a tourist attraction, decided to press ahead regardless. As a result, in 1980, builder T. G. Fernihough was contracted to undertake the major restoration of the chapel for an estimated cost of $17,000. Mr Warwick Broomfield, who was appointed as architect, was given the brief to restore the building as close as possible to the original. [30]

To represent the order, a group of Dominican Sisters and former Yalgoo teachers travelled from various centres to attend the opening of the restored chapel. Concelebrating with the newly-ordained Father Michael Morrissey, son of local identities Harry and Margaret Morrissey from Noongall Station, was Father Peter McCrann, whose father was at one stage postmaster at Yalgoo, and Father Robert Cross, a fellow student at the seminary. The official re-opening of St Hyacinth's Dominican chapel took place on Sunday, 7 June 1981, before a crowd of some 500 people, including the guest of honour, the Premier of Western Australia, Sir Charles Court. Vicar General, Monsignor Bryan, who at the time was parish priest of the Mullewa parish, reflected on the use of the name St Hyacinth, who as a martyr for his faith was put to death in A.D. 269. Both Monsignor Bryan and Sir Charles then paid homage to John Hawes, the man responsible for the creation of the original chapel, as well as the dedicated Dominican Sisters who, as Sir Charles stated, 'carried the arts to the country' – a view endorsed by tens of thousands of Western Australians who had or have benefited from being taught music, singing, painting, craft-work, literature, languages, art of speech, and drama by religious teachers in convent schools.

The Shire undertook the $24,000 project, $10,000 of which was a grant from the Heritage Commission, and the State Government, through the Premier, donated a further $5000. After years of silence, as the plaque was unveiled, the long forgotten peal of the chapel bells rang out from the restored tower and for a short while it seemed as though time had stood still. [31]

87. Opening of restored Dominican Chapel, Yalgoo, 1981
L. to R. Back Row: Sisters Mary Ryan, Regina O'Neill, Gemma Seaman, Margaret Scharf, Anthony Sachse, Bernardine Hanafin,
Middle: Sisters Helen O'Connor, Dominic Galvin, Anne Graham, Bernadette Punch,
Front: Sisters Margaret Vance, Teresa Martelli, Edith Murphy, Xavier Ryan

## SANTA SABINA CONVENT AND ST JOSEPH'S SCHOOL, MINGENEW

The wheatbelt town of Mingenew, situated 38 miles east of Dongara, was originally part of large land holdings leased at different times to a number of well-known pioneers. Two of these, Samuel Pole Phillips and Edward Hamersley, had selected the first two leases in the Upper Irwin region (Mingenew) as early as September 1850 and on each 20,000 acre lease of 'finely grassed and well-watered land' they initially ran cattle. [1] Later, in partnership with other well-known colonists Vigors and Burges, a successful cattle breeding company was formed. In the 1870s, taking advantage of the excellent grazing lands that existed in the area, sheep farming took hold in the Mingenew district and pastoral leases continued to increase in numbers throughout the 1890s. The international demand for wool continued to rise during the post-war period and, by the 1930s, the pastoral industry, earlier established in the Mingenew region, had become a highly successful commercial venture. Prominent among those who followed in the wake of the first settlers and have had a long association with the district, are the names of Broad, Whitfield, du Boulay, Morrissey, Pearse, Fane, Foss, Smith and Lee Steere. [2]

The name Mingenew, was said to have originated from either the Aboriginal word 'Mininoo', meaning 'place of many waters', or 'Minganu', 'place of many ants'. [3] As well as being on an important stock route, Mingenew was also a significant depot for the Murchison goldfields, which were proclaimed in 1891, and as predicted, had an enormous impact on the development of towns and districts north and north-east of Perth. As mentioned earlier, by 1909, large tracts of land had been selected and cleared along the railway line between Mingenew and Carnamah. Described as 'a magnificent belt of country', [4] the land in question, which was suitable for agriculture and in close proximity to both the railway and port, was commercially developed on a large scale over the years to support a successful wheat growing industry. Gradually the township began showing signs of residential growth and the expectations of an increasing population eventually began to dictate the size and shape of the town boundaries. At the turn of the century, the township, by then 10 years old, had two hotels, four general stores, three blacksmiths and wheelwrights. The foundation stone for an Anglican church had been laid, and, between 1908 and 1912, a group of Methodists completed a church on the corner of Irwin and Victoria Streets. At that stage, Catholic residents, although keen to build their own church, still attended monthly Mass in the local hall. [5]

On 22 September 1910, a fund-raising event in the form of a bazaar was organised by Mesdames Rayner, Beckett, Black, Linthorne and O'Connor and the Misses Craig, Grave, Beckett and O'Connor, and on that occasion the ladies managed to raise £54 in aid of the church fund. The Catholic population at Mingenew was not large, however, and at that time most settlers were trying to establish properties and therefore had little time, or money, to spare. Father O'Hare, in charge of Dongara, was aware of the problems they faced and in November 1910, he was persuaded to appeal to the readers of the *Sower* to help with contributions towards a church at Mingenew. At the same time, he also acknowledged the generous gifts already donated by Mrs Rayner (a silver chalice), Mrs Black (altar cruets), Mr O'Halloran (altar charts), Miss Craig (a set of vestments purchased from the £4 she had earlier raised), and members of the church committee, who had bought an altar stone, missal and stand with the proceeds of a successful euchre party. [6]

88. First St Joseph's Church, Mingenew

As with many other towns in the Geraldton diocese, Mingenew celebrated St Patrick's Day with great enthusiasm. Catholic parishioners with Irish backgrounds were extremely proud of their origins, and the traditional holiday generally served as a nostalgic reminder of the past. The gala family event, on 17 March 1912, arranged by members of St Joseph's Church, not only raised much-needed funds, but practically brought the township to a standstill. A member of the Geraldton press captured the mood of the day soon afterwards:

*St Patrick's Day was celebrated here by one of the most successful day's sports held in Mingenew. The weather was all that could be desired for the holiday seekers, who came for miles around. It was quite a fete day. The business places closed at noon, and the anniversary of the Patron Saint was honoured by all classes. If a ballot had been taken in Mingenew that day for Home Rule it would have been carried by a large majority. There were eight events on the programme and all passed off without a hitch, which speaks well for the handicapper, Mr W. Linthorne. The stewards also are to be complimented on the manner in which they fulfilled their duties. The "books" did a fair amount of business and also the booths which were in the capable hands of Mr R. Humerston, of the Mingenew Hotel. Roulette and other harmless but exciting games were in evidence. The beaming and benevolent countenance of the Rev. Father Hilly was seen to be smiling on all denominations, and it was in aid of funds for his church that the large crowd had come together. The whole of the events of the day and the dance and concert given in the evening, were under the directorship of the Hon. Secretary, Mr W. Kearney, and too much praise cannot be given for the indefatigable and courteous manner in which he brought to a successful issue one of the most enjoyable programmes given in Mingenew. In the evening a most enjoyable and successful dance, interspersed with song, was held in the local hall, and largely attended. The duties of M.C. were carried out in Mr Jacob Herbert's usual obliging and courteous manner, while the musical portion was left in the hands of Mr S. Bennett, who fulfilled his duties in a capable manner, leaving nothing to be desired at the termination of a very pleasant evening.* [7]

In 1912, the first St Joseph's Catholic Church, a modest timber and iron structure, was erected on the corner of Irwin and William Streets. Visiting priests continued to celebrate Mass once a month and when necessary arranged to conduct other important services. Early priests, besides Fathers C. O'Hare and T. Hilly were Father R. Scanlan, an Irish priest, who in the 1920s travelled monthly by train from Moora, and popular Father J. Hawes, who used to ride from Mullewa to Mingenew on his black horse. By 1922, Father J. Tymens had taken charge of the district followed by Father J. Flavahan and once again Father C. O'Hare. Father Michael Lynch, the proud owner of a new single-seater Chrysler motor car, was appointed in 1928 and remained in the area until 1944. [8] Like Monsignor Hawes, the future Dean Lynch had an interest in horse-racing. An oft-repeated story is told about the time he purchased a horse from a breeder at Three Springs. Thinking to dissuade backers and receive a good price from the bookies, he named the animal, 'Poor Softy'. To everyone's surprise the title he chose belied the horse's efforts and good breeding showed through when it won races at Mingenew, Arrino and Yandanooka as well as the Three Springs Cup. [9]

In 1932, people in the town witnessed the establishment of yet another Dominican foundation in the Geraldton diocese when Bishop O'Collins, assisted by Father Lynch, blessed and opened St Joseph's

89. Original convent, Mingenew

convent school at Mingenew on 20 February 1932. Accommodation had earlier been arranged for Sisters Aquin Inglis, Berchmans Wilson, Pius Nolan and Evangelist Graham, the four founding members of the community, in a house close to the church-school. In 1931, in anticipation of the Sisters' arrival, the original old wood and iron Catholic Church at Strawberry, used in 1918 to house the school at Strawberry Siding, was transported to Mingenew and added to the east wall of St Joseph's Church for use as an additional classroom. [10] According to one of the original pupils, a number of Catholic children transferred from the government school at the time of opening. [11] The decision to recycle the old building was therefore justified.

In keeping with the majority of early convent schools founded in country areas, a concert was the first major activity organised by the Sisters at Mingenew. The event not only helped financially, but it also alerted non-Catholic parents to the wide range of artistic subjects available through private tuition. Sister Bertrand O'Connor, a past pupil, recalled some of the 'behind the scenes' incidents that were never apparent to the audience. On one occasion, it seems that her small brother had been given the part of the bridegroom in a performance of *The Wedding of the Painted Doll*. The children had gathered in the hall at 2.30 p.m. for the rehearsal when it became obvious that the star performer had disappeared. Upon his unexpected arrival home, a surprised Mrs O'Connor enquired why he was not at school. Cornered, the unhappy youngster replied, 'If they think that I'm going to marry that girl, I won't do it, so there!'. A simple explanation and a word of encouragement from his mother saw the young boy reluctantly return to his 'bride' and the 'wedding', much to everyone's amusement. [12]

In 1944, Father Brian Gallagher, the parish priest of Three Springs, took charge of the district and until his departure in 1951, when Father George Sharry replaced him, he formed a close-knit relationship with his parishioners. The number of pupils in attendance at St Joseph's fluctuated during the Second World War. In 1945, only 15 children were enrolled in the school and yet, despite the low numbers and unsettled times, the Sisters continued to teach. Although class numbers had still not increased by 1947, the school inspector's report for that year pointed out that with 40 per cent of pupils listed as Aboriginal, teachers at St Joseph's had spent a great deal of their spare time providing extra assistance to improve their skills. The report also stated that, whilst the present accommodation was more than adequate for the size of the enrolment, the teachers were handicapped by the lack of a suitable building and equipment. [13]

Mingenew's temperature changed markedly from near to freezing point at times in winter to extremely hot during the summer months. It has, factually or otherwise, the reputation of being the hottest place in Western Australia after Marble Bar and Meekatharra, and with few improvements made over the years, conditions in the original timber and iron church were exceptionally trying in both seasons. By April 1950, the roll call recorded 22 children in classes ranging from Infants to Grade VI. In a move to rectify some of the inadequacies earlier mentioned, Father Gallagher and Perth architect Mr Summerhayes, met in September 1950 to discuss plans to erect a new Dominican school and to select a suitable site. [14]

The new one-room schoolhouse, built in William Street, drew favourable comments when it opened for classes in 1951, and in view of the number of pupils in attendance its size was considered to be more than adequate. The sudden expansion of the Mingenew district during the 1950s, however, meant that within 10 months the enrolments at St Joseph's had increased to a total of 32 children. A half-yearly class report, written in 1952, applauded the teaching efforts of Sister Xavier Ryan and Sister Teresa McQuillan, but warned that, whilst the standard and condition of the building was excellent, the room was beginning to show signs of overcrowding. [15] To meet the needs of a growing community, an additional classroom was therefore erected the following year at a cost of £1700. Mr A. H. Trotman, the District Superintendent of Schools, examined St Joseph's pupils in 1953 and under the two headings 'Accommodation' and 'General' added the following comments to his 3 June report:

90. St Joseph's School, Mingenew, 1960
Courtesy Mingenew Shire

91. Winners of Inter-Schools Sports, St Joseph's School, Mingenew, 1966

*With the completion of the second classroom now in the course of construction a most pleasing educational establishment will be added to the district. The completed classroom, with its modern furnishings and abundance of teaching aids and general air of efficiency is a delight... Both teachers are to be commended for their application. The school is performing a valuable service for the community and for this the teachers are to be highly commended. Noticeable features are the very fine school tone and the attempt to build up academic attainment in both skills and cultural subjects.* [16]

Mr Trotman's summary of the higher classes continued, 'there is a splendid working spirit and a pleasant friendly atmosphere in this room. Sr Berchmans Wilson has organised well and taught most efficiently'. Similarly, Mr Trotman noted that in the lower classes, 'good habit training is a feature. Sr Teresa McQuillan's efforts on behalf of these children are most praiseworthy. Much good work has been done'. [17]

In November 1954, the Bishop of Geraldton, Dr A. J. Gummer, officially blessed and opened the newly-completed Santa Sabina Dominican Convent in Irwin Street. The building, erected at a cost of £6300 by one of the Church's regular building contractors, Stan Costello of Kalamunda, followed in the wake of the new school extensions. Members of the Catholic community, who had enthusiastically supported both projects, volunteered to cart bricks from the Irwin brickworks in readiness for the builder to commence the new convent. The Sisters, who for over 20 years had occupied a small house in Victoria Street, were overjoyed with their new quarters. Not only were members of the Mingenew Dominican community at that time, Sisters Dominic Galvin, Teresa McQuillan, Augustine Corbett and Brigid Kelly, in a position to enjoy the comfort of a modern brick and tile building, which included a private chapel and wide verandahs, but the three teachers among them had the added bonus of being able to teach in spacious new classrooms of the latest design. Sister Dominic, who spent her first and only year at Mingenew in 1954, recalled that the recently-completed school building had special ceilings fitted to reduce the noise, a set of flush toilets close to the end of the building, and in front of the blackboard a raised platform for better pupil viewing. By then attendance had reached the 60 mark. [18]

Mingenew, which had previously been included in the parish of Three Springs, became an independent parish in 1957, when Father Keith Spain was transferred from Three Springs and appointed the first resident parish priest. To complete Mingenew's Catholic complex, a small dwelling for the priest, built opposite the police station, and a new St Joseph's Church were officially opened by Bishop Gummer on 28 June 1959. Designed in a traditional style with a slight Dutch influence, the cream brick building, constructed by Geraldton builder Mr W. Marcolina, featured green terracotta tiles and an unusual cone shaped bell tower. [19]

In the 1960s, the area administered by the Mingenew Road Board had a population of some 1000 persons, approximately half of whom lived in the town. By then the town centre was well-established and comprised most of the public buildings usually found in

Western Australian wheatbelt towns. Father Spain withdrew from the parish in 1961 and, for the brief time that Mingenew was without a resident priest, members of the Catholic Ladies' Guild met regularly to keep the parish intact. It was during the appointment of Father Paul Fitzgerald, between 1961 and 1962, that a decision was made to purchase the residence belonging to the Oliver family, opposite the Catholic Church, for use as a presbytery. As usual St Joseph's parishioners were quick to offer assistance, and during the time that it took to renovate the building there was no shortage of volunteer labour. Unfortunately, parish expenses did not end there, for when the number of pupils attending St Joseph's School exceeded 86, the parish priest, Father M. O'Flaherty, became responsible in 1963 for the building of a third classroom to cope with a further influx of pupils. [20]

The news that Father Keith Spain had been re-appointed in 1972, was met with great enthusiasm by many people, including members of the Dominican community, Sisters Bertrand O'Connor, Dolores Cummins and Margaret Vance. The priest, often described as a humble and generous man, was involved over the years in many worthwhile diocesan projects, including the Bushies' School and the introduction of the lay missionary scheme. An active sportsman, he enjoyed tennis, golf, bowls, fishing and chess, and was an ardent follower of both football and cricket. These interests gave him the opportunity to mix with others in an ecumenical setting and also earned him the respect of many young people who tried to emulate his sporting achievements. It could be assumed that some of his fervour for competitive sports and the encouragement he gave to St Joseph pupils paid dividends when, to everyone's delight, the Dominican school at Mingenew won the shield at the Irwin Districts School Sports in 1972 and for the next three years.

A turning point in the Dominican Sisters' long involvement with the Geraldton diocese came in the 1970s. Confronted by a decrease in the number of postulants joining the order and the closure of the Priory

92. Pupils and staff, St Joseph's School, Mingenew, 1978
L. to R.: Sister Imelda Ryan, Miss Anne Seeber,

and Dominican Ladies' College at Dongara in 1971, the Sisters, who by then had established new foundations in Perth, found it increasingly difficult to spread their numbers. It therefore came as no surprise when, on 15 March 1978, the Prioress Provincial Mother Assumpta Moriarty, informed Father Spain that the community would be unable to staff the Mingenew school in 1979. Five days later, the chairman of St Joseph's School Board, the chairman of the Catholic Education Commission and Bishop Francis Xavier Thomas were also notified. Towards the end of 1978, Sister Anne Graham and Sister Imelda Ryan finalised the packing and closure of the convent. St Joseph's continued to function as a school when, under the guidance of the parish priest, two lay teachers were employed to take charge. Arrangements were made for the parish-owned school and former Oliver house to be sold and for the former convent to be rented out by the parish.

93. New Santa Sabina Convent, Mingenew

Although no longer associated with the district, the Sisters have fond memories of the 46 years spent at Mingenew, teaching the children and nurturing their faith. Former members of the Santa Sabina Convent community still recognise and value the contribution made by local families during the time they lived there. These included Mr and Mrs Cecil Newton, Mr and Mrs Tracy Cole, Mr and Mrs Paddy Lynch, Mesdames Dorothy Dowd and Frances Downes and all members of the Parents' and Friends' Association, in particular Messrs Eddie Stevens and John Rowe. Many residents, formerly associated with the Sisters, likewise remember the Dominican's who taught, counselled and befriended them over the years.

## OUR LADY HELP OF CHRISTIANS CONVENT AND SCHOOL, REEDY

On 22 December 1941, the Bishop of Geraldton officially blessed and opened the first Catholic church at Reedy, a mining township, 30 miles east of Cue, 50 miles south of Meekatharra and 18 miles from the railway at Tuckanarra. The three Murchison towns of Cue, Big Bell and Reedy (earlier listed as Reedy's),

94. Catholic church-school, Reedy

were significant gold mining centres during the 1930s and until the demise of Reedy after the Second World War and the closure of Big Bell in 1955, Cue benefited commercially from their prosperity and remained a bustling town. [1]

Having earlier accepted an invitation from Bishop O'Collins and the parish priest, Father Owen O'Connor, to establish a school at Reedy, three Dominican Sisters, Bernadette Punch, Stanislaus McDonough and Brigid Kelly, took up residence in September 1941, in the small corrugated iron, two-bedroom cottage provided for them. Sister Bernadette recalled later, that as foundation members they were warmly welcomed by the parishioners and given every assistance. Parents, obviously pleased that they could at last enrol their children at a convent school, decided to make a practical show of support and each week donated a grocery item, which was placed in a box at the shop and delivered to the convent every Friday. Shortly after the Sisters' arrival, classes commenced in the recently-completed church, and the initial roll call of approximately 40 pupils, the majority of them from the government school, more than vindicated the Sisters' move to Reedy. [2]

With the exception of a series of tragedies that touched their lives, the Sisters, on reflection, saw the foundation years at Reedy as being both a rewarding and happy experience. As with all mining developments, unexpected accidents were part of the daily risk that mining families constantly faced and because Reedy's close-knit population was small, a sudden bereavement cast a pall over the entire town. As it happened, the news of a mine fatality broke on the Saturday following the Dominicans arrival, which meant that, understandably, a fête organised to take place that afternoon was understandably cancelled. The victim, a near neighbour of the Sisters, was also the husband of a former boarder at the Dominican Ladies' College at Dongara and members of the convent community, whilst in a position to comfort, were also directly touched by his passing. Deaths involving young children were also commonplace and several young family members lost their lives during the Dominican Sisters first two years at Reedy. One of these, the son of another past pupil from Dongara, had died from burns and two young pupils, enrolled with the Dominican Sisters at Our Lady Help of Christians in Reedy, took ill and later died in hospital. [3]

95. Our Lady Help of Christians' Convent, Reedy

Although far from the bombing raids that took place at Darwin, Port Hedland and Broome, the Benedictine's Drysdale River Mission at Kalumburu and Broome, the fear of a Japanese invasion still affected those living in isolation on the Murchison. On 28 March 1942, under the headline 'Battle for Australia', readers of the *Murchison Times and Cue – Big bell – Reedy Advocate* were informed, 'The whole world is focussed on the impending battle for Australia – to forestall Japanese hopes of completely dominating the Pacific'. [4] In line with the remainder of Australia, various restrictions, including petrol rationing, were introduced and the question of evacuation was discussed at some length. In August 1942, the remaining population at Reedy were advised that the mine was about to close and families wishing to leave town were entitled to apply for emergency petrol. The sudden exodus of able-bodied men leaving the fields to join up and the loss of migrant workers, who for security reasons were interned for the duration of the war, meant that manpower was at a minimum. By the end of that year, the effects of the war had taken its toll and the mines at both Big Bell and Reedy had ceased to operate. [5]

The population of the district in 1944 was, Cue 414, Reedy 108, Tuckanarra 57, Big Bell 49 and Day Dawn 28, with some 86 persons living on neighbouring stations. [6] For members of the Dominican community living at Reedy towards the end of the war, life was very different from that experienced by the foundation members. Sisters Dominica Murphy, Xavier Ryan and Brigid Kelly found the town almost deserted and general living conditions poor when they arrived in 1944. The sanitary system by then was non-existent and residents were forced to make their own arrangements. Health, always a major concern in the outback, was even more of a problem during war-time and long-standing efforts to engage a doctor were not successful until, in 1944, Doctor Jury took up the challenge at Big Bell. Money was scarce and the Sisters, like other townspeople, had little to spare. Sister Xavier recalled the dilemma they were placed in on arrival, when they were each expected to pay 10 shillings fare to a man who had driven them from Tuckanarra to Reedy. At the time the local Superior had only a meagre £5 in her possession and after settling with the driver she was left in a vulnerable position the next morning when presented with an account for water rates which amounted to 30 shillings.

Only 12 pupils enrolled when the school opened in 1944, and although several families were able to pay the set school fee of one shilling a week, others were not in a position to contribute. In such cases parents generally showed their gratitude by delivering home-made scones and cakes and various perishables, whenever they could spare them. Apart from the priest who came out from Cue on Saturday afternoons and returned after Mass on Sundays, the Sisters saw few people and the distance from Cue and Dongara meant that for some the loneliness was at times a hardship difficult to overcome. [7]

The unexpected return of families to the district in 1947, meant that enrolments at Our Lady Help of Christians School that year increased to 31. Although encouraged by the sudden rise in numbers, the Sisters were also confronted with the immediate problem of accommodating so many children in the church. To overcome the crisis, it was decided that extra classes would be held on a narrow verandah enclosed with iron and hessian. Unfortunately, the space was limited and at times the teacher found it difficult to ease herself between the desks, let alone turn around to return to her desk. In addition to other inconveniences, the lighting in the church was less than satisfactory during dull weather, and in the summer months the heat concentrated in such a confined space often proved insufferable. Apart from working in less than comfortable conditions for seven years, all Sisters assigned to Reedy had the added burden of having to remove school furniture from the classroom each Friday in preparation for weekend Mass, and returning it again before lessons commenced on the Monday. [8]

The quality of the lessons given though, was never in question. A report, furnished by Education Inspector S. F. Thornbury on 30 July in 1947, informed the Dominican Prioress at Dongara that Sister Gabriel Barden was to be congratulated on the work she had achieved under such trying circumstances. His assessment report that year also stated that, in his opinion, the second member of staff, Sister Albertus Bain, had 'a good grip on her classes and was a teacher who thoroughly understood her pupils needs'. [9] When Sister Xavier returned to Reedy the following year, the community again included Sister Peter Geeson and Sister Brigid Kelly. By then, pupil numbers had increased to 40, three of these being first year high school students. At that time Sr Peter taught the lower classes and Sr Xavier was in charge of the upper classes.

The Dominican foundation, despite rising numbers, experienced only a brief resurgence. By the end of 1948, without warning, the mine had suddenly closed, and almost overnight Reedy's population disappeared, leaving less than 10 pupils in attendance at the school. Under these circumstances, the Dominican Sisters had no option, but to close Our Lady Help of Christians School and return to Dongara. Although not surviving long when compared to other foundations, the years spent at Reedy were extremely worthwhile. During that time, the Sisters not only provided religious education to children living in isolation, but they also gave support and spiritual comfort to families experiencing economic hardships and uncertainty during the difficult war years. Apart from the three foundation Sisters who established the Dominican convent and school at Reedy – Stanislaus McDonough, Bernadette Punch and Brigid Kelly – the other members who followed were, Sisters Albertus Bain, Bertrand O'Connor, Dominica Murphy, Peter Geeson, Pius Nolan, Teresa McQuillan and Xavier Ryan.

It did not take long for the town to fold and even less time for the population to desert their homes and businesses. A brief description of Reedy, written one year after the Dominican Sisters withdrew from of Our Lady Help of Christians Convent School, appears in Philip Heydon's history on the Murchison. Penned by the secretary of the then Cue Roads Board, the report leaves no illusions as to the fate of the once-lively goldfields town:

*I went out to Reedys and checked on all the places that had been dismantled during recent months and I have to report that there are very few buildings standing, only the Hotel, Barber's Shop, Eve's Store, Webster's old store, a store on the corner, Post office, RC Convent and Church, the C of E and a few dwellings, also a few mine houses, which I understand have nearly all been sold.* [10]

## MARIAN CONVENT AND SCHOOL, MORAWA, ST JOSEPH'S SCHOOL, PERENJORI AND THE MOTOR MISSION

The Dominican Sisters founded their last wheatbelt school in the Geraldton diocese in 1955, when the Prioress accepted an invitation to establish a new community at Morawa, 365 kilometres from Perth, via Three Springs, and 187 kilometres from Geraldton.

Before a parish was created at Morawa, Catholics living in the district relied on visiting priests from New Norcia, Tardun, Mullewa, Three Springs and Geraldton to celebrate the liturgy in the homes of various local residents, namely those of Messrs S. Valentine, C. Cole and T. Kramer. Later, as the township developed, the Morawa Hall was used as a temporary place of worship. The first visit of a priest to say Mass locally, was recorded in 1917 when Father John Hawes rode his bicycle from Mullewa to Merkanooka, calling on outlying farming properties en route. Other early priests associated with the foundation of the Catholic Church at Morawa were Fathers Michael Lynch, Augustine Spangenberg SAC, Albert Scherzinger SAC, Leo Hornung SAC, Franz Girke SAC, Anton Wellems SAC and Edward (Ted) Bryan. [1]

Along with Coorow and Mingenew, both Morawa and Perenjori became part of the Three Springs parish

96. Church of the Holy Cross, Morawa

in 1921, with Father Hart appointed as the first parish priest. In 1924, an enthusiastic group of Catholics, the majority of them from Merkanooka, called a meeting in the local hall at Morawa to establish a fund-raising committee to finance the erection of a parish church. The outcome of the evening's gathering was the formation of a strong body of members, namely: T. Kramer, C. Cole, J. Doody, H. Hepworth, N. Gill, M. Neagle, J. McCarthy, C. Valentine, S. Valentine, P. Haddock, J. Powell, M. and G. White and T. Bradley, who agreed to become the group's secretary. Although busy trying to establish their farms and businesses, the committee members grasped every opportunity over the next few years to hold various fund-raising events. By 1926, when the balance of the special account held at the Commonwealth Bank reached the sum of £131.3.7, the members felt confident enough to press forward with plans to build a church at Morawa. [2]

Land had been set aside east of the railway line, but the decision to clear the ground was quickly revoked after an inspection proved that the site was not suitable. Instead, the committee applied to the Lands Department to have another block surveyed on the western side of Morawa and, as a result, the present church land, together with the adjoining blocks, on which the presbytery, the Marian Convent and school oval were later built, was gazetted on 21 March 1930. [3] On 5 January the following year, Father Albert Scherzinger, a Pallottine priest from Tardun, was appointed parish priest of Morawa, with the added responsibility of Perenjori, Latham and Buntine.

Finally, in 1932, the Church Committee approached Dean Hawes regarding a set of plans and specifications for the erection of a Catholic church in Morawa. In July, during Bishop O'Collins's first visit to the town, Mr Tom Bradley, secretary of the Church Committee, took the matter one step further when he outlined the members' future plans and reported to the bishop on the current state of affairs. Impressed by the committee's business-like approach, the Bishop of Geraldton did not hesitate to sanction their arrangements. [4] Subsequently, 12 months later on Sunday, 2 July 1933, Bishop J. O'Collins blessed and officially opened the newly-erected Church of the

97. Hermitage presbytery, Morawa

98. St Joseph's Church, Perenjori

Holy Cross in Davis Street. The building, distinctively Hawes in style, is early Italian Renaissance in appearance and is in many ways reminiscent of the Church of San Domenico in Siena, Italy. The church featured a roof of red pantiles (Cordoba tiles), a small campanile, and the walls were constructed of local stone, which the builder, W. Oman, had arranged to have quarried from properties owned by G. Agar and T. Neagle of Merkanooka. In a team effort to save money, the stone was transported to the site by local residents, Messrs Regan, Handcock and Hall. [5]

Described as being 'warm with colour', the original interior of the Church of the Holy Cross had alternate bands of grey and white running along the length of the walls, with a brighter touch of blue around the Gothic window arches and zebra stripes over the sanctuary arch. [6] Later, when additions became necessary, there was deep concern expressed about destroying the appearance of the unique Hawes designed building. Bishop Thomas opened the extensions on 26 June 1966, and it is widely agreed that, by completing them with stone from the original quarry, the designers in no way sacrificed the church's beauty. The quaint stone hermitage, built by Hawes in 1933 behind the Church of the Holy Cross, is another example of the English priest's unusual talents. The tiny, one-room building, with just enough room for a bed, is alleged to be the smallest architect-designed presbytery in the world. [7] Four local girls, from the Morawa district, who were well-acquainted with the Church of the Holy Cross, and had received their education from the Dominican Sisters, later entered the novitiate at Dongara and became valued members of the Dominican community. These young ladies were the Misses Suzanne Vandeleur (Sr Julian), Bernice Gill (Sr Perpetua), Frances Haddock (Sr Francesca) and Andrea Lane (Sr Augustine).

Morawa's population increased during the post-war period, when migrants and their families, mainly from the Baltic States, arrived in the town to await resettlement. Many were Catholics and they were extremely grateful when, in 1953, Mrs N. Gill made arrangements for a Polish priest, Father Dzieuciol, to say Mass in their own language. [8] Eventually, under the leadership of Father Bryan, a firm of architects was commissioned to draw up plans for a convent and school and in order to lower the construction costs, several parishioners generously offered to cart the bricks needed for the building from the Irwin brickworks. The new buildings, designed by architects Summerhayes and Associates, were completed by contractors Berry Bros of Mt Hawthorn, Perth, at a cost of £21,000. [9]

On 27 March 1955, the Bishop of Geraldton, A. J. Gummer, officially opened the Marian Convent and school buildings in the presence of the Dominican foundation members, Sisters Augustine Corbett, Gabriel Barden, Antoninus Campbell, Mercedes Clune and a large crowd of some 400 people. As soon as the debt on the school building had been substantially reduced, boarding accommodation was provided for several boys and girls, who had been earlier accepted by the Dominican Sisters as weekly boarders. These children generally lived too far away to travel to Morawa daily, yet close enough to return home on weekends. Later, when better transport arrangements made the school more accessible, the boarding section of the Marian Convent School was phased out.

99. Marian School, Morawa

In 1956, Sister Declan Callaly was assigned to Morawa and over a period of eight years, although not consecutively, she taught at both the Marian School, Morawa and St Joseph's in Perenjori. Looking back on the time she spent in the wheatbelt town, she later wrote, 'Morawa was, for me, a great teaching experience. I enjoyed life there just as much as I had enjoyed Dongara. It was a very different type of set-up in that we were involved with the local community. Dongara was a boarding school so we didn't see the parents very much.I received a great deal of encouragement from the parents and local community in Morawa'. [10] According to Sister Declan, the parishioners were extremely generous and they made sure that the members of the Dominican community did not want for anything in the way of food or school resources.

Until the mid-1960s, the Marian school at Morawa consisted of a two-roomed brick building with sufficient space to cater for local needs. Additional rooms were needed, however, when the Western Mining Corporation commenced iron ore mining in the area and enrolments suddenly increased. To cater for the extra pupils, a decision was made to

100. Community, Marian Convent, Morawa, 1969
L. to R.: Sisters Consilii Costello, Emmanuel Lynch, Marlene Laracy, Aquin Inglis, Paul O'Connor, Myrtle Anstey

purchase three former classrooms from the government school and with a minimum of effort, paint and polish, these buildings were soon converted into an attractive air-conditioned classroom, a combined hall and library and an arts and craft room.

The Dominican Sisters attached to Morawa also staffed St Joseph's, a small Catholic school at nearby Perenjori. The town, its name taken from the Aboriginal word for water hole, is situated on the main north-south route which from Dalwallinu and Wubin in the south, to Mullewa and Tardun in the north, is known as the Wildflower Way. Over a period of some 10 years, Sisters Andrew Murphy (Sr Edith), Rosarii Keenan, Declan Callaly, Martin Doyle (Sr Treasa), Benvenuta Brophy (Sr Catherine), Consilii Costello (Sr Anne) and Paul O'Connor, at different times made the 26-mile journey each day from Morawa to Perenjori to teach at St Joseph's school. They found the same level of enthusiasm and support in this small country town as in Morawa. So much so, in fact, that one non-Catholic volunteer, who willingly did most of the school repairs, found himself in trouble at home for neglecting some of his domestic chores. Feeling neglected, the man's wife approached one of the Sisters and asked, 'If I bring my broken brooms to school will you leave them with yours so that I can get them mended?'. [11]

St Joseph's school continued to operate until 1970, when lack of staff and decreasing pupil numbers forced its closure.

With the introduction of the 1970s came many changes, both socially and within the Dominican Order. The unfortunate closure of religious foundations in a number of once-significant mining and agricultural towns in the Geraldton diocese left many Catholic children without the benefit of religious instruction. To correct this unhappy situation, in 1972, a Motor Mission was formed at Morawa and later at Three Springs. Two members of the Dominican community, Sister Bernadette and Sister Bernardine, agreed to visit selected mid-west towns to provide religious instruction to Catholic pupils at government schools. Recalling this trip Sr Bernadette later wrote:

*Our first visit was to Yalgoo. In this school most of the children were Aboriginals. Monsignor Bryan accompanied us on this first visit and at lunchtime asked if we had any "Carnamah Kids". When we asked the Principal where they were he was horrified – "Good Lord that's too far away'. (He was new to the school and to Aboriginals). The following week we decided to go looking for these children and as we approached the "camp" a lass was sweeping the ground with twigs tied together (and making a good job of it). "Are you Mrs Carnamah?" Sister asked. "No I am Miss Dongara!".* *

* It was not uncommon for Aboriginal families to take the name of a local town.

*Our weekly itinerary: Monday – to Yalgoo on the back road, 75 miles, and returned through Mullewa, 135 miles, where we had both Primary and Secondary Classes. Tuesday – to Buntine, 68 miles, and returned to Morawa – taking classes at Perenjori on the way. That evening we travelled to Three Springs, 40 miles, and on Wednesday drove to Coorow, 35 miles, for classes at 9.00 a.m. and returned to Carnamah, for Primary classes in the morning and High School in the afternoon. Thursday – it was to Eneabba, approx. 40 miles, then on to Dongara, 50 miles, and to Walkaway, 30 miles, in the afternoon and returned through Mingenew to Morawa.* [12]

In 1974, Sister Alphonse-Marie de Kuyer replaced Sister Bernardine and a request that year from Father Brymora saw the Sisters include a monthly visit to Meekatharra and Cue. Regardless of the distance, they complied with this request for 12 months. For the next 12 years, two Sisters regularly visited schools in Morawa, Perenjori, Buntine, Yuna, Nabawa, Walkaway and Dongara. These dedicated women often travelled over 1000 kilometres a week and before setting out, spent many hours preparing home programs to distribute whilst on tour. The parishes where the Sisters were based, generally provided a stipend and also a large contribution towards a suitable vehicle and running expenses. When possible, other parishes contributed. The numerous services offered by the Sisters operating the Motor Mission included

101. Motor Mission Group, Perenjori
L. to R.: Sisters Bernardine Hanafin and Bernadette Punch

visiting homes, preparing groups of children for communion and confirmation, conducting catechism classes, Bible study meetings and Majellan groups, as well as overseeing training days for catechists. Between the Sisters' visits, the children often completed their exercises at home with some guidance from the parents. Individual Sisters often used their talents to further advance the scheme. Sister Margaret Scharf, for example, often reached the young through her guitar. Sister began her music career with a folk group in the Bentley parish, wrote her first rock Mass at the age of 16 years, and her second when she was studying at Churchlands College of Advanced Education in 1976. Sister Margaret's liturgical cassette, 'I Hear You Calling', has been widely used in schools and parishes. [13]

'Motor Mission work generally seems to be something that cannot be tangibly assessed', stated an article in the *Cathedral Chronicle*. [14] It is certainly true that one would have to cast the net wide to record the spiritual and personal assistance given to families by the following Sisters who kept the Motor Mission going for the 12 years of its operation:

| | |
|---|---|
| 1972 | Sister Bernadette Punch and Sister Bernardine Hanafin |
| 1974 | Sister Bernadette Punch and Sister Alphonse-Marie de Kuyer |
| 1975 | Sister Helen O'Connor and Sister Augustine Lane |
| 1976 | Sister Helen O'Connor and Sister Bernadette Punch |
| 1977 | Sister Bernardine Hanafin and Sister Thomas Short |
| 1978 | Sister Bernardine Hanafin and Sister Anne Larney |
| 1980 | Sister Alphonse-Marie de Kuyer and Sister Myrtle Anstey |
| 1981 | Sister Regina O'Neill and Sister Margaret Vance |
| 1983 | Sister Margaret Vance |
| 1984-1986 | Sister Margaret Scharf [15] |

The Dominican Sisters continued to serve the Morawa district well into the next decade. In 1976, six Sisters resided in the Marian Convent. Of these, Sisters Augustine Lane, Diane Ross and Margaret Vance taught in the school, Sister Helen O'Connor and Sister Bernardine Hanafin were involved in the Motor Mission and Sister Norbert Burke (Sr Pauline) was responsible for household duties. From 1978 onwards, a number of lay teachers were employed at the Marian school. These included former Marian school pupil, Nancy Norton, Newman Siena College ex-student, Anne Carr, and Kim Elson who was educated first at St Dominic's Innaloo and then at Newman Siena.

In 1984, the Marian school re-opened with a staff consisting of Sister Eileen Leahy (Sr Reginald), Sister Diane Ross (Sr Pierre) and Mr Peter Baldry and an enrolment of 43 pupils. The principal, Sr Eileen, who taught Years 6 and 7, was described in a 1985 teacher evaluation report as having 'a very good teaching manner and able to extend the children to achieve their best'. [16] Eileen Leahy, born in Brosna, County Kerry, Ireland, volunteered to join the West Australian mission after meeting Sisters Laurence and Ignatius Prendiville during their visit to Ireland in 1950. On her acceptance into the novitiate at Dongara in May 1953, Miss Leahy received the religious name Sister Mary Reginald and 12 months later made her profession. A prayerful, studious person, she completed her studies for teacher qualification externally while teaching full-time in country schools, and later continued studying externally to obtain a Bachelor of Education Degree. A former principal at Bentley, Scarborough and Morawa, Sr Eileen, 'a true daughter of Ireland', has a great love of Irish history and literature and a much-envied flair for creative cooking which she developed over the years.

By 1986, the total number of pupils attending the Marian School had fallen to 25. At that time, country areas were suffering from the effects of a rural recession and the Dominican community from a paucity of staff. When the Sisters' concerns regarding the situation were relayed to the Catholic Education Commission, it was agreed that a meeting should be called to notify parents about the changes that might take place. The meeting was held on 5 December 1985 and chaired by Mr Paul Gair from the Catholic Education Office. As chairperson he spoke for the Sisters, outlining their difficulties and their decision to withdraw at the end of 1986. After lengthy discussion, the majority of those present optimistically made a strong commitment to see that the work begun by the Sisters 32 years earlier continued.

In recognition of the Sisters' lengthy service to the town, a farewell presentation was held in the Shire Council Chambers and in the weeks preceding their departure, the Morawa and Perenjori parishes gave similar farewells.

102. Consecration of St Joseph's Church, Perenjori, 1982
L. to R.: Sisters Leonie Connolly RSJ, Eileen Leahy, Anne Graham

In Morawa, Bishop Barry Hickey, assisted by the parish priest, Father O'Flaherty, celebrated Mass for the Sisters in the presence of a number of parishioners. The ceremony was later followed by a reception in the Town Hall. The last three members to reside in the convent were Sisters Vianney O'Brien, Diane Ross and Margaret Scharf (Motor Mission). The Dominican Sisters finally departed on 17 December 1986, after ensuring that the former convent was in a spotless condition for Sonia Fitzpatrick, the school's first appointed lay principal. As the three Sisters drove away from the township, their mixed feelings were reflected in the words of the last entry to appear in the annals of the Marian Convent:

*We are leaving with regret because we are unable to supply the Sisters for the school. The same thing is happening all over the State. There are just not the people entering religious life. Sisters Vianney, Margaret and I [Sr Diane] left with heavy hearts, but talked about how generous the people have always been and how accepted we have always felt in the town. There has been a wonderful spirit between the churches and the ministers, which one doesn't experience elsewhere. Thus ends thirty-two years of Dominican service in Morawa.* [17]

103. Last community at Morawa, 1986
L. to R.: Sisters Vianney O'Brien, Diane Ross, Margaret Scharf

CHAPTER 7

# Reaping the Harvest

## ST DOMINIC'S CONVENT, ST PETER'S SCHOOL AND ST THOMAS AQUINAS COLLEGE, BEDFORD PARK

The possibility of establishing a Dominican foundation in the Perth diocese was first raised as early as 1933. The world-wide economic depression experienced between the years 1929 and 1933 had unfortunately taken its toll on a wide range of enterprises including the pastoral, cattle, agricultural and mining industries. The far-reaching financial downturn meant that unemployment was rife and people were hesitant to plan their futures. During that period the Dominican Sisters established only one new foundation, Mingenew.

In mooting the idea of a Dominican college in the metropolitan area, Mother Laurence would, in all probability, have been influenced by the strong tradition from the earliest days of the Dominican Order of making foundations in the university cities of Europe. Given, too, the fact that study has always been regarded as a very important aspect of Dominican life, she would have recognised the greater opportunities available to the Sisters in the city to pursue a variety of studies. She may also have felt that it would be possible to more readily take advantage of these opportunities while her brother, the future Archbishop of Perth, was in a position to advise and assist the Sisters. Dr Redmond Prendiville, a highly-qualified academic and enthusiastic sportsman, had had a meteoric rise in his ecclesiastical career when, four years after his arrival in Western Australia in 1925, he was appointed Administrator of the Cathedral in the Archdiocese of Perth and on 11 July 1933, Coadjutor to Archbishop Clune.[1]

When first approached about the establishment of a Dominican foundation in Perth, Archbishop Clune was hesitant. He already had a number of teaching orders operating within the archdiocese and felt that he could not justify the introduction of another group at that time. It was not until Archbishop Prendiville was installed, that the idea took root. There were certain problems to be solved, however. The archbishop had to first find a locality where the right facilities existed, at the same time making sure that a new foundation would not encroach on an area close to an established school.

St Peter's was the first church building to be erected in the new parish of Bedford Park-Bayswater. Well-lit and attractively designed by architects Messrs Howard, Bonner and Tracey, the hall, which was built by contractor

104. St Peter's Church-school, Bedford Park, 1941

Mr G. Hallier for under £2000, was officially opened early in 1938. Archbishop Prendiville was pleased with the classic style of the building and in his opening speech informed those present that it was his intention to eventually use St Peter's Church for a school. He explained that the hall was designed in such a manner that, when a proper church was built, the present building could be easily divided into three large classrooms. The Archbishop also revealed that, depending on the number of enrolments, he hoped one day to see a religious foundation established alongside the proposed school. Furthermore, 'if all went well the convent would be built before the beginning of the 1939 school term and the school would then be staffed by resident Sisters'. [2] St Peter's church in Bedford Park was initially offered to the Dominican community, but was refused by Mother Laurence when she discovered that, although reasonably close to the centre of the city, the hall was surrounded by bushland and not connected to either the water or electricity supplies. [3]

In the period between the end of the Depression years and the beginning of World War II, the Dominican community increased dramatically when a number of talented postulants from New Zealand, Ireland and Western Australia entered the novitiate at Dongara. These young women included the Misses Rosalind Bain (Sr Albertus), Mollie Ryan (Sr Veronica), Mary Lynch (Sr Emmanuel), Violet Sharman (Sr Marie-Therese), Kathleen Galvin (Sr Dominic), Hannah Prendiville (Sr Ignatius), Ann Ryan (Sr Xavier), Joan Punch (Sr Bernadette), Dorothy Dominish (Sr Gertrude), Patricia Sachse (Sr Anthony), Gladys Ashleigh (Sr Immaculate), Mary O'Connor (Sr Joseph), Dorothy Lewis (Sr Magdalen), Ellen Heron (Sr Imelda) and Gladys O'Connor (Sr Bertrand). In 1939, Mother Laurence completed her term of office as Prioress and became Mistress of Schools. Despite her change in roles, she lost none of her enthusiasm about a Dominican foundation in Perth and continued to raise the subject with her brother at every opportunity. Dr Prendiville, who was ordained Archbishop of Perth in 1935, would no doubt have found himself in an invidious position, not only because of a personal involvement, but because the Sisters transfer to Perth reduced the staff capacity in the Geraldton Diocese.

On 4 August 1940, the parish priest of Bedford Park, Father E. McBride, sent a letter to the Archbishop on behalf of his parishioners in which he expressed 'their desire to open a school in that district in February of next year'. Among the various reasons put forward was the fact that most residents in the area were young and to attend the nearest Catholic school their children would have to travel part of the way through busy traffic. [4] Two days later the new Prioress, Mother Vincent Colgan, received from Archbishop Prendiville a copy of the letter from Father McBride. The Archbishop also enclosed a note which stated: 'If you decide to accede to this request, to open a school in Bedford Park in February next year, it will be necessary for you to make arrangements as quickly as possible for the erection of the Convent. I will be pleased to hear from you as soon as possible'. [5]

Mother Vincent and Sister Ceslaus Freed visited Perth shortly after to examine the site. The suburb of

Bedford Park was then still in its infancy and, although in certain sections streets had been formed and a number of new houses boasted lawns, the proposed school site was surrounded by virgin bush. Surprisingly, Bishop O'Collins granted the Prioress permission to commence a school at Bedford Park, although, to protect his own interests, he also made it clear that only four Dominican Sisters could work in the Perth diocese at one time. Mother Vincent was also informed that under no circumstances was money to be transferred from the Geraldton diocese. [6]

The year 1941 was exceptionally busy for the Dominican Sisters. Apart from founding St Peter's at Bedford Park, they had returned to Leonora and Gwalia after an absence of 17 years and had also opened a school and convent at Reedy. In retrospect, it was an opportune time for the Dominican Sisters to establish a foundation in the Perth diocese, for under the building program fostered by Archbishop Prendiville between 1935 and 1946, many new parishes were formed and churches and chapels opened. In what proved to be a decade of growth in the archdiocese, a number of fine institutions, hospitals, convents, colleges and parochial schools were constructed and, of significant interest to Catholic teaching orders, the Mater Dei Teacher Training College was established at Victoria Square in 1938. Besides the Dominicans, the Archbishop also introduced several other religious communities to the Perth diocese. These included the Jesuits in 1938, the Brigidines in 1942 and two years later the Pallottine Fathers, who had already staffed Tardun.

105. Sisters' original house, Wood Street, Bedford Park, 1941

A rented brick house at 38 Wood Street, for which the Dominican Sisters paid 27 shillings and sixpence a week, was used as a temporary convent to accommodate Sisters Laurence Prendiville, Marie-Therese Sharman, Albertus Bain and Rose McCusker. The group left Dongara on 24 January 1941, almost immediately after the completion of the annual retreat, and accompanied by Father Brennan they drove south on what proved to be an exceptionally hot day. Sister Laurence had unfortunately broken her arm prior to leaving and for a time was unable to assist physically in setting up the new convent and school. Born at Castleisland in County Kerry, Ellen Prendiville (Sr Laurence), one of a family of 16, joined three of her brothers, John, Peter and Gerald in Perth in 1910. On arrival she worked for the legal firm Lavan and Walsh and decided to remain with the rest of her family in Western Australia after her eldest brother John returned to Ireland. Following in the steps of two of her relatives, who became Dominicans in France and England, Ellen entered the Dominican novitiate at Dongara in February 1917 and was professed six years before her brother Redmond arrived in Western Australia. A skilled linguist, Sr Laurence also specialised in the teaching of English and, although she spent the major part of her early religious life attached to the Dominican Ladies' College at Dongara, she also taught for a time at the Holy Rosary Convent, Meekatharra, and St Catherine's Convent, Leonora. [7]

The second member of the group, Sister Marie-Therese Sharman, was another highly-respected teacher. Baptised Violet Josephine, Sr Marie-Therese was the eldest of three children born to Annie and Henry Sharman. She received her early education at the local Bassendean State School, where she proved to be a proficient student gaining in her final primary school year a scholarship to the prestigious Perth Modern School. As a young adult, Violet graduated from the Claremont Teachers' College and later obtained both her A Mus A and teaching diploma for Speech and Drama (Associate Trinity College of London). On completion of her studies, she joined the Education Department and taught at various schools around the state, including the Dongara State School. Whilst there she offered to teach eurhythmics at the Dominican Ladies' College and after accepting that she had a vocation, entered the Dominican Convent in 1935. Sister Marie-Therese later taught at Cue, Meekatharra, Dongara and Three Springs before being assigned to Bedford Park (Inglewood). In all those places she displayed a special talent for teaching and an excellent rapport with the children enrolled in the junior primary classes. As a member of the General Council, she resided in Canberra for a time, where she took on the role of lecturer at Signadou, the newly-established Dominican Teachers' College. [8]

106. Foundation Sisters, Bedford Park, 1941
L. to R.: Sisters Laurence Prendiville, Rose McCusker, Marie-Therese Sharman, Albertus Bain

Rosalind Bain (Sr Albertus), who later became a well-known author and historian, was born at Kurow, a village on the banks of the Waitaki River in the South Island of New Zealand. After taking a position in Dunedin and studying ancient and medieval history part-time, she made a decision, at the age of 24 years, to enter the Dominican Order in Western Australia. Sister Albertus, who originally taught junior primary pupils at St Peter's church school, later completed an Arts

107. Sister Albertus Bain

degree at The University of Western Australia and for many years taught history, economics and biology at secondary school level. She was also a highly-successful teacher of Art of Speech and Verse Speaking, her students consistently gaining Honours awards in these areas. [9] The fourth member of the community, Sister Rose McCusker, joined the Dominican community at Dongara in 1910, after being recruited by two of the foundation members, Sisters di Pazzi Miscall and Dominica Murphy, during their quest for postulants in the eastern states. A much-loved and capable lay Sister, she mainly had charge of the boarders' and priests' dining rooms at Dongara and when assigned to Bedford Park she continued to take care of the domestic arrangements. Sister Rose died in 1970 at the age of 80.

Despite being unimpressed by their first sight of the tiny house with its unkempt lawn and a stretch of black sand running to the back of the property, the Sisters were overwhelmed by the reception they received. Mr and Mrs Sachse had managed to secure the essential pieces of furniture second-hand, and Mrs Cranley provided a dining room suite and two autumn-toned druggets. Towels and blankets, crockery and cooking utensils, as well as six prie-dieux were also supplied and Eileen Boyle, in memory of the pioneer Sister Baptist Hall, donated a tabernacle, altar linens and vestments. A welcome meal was supplied and the house was made presentable by a hospitable group of workers. Listed also among the many benefactors who assisted the Dominican Sisters in their foundation years at Bedford Park were Mesdames Punch, Virgo, Nolan, Doyle, O'Neill and Prendiville. The Sisters' luggage, sent ahead by train, unfortunately did not arrive and for the first few days this additional inconvenience meant that members of the community had to improvise. In the meantime, the Sisters changed the furniture around to suit their needs. One of the two front rooms became a parlour, which was used to receive visitors, while doubling as a dining room for visiting priests. The second room, which featured double glass doors, was turned into a chapel and arrangements were made for a builder to enclose the fireplace so that an altar could be put in place. [10]

The Sisters had expected to enrol at least 50 pupils on the first day of school, hence they were somewhat disappointed to find that only 26 children turned up for classes ranging from Infants to Grade VI. Terry Eaton, the sole student enrolled in the higher class, was hoping to gain a government scholarship and it was a rewarding situation for both teacher and pupil when he achieved his objective at the end of that year. Other secondary students, Pam and Norma Saunders, Pam Inglis and Emma Wuest, later joined Doreen Forrest studying for her Junior Certificate in the tiny classroom set aside at the front of St Peter's hall. This group formed the nucleus of what would later become a large secondary college at Bedford Park. Prospects quickly improved when parents realised that within easy distance of their homes their children could receive almost individual tuition in basic and extra subjects from highly-qualified teachers.

There were, of course, many drawbacks, but in those days, as with the majority of early religious foundations, people living in country and developing areas did not expect modern classrooms and sophisticated teaching methods. Most Catholic parents were interested in their schools providing a Christian ethos, good manners and confidence, as well as a range of cultural and academic subjects. School requisites at St Peter's, in the beginning were few, and for many years the Sisters were inconvenienced by the common practice of having to remove school desks and large wall charts each week for Sunday Mass. This procedure was duplicated every Wednesday evening when the hall was used for fund-raising events aimed at paying off the interest on the building debt. To make ends meet it was necessary to set Bedford Park school fees at one shilling a week despite most other parochial schools charging less than half that sum. [11] Even so, there were times when the Sisters received far less than the calculated weekly fees, although they counted themselves blessed with the regular assistance they received from many parents.

The community's economic position improved after the Sisters (on the advice of well-known Perth music and elocution teacher Mrs Sutherland Groom), purchased a Ronisch piano for £50. The number of pupils seeking music and elocution tuition from the Dominican Sisters increased dramatically and to provide extra accommodation, the small, sparsely-furnished staff room was turned into a makeshift music room. Fees for private music and art of speech lessons conducted after school hours by Sister Marie-Therese Sharman and Sister Albertus Bain, were set at two guineas for a 13-week term. By the end of the first year, the speech class at St Peter's was awarded Honours in the Trinity College of London Examinations and in the following year the school's first singing class gained a Credit award. [12]

The Sisters walked to St Peter's carrying the items they needed for their day's work. 'We must have looked strange figures as we went along Wood Street to the school on many a morning', wrote Sister Marie-Therese, 'we had the long cream serge habits, the black cappas, and under these, a Chinese basket for wood, a violin, a stand and case'. Many wood-yards had closed during the war years and wood was difficult to get, so, in keeping with most householders, the Sisters collected roots from the nearby bush for use in the stove or fireplace. They generally only made the one trip to and from school as Sister Rose frequently sent a midday meal across to be heated on a small methylated spirit stove kept on the premises.

The road stopped well short of the building, leaving only bushland to be negotiated by the Sisters and pupils before reaching a small bitumen path leading to the front steps. In some respects the isolation of the grounds had its advantages, for with little traffic the students were able to use the end of the road as a netball court. Sister Laurence and Father McBride arranged a meeting to form a Parents' and Friends' Association, and subsequently a decision was made to cover a section of land on the left-hand side of the building with gravel for sporting events. During those formative years, costs were often minimised with the use of volunteer labour, and a great deal of effort also went into organising a variety of fund-raising activities to provide many of the amenities lacking in the school. The early annals record the names of many parishioners who regularly offered their services, among these were: Mr and Mrs Maidment, Mr and Mrs Ives, Mr and Mrs Wall and Mesdames Matson, Tory, Cutler, Thomas, Wellington, McDonald, Eaton, Purkis and Ross.

As is often the case where young children are involved, teachers have an endless store of anecdotes to draw on. Sister Marie-Therese later recalled the occasion when Sister M. Laurence was confronted by a curious six-year-old pupil, obviously not used to nuns. 'What's your name?', the child asked, to which the surprised Superior retorted, 'What do you want to know for?'. 'My mother wanted to know', was the reply, 'I told her that if the man that comes to the school is Father McBride – then you must be Mother McBride'. [13] By the end of 1941, St Peter's boasted a roll call of about 50 children and according to the School Inspector's report, the results achieved by the Dominican Sisters during their first year were extremely pleasing. Indeed, Father McBride considered Inspector Worner's glowing remarks to be such an excellent advertisement for the school that he could not resist sharing them with the congregation at Mass.

The school's first annual concert, which was successfully held on a Saturday afternoon, was memorable for another reason. On that day, former Dominican student Miss Kath Levitzke, who attended the event, approached Sister Laurence about becoming a postulant. West Australian-born, Miss Levitzke was the second young woman to apply that year and, accompanied by Miss Mary Patterson (Sr de Sales), she entered the Dominican novitiate at Dongara on 6 January 1942. Both these teachers later taught at St Thomas Aquinas Secondary College at Bedford Park and are still held in high esteem by their former pupils. Sister di Ricci (Sr Kath), a person interested in everything and everybody, had a special gift for reaching out to the young, especially those in need of her support and encouragement. Strict, but fair, she spread her teaching talents and compassion over many areas and is remembered with affection by the pupils she taught in country and metropolitan schools and by those who attended her religious education and English as a Second Language classes (ESL). Sister de Sales Patterson (Sr Mary), an extremely capable, widely-read person, whose background is described in a later chapter, occupied many positions of responsibility within the congregation, including that of Prioress of St Dominic's Convent and Sister-in-Charge of St Thomas Aquinas School.

In the meantime, Archbishop Prendiville had provided a block of land near the school hall and throughout 1941 the possibility of building a two-storey Dominican Convent on the site was often raised. The 1940s, however, proved to be one of the most dramatic and worrying periods in Australia's history and war-time restrictions created many unforeseen pressures. In February 1942, the unexpected fall of Singapore, one of the state's northern neighbours, saw people's lifestyle change almost overnight. Ration books, entitling each person to a limited number of coupons to purchase clothing, meat, tea, butter, petrol and other essentials, were distributed. Blackouts were compulsory and glass windows in residences, shop-fronts, schools and public buildings were taped or papered over to avoid damage in the event of a bomb blast. The growing threat of a Japanese invasion also saw precautionary measures being taken in the form of evacuation. Religious Sisters were advised to pack suitcases and make plans for a quick exodus in case this occurred and bomb shelters and slit trenches were prepared in cities and towns and on both public and private properties. With a large proportion of the menfolk in the armed forces and many women enlisting or taking positions previously held by males, family life assumed a new direction.

A state-wide shortage of building materials meant that a permit was necessary before a contractor could commence work. Towards the end of 1941, the authorities approved the Dominican community's request for permission to build, but only on the understanding that the building would be designed as a private house rather than as a convent, and that the cost would not exceed £3000. The original size, therefore, had to be restricted and in the final re-draw of the plans the back verandah and fence were deleted and four of the proposed bedrooms became one large dormitory. Due to lack of manpower and delays caused by delivery trucks becoming bogged in sand, it was six months before the building was completed. The Sisters finally moved into their new residence on 3 June 1942, and prepared for the official opening four days later. By then, Father Hennebry, who had known the Dominicans in Leonora, had replaced Father McBride and he offered to assist members of the community when they transferred from 38 Wood Street to the new St Dominic's Convent at number 103.

108. St Dominic's Convent, Bedford Park

Despite their obvious excitement, it was not an auspicious day and the Sisters could well have done without some of their experiences. Sister Rose was suffering from a burnt hand; Sister Marie-Therese had influenza, and they were all inconvenienced by incessant rain. Adding to their misfortunes, the truck, which had no covering, ground to a halt in the mud and the furniture was thoroughly drenched after it was temporarily deposited on the side of the track. Mrs Hart, a neighbour, had thoughtfully provided a welcome billycan of soup, but still Dame Fortune refused to smile. The wood was too wet to light a fire for heating the food and when Sister Albertus connected the new electric jug, given to them by Father McBride, it blew the fuse. [14]

The Prioress General M. Vincent Colgan and Sister Ceslaus Freed from Dongara attended the opening ceremony performed by Archbishop Prendiville on 7 June which, coincidentally, marked the forty-third anniversary of the order's foundation in Western Australia. Despite war-time conditions, an appeal for donations that day proved highly successful, however, a £500 cheque handed over to the Bedford community by the Dominican Prioress General again raised the question of the order's pontifical status. Believing that the Sisters were diocesan, and under his jurisdiction, the Bishop of Geraldton insisted that the sum of money be returned to the community at Dongara. [15]

Because the Sisters had to rely entirely on bore water, there was still a great deal of manual work to be carried out. Consequently, busy-bees were arranged to excavate trenches to lay water pipes from the top of the hill, and also for telephone cables. A school canteen was organised and the money derived from sales was used to purchase library books for the 90 children enrolled in 1942. In the meantime, a cement verandah was added to the building and a fence, part brick and part wood, was erected to provide more privacy. The grounds, which were still in their natural state, were eventually levelled, and on the Archbishop's recommendation State Botanist and author, Charles Gardiner, generously gave advice on landscaping the gardens.

As the road system gradually improved in the district and neighbouring suburbs, land became more accessible and with the completion of a number of project homes and groups of State Housing Commission settlements, the population rapidly increased. By then, the church hall had become overcrowded and, to cater for the extra children seeking enrolment, a decision was made to erect a separate building. The newly-completed St Peter's Primary School, consisting of five classrooms, an office and a small enclosed hall, was officially opened in July 1953 with a total enrolment of 253 pupils, including a number of secondary students. By then, the school was divided into two sections with Sister Marie-Therese remaining in charge of the primary school and Sister Aloysius O'Neill, a former fully qualified lay teacher, appointed head of the secondary school. [16] Sister Aloysius, who had had many years experience in state schools, came to Bedford Park in 1953, after a period of several years as Mistress of Novices at the novitiate and Sister-in-Charge of the Dominican Ladies' College at Dongara. Her positive approach and personal interest did much to empower her students to believe in their gifts and develop them. Sisters who were guided by her in their early teaching careers, and later became independent educators in their own right, recall her encouragement to keep the Dominican ideals in education in mind as she assisted them with everyday classroom management.

For some time, a number of parents had expressed a keen interest in the Dominican Sisters establishing a kindergarten. The parish priest during the early 1950s, Tralee-born Father J. V. O'Sullivan, noted for his Irish wit and infectious optimism, felt that the income from such a venture might go a long way towards financing a much-needed secondary school, and he encouraged this idea. As a result, a generously-proportioned community room, earlier added to the rear of the convent, was set aside for pre-school children. The kindergarten opened in February 1955, with future Dominican Prioress, Sister Damian Carville (Sr Joan) in charge, followed in 1957 by Sister Christine Fogarty. In that same year, the Dominican Sisters established, at a cost close to £10,000, St Thomas Aquinas

Secondary School, for girls from Years 8 to 12. The new building in Salisbury Street, Bedford Park, consisting of three classrooms, an office, two small rooms for senior students, a library and a large kindergarten room, ran parallel with and adjacent to Wood Street. A Board of Management was formed and Sister Laurence Prendiville

109. New St Thomas Aquinas Secondary School, 1955

returned as Prioress to become the first Sister-in-Charge of the new school.

In July 1959, a new kindergarten was completed facing Salisbury Street. [17] Sister Christine Fogarty continued as Sister-in-Charge until 1962, when Sister Edith Murphy was assigned to take her place for one year. For the next six years, the kindergarten was privately run under the umbrella of the Education Department's Early Childhood Education Programme. Mrs Sadie Mulhern, teacher-in-charge from 1964 until her sudden death in 1969, is remembered as a caring, capable teacher, respected and well-liked by all who were associated with her.

Apart from the heavy burden of re-building and running two schools, the Dominican Sisters from Bedford Park were also involved in St Therese's Primary School, Gwelup (1952), Santa Clara Primary School, Bentley (1953) and the School of the Infant Jesus at Morley Park (1956). In April 1959, during the first visit made to the Holy Family Province by the Mother Prioress General, both the Santa Sabina Convent at Scarborough and St Dominic's, Bedford Park, were raised to the status of priories. In 1961, Sister Laurence was replaced by Sister Ignatius Prendiville and transferred to St John's, Scarborough. From 1961 to 1967 inclusive, the Prioress of St Dominic's Convent was also Sister-in-Charge of St Thomas Aquinas School. The last person to maintain this dual role was Sister de Sales Patterson, who succeeded Sr Ignatius. In turn, her successor as Prioress was Irish-born Sister Regina O'Neill, one of the postulants who accompanied Mother Laurence on her return to Western Australia in 1950. As a teacher, Sr Regina O'Neill had the respect of her students and made a strong contribution. Later she became involved in counselling.

She entered this field in 1985, when she accepted the position of Student Counsellor at Newman College Senior School, advising students on personal matters and careers choice. In 1996, Sr Regina was appointed Student Advisor at Mater Dei, a Catholic Education Commission School in the northern suburb of Edgewater.

Sister Anita Wilmott, was appointed principal of St Thomas Aquinas School in 1968, the first Sister to hold this position separately from that of Prioress. A West Australian by birth and a former student of the Dominican Ladies' College in Dongara, Sr Anita's years of study and teaching prepared her well for the task of school principal. Her organisational skills and her efficiency made for a highly-successful school. At a time when there was limited financial assistance from governments and consequent lack of sporting and other facilities, St Thomas Aquinas excelled in athletics and other sports, becoming a strong competitor in inter-school competitions. Culturally, the emphasis given to art, music, speech and singing, combined with sound teaching upheld the reputation gained over the years by the school. Sister Anita continued as principal until 1974, when she was granted study leave which was taken at the National Pastoral Institute in Melbourne, Victoria.

110. Principal, Sister Anita Willmott with a group of STA secondary students,

111. Presentation of Inter-Schools Athletics Shield, 1970

Many improvements were made to the schools, convent and grounds during the 1960s, including the extension of a brick wall along the Wood Street entrance to the newly-constructed parish church, the original church-school by then having become the parish hall. As the demand for commercial courses increased, the St Thomas Aquinas School building was altered to make two extra classrooms, one for third year students enrolled for professional courses, the other for those preferring commercial studies. The popularity of commercial subjects resulted in further extensions being agreed to in June 1965. By September, the architect's plans had been approved and permission was also given to organise the purchase of extra equipment. [18]

At that time St Peter's, under the principalship of Sister Damian (Sr Joan), accepted boys and girls to Grade III, but only girls beyond that standard. In 1967, St Peter's primary school had a total enrolment of 274 children (206 girls and 68 boys), the staff at that time being Sisters Damian Carville (Sr Joan), Ambrose Bernet, Christine Fogarty, Augustine Lane, with Mrs Van Hauen and Mrs Carpenter. In September that year, a pleasing report presented by the Education Department's district superintendent, Mr J. West, gave the Dominican school his seal of approval:

*Accommodated in excellent buildings, St Peter's is an impressive school. Because of rather large classrooms, their extreme tidiness, the excellent appearance and attitude of the students and the fine tone prevailing, it is not obvious that many classes are large by present standards. It is clear too, that since Grade I is already reasonably accommodated in the Parish Hall, it will not be easy to provide another room. However it is suggested that a seventh teacher and room is desirable if present enrolment is maintained and increased. The work done at the school is of a high order. Contact was made with all the classes and lots of children's work seen and heard. It was noted that the large Grade I class was making an excellent start in school work and that in all classes splendid work was being done. Particular mention is made of the outstanding singing and speech in the upper classes.*

*A staff conference was conducted after school. Matters discussed included new draft syllabuses, recent changes in some subjects and topics raised by the teachers. Appreciation is recorded of the fine work of the teachers, the interest of the staff in recent educational trends and the courtesy and hospitality extended during the visit.* [19]

It was during 1970, that the inaugural Parents' and Friends' Association was formed and the necessary funds were raised to provide teaching aids, furniture and equipment for the various subject areas. At the same time, members, such as Mr Joe Tavelli and others, proved invaluable in keeping repairs and building costs to a minimum. These people, along with the many members who served on the various committees over the years were the pivot around which the development of the school revolved. The list is long and it is impossible to record the names of all the volunteers, however, the following are representative of all those who contributed their skills and time, saving the school and the school community a substantial sum of money: Messrs John Metcalf,

John Hilton, Joe Fedele, and Mrs Caryl Cairns from the Parents' and Friends' Association, Mesdames Henningheim, Robyn Hollands, Frances Hilton and Rosemary Ovenden who voluntarily ran the uniform shop. Also deserving of a special mention are Mrs Joy Wilkes, the canteen manageress and Mrs Marion Castelanelli and her husband Joe, who persevered in the face of difficulties to hold regular Bingo evenings which provided a constant source of funds.

In November 1970, the Dominican Council investigated the possibility of closing the kindergarten and converting the building into a science laboratory and after a lengthy discussion on the wisdom of such a move, a decision was made to press ahead with the project at the end of that year. The Achievement Certificate, which had been introduced in 1971, was well and truly entrenched by 1974 and with an ever-increasing enrolment of students attending the school, the completion that year of five new classrooms, a library and two science laboratories was of prime importance. The new school building opened in 1974, with a roll call of 177 pupils. The original building, erected in 1955, then became the administration block. Two years later, the on-going building program included the erection of modular classrooms, intended to relieve overcrowding problems. Although provided as a temporary measure they were in fact part of the school for many years.

Progress during the 1970s brought about a significant number of policy changes. On 29 April 1975, a meeting was held at Bedford Park between the principal, Sister Treasa Doyle, Sister Assumpta Moriarty, the Provincial of the Dominican Sisters, Brother Woodruff, the Provincial of the Christian Brothers, and Brother Hall, to discuss the long-term likelihood of St Thomas Aquinas School forming a co-educational senior school in conjunction with the Christian Brothers' St Mark's College. In 1978, major staff changes were introduced at St Thomas Aquinas School, when Mr Graham Cooney was appointed the school's first lay principal and Sister Antoninus Campbell, an experienced administrator, became the deputy principal. As deputy, Sr Antoninus played an important role in the transition year, being responsible for the time-tabling for the whole school, for student welfare and for other associated duties.

112. Student Representative Council, 1978
L. to R.: Veronica Shakhovskoy, Hetty Child, Jill Ryan, Maria Pizzino, Lynette Jutte, Joanne McGowan, Eva Cicmirko

A larger roll call saw the junior secondary classes expand into three streams in 1978. Reflecting on his first year in office Mr Cooney stated: 'It is only right that a tribute should be paid to the splendid work done by Sr Treasa Doyle, Principal of S. T. A. from 1975 to 1977, and to those other Dominican Sisters and their dedicated lay assistants, who over the years have brought this school community to its present level of vibrant growth'. [20]

113. St Thomas Aquinas School staff, 1979
L. to R.: Sister Regina O'Neill (R.E. Co-ord.), G. Cooney (Principal), Sister Antoninus Campbell (Deputy)

In 1981, enrolment at the college fluctuated around 470 students and within three years this figure had risen to 543 enrolled students with a teaching staff of 47, administration staff of five, a similar number of service staff, a deputy principal and a principal. In 1981, a Business Studies Course for students who had completed Year 10 was introduced and in August the construction of new facilities for home economics, additional classrooms, science laboratories, toilets, change room and undercroft were commenced. [21]

In December 1980, the premature death of Monsignor Goody's successor at Bedford Park, Father Vincent O'Sullivan, was a great loss to the parish. Father Vincent O'Sullivan, easy going and well-liked, loved mixing socially with his parishioners. It is said that he was the first to suggest to the Archbishop the idea of using acolytes to replace some of the priest's duties and could, therefore be regarded as the instigator of the acolyte ministry in Western Australia. Certainly, the parishioners in Bedford Park were among the first to benefit from the appointment of acolytes in their parish. Father O'Sullivan's illness before his death, was made easier when Sister Josephine Hanafin, who was responsible for the cooking and household duties in the convent, extended her care to the ailing parish priest. She prepared his meals, and ensured that all was in readiness for him to offer his own private Mass in the presbytery each day until he could no longer do so. Sister Josephine, one of two sisters who entered the Dongara novitiate from County Kerry, Ireland, followed in the footsteps of her sibling, Sister Bernardine Hanafin, who had joined the Dominican community two years earlier. Both excellent cooks Sr Josephine continued to excel in this role at the Santa Sabina Convent in Scarborough and Sr Bernardine, resident at Veritas House in Scarborough, was appointed to the Home Economic Department at Newman Siena.

Mr Laurie Mayne was appointed St Peter's first lay principal in 1979 and until such time as the Sisters finally withdrew from St Peter's School at the end of 1982, two Dominican teachers continued on staff: Sister Imelda Ryan from 1979 to 1981 and Sister Mary Ryan during 1982.

The extensive building program carried out for St Thomas Aquinas College* during the late 1970s was made possible by the funds granted by the Commonwealth Government and the Catholic Education Commission, as well as funds generated by the School Building Fund. The success of such a venture can be attributed to the constant and careful management of these funds by Sister Margaret Robson, the Congregational Bursar and later by successive Boards of Management whose members gave their services freely to ensure that the school maintained a sound financial base. Initially the Board consisted of Sisters only, with the Prioress of the congregation as chairperson. This was altered in 1982, when the Board was expanded to include a number of parents, with Mr Cooney, the principal as chairperson. In 1983, the Dominican Sisters appointed Mr Herb Duckett chairperson and Mr Peter Chapman was elected treasurer. During the year, a School Building Fund was set up by Messrs Jim McNamara, Alan Lean and John Ardagh, assisted by Mr Ross McLean. [22]

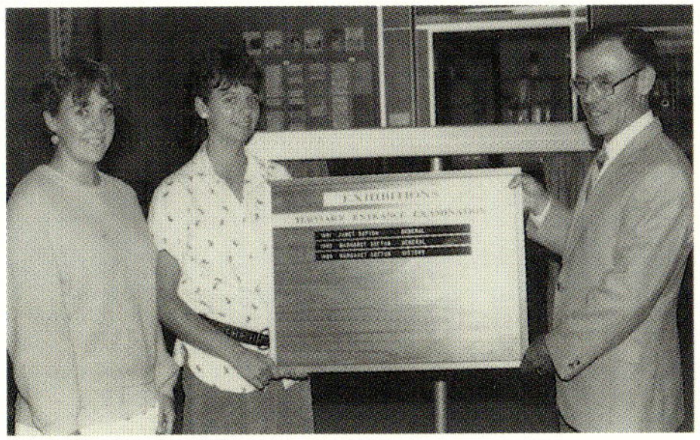

114. Mr G Cooney honouring Margaret and Janet Sefton's academic achievements, 1985

In keeping with current educational trends, in August 1984, the subject of secondary school rationalisation in the Bedford Park-Highgate area was discussed by the principal of St Thomas Aquinas School, Mr G. Cooney, the Provincial of the Dominican Sisters, Sister Mary Patterson, and the Provincial of the Christian Brothers in Manning, Brother G. Faulkner. [23] A working party was subsequently established and various models of the proposed merger were offered for consideration. On 24 July the following year, the then Provincial, Sister Concepta Flattery, wrote from St Catherine's Dominican Convent in Doubleview, 'We can see many educational, social, spiritual and psychological advantages to having co-education at the

115. Successful National Levels Gymnasts, Pene and Kathryn Hambrook, 1987

* Thomas Aquinas Secondary School was re-named St Thomas Aquinas College in 1985

Senior School level. Our experience has convinced us that it is advantageous to students of both sexes. Because of this we firmly endorse the idea'. [24]

In 1986, Mr Jim McNamara was elected chairperson of the College Board and Peter Kora, treasurer. The composition of the College Board in 1988, the last year of the Sisters' involvement with the college,

116. St Thomas Aquinas College Board, 1986
L. to R.: Back Row: Jim McNamara, Joe Tavelli, Rob Devenish, Peter Kora
Front: Sister Margaret Robson, Deidre Appelbee, Sister Perpetua Gill, Graham Cooney

was: Mr Peter Kora (Chairperson), Sister Margaret Robson (Provincial Bursar) and members: Sister Anita Wilmott, Mrs Deirdre Appelbee, Mrs Judy Sluchniak, Mr John McDonald-Smith, Mr Joe Tavelli, Mr Walter Bamford and Mr Rob Devenish (College Business Manager). Negotiations that took place in 1987 with Mr D. O'Sullivan, representing the Catholic Education Office and Monsignor P. McCrann, representing the Archdiocese, were finalised on 11 March 1988, when the interim Chisholm Board accepted the terms offered. The interim Board, set up with Mr Jim McNamara as chairperson, consisted of members of the St Aquinas College Board and the St Mark's College Board. Its function was to ensure the smooth transition of the two colleges to an amalgamated institution under the name Chisholm College by the beginning of 1989. This was achieved most effectively. [25]

On 9 April 1988, prior to the proposed co-educational college becoming a reality, the Dominican Sisters finally withdrew from St Dominic's Priory, Bedford Park, knowing that the schools they founded were in the safe hands of Mr G. Cooney, and a dedicated lay staff. Members of the last community to serve at Bedford Park were Sisters Concepta Flattery, Eileen Leahy (Sr Reginald), Dominica Davis, Joan Carville (Sr Damian) and Kath Levitzke (Sr di Ricci), who was also the longest-serving Sister on the staff at St Thomas Aquinas. It was the beginning of a new era for the Dominican Sisters when the keys were handed over on 11 April, leaving the buildings free.

Chisholm College, named after Caroline Chisholm, noted early Australian colonist whose work with female immigrants in New South Wales was widely acclaimed, opened its doors in 1989 with a roll call of over 1000 students. The new Catholic co-educational college, controlled by the Catholic Education Commission, was the result of an amalgamation between the Dominican Sisters' foundation, St Thomas Aquinas College and the Christian Brothers' St Mark's College. During his 10 years as principal of St Thomas Aquinas, Mr Graham Cooney had shown himself to be a competent administrator and a fine teacher and it was no surprise, therefore, when he was appointed principal of the new education centre. Mrs Cynthia Brown, who spent a total of 14 years on the staff of St Thomas Aquinas is well-qualified to comment on Mr Cooney's contribution to the success of the college. She stated: 'Graham is a true educator. A deeply spiritual person with a great sense of compassion he is thoroughly committed to building a school community which continually seeks improved ways of providing students with a solid grounding in Christian values, an excellent learning environment and a broad range of opportunities for physical and social development'. [26]

Years 11 and 12 occupied the former St Thomas Aquinas College building to form the Wood Street Campus, whilst Years 8, 9 and 10 became part of the Beaufort Street Campus, in what was originally St Mark's College in Bedford Park. Enrolled students came from regional Catholic feeder schools at Bayswater, Bedford Park, Dianella, Highgate, Morley Park and Mt Lawley. The college placed a strong emphasis on student development and equality, and in line with the majority of Catholic schools, no students were turned away because their parents could not afford to pay the fees. From their small rented house in Wood Street, the original group of Sisters could not have anticipated the end results of their efforts. They would be the first to admit, however, that these goals could not have been achieved without the close co-operation of dedicated staff and parents. The recent celebrations of the sixtieth anniversary of the parish brought together friends and helpers of the Sisters. The Kearneys, Creightons, Smiths and Corbetts are representative of the many such people involved over the years. Looking back on those times, Sister Assumpta Moriarty recently reminisced:

*As in any family group the life of a school encompasses its highlights, but is much more than that. One has to live through a school year as a member of staff or as a student to know and appreciate the ethos, the characteristic spirit of a school. This is true of St Thomas Aquinas, now a component of Chisholm College. St Thomas Aquinas was a happy school. As in any good school many friendships were engendered there which have stood the test of time. Noteworthy is the relationship which exists between students and Sisters as well as other staff members, a relationship which continues to this day. The achievements were solid: religious, cultural, sporting, academic and social and the Dominican Sisters are happy to have been part of it. They include their years at St Thomas Aquinas among their great memories.* [27]

PRIORESSES OF ST DOMINIC'S CONVENT, BEDFORD PARK

| | |
|---|---|
| 1941 | Sr Laurence Prendiville |
| 1945 | Sr Augustine Corbett |
| 1948 | Sr Laurence Prendiville |
| 1949 | Sr Marie Therese Sharman |
| 1955 | Sr Laurence Prendiville |
| 1961 | Sr Ignatius Prendiville |
| 1964 | Sr de Sales Patterson |
| 1967 | Sr Regina O'Neill |
| 1970 | Sr Declan Callaly |
| 1973 | Sr Ambrose Bernet |
| 1974 | Sr St Anne Graham |
| 1977 | Sr Regina O'Neill |
| 1981 | Sr Cecilia Murphy |
| 1984 | Sr Concepta Flattery |
| 1985 | Sr Gemma Seaman |
| 1987 | Sr Eileen Leahy |

PRINCIPALS OF ST PETER'S SCHOOL, BEDFORD PARK

| | |
|---|---|
| 1949 | Sr Marie Therese Sharman |
| 1956 | Sr Paul O'Connor |
| 1961 | Sr Gemma Seaman |
| 1964 | Sr Paul O'Connor |
| 1965 | Sr Dolores Cummins |
| 1967 | Sr Damien Carville (Sr Joan) |
| 1969 | Sr Jerome O'Connor (Sr Helen) |
| 1975 | Sr Benvenuta Brophy (Sr Catherine) |
| 1979 | Mr Laurie Mayne |

## SIENA CONVENT AND SANTA CLARA SCHOOL, BENTLEY

For the first three years of foundation, Sister di Ricci Levitzke (Sr Kath), and Sister Anthony Sachse, travelled daily from St Dominic's Convent at Bedford Park to teach at the Santa Clara Primary School in Bentley. The suburb, named after John Bentley, an early convict warder, was typical of many developing localities – sandy and interspersed with scrub and lightly-timbered bushland. Now a heavily populated district, Bentley was initially settled by a handful of post-war migrants who came from various parts of Europe in the late 1940s. During the time that they took to build their homes, the majority of these hard-working settlers temporarily lived in sheds, tents or caravans.

To attend Mass, the Catholics among them generally followed sandy tracks to reach earlier-established churches at either East Victoria Park or Queen's Park. Although a pleasant enough stroll in moderate conditions, the parish priest of East Victoria Park, Father Frank O'Connor, was mindful of the fact that inclement weather and the searing heat of summer made these long treks rather trying. Consequently, in order to bring church services to the Bentley area, the priest decided to seek donations towards the purchase of a marquee. The 'tent-church', erected on an undeveloped portion of Mr and Mrs Sarich's land, was capable of holding some 60 persons and it served its purpose until heavy winter rains and winds in 1952 wreaked havoc on the canvas. [1]

On 17 August 1952, the official opening of a church-school, built on an acre of land in Palmerston Street, was seen as a progressive step forward for 200 or more New Australian settlers trying to cope with a new environment and language. The first Mass was celebrated in the new building shortly afterwards by Father O'Farrell in the presence of Archbishop Prendiville. Even though the premises were furnished in readiness to accept the enrolment of pupils, the task of finding a religious order with sufficient numbers to staff a parish school was not easy. The priest and parishioners were jubilant, therefore, when members of the Dominican order agreed to utilise the existing building to establish a Catholic primary school. Opening day in February 1954, proved to be a highly-successful event with a roll call of 66 pupils. This number increased during the year when a further 22 pupils enrolled for classes. [2]

The Santa Clara Primary School's first general report, presented on 30 June 1954, by the Superintendent of Schools, Mr Edgar Logan, was extremely gratifying. It noted that the term exams had already been successfully held and that all school records and programmes were up-to-date. After making a thorough inspection of the Dominican primary school, Mr Logan recommended that it be registered as an 'Efficient School' under the Education Act. His submission stated:

*...the Sisters deserve great credit for the very healthy school tone and spirit already developed. The standard of achievement reached is a very satisfactory one, and, despite the fact that there are twenty-eight New Australians, very good study habits are being developed. Children are extremely well behaved, are eager to work, and all appear to be working to full capacity.* [3]

Father Patrick Dunne was appointed the first parish priest of Bentley in November 1954, although he continued to live at Queen's Park until a presbytery was constructed in the new parish in 1955. Despite not living in the district, Fr Dunne managed to establish a valuable link with the Sisters and his parishioners, and throughout his term of office was daily encouraged by their willingness to support him in his parish duties. He, in turn, was extremely supportive of them. His dry sense of humour was a source of great enjoyment and his premature, sudden death was a shock to all who knew and admired him.

From the time of its opening, a constant stream of parents sought admittance to the school for their children, and the teaching staff was hard-pressed to prevent overcrowding. The original church-school at Bentley consisted of two rather large rooms divided by sliding doors, and towards the end of 1956, to meet the needs of a fast-growing population, it was decided to make additions. The dual-purpose brick and tile extensions, built at right angles to the existing building, were completed early the following year with great personal input from local families. On weekdays the hall was sub-divided into three classrooms and on Sundays it was converted for use as a church. [4]

The problem associated with the Sisters having to travel each day to Bentley from St Dominic's Convent, Bedford Park, was eventually raised and, taking in to account the time it took to make the long tiring journey, a decision was made, in July 1957, to build a Dominican Convent on a block of land donated by the parish. The building of the Siena Dominican Convent at Bentley commenced in September and, until it was occupied in March 1958, Father Dunne kindly moved out of his presbytery to provide accommodation for the Dominican Sisters. In the meantime, Sister Anthony Sachse was appointed Superior of the new convent and joining her were Sisters Reginald Leahy, Annunciata Kelly and Mercedes Clune. Although Sr Anthony remained in charge, in 1961 the other members of the Bentley community were replaced by Sisters Evangelist Graham, Xavier Ryan, Dolores Cummins and Columba Wilkinson. [5] A further increase in both pupils and parishioners meant that, by the 1960s, extra space was again needed to cater for the needs of both parties. As the parish was not in a position to afford the estimated cost of a complete new church, it was decided to erect the building in stages and to sub-contract the work with the help of volunteer labour. Construction began on the first section of the new Santa Clara Church in October 1962 and the building was completed the following May. By February 1963, there were 250 children being educated at the Santa Clara school. [6]

117. Siena Convent, Bentley

118. Siena Convent chapel, Bentley

Fortunately, many of the parishioners were tradesmen and not only did they supply free labour after work and on weekends, but the womenfolk also joined forces to provide the necessary refreshments. During the construction period, a great many families generously put their own household maintenance on hold until after their commitment to the project was completed. Involvement in the new building did not prevent local people from showing their gratitude by showering attention on the Sisters. Fruit, vegetables and an assortment of small luxuries were often delivered to the convent and, for a period of some 20 years, one local lady, Mrs Plackett, donated a dessert every Friday night, and cakes and the sweets for dinner on Sundays. When the Sisters first moved into the convent, parishioners thoughtfully provided them with a television set. Having no car, the Sisters for a time had to rely on various parents for transport. In the mid-1960s, much to the Sisters' delight, one benefactor made a Holden car available for a period of two or three years. Later the parish priest, Father Dunne, a man remembered by the Sisters and parishioners for his friendliness and compassion, sought donations towards the purchase of a second-hand vehicle for the convent.

Apart from concentrating on their academic and cultural studies, the students were extremely enthusiastic about sports. Constant practice, keen supervision and encouragement resulted in Santa Clara winning the Athletic Shield in 1966 at the Inter-school Sports. By 1967, a large section of lawn had been planted and a colourful display of flowers made it difficult to recall the sandy location of earlier years. Staff at that time consisted of Sisters Gemma Seaman (Superior, school principal and teacher in charge of Grades VI and VII), Xavier Ryan (bursar and teacher of Grades IV and V), Bernard Larney (Grade II), Mark Laracy (Grade I), Stanislaus O'Donough (music) and Eymard Regan, who cared assiduously for the house and the Sisters' well-being. Two years later, due to a shortage of Dominican Sisters, an extra lay teacher, Miss Grace, joined Mrs Murphy who had been on the teaching staff of Santa Clara for almost eight years. [7]

Local improvements in the district included an aquatic centre, which opened towards the end of 1969, and the construction of a huge State Housing Commission complex in 1970. The Olympic-sized pool, within walking distance from the school, proved to be a great boon to the pupils of Santa Clara, particularly during the summer months. When 320 units in the block of flats known as 'Brownlie Towers' were finally completed, they provided accommodation for a large number of families. Although some residents stayed only for a short period before moving into a home of their own, the location of the building placed further pressure on the parish to increase the size of the church and school. At the same time Sisters who were retired, or not engaged in teaching, often visited the elderly people living in the flats. Among these were Sisters Mary Anne Graham, Pauline Burke and Ambrose Bernet. The Sisters joined the tenants in weekly Mass, shared their joys and concerns and brought at least some warmth into their restricted lives.

119. Bentley Community, 1969
L. to R.: Back Row: Sisters Mercedes Clune, Xavier Ryan
Front: Sisters Anunciata Kelly, Eymard Regan

In 1974, the Santa Clara Primary School received a grant of $8400 from the Australian Schools Commission and Catholic Education Commission towards the cost of renovations. This amount was topped-up by $3900 contributed by the parish. Long steel girders were negotiated through doorways and jacked up to ceiling height for fixing, new acoustic doors in aluminium frames replaced the original heavy partitions dividing the classrooms and clear glass windows in aluminium frames were fitted instead of louvres. Other improvements included the installation of carpet and two acoustic ceilings, the rewiring of the building, and a considerable amount of refurbishing.

The Bentley parishioners were again fortunate to have as their parish priest, 'a man of the people'. Father James Patrick Petry MBE, served as a Chaplain in the British Army in England, Europe and Asia between 1950 and 1957, and after arriving in Western Australia in 1957 took up appointments in the south-west of the state before moving to Perth in 1966. He had a positive approach to life and according to those who knew him, encouraged others to be more positive about themselves. A regular attendance of approximately 600 persons at Mass persuaded Fr Petry and members of the Parish Council (formed in 1971, along with a branch of the Parents' and Friends' Association), to enlarge and renovate the Santa Clara Church in 1977. That same year, in view of a decision to accept boys to Grade VII, a modular classroom was erected between the convent and the presbytery and one of the earlier classrooms was converted into a library. Other developments involved the 1978 purchase of a residence in Palmerston Street for use as a pre-primary school, and the acquisition of a much-needed playing field.

During the 1980s, growing concerns were expressed about the need to constantly maintain the existing buildings and, in view of this situation, a practical decision was made to erect a new school. The First Stage of the project, a two-storey wing consisting of six classrooms, was funded by the Commonwealth Grants Commission, the Catholic Education Office and the Diocesan Resource Committee and completed in September 1988, at a cost of $378,400. In 1990, the school year commenced with an enrolment that had increased to 208 pupils. By then, the Second Stage of Santa Clara's redevelopment was in progress and expected to be completed within six to eight weeks. To make way for the new buildings, which were designed to house a library, an administration block, a canteen and an ESL (English as a Second Language) room, the old library and several classrooms were gradually demolished. With almost 50 per cent of the district's population coming from an ethnic background, the majority of migrant children needed special tuition and extra space was urgently needed to cater effectively for the situation. [8]

The new development was blessed by Archbishop Hickey and officially opened by Dr G. Gallop MLA on St Patrick's Day, 17 March 1992, before a crowd of about 500 onlookers. Invited guests who took their places on the dais were the Dominican Prioress, Sister Joan Carville, Sister Joan Buchanan, representing the Catholic Education Commission, and members of the Norbertine community, Fathers McNulty, William, Martin and Reynolds. By 1992, extra subjects had been added to the curriculum and there were 18 teachers on the staff of the primary school, including some part-time teachers and Sister Bertrand O'Connor, who assisted the librarian, Mrs Quigley, three mornings a week. On one section of the building is a plaque bearing the inscription: 'This Library is dedicated to Sister Anne Larney OP in recognition of her many years of service to Santa Clara School, Bentley, 17 March 1992'.

Dublin-born, Sister Anne Larney was professed in 1960, and during her religious life taught at Scarborough, Three Springs, Gwelup, Innaloo, Bedford Park (St Peter's), Bentley, Wembley Downs, Morley Park and Doubleview (Holy Rosary). She was the principal at Bentley during the stressful period involving the extensive redevelopment program. It was a time which required constant close co-operation with the Catholic Education Office, and regular negotiation with government authorities, architects and builders. Sister Anne, a dedicated teacher, handled the additional work quietly and with competence. A pastoral person, she related well to the various sections of the school community. 'There was', she reflected, 'a good relationship between the Sisters and the families at Bentley. The parents were "salt of the earth people", poor, but rich in goodness and generosity, very hospitable, simple and hard-working with few amenities. The children were very friendly, happy and full of life, enthusiastic and sports-loving'. [9]

When the parish priest of Bentley, Father T. McDonald, took up an appointment as Dean and Administrator of St Mary's Cathedral, Perth, in February

120. Santa Clara staff, Bentley, 1992
L. to R.: Back Row: S. Kelly, J. Trevenen, E. Battel
Middle: D. de Cinque, C. Rapanaro, C. Rebello, C. Trevenen, Sister Bertrand O'Connor
Front: D. Moriarty, S. Bryant, A. Szabo, Sister Anne Larney, J. Freeman, S. Quigley, A. Puglia

1992, the Norbertine Fathers from nearby Queen's Park took charge of the parish. Decreasing numbers in the Dominican community, and the retirement of many earlier teachers, meant that after a long and happy association with the district and its people, the Sisters found it necessary to withdraw from the school at the close of 1992. From the small parish church-school founded in 1954, Santa Clara has developed into a modern complex with a current enrolment of 250 pupils from kindergarten to Year 7. Although no longer involved in administration and teaching side of the school, the Dominican Sisters' links remain. Sister Anne, as pastoral assistant to the parish priest, continues to maintain a Dominican presence at Santa Clara by providing pastoral care for the school and parish communities. Sisters-in-Charge of the Santa Clara School were:

| | |
|---|---|
| 1958 | Sr Anthony Sachse |
| 1964 | Sr Rosarii Keenan |
| 1965 | Sr Joseph O'Connor |
| 1966 | Sr Gemma Seaman |
| 1969 | Sr Mercedes Clune |
| 1972 | Sr Eileen Leahy |
| 1978 | Sr Dolores Cummins |
| 1983 –1992 | Sr Anne Larney |

## INFANT JESUS SCHOOL, MORLEY PARK

At the beginning of 1955, two Dominican Sisters from St Dominic's Convent in Bedford Park opened a primary school in St Paul's Church in Walter Road, Morley Park, with an enrolment of 58 children, only eight of those being Australian. Morley Park, almost on the border of Bedford Park, was then just beginning to evolve as a promising suburb. It was populated mainly by migrants, a large proportion having come from Italy, Holland and Hungary. Sister Joseph O'Connor and Sister Dominic Galvin, had been involved in a number of new foundations in the Geraldton diocese and therefore were experienced in the development of primary schools.

The parish of St Paul's in Morley Park, which had been established in 1954, was placed in the care of the Carmelite Fathers in the following year. The elongated brick church building was built with a small room at either end. One of these was used as a cloakroom, the other as a store area for the altar, which was on wheels and could be rolled out of the church when classes were held during the week. A blackboard was positioned on one end wall and 80 wooden chairs, normally used by parishioners attending Mass, were used as temporary seats and desks until the proper classroom furniture was delivered. The building was divided into two classrooms by a hinged partition which was folded back for Mass on Sundays.

In 1960, there were 102 pupils being taught by the Dominican Sisters and a decision was made to erect a new school as soon as possible. All those involved in the discussion agreed that the land on which the church stood had a number of obvious drawbacks. Not only was the site too small and the grounds boggy in winter, but Walter Road created serious traffic problems as it gained prominence as a major thoroughfare. Subsequently, a replacement block was purchased for £3500 on the corner of Smith and Russell Streets, and, in November 1960, the construction of a new school building commenced on the four-acre site at an estimated cost of £14,500. By that stage, the new Infant Jesus School was regarded as a full primary school with enrolments being accepted to Grade VII. [1]

121. Original school, St Paul's, Morley Park, 1955

To prevent overcrowding during the time that the building was in progress, the Sisters were forced to make a number of temporary arrangements. These inconveniences were soon forgotten, however, when, at the beginning of 1962, the first Dominican pupils took their places in well-lit, airy classrooms. The new, white brick, single-storey construction was an enormous improvement, for although the original St Paul's School had a pleasing appearance, the building was inadequate as a school. The new primary school, which consisted of four modern classrooms and a small combined office and staff room, was sensibly designed with low maintenance steel-framed windows and sliding doors, most of which were protected by a long verandah featuring a set of glass panels. A paved bitumen section, running the entire length of the school building, was an ideal place in which to play and the grounds were well supplied with drinking fountains. [2]

Depending on the availability of places at nearby boys' colleges, male pupils usually remained with the Sisters until they reached Grades IV or V. In 1962, arrangements were made to transfer the first 20 Grade V boys from the Infant Jesus Primary School to nearby St Mark's Christian Brothers' School at Bedford Park. A hard-working Parents' and Friends' Association was established that same year and when the parents of Grade I pupils were invited to contribute 10 shillings towards the cost of the newly introduced Cuisenaire system (coloured rods used as an aid in teaching numeracy), the committee readily paid the balance. Within two years, a parish kindergarten had opened with about 50 small children registered, and enrolments at the Infant Jesus School had reached a total of 190 pupils.

As with the majority of religious schools established in new areas where young Catholic families were purchasing or renting homes, enrolments increased rapidly on a yearly basis. By 1965, there were 250 pupils in attendance at the Infant Jesus Primary School, and to cater for their needs two more classrooms were built and opened in time for the beginning of the second term. Until the end of 1969, a group of mothers were rostered to ferry the Sisters back and forth from the convent at Bedford Park to the school in Morley Park. This arrangement changed with the purchase of a splendid new Holden Torana. The Sisters, despite a nervous Sister Ambrose Bernet at the wheel, soon gained a new-found sense of independence, previously unknown to them. [3]

Sister Helen O'Connor, the last Dominican Sister to serve as principal at Infant Jesus, Morley Park, remembers the suburb in its infancy. As a young Sister, fresh from the Dongara novitiate she was assigned to the school in September 1956, and recalls that on her first impression she likened the appointment to a missionary outpost. The Carmelite Fathers had, at that time, just accepted the responsibility of the recently established parish and Father O'Leary's place had been taken by Father Hilary Doran ODC. Catechism classes were conducted on Saturdays in a bushland setting under the shade of a tree when Fr Hilary, accompanied by two Dominican Sisters, gathered a group of children together in the Hampton parish. The lessons, although of a serious nature, were informal and Sr Helen recalls youngsters coming through the bush bare-footed and eager. Recently looking back on those early days Sr Helen wrote: 'Like all beginnings nothing was easy, yet I found it a privileged place to begin my teaching apostolate. By 1964 the site of our earlier labours was in the hands of developers for a shopping complex and on my return to the school in 1964, as principal, I was introduced to a modern school building on a new location, plus a Carmelite church a short distance away. The local community had done wonders!'. [4]

Whenever finances allowed, various school amenities, such as a Jungle Jim combination and monkey bars and, more importantly, tennis courts were added over the years. The popularity and successful growth of the

122. First lay principal, Mr J. Hollands, Sisters Catherine Brophy, Margaret Vance and lay staff, Infant Jesus School, 1980

school was evidenced by the fact that, by 1975, the staff consisted of two Dominican Sisters, eight lay teachers and a full-time secretary, headed by the first appointed lay principal, Mr John Hollands. In 1978, a new resource centre and two more classrooms were added to the school complex to accommodate a further increase in the number of pupils. The Dominican Sisters who taught at Morley Park from 1976 until the community's withdrawal were: Anne Larney, Imelda Ryan, Mary Ryan, Margaret Vance, Catherine Brophy and Alphonse-Marie de Kuyer.

Several innovations were introduced during the 1980s to meet the criteria expected in modern educational centres. For example, children were instructed in the use of computers and a new general-purpose room was erected to accommodate the equipment. Boys attending the Infant Jesus School were given permission to complete their primary school education at the same school. This move later resulted in double stream classes and to cope with the extra numbers, staff levels were increased to include 18 teachers, two office and five ancillary members of staff, as well as the lay principal. Although the school still continued to operate, the year 1986 hailed the end of an era when, for the first time in 30 years, the Infant Jesus School at Morley Park commenced classes without any Dominican Sisters being present.

## OUR LADY'S ASSUMPTION SCHOOL, DIANELLA

The building of a parish school at Dianella in 1967, was truly a fine example of local co-operation and generosity. Our Lady's Assumption Church, which had been blessed and opened two years earlier to suit the needs of a newly-formed parish, was then under the guidance of the first appointed priest, Father Patrick O'Mara. At the time, Dianella recorded some 300 Catholic parishioners and, because many were young people with families, the possibility of opening a religious-based primary school in the district was discussed at some length by members of the Parish Finance Committee. The parish priest had first approached the Dominican Sisters in June 1965, in the hope that they might supply teaching staff for a school in 1966. Unfortunately, the Prioress was unable to spare a member of the community at the time and it was July 1966 before she could demonstrate her willingness to send a teacher the following year. [1]

Prior to the Dominicans' involvement, the majority of Catholic children attended the parish school at Bedford Park, and when a decision was made, early in 1966, to build a new school at Dianella, the project had the full support of the parish. The committee's request for assistance was highly successful when 77 volunteers, 29 of these being tradesmen, generously offered their services free of charge. Father O'Mara, a pleasant-natured Irishman from County West Meath, remained in the parish during the time that the Dominican Sisters taught at Dianella. He was not only approachable and interested in the school, but a competent financial manager of archdiocesan funds. To his credit, he initiated and organised the extensive building program for Our Lady's Assumption School and often assisted the team of voluntary workers.

The new school building, designed by G. Mazak and to be constructed by A. McGlinchy, commenced on 7 December 1966, and was completed after just eight weeks for a total cost of $16,400. [2] Among the numerous contributors who provided support and volunteered their time were: J. Boland (engineer); M. McKinnie and S. Aldridge (surveyors); R. Lamb, R. Appelbee, K. Kubcek and P. Kerrigan (electricians); D. Colley, A. Dunsire, F. Krepp and J. Durbridge (plumbers); E. Deans and J. Wicks (welders); M. Meaney, G. Hille, F. Colman, M. Dragicevich, R. Schofield and N. Ewing (carpenters); A. Hodes and R. Mackiewicz (cabinet makers); E. Bowers and A. Ammonini (granolithic workers); A. Branca (plasterer) and H. Leber (painter). [3] Sharing their skills and providing support were: G. Durkin, N. Carter, R. Omodei, K. Parker, D. O'Brien, J. Ryan, J. Shimmings, W. Cassidy, R. Williamson, P. Perich, P. Wilson, R. Worthington, A. Thomson, T. Hawkes, P. Mahoney, L. McComish, G. Edmondson, J. Norton, W. Cobby, G. O'Connor, V. Richardson, R. Waters, J. McNamara, R. Russell Brown, R. Tinkler, T. Dwyer, K. Thomas, G. Power, D. McCullagh, J. Hawke, L. Bevis, R. Elton, M. Boswood, J. Kennedy, K. Martin, B. Bonwick, J. Grant, K. Brown, M. Gatti, J. Buckland, D. Bailey, S. Bardon, G. de Vos, W. Hendricks, R. Devereux, A. Smith and

J. Kapuscik. It was said that even the small children were involved in the busy-bees that took place, and for part of the day they worked happily alongside the adults carrying little buckets of sand or trundling broken bricks in their small toy barrows. [4]

After the completion of Our Lady's Assumption School in 1967, Sister Maria Goretti Power, a member of the Dominican community based at nearby Bedford Park, was appointed the school's first principal. Miss Norma Gianotti, a qualified lay teacher and ex-student of both St Thomas Aquinas and the Dominican Ladies' College at Dongara, was employed by the parish as class teacher for pupils in Year One.

Patricia Power (Sr Maria Goretti), the daughter of Margaret and William Power, was born in Dublin, Ireland. She arrived in Western Australia in March 1954 and nine months later was accepted into the Dominican novitiate at Dongara. After making her final profession of vows in 1961, Sister Maria served in a number of schools in both country and metropolitan areas. These included the Marian School at Morawa, St Paul's at Three Springs, Holy Rosary at Doubleview, Our Lady's Assumption at Dianella and the Infant Jesus School at Morley Park, until a spinal injury resulted in her having to terminate her teaching career. Between the years 1981 and 1983, she was the Prioress of the Santa Sabina Priory in Scarborough and, in 1981, she became a receptionist at Newman Siena College in Doubleview serving for a period of 16 years. Described as a meticulous worker and a compassionate listener, she was kept busy in her new role welcoming parents and visitors, performing clerical duties and offering pastoral care to students.

123. Foundation pupils with first principal, Sister Maria Power, Our Lady's Assumption School, Dianella

The new school building, which was officially opened on Sunday, 28 May 1967, by Bishop Myles McKeon, consisted of two classrooms, an office, a storeroom and a protected outside area with suitable seating and modern facilities for both the boys and girls, as well as for the staff members. School fees were kept to a minimum of one dollar a week for a family, and in an effort to economise, the desks and chairs needed to furnish the classrooms were purchased from the government disposals office for the bargain price of 12 cents and 18 cents respectively.

Towards the end of 1968, two additional classrooms were erected to cope with the mounting number of enrolments. The community spirit that had been evident from the beginning continued to grow, and by the time the construction of a new two-storey building commenced, members of the volunteer force, who had offered assistance, had increased to some 102 persons. When the new classrooms opened at the beginning of 1969, Sister Eileen Leahy (Sr Reginald) was appointed principal of Our Lady's Assumption School, Dianella, in charge of the 142 pupils who were enrolled that year.

The completion of the Third Stage of the building program in 1970, a double-storey complex consisting of three classrooms and a tuck shop, was timely, for in following year it was estimated that 650 families lived in the parish. To cater for the 238 pupils attending classes at Dianella in 1971, five lay teachers joined the staff and classes were extended to Grade 6. It seems that members of the original parish busy-bee decided not to disband after the first and second projects were completed, and over the years an army of 232 hardworking volunteers, including 77 parish ladies, gradually changed the face of the Dianella parish.

On 5 June 1972, a large crowd gathered to witness Archbishop Launcelot Goody (later Sir Launcelot) bless and officially open the impressive extensions made to the school. The new building consisted of a school hall, four extra classrooms on the upper level, a kitchen, a storeroom and a self-contained flat for the caretaker, Mr John Walsh. Two of the classrooms had been completed earlier, in time for the opening of school in February 1972. The huge savings made through parish participation meant that the cost of the latest extensions amounted to the sum of only $49,000. Using the same volunteer labour force, another wing was added to the school building in 1978. The total cost of this new addition amounted to approximately $34,000, $6000 of which was provided by the Schools Commission towards capital costs. [5]

One year later the Dominican Sisters, who along with other religious orders were experiencing a shortage in vocations, had no choice but to withdraw from the school at Dianella. For much the same reason that many foundations scattered throughout the state had closed, the Sisters had to rationalise their resources to the best possible advantage. Between 1967 and 1979, the following Sisters staffed Our Lady's Assumption School:

Maria Goretti Power (first principal), Ambrose Bernet, Jacinta Vance (Sr Margaret), Pierre Ross (Sr Diane), Agnes Leeson (principal), Reginald Leahy (Sr Eileen, principal) and Francesca Haddock (the last Dominican principal).

From the beginning, the school benefited from community involvement and the Sisters were grateful and ever mindful of the part parents played in its development. An extract taken from an educational study, published in 1973, could well have had Our Lady's Assumption School in mind:

*...it is the parents who evolve the family system of values about education; it is the parents who reject or accept school values. Schools are staffed by qualified teachers and are equipped with an ever-increasing variety of modern technology. Despite all this expenditure of effort and resources, the whole enterprise appears to stand or fall according to the support or opposition of parents.* [6]

Judged on this opinion, Our Lady's Assumption School indeed stands tall.

## SANTA SABINA CONVENT AND ST JOHN'S SCHOOL, SCARBOROUGH

Despite its dangerous seasonal ocean currents and comparative isolation, Scarborough became a popular fishing spot for campers and a summer resort for families long before the suburb became residential. Colonist John Hughes became the earliest known resident when he farmed a section of land in the area during the 1850s. Although he did not own the original property, he later purchased 40 acres of Crown land close to the coast in 1869. The few settlers who were attracted to the valleys and swamps that existed behind the sand dunes, were mainly dairy farmers interested in grazing. Until such time as the names Wattle Park and Scarborough Park were introduced for real estate purposes, the district often took its name from Hughes's property, Blue Hole Farm, said to have been chosen because of the bluish reeds growing in the local swamp. Among other families to have an early association with the area were the Butlers, Corbetts and Mannings. [1]

A public sale of land at Scarborough Beach, described by several real estate agents as the 'Queen of West Australian watering places', was heavily promoted by developers as early as 1886. Potential buyers, interested in viewing the one-acre blocks of land, were advised that they could reach the 'marine retreat' from Perth, within one hour on horseback or in two hours if driving a conveyance. [2] The locality's gradual emergence as a top surfing beach and holiday spot, however, soon demanded better travelling conditions and, to satisfy the influx of visitors making their way to the coast, the main arterial route, North Beach Road, was re-routed along Killarney Road to the beach and, in 1925, renamed Scarborough Beach Road. Hubert Baker's privately owned Excelsior Motor Service, which began in 1916 and operated until the late 1920s, was one of several small family enterprises formed to transport day-trippers to the beach during the 1920s and 1930s. [3]

Several unfortunate drownings took place during those years and, to safeguard swimmers, a Surf Life Saving Club was formed with volunteers in 1928. Within three years, Scarborough had become more attractive to a wider range of visitors. By then, the beach was floodlit and waterfront improvements included impressive retaining walls, a promenade and new bathing facilities. Scarborough became even more popular after December 1932, when the 'Art Deco' Scarborough Hotel, acclaimed for its select accommodation and extensive and uninterrupted ocean views, opened its doors in time to capture the Christmas trade. During the 1930s, the area continued to gain popularity and, with the introduction of better roads and more facilities, many permanent residences were beginning to appear alongside the original holiday cottages.

Scarborough, once part of the Leederville parish, was mostly serviced throughout the 1930s by Catholic priests attached to Osborne Park and Leederville. In summer time, Mass was celebrated for holiday-makers and a number of residents in Peter Rinaldi's Silver Bells Tea-rooms on the beach-front. With the gradual expansion of the population, Monsignor Moloney, the priest in charge of Leederville, commissioned the building of a hall on Scarborough Beach Road within walking distance to the beach. The wooden building, which cost £740 to erect, was officially opened and blessed by Archbishop Prendiville in December 1936. In the early 1940s, after Scarborough became an adjunct of Osborne Park, Mass was held regularly in the hall every Sunday before a small group of locals and a large crowd of beach-goers. Understandably, during winter the attendance diminished. [4]

The residential side of Scarborough really started to develop during the post-war period and with the arrival of more families came the usual call for churches and schools. Taking into account the increased population, Archbishop Prendiville canonically erected the parish of St John the Evangelist, Scarborough, on 8 February 1948, and appointed Father E. McBride as parish priest. At the same time, the Sisters of Mercy commenced St John's Primary School with an enrolment of 44 children. Foundation Sisters, Celine O'Farrell and de Lourdes Frawley, each day travelled by bus from the Mercy Convent at West Perth to teach in the local Catholic hall. On schooldays, the sanctuary was separated from the rest of the hall by curtains and the remainder of the space was divided into two classrooms by free-standing blackboards. Sister de Lourdes taught 28 pupils in Grades III to VI and, to augment the two shillings paid per week for school fees, she provided music lessons before and after school, during lunch recess and again on Saturdays. Her companion, Sister Celine, conducted classes for 16 children in Grades I and II and also taught Theory of Music before school commenced. [5]

According to the original school register, the first children to enrol at St John's, on 2 February 1948, were Anne and Peter Samuels, Edna Wells, Thelma and Yvonne James, Kathleen Drew, Anne and Mary Adam, Bryan Tapsell, George and Thomas Drew, Gloria and Leslie Lynch, Rodney and Lionel McPherson, Judith and Fay Taylor, Dawn and Olive Fee, Pauline and Garrett Stack, Peter Rose, Janice Orr, Ronald Smith, Patricia and Lawrence Horner, Judith MacRae, Julitta and Neil Fisher, Mary Ryan, Anthony Barret, Terence Mahony, Peter Kenny, Ronald and Wayne Kirk and Stewart Pedley. It is also interesting to note that Marlene Laracy, who later became a Dominican and took the religious name Sr Mark, enrolled as a pupil at St John's the following year. At the beginning of 1950, a total of 79 primary school children arrived for classes and three Sisters of Mercy (Sisters Brendan, Kevin and Eucharia), took the place of the original staff and continued to teach until the Dominicans took charge of the Scarborough school some six months later. [6]

In August 1950, after accepting Archbishop Prendiville's invitation to form a Dominican community at Scarborough, Sisters Albertus Bain, Anthony Sachse and Francis Huntsman, moved into a neat asbestos and tile house purchased for them in nearby Clifton Street. On school days, the group left home each morning at 6.00 a.m. to walk to Mass carrying their breakfast with them. This was shared afterwards in a tiny room at the back of the church-school, which was used at various times as a sacristy, a confessional, a store, and a staff or music room. Music lessons followed until it was time for classes to begin and with only a brief moment to spare for a cup of tea, the Sisters again gave speech and music lessons after school before leaving to walk home for evening prayers and a meal. [7]

124. First convent, Clifton St, Scarborough, 1950

At first, the original church-hall was considered to be more than adequate for the number of children expected to enrol. As enrolments increased, it became obvious to those in charge that any future intake of pupils would have to be limited, unless the premises were extended. Action was taken to remedy this situation when, towards the close of St John's first year as a Dominican school, approval was granted to commence additions. By the time two new classrooms, a storeroom for school equipment, and a small front office were blessed and opened on 4 February 1951, the number of pupils in attendance had reached 100 and Sister Ignatius Prendiville had replaced Sister Anthony as a member of staff. The decision to expand the school's accommodation was timely, for during the year the number of pupils enrolled at St John's had risen by a further 40 and, for the first time, both primary and secondary subjects were included in the curriculum when a small group of girls commenced secondary studies. Boys who were accepted for Infants and Grades I to III usually continued the remainder of their education at the Christian Brothers' College in Leederville.

State Housing Commission rental and War Service homes built in the Scarborough-Doubleview area during the 1950s, had a huge impact on the development of the area. Many New Australians who had settled in the district, particularly those from Holland, such as the Gradisen, Uijen, Stoffels, Van Grootel, Vermeer and VanderMark families sent their children to be educated by the Dominican Sisters at St John's. Happy to learn the language and make friends with their neighbours, many became involved in the school's progress and were always willing to assist. As one Sister later observed, 'They brought with them a new and valuable dimension to the parish school'. [8]

An exceptionally busy year for the Dominican Sisters in Western Australia proved to be 1952, for not only were they still teaching at Scarborough, Dongara, Cue,

125. Pupils, St John's School, Scarborough, 1952
L. to R.: Back Row: N. Swarbrick, J. Orr, P. Masters, A. Hulbert, M. Morrissey, J. Beer, A. Gradisen, S. O'Neil, C. Milne, P. Horner
3rd Row: K. Serventy, G. Symons, P. Stack, R. Mayne, J. Hayward, A. Hinde, J. Whitby, O. Fee, C. Willesee, J. Fisher, G. Murray, S. Leeson
2nd Row: A. Harnett, H. Hoskins, M. McGuire, A. Beech, P. Aquino, L. Hoskins, E. Flanagan, M. Fisher M. Doherty, J. Pickford, F. Ryan
Front Row: B. Tapsall, J. Lippa,..., C. Trestrail, G. Gradisen, G. Lane, B. Gradisen, M. Kinsella...., E. James

Leonora, Gwalia, Meekatharra, Three Springs, Mingenew and Bedford Park, but in May the previous year they had also taken over the Sisters of Mercy small school at nearby Gwelup. With an increased enrolment that year of 175 pupils, Sister di Ricci Levitzke (Sr Kath) joined the foundation Sisters to cope with the extra numbers attending the school. By then, the nuns' residence in Clifton Street was 'home' to seven members of the community – Sisters Albertus Bain, Francis Huntsman, Ignatius Prendiville and di Ricci Levitzke, who were on the staff at St John's and Sisters St Anne Graham and Joseph O'Connor who taught at Gwelup. The seventh person, Sister Agnes Leddin, an excellent cook, had charge of the household. It was said that Sr Agnes readily added a dash of humour to most situations and that for most of her religious life she seemed to rotate between the chapel, the kitchen and the laundry. [9] By 1952, the use of the Clifton Street house was nearing its end, for plans were already being made for the construction of a new convent on the corner of Deanmore and Lalor Streets.

St John's School had 220 pupils on the roll in 1953, and by then it was necessary to augment the existing teaching staff with two more experienced teachers, Sister Ambrose Bernet and Sister Perpetua Gill. The cooking and the domestic side of convent life was, at that time, shared by two elderly, dedicated and hard-working lay Sisters, Rose McCusker and Evangelist Graham. Sister Ambrose, a talented musician, was described as 'an unassuming, gentle and prayerful person'. The daughter of Swiss parents, she received her early education from the Mercy Sisters at Victoria Square, commencing music lessons at an early age. Later, as a Dominican Sister, she studied at an advanced level under Vaughan Hanley and during her lifetime gained many awards for violin. Over the years, Sr Ambrose patiently shared her talents with many pupils. Estelle Dragun (née Bedford), her brother Lewis and later in 1980, her son Matthew, were three pupils who benefited greatly from the tuition they received from this fine musician. When asked to comment on her former teacher Estelle stated, 'You always listened attentively to her every word because of her very strong Swiss accent. As we lived close to the convent, Sister, when walking on a summer's afternoon, would often call in and have a cup of tea with my mother. Music, among other things, was always discussed and she loved to reminisce about Switzerland and her family'. When Estelle took her son to learn the violin at the convent in Bentley, she discovered that her former mentor had been researching teaching methods of bowing technique with Mr Hanley. Impressed, she recalled:

*Sister Ambrose's enthusiasm to trial a particular method was great and we had a lot of fun learning. Sister was my first teacher, teaching me in Grade I at St John's School in Scarborough. Her deep faith and love of her work reflected in her teaching, and she certainly contributed to the understanding of my own faith. I will always remember her warm smile and her encouraging way. She was a shining example of the Dominican way.* [10]

Sister Perpetua Gill, a highly-respected member of the Dominican community, remained on the teaching staff at St John's for eight years and later, when she took up her appointment as principal of Newman Siena, her expertise was successfully channelled into a number of worthwhile directions. When speaking of past teaching methods, Sr Perpetua recalled:

*The combined classes, sometimes two – sometimes three, or even more, also meant that the teachers had to work harder to provide a double and, in fact, often triple number of teaching lessons, but this was accepted as part of the commitment to Catholic Education and, after teaching for 50 years in many situations, I still believe the students were well taught and high standards maintained. Many of them continued into Upper Secondary School and their results compared more than favourably with those of other Catholic and Government Schools.* [11]

Improved living conditions for the Sisters began to look more promising when foundations for the new convent were laid in 1953. Work also began that year on the construction of a modern church, more in keeping with a progressive suburb. The new Santa Sabina Convent, designed by architect Mr A. O'Hara and built by Berry Bros, consisted of 10 monastic cells (bedrooms), a parlour and community room and a small chapel with seating to accommodate 15 Sisters. A magnificent painting of Mary,

126. Santa Sabina Convent chapel, Scarborough

by Greek artist A. Karafylakis, dominates the wall behind the altar, adding colour and a sense of reverence to the sanctuary. After delays caused by the amount of limestone present on the site, members of the Dominican community,

Sisters Albertus, di Ricci, Francis, Ambrose, Perpetua, Rose and Evangelist, shifted from Clifton Street and took up residence in their new quarters in late October 1953. In what appears to have been a well-organised team effort, students, parents and friends assisted with the transfer of goods and furniture and the Sisters have never forgotten the kindness of people like Mrs Geita Peterkin and Mrs Lorrie Tracey who thoughtfully welcomed the seven occupants to their new home with a delightful afternoon tea. Towards the end of 1953, new ground was broken at St John's when Faye Taylor, Geraldine Haywood, Mary Milne, Loretta Serventy and Pat Elphick became the first candidates to sit for the Junior Certificate Examination. [12]

Built in a prominent position on the crest of a hill at the corner of Scarborough Beach Road and Deanmore Street, the nave of the Immaculate Heart of Mary Church was officially opened and blessed by the Auxiliary Bishop of Perth, Dr Goody, on 22 November 1953. The construction of Stage One was the result of a great deal of fund-raising on the part of Scarborough's parishioners, who later worked tirelessly to reduce the parish debt. Fifteen years later, much to everyone's satisfaction, the church, which featured a series of specially designed stained glass windows, was eventually completed. The man behind the development of Scarborough's church precinct was Kalgoorlie-born Father Eddie McBride. Described by those

127. Presentation by Shire representative, W. Stewart, to Father Henry Byrne at Scarborough parish Golden Jubilee celebrations; photograph of former parish priests in background

who knew him as a 'practical, approachable person', blessed with a 'keen sense of humour', he was part of the parish scene for some 20 years.

Father Ed McBride was educated in the goldfields, first by the Sisters of Mercy, and then by the Christian Brothers in Kalgoorlie. Later he studied for the priesthood in Victoria and was ordained in Perth in 1937. Serving first as assistant priest at Palmyra, he became parish priest of Bedford Park-Bayswater in 1940, before taking up an appointment two years later as vice-rector of St Charles Seminary in Guildford. His appointment at Scarborough coincided with the separation of that parish from Osborne Park and during his long term of office in the district, he witnessed the birth of the neighbouring parishes of North Beach, Innaloo, Doubleview, Karrinyup and

Wembley Downs. Father McBride was ordained Monsignor six years before he died in 1972, and priests who succeeded him in the parish included Monsignor John Murphy (1969), Father Frank Dillon (1974) and Father Henry Byrne (1985). [13]

It has been said that convent-educated girls can often be identified by their manners and distinctive speech. If these observations are correct, then the fact that many religious Sisters have also taught small boys means that young male pupils educated at convents must also share these attributes. It is well-known that self-expression and a deep love of literature and the spoken word, have always been encouraged by members of religious teaching orders. This was certainly true of the Dominican Sisters, as evidenced by the attention given to music, speech, singing, drama, debating and public speaking. The emphasis placed on fluency, elocution and the need for clarity in reading, means that, at some stage of their education, most convent pupils have been subjected to practical experience in voice production. Participation in annual school concerts, verse speaking choirs and The University of Western Australia and Trinity College of London speech and music examinations usually commenced at primary school level and continued through high school. It is not surprising, therefore, that so many parents have taken advantage of the convent school system. Indeed, a number of today's public speakers, lecturers, actors and news-readers learnt their basic skills from the Sisters. One such person, Terry Willesee, a journalist and high-profile television presenter, readily admits that, during the 1950s, his former teachers, the Dominican Sisters, played an important role in his future career:

*My memories of school at St John's are all pleasant. That from someone who had a phobia about school is saying a lot. Aged 10 and still unable to read, I was sent to St John's for urgent help. It came in the form of Sister Mary di Ricci [Levitzke], she showered me with love and care and had me reading in weeks. I will never forget her and the spirit of the Dominican nuns.* [14]

Attendance at the school increased to 280 pupils at the commencement of 1954, and by the time the new convent was officially opened in February that year, there were 11 Sisters living at Santa Sabina, including Sister Assumpta Moriarty and Sister Regina O'Neill, who were studying for degrees at The University of Western Australia. [15] On 19 July, Dominican Father Fintan Campbell, who had arrived in Perth to establish the new parish of Innaloo, moved into the presbytery at Scarborough and, during Father McBride's absence, temporarily took charge of the parish. By October, work had begun on St Dominic's primary school in nearby Innaloo (North Doubleview).

In 1955, eight extra rooms were added to the Santa Sabina Convent giving the Sisters a total of 18 bedrooms to cater for additional staff and visiting Dominican guests. By then, St John's roll call recorded 310 pupils, despite the expectation that numbers could have been affected by the opening of St Dominic's School at Innaloo. In May, when foundation Superior Sister Albertus Bain returned to Bedford Park to join the staff at St Thomas Aquinas Secondary College, Sister de Sales Patterson (Sr Mary), was appointed Superior and Sister-in-Charge of the Santa Sabina Convent and St John's School. Another 20 pupils' names were added to the roll in 1956, and to cater for the increased enrolments, two more classrooms were erected by voluntary labour and completed by June. In November, the school's sole senior student, Geraldine Haywood, succeeded in gaining a Leaving Certificate and another five girls entered for the Junior Certificate. [16]

Although not having their own playing fields at St John's might have at times inconvenienced the pupils, the situation did not prevent them from excelling at sports. For a number of years, the school's Annual Sports Day was held locally at Abbett Park and, as usual, parents were totally supportive of the day's activities. Apart from participating in this yearly event, which at one time involved eight teams, each with more than 50 pupils, the school also took part in an Inter Dominican Inter-Schools Sports Day, inaugurated in 1955. Thereafter, for three consecutive years, St John's won the Primary Schools Athletic Shield. In 1956, they also won the Secondary Schools Athletic Shield and, in 1959, the Secondary Schools' Marching Trophy. [17]

The wearing of school uniforms has long been a custom followed by convent schools, and over the years it has been easy to identify a particular school or college by a colour, badge or motto. Although many Dominican schools around the world, including the Dominican Ladies' College at Dongara, chose the ancient Dominican combination of black and white for school uniforms, St John's followed a more modern trend. In summer, students wore a fawn (beige) dress with a blue collar and buttons, topped by a fawn bolero and a Panama hat, which featured a rust-coloured band and metal badge, inscribed with the Dominican motto *Veritas*. During the winter months, this outfit was replaced by a rust-coloured school uniform, a blazer and matching stitched beret.

In terms of change, 1958 heralded an historic year for all Dominican Sisters when the four autonomous congregations of the Dominican Order in Australia amalgamated into one congregation under one Mother Prioress General (Mother Philomena Waite), based in Canberra. That same year, enrolments at St John's increased to more than 410 (over 90 of these children being enrolled in Grade I classes), and, for the first time, the school employed a lay teacher, Mrs West. To keep pace with the growth in pupil numbers, further improvements were made to the Scarborough complex in 1958. Not only was a domestic science room, a tuck shop and a new toilet block erected at St John's, but additional cells and a new laundry were also added to the convent. [18] Space continued to be at a premium until other Dominican schools were established in nearby parishes, and so, to avoid overcrowding, alternative arrangements occasionally had to be made. For example, in 1958, first year high school students were temporarily housed in the local Returned Servicemen's League hall on the corner of Grand Promenade and Brighton Road, and use was later made of Mr and Mrs Donnelly's vacant garage at 19 Stanley Street. When these premises were no longer available, Father Campbell OP helped relieve the situation by offering 27 of St John's secondary school students short-term accommodation in a vacant room at the new Holy Rosary School at Doubleview. Sister Regina O'Neill accompanied this group of students when they were transferred from Scarborough to Doubleview in February 1959.

Classes for other secondary school students were also held in Santa Sabina's 'Green Parlour' and, during 1959, use was also made of a free-standing room at the back of the Finnegan family home in Deanmore Street. In this small studio, two Leaving students, Margaret Doherty and Rita Wark, and three Sub-Leaving girls, Jill Hopkins, Judith Francisco and Elaine Flanagan were prepared for their Leaving (TEE) exams.[19] Lack of facilities obviously did not affect the students' studies, for one of these girls, Margaret Doherty, later graduated as a doctor. The Sisters involved in teaching secondary school students at that time were Ignatius Prendiville, Perpetua Gill and Regina O'Neill. Primary school teachers at St John's included Sisters Emmanuel Lynch, Cecilia Murphy, Antoninus Campbell, Dominica Davis, Thomas Short, de Montfort Evans and Jerome O'Connor (Sr Helen).

128. The senior girls' temporary classroom, 1959
L. to R.: M. Doherty, J. Hopkins, E. Flanagan, R. Wark, J. Francisco

Members of the Scarborough community were particularly pleased when, in January 1959, a past pupil from St John's, Anne Hulbert (Sr Stephen) entered the Dominican novitiate at Wahroonga, New South Wales. They were even more delighted when a further three former pupils, Marlene Laracy (Sr Mark), Edith Murphy (Sr Andrew), and Sally Leeson (Sr Agnes), joined them in February the following year. In May 1959, during the first visit to Western Australia by the Dominican Congregation's Mother Prioress General, the Santa Sabina Convent in Scarborough was constituted a Priory and Sister Emmanuel Lynch was appointed the Prioress with Sister Assumpta Moriarty as Sub-Prioress. [20]

Mary Lynch (Sr Emmanuel), the youngest child of Sarah and Philip Lynch, a farmer, was born at Three Springs on 19 July 1913. Having lost her mother prematurely, she was enrolled, at an early age, as a boarder at the Sacred Heart Convent in Three Springs and later at St Dominic's College in Dongara, where she completed her Leaving Certificate. The future Sister Emmanuel, entered the novitiate at St Dominic's Priory when she was 21 years of age and during the 1930s obtained her Teachers' Certificate and studied towards an Arts Degree at The University of Western Australia. Widely recognised for the hospitality she extended throughout her life and noted for her keen sense of humour, a heritage of her Irish ancestry, Sr Emmanuel held many significant positions within the community, including those of Mistress of Schools, Prioress and also Prioress Provincial, a title she held for eight years. She was described by her contemporaries as a considerate and humble Superior, who readily sought advice from others whose expertise she regarded as greater than hers.

On 20 December 1960, a reunion of past pupils was held at St John's for the first time when 55 girls attended a buffet tea in 'the grove' which was followed by Benediction. The following year, a Parents' and Friends' Association was established and their collective support made it possible to upgrade many of the school's facilities. In 1961, there were 20 religious living in the Santa Sabina Convent at Scarborough, with Sister Assumpta Moriarty as Prioress and Sister Laurence Prendiville as Sub-Prioress. Ten Sisters taught at St John's, including Sister Consilii Costello, who, by then, was Mistress of Schools. Two others travelled from Santa Sabina to teach at the new Holy Rosary School at Doubleview and five other members of the community journeyed each day to St Dominic's at Innaloo. At that time, two Sisters were attending university, one part-time and the second, a full-time student, was preparing a thesis for her Master of Arts Degree. [21]

St John's re-opened in 1961, with an enrolment of 370 primary school pupils and 80 secondary students and from that group seven girls successfully sat for the Junior

Certificate and four for the Leaving Certificate. The announcement that one student, Elizabeth Doherty, had not only passed in seven subjects with five distinctions, but had also received a Commonwealth Bursary and gained a Government Exhibition, was greeted with great enthusiasm. In May 1962, after the Dominican Sisters had opened their new Girls' High School, Siena, at Doubleview, the school at Scarborough underwent several major changes. Instead of continuing their secondary studies at St John's, the senior students were transferred to Siena, thus creating the opportunity for St John's to revert to its original primary school status.

129. St John's School, Scarborough

When the Prioress Assumpta Moriarty also became principal of Siena in 1962, Sister Dominica Davis became the new Mistress of Schools at St John's, with the authority to handle school matters that would normally be the province of the Prioress. Sister Dominica, an outstanding educationalist in a wide range of subjects, had experienced teaching and community life in both the country and metropolitan areas and was as well-known to pupils in Dongara, Mingenew, Bedford Park, Innaloo, Wembley Downs and Doubleview, as she was at Scarborough. Born at Wilga, Western Australia, on 29 September 1914, and christened Dorothy Ellen Letitia, she was the eldest of two children born to Charlotte and William Davis. After completing her education with Our Lady of the Mission Sisters at Highgate, she studied at Claremont Teachers' Training College and taught for a number of years in government schools before entering the convent. A highly-principled, decisive person, Sr Dominica set high standards for herself and others, not only in teaching and administration, but also in the fine needlework she produced and the gardens she created.

She is credited with having planned and developed the gardens at the Scarborough and Doubleview convents and also the oval at Newman Siena College. During an interview in 1988, Sr Dominica made an interesting comparison between past and present pupils:

*In 1958 when I joined St John's I had a Grade One class of 90 or 91…Sister Mary Cecilia joined me, and we did it between us. We had a great year...I think now teachers have to be on the ball all the time. It's a different type of child. They can't use things over and over again. You've always got to think of something new; whereas children accepted what we put up in front of them in those days.* [22]

By 1963, the Santa Sabina Convent was full to overflowing. All 20 rooms, as well as an office, were needed to accommodate the 21 Sisters in residence and there was little room to spare in the chapel and refectory. At that stage, six Sisters taught at St John's (360 pupils), six at Siena (104 pupils), four at St Dominic's (270 pupils), another four at Holy Rosary School (172 pupils) and one Sister was in charge of the household. Sister Anthony Sachse, who left St John's in 1958 to take up an appointment as Sister-in-Charge of Santa Clara School, Bentley, returned to Scarborough in 1964 as principal and was struck by the growth in population and the physical changes made to the school and suburb. She was most impressed to find that the school's amenities had improved beyond belief and that no longer did the pupils and Sisters have the onerous task of pulling heavy desks aside to clear the hall. [23] Frances Patricia (Sr Anthony), the daughter of Mary and Herbert Sachse, was born at Cottesloe in the 1920s. Her father, a well-known chef in Perth, was said to be the creator of Australia's best-known dessert, the Pavlova, and since his death the international acceptance of this meringue-style creation has assured his place in cuisine history. Sister Anthony, a meticulous person, taught at Cue, Meekatharra, Dongara, Three Springs, Morawa, Leonora, Scarborough, Bedford Park, Bentley and Doubleview and served as Prioress in three of these foundations and as principal in four of the schools. Sister Dolores Cummins replaced Sr Anthony as principal of St John's in 1967 and, in 1970, Sister Xavier Ryan assumed that role. Sister Xavier later proclaimed that one of her proudest achievements during her term of office was the establishment of a well-stocked library at the school.

In what was described by one person as 'the dark days', St John's Primary School almost faced closure during the 1970s. At the time, Scarborough had an ageing population, and because enrolments at the Dominican primary school were affected by the development of new schools in the northern suburbs, the Sisters were forced to seriously consider the future viability of St John's. Meetings were held in an attempt to clarify the situation, and although opinions were divided about the school's future, it was finally decided that the majority of parishioners wished to retain the school. Many of those present agreed that they would be willing to increase fees threefold rather than close St John's, whose numbers by then had reached an all-time low of 74 pupils in

130. Staff, St John's School, Scarborough, 1979
L. to R.: Misses N. Genovese, T. Hills, Sisters Eileen Leahy, Marie Therese Sharman, Miss H. Patchett

attendance. A wise decision to purchase a school bus to transport children from neighbouring suburbs eventually solved the problem. Mrs Jan Morris (née Ibbotson), secretary of the School Board and a former student of St John's, later wrote, 'The school is now on the up and up, numbers continue to rise. We have excellent teachers. I can't see St John's doing anything but going from strength to strength'. [24]

In 1981, Sister Eileen Leahy (formerly Sr Reginald), the last religious principal to serve at the primary school, was succeeded by St John's first lay principal Miss Nancy Genovese, and with her appointment the Dominican Sisters' involvement with the school gradually lessened. Miss Genovese, a committed Catholic and dedicated teacher, continued to maintain the spirit of the Dominican Sisters, assisted during the 1980s by the presence of Sister Diane Ross and Sister Edith Murphy. Sister Catherine Brophy, who followed as religious co-ordinator, was the last Dominican Sister to be attached to the staff at St John's. It was during this period that a special project was initiated for autistic children from other schools who were given the opportunity of integrated learning at St John's. The program was not only beneficial to the young participants, but also to the staff and other pupils who were involved in the experience. The return of young families to the district, and the 1989 decision by St John's School Board to adopt a capital development program, saw a large increase in enrolments. With assistance from the parish and the State and Commonwealth Governments, the school was re-developed, upgraded and refurbished over a series of six or more stages. By 1999, the staff had grown to 22 and information technology now plays an important part in classroom activity.

131. Santa Sabina Convent, Scarborough, 1999

On reflection, both the Sisters of Mercy and the Dominican Sisters agree that the most enduring memory they have of St John's founding years is the friendliness, enthusiasm and warmth generated by the Scarborough residents. At a time when government grants were non-existent, and fees too low to support a religious community, the members were dependent on the generosity of parents for involvement in fund-raising projects, repairs, busy-bees and the school canteen. The fact that many families were new to the district and keen to form friendly relationships, helped foster among them a strong community spirit. That spirit benefited both the Sisters and the school, and past Sisters have nothing but praise to offer those who unselfishly contributed.

Their names are too numerous to list, but two whose generosity to the Sisters began with the opening of the school and has been ongoing, are Mrs May Lane and Mr Stan Rose, who are representative of the many residents whose help in former years was indispensable.

According to early pupils and former members of staff, St John's was a very happy school, despite its initial lack of modern facilities. During the 1950s, Scarborough still possessed a large amount of virgin bush, and the swamp near the site, now occupied by the Sportsman's Club, attracted the adventurous – especially boys. It was, as one Sister described, 'a paradise for young people and a nightmare for teachers who had to keep an eagle eye on pupils who liked nothing better than to disappear to catch "taddies"'. [25] With little prompting, past pupils readily recall special St Dominic's Days and St Patrick's Day celebrations at Leederville Oval, fancy dress balls, concerts, picnics and nature excursions to the nearby beach and swamp, and for Catholic pupils their First Communion Day, followed by a celebratory breakfast.

For more than 30 years, the Dominican Sisters, in keeping with their apostolate, provided the children of Scarborough with strong Christian principles and a sound academic education in the hope that as adults their pupils would be better equipped to face the realities of life. St John's continued to build on this foundation under the competent leadership of Mr Shane Baker, a past Dominican pupil from the Holy Rosary School. Mr Baker, and a committed group of lay teachers under the watchful eye of an interested and caring priest, Father Henry Byrne, have continued to uphold the values set by their predecessors.

## ST THERESE'S SCHOOL, LAKE GWELUP

Lake Gwelup, until recently a semi-rural area, was once the heart of the market garden industry in the northern districts. The locality was mainly inhabited by non-English speaking Yugoslav, Croatian and Italian migrants who were prepared to work long hours in primitive conditions to establish a business of their own. Many of the families were Catholic and, prior to St Therese's Church being erected by Mr J. Malony in 1937, most people in the district, including those living at North Beach, Trigg Island and Waterman's Bay, had to drive long distances to attend Mass at Leederville. The small church at Gwelup, originally known by its Italian title, 'St Teresa's', was situated on a rise overlooking a tranquil lake on the undeveloped outskirts of Perth City. The building, situated close to the market gardens, seemed to be a likely place to establish a parish school for the growing number of school-age children living in the area.

In 1935, the Sisters of Mercy from West Perth established St Anthony's School at Wanneroo, and, three years later, arrangements were made for members of that order to open a small primary school in the newly-completed St Teresa's Church at Gwelup. Until the North Beach parish was formed in 1951, Gwelup was attached to Osborne Park, which, in the 1930s was also responsible for the districts of Wanneroo, Yanchep, North Beach and Scarborough. Father Albert Langmead, from St Kieran's, Osborne Park, took charge of the new Gwelup church in 1938. He became a familiar figure to the pupils and teachers attending St Teresa's (Therese) school and, regardless of creed, was soon on friendly terms with residents, fishermen and local market gardeners alike.

Classes began in the church-school in February 1937, with an enrolment of 34 children and, because there was no convent available, Sister Pius Stanley and her companion, Sister John, initially travelled to Balcatta Beach Road from Leederville and then later from Osborne Park. To subsidise the cost of petrol for 'Leaping Lena', the old 'T' Model Ford they used for transport, the two Sisters of Mercy gave music lessons out of school hours, which meant that their days were usually long and tiring. Unfortunately, although convenient, the car was not always reliable and pushing it up to the top of the quarry hill in order to reach the church often became part of the day's activities. [1]

132. St Therese's Church-school, Gwelup, 1939
Courtesy Sisters of Mercy, Perth

School fees were set at sixpence a week. However, because it was felt that many settlers were still trying to put down roots in their adopted country and had little money to spare, the Mercy Sisters were given strict instructions by Monsignor Moloney, not to request payment or insist on the wearing of school uniforms and shoes. As with future teachers, the Sisters were showered with home-grown and home-made gifts in lieu of fees. By 1947, there were 100 pupils attending the school at Gwelup and the Sisters of Mercy continued to conduct classes in the church until the Dominican Sisters from Scarborough assumed control in 1951. [2]

On 1 January 1951, Archbishop Prendiville wrote to his sister, the Dominican Prioress General, Mother Laurence Prendiville, and suggested that members of her community might consider replacing the Sisters of

Mercy at Gwelup and also at Scarborough. He explained that the Sisters of Mercy had agreed to establish a foundation at Kojonup, and possibly Tambellup, on condition that they were relieved of their schools in the northern suburbs. [3] Mother Laurence and her Council agreed to the proposal, and in May 1951 two Dominican Sisters, Sister Joseph O'Connor and Sister St Anne Graham, took over the responsibility of the small church-school at Gwelup. To reach Lake Gwelup, the Sisters had to travel daily on public transport. This entailed walking from a house occupied by the community in Clifton Street, to a bus stop in Scarborough Beach Road and catching a bus to Gwelup.

The classrooms were furnished with lengthy, old fashioned-desks with benches attached and because so many of the early schools were also churches, the Sisters were well used to re-arranging the furniture after classes had finished on Friday, for Sunday Mass. Sister St Anne, as principal, taught the top primary groups, Grades IV to VII, and Sister Joseph took charge of the junior primary Grades I to III. [4] Initially the teaching staff at Gwelup was somewhat apprehensive about stepping into classes where for the first three months of the year the children had been taught by members of a different religious order. Sister Joseph explained:

*It was very strange and new at first – going into a new situation after the May holidays to take over an empty school... The biggest difference was facing up to a crowd of little, and not so little, bodies, looking apprehensively at these strange new people who had suddenly invaded their world, usurped the place of, and driven out "our Sisters"...It was a case of summing each other up for a while, but the Gwelup children were genuine, as most children are, and I admired their loyalty to their former teachers, something they soon came to extend to us. They proved to be amongst the most lovable pupils I ever taught.*

*Our day went like this: Rise 5.30 a.m. say the Office in the chapel, take our bags and needs for the day and walk down to St John's Church, Meditation and Mass followed by breakfast. It seemed a long walk from the Clifton Street house, dressed in our long habits and laden with our school requirements and our breakfast, especially on the cold, dark and sometimes rainy, winter mornings...After a quick breakfast, we caught a bus on Scarborough Beach Road to go to Gwelup, while the other Sisters spent the time giving music lessons, until it was time for school classes to begin at 9.00 a.m.* [5]

With so many market growers living in the district, it was not surprising that the Dominican Sisters, as were the Sisters of Mercy before them, often inundated with fresh vegetables. In view of the community's lack of regular income, the produce was most welcome, but carrying the goods home was another matter. Sister Joseph recalls that on one occasion a badly secured bag of vegetables tipped over in the bus. The incident not only caused embarrassment, but a certain amount of light-hearted amusement when a number of passengers started to scramble for potatoes and other items that had rolled under the seats and down the aisle. 'Here's a lettuce and potato, Sister!', or 'Here's a carrot, Sister!', they cried out, trying to be helpful. [6]

When Sister St Anne was transferred to another school in 1952, Sister Joseph O'Connor was appointed Sister-in-Charge of St Therese's church-school and Sister Immaculate Ashleigh joined the staff. By then, they had become part of the Bedford Park community and travelled each day from that suburb. Of the 44 children enrolled in the senior classes conducted by Sr Joseph, only four were members of English-speaking families. Twenty-eight had a foreign language background, but had the experience of having lived in Australia for some years. The remaining 12 pupils were recent arrivals and because they spoke only in their native tongue, both class teachers needed a great deal of patience. The following year, School Inspector Mr W. Rourke reported, 'The work is some of the best I have seen…I cannot stress too strongly the fine work being done by the Sisters in this school. They have not only to understand the problems of the child, but their parents also…Sr Immaculate, Sr Anthony and Sr Paul have worked together as a happy, efficient team and all are to be commended for their fine work'. [7]

In 1954, Gwelup was removed from the North Beach parish and parishioners were, therefore, in a better position to service their own needs. St Therese's Day, in honour of the 'Little Flower', St Therese of Lisieux, was always an annual gala event. On that day, 3 October (now 1 October), the Archbishop of Perth and members of the clergy generally participated in a special Mass, which incorporated children making their first communion and confirmation. A celebratory lunch, provided by the ladies of the Gwelup and North Beach parishes, gave the people in the district, and their friends and relatives, an opportunity to meet and joyously share in the day. The festival always finished with a procession around the grounds with six able- bodied men bearing a large statue of St Therese on their shoulders. In European-style, the platform beneath the figure was artistically strewn with flowers and ribbons, amongst which paper money of all denominations was pinned. The festive occasion usually drew to a close with the reciting of the Rosary, followed by band music and a colourful display of fireworks.

In 1958, the Sisters teaching at Gwelup lived in the convent at North Beach. In that particular year, there was only one Australian child enrolled at the school and, because most of the fees were paid in kind, the Sisters often depended on the two shillings and sixpence paid weekly by his parents to buy eggs for the convent. Sister Declan Callaly, who taught at Gwelup in the final year before the Dominican Sisters withdrew, recalled that, despite working in the market gardens before school, the children rarely missed class and were a delight to teach. Years later when she was teaching at Newman College, Churchlands, Sr Declan had the privilege of teaching some of the children of her former pupils at St Therese's. 'Their parents', she stated, 'had worked hard, established themselves and were obviously determined to give their children a sound education'. [8]

In December 1958, the Dominican Sisters handed over the school to the American Sisters of the Holy Family of Nazareth, who also took charge of a second Dominican foundation at North Beach. Sisters who taught at St Therese's, Gwelup, from the time of foundation were as follows:

| | |
|---|---|
| 1951 | Sr St Anne Graham and Sr Joseph O'Connor |
| 1952 | Sr Joseph O'Connor and Sr Immaculate Ashleigh |
| 1953 | Sr Immaculate Ashleigh, Sr Anthony Sachse and Sr Paul O'Connor |
| 1954 | Sr Immaculate Ashleigh and Sr Paul O'Connor |
| 1955 | Sr Immaculate Ashleigh, Sr Benvenuta (Sr Catherine) Brophy and Sr Antoninus Campbell |
| 1956 | Sr Dolores Cummins and Sr Immaculate Ashleigh |
| 1957 | Sr Dolores Cummins and Sr Bernard Larney (Sr Anne) |
| 1958 | Sr Declan Callaly and Sr Bernard Larney. |

## OUR LADY OF GRACE CONVENT AND SCHOOL, NORTH BEACH

Despite magnificent ocean views, early settlement at North Beach was discouraged by the lack of easy access, poor soil and the absence of potable water. Although the locality gained popularity in the 1920s and 1930s as a fishing, swimming and holiday spot, residential development of the area was in fact extremely slow. The opening of the West Coast Highway extension in 1940, from Scarborough to North Beach, via Trigg Island, and the construction, two years later, of the Mt Flora water tower, however, had a significant impact on the beachside suburb during the post-war years.

Guildford property owner, Edward Hamersley, one of the colony's early pioneers, was the first to build a substantial residence at North Beach. With his French-born wife, Ann Louise (Elvire), and family of six sons and two daughters, he spent regular vacations in the white limestone bungalow, over-looking the coast, which he built in the 1860s. It was no easy feat to reach 'the Castle', the local name given to the Hamersley residence. The family, accompanied by their retainers, milking cows and horses, and a cart loaded with supplies, had first to travel via the coast from the Swan Valley to the Wanneroo Road before turning off at the seven-mile peg to follow a sand track to Balcatta (the original name for North Beach). The Hamersley name, and those of family members, have been perpetuated in the neighbouring suburb of Hamersley, as well as in a popular ocean swimming pool and local streets. 'The Castle' had a chequered history. In 1896, it was leased to the government and used as a quarantine station for Afghan drivers and camels en route to the Murchison goldfields, and, at the turn of the century, the building became the district's only hotel. [1] The area remained isolated for many years, as is evidenced by a picnicker's description published in 1911, 'the party drove through the scrub, past Lake Gwelup where picturesque views of the virgin bush were obtained. After a walk through the sand for some distance, the waters of the Indian Ocean and the scattered settlement of North Beach came into view '. [2]

Land previously owned by the Hamersleys was later sub-divided to form the Mount Flora Estates, and, in 1918, estate agents offered 212 choice building lots on 10 per cent deposit, with the balance to be paid over 48 months, free of interest. Although the suburb was still sparsely settled, its popularity as one of Perth's favourite and safest family swimming beaches continued to increase. In 1923, plans were put out to tender for a seaside jetty and, for the time that the wooden structure existed, it gave immense pleasure to weekenders and countless visitors attracted by the peaceful beach life that existed in North Beach. [3]

During the 1920s, Catholics living at North Beach and the surrounding districts usually journeyed to Leederville to attend Sunday Mass. This weekly routine changed in 1937, when a small Catholic church was built at nearby Gwelup. Previously, Mass had been celebrated at North Beach only during the Christmas holidays. Some older residents still recall one particular Christmas Eve when a group of parishioners, filled with the joy of Christmas, assumed the role of carol singers and took to the streets of North Beach, using a piano on the back of a truck to provide the accompanying music. Mass was celebrated at North Beach for the first time during the 1940s, when visiting priests made use of a wood and corrugated iron holiday cottage owned by the Sisters of Mercy. The building, situated on North Beach Road (approximately on the site of the present Ampol service station), with its front verandah partially enclosed with lattice, was of a simple design in keeping with other beach structures at that time. A similar one-room shack with a lean-to kitchen, also the property of the Sisters, served as the original presbytery. Rust, caused by the heavy salt air, had created holes in the walls of the makeshift church, which allowed the welcome sea breezes to enter during summer and the not so welcome coastal winds to cause a draught in winter. It was not unknown for church-goers to put their feet through the rotting timber floor when going to Communion and if the space inside was crowded, some spilled over into the verandah. [4] People joked about these inconveniences, but to them the all-important issue was being able to attend Mass locally.

Until the first parish priest, Father Tom Prendiville, was appointed in 1951, North Beach relied on a number of priests, most of whom made a lasting impression on residents and holiday-makers alike. Among the first celebrants to say Mass in the area were Father Edward McBride from Scarborough, Father (later Monsignor) Albert Langmead, parish priest at Gwelup, and ex-Aquinian Father John Chokolich, a curate at Osborne Park, who was a familiar sight in those days travelling to and from North Beach on his motor bike. On at least one occasion Father James Knox, the future Australian Cardinal, said Mass in the locality. [5] On 6 January 1946, two years prior to North Beach being separated from the parish of Osborne Park in order to form a new parish with Scarborough, an appeal was made for funds to build a parish church. In May 1947, consideration was given for the purchase of a half-acre block of land on offer for £80. Archbishop Prendiville established the North Beach parish of Our Lady of Grace, which included the suburbs of Trigg Island, Waterman's Bay, Marmion and Lake Gwelup, in March 1951. Due to setbacks involving the land earlier selected, an approach was made to the government with a view to obtaining an alternative site for a church. As a result, three acres of land was set aside from the Kitchener Street reserve and purchased by the parish in 1953.

The first appointed parish priest, Father Tom Prendiville, worked tirelessly to make the project a reality. The fact that he was the nephew of Archbishop Redmond Prendiville, no doubt gave him a certain amount of status, however, the parishioners quickly discovered that he was an unpretentious person, determined to meet the needs of a struggling parish. His habit of playing the melodeon after services not only provided him with an appreciative audience, but also gave his parishioners the opportunity to get to know him on a personal level. Father Prendiville's plan to build a suitable place of worship, and hopefully open a church-school, was realised the following year when Mr Stan Costello, a contractor with a background in the construction of church buildings, completed Our Lady of Grace Church in time for the official blessing and opening by the Archbishop on 7 March 1954. [6] Within walking distance of holiday cottages on the sea-front, the first North Beach Catholic church, a solid structure built in brick, was designed with folding doors that could either divide the interior into three rooms or remain open as a hall. The original building has survived and is now part of the present school complex.

Our Lady Of Grace School had opened a few weeks earlier, when a group of Dominican Sisters, de Sales Patterson (Sr Mary), Evangelist Graham, Bernadette Punch, Immaculate Ashleigh and Paul O'Connor, moved into the Dominican convent at 2 Kitchener Street, North Beach. School fees had been set at 30 shillings a term, although there was no guarantee that all parents would be in a position to pay this amount, [7] and for the first few weeks, classes were held in the still incomplete church. The Sisters' decision to open the school in February, before the building was finished, was more than justified when 46 children sought enrolment in classes ranging from Grades I to VI. The first day was not as orderly as the Sisters would have liked; no sooner had they coped with the registration of names and the collection of new books, than painters arrived to commence their work. In the meantime, two members of the community, Sister Immaculate Ashleigh and Sister Paul O'Connor, caught the bus each day to teach at St Therese's church-school at Gwelup, which by then was no longer part of the North Beach parish. [8]

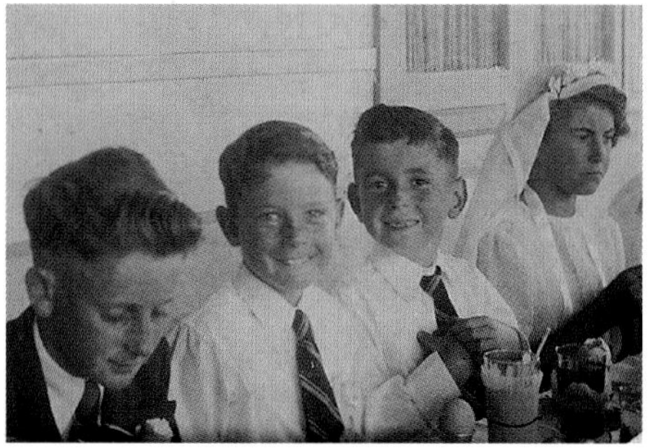

133. First Communion Day, Our Lady of Grace, North Beach, 1954
L. to R.: ..., K. Watters, M. Willey, C. Kiely

Father Prendiville was extremely supportive of both the Sisters and pupils and, until such time as the new church was opened, he used to drive them to the old Mercy cottage in North Beach Road to attend Mass each morning. Unfortunately, the finishing touches being made to the Sisters' house in Kitchener Street were not to be completed for at least another two weeks and being confronted by workmen each day left little room for privacy. The new convent was not large. One room was used as a parlour, another as a chapel, and the remainder of the building consisted of a kitchen, a laundry, a bathroom and a sleep-out that was divided into five cubicles. Sister Bernadette recalls that when they first moved into Kitchener Street the community's sleeping arrangements were in a complete state of disarray. Not only was it difficult to find enough floor space on which to place a bed, but even after the Sisters' sleeping cubicles were ready for use, they still had to negotiate the scaffolding left in the laundry before they could retire. [9]

The parish was far from prosperous and both the Sisters and parish priest often had reason to be grateful to caring parishioners such as the de Mamiel, Rayner, O'Loughlin, O'Rourke, Byrom, Vliek, Carr, Hooper, Butler, Parlevliet, Van de Verve and Wall families and other supporters too numerous to mention. From the beginning, the Sisters were made to feel welcome. Indeed, Sister Bernadette has told of an unexpected gesture that proved to be the first of many kind acts ministered by the North Beach residents. On this occasion, the Sisters had just commenced saying the Office on the feast of St Catherine, when they discovered that the community's first load of wood had been delivered in such a way that it blocked the road. Under the circumstances, the Sisters felt obliged to immediately remove the logs, and so the five community members, without the aid of a wheelbarrow, began to transfer the heavy load. They were both pleased and touched when a pupil's father, making his way home, insisted on completing the irksome job. [10] Similarly, when the parish ladies organised a Christmas tree for the children at the end of the Dominicans' first year at Our Lady of Grace, the Sisters were not forgotten. To their surprise they were presented with a huge stocking full of tinned food to tide them over the holiday period.

Although the Sisters did not remain in the district for long, they formed many friendships during the five years they spent at North Beach, and, despite their relatively enclosed style of living, were well-known throughout the district. Sister Benedict Lyons, who together with Sisters Joseph O'Connor, Columba Wilkinson, Declan Callaly and Bernard Larney (Sr Anne), resided at the North Beach convent in 1958, was an affable person, regarded as somewhat of a character by those who remember her. Always practical and inclined to be independent, she was born in the dairying district of South Australia, and, after joining the order, spent many years working on the farm attached to the Priory at Dongara. Sister worked very hard, rising early each morning to milk the cows and perform other duties associated with the property. Used to a busy country life, Sr Benedict at first found it difficult to adapt to life in the suburbs and to fill in the time spent long hours making cakes and scones for raffles, and useful layettes for new-born babies. Her endearing habit of providing chairs for people waiting at

134. Mrs Cathleen de Mamiel, staunch supporter of the North Beach Parish

the bus stop in front of the house was not only thoughtful, but provided her with a heaven-sent opportunity to pass the time of day and have a friendly chat. [11]

For some time, the Sisters had been keen to transfer members of the North Beach community to the Santa Sabina Convent at Scarborough, in order to concentrate their efforts on the new foundation at Doubleview. In September 1958, they paid a visit to Dr Prendiville to discuss the likelihood of closing the convent in Kitchener Street and were surprised to find that Archbishop had anticipated their request and was more than willing to sanction their withdrawal from both North Beach and Gwelup.

The Dominican community at North Beach eventually departed on 10 December 1958, and shortly afterwards the premises in Kitchener Street were valued and put up for sale. [12] The following year an American order, the Sisters of the Holy Family of Nazareth, who had established a foundation in North Perth, took charge of the former Dominican schools at North Beach and Gwelup. Until a fine two-storey convent in Kitchener Street was officially opened on 19 April 1964, members of the new community travelled daily by car from their foundation in North Perth, to conduct classes at both schools. Subsequently, the Catholic Church precinct at North Beach included new school buildings, a brick presbytery and a contemporary modern-style church and associated offices.

Following in the footsteps of popular Father Tom Prendiville (1951-1957), priests appointed to Our Lady of Grace parish over the years have maintained a close relationship with the people, and at the same time met the needs of a fast-growing, heavily populated parish. Since Father Prendiville's departure the following seven priests have served the parish of North Beach: Father C. Nolan (1957-1958), Father J. Depiazzi (1959-1966), Father J. Chokolich (1966-1969), Father R. O'Reilly (1969-1973), Father J. Mullins, (1974-1982), Father Ken Keating (1982). [13] The Dominican Sisters who were members of the North Beach community were:

| | |
|---|---|
| 1954 | Sr Bernadette Punch,<br>Sr de Sales Patterson (Sr Mary),<br>Sr Evangelist Graham |
| 1955 | Sr Emmanuel Lynch,<br>Sr de Sales Patterson, Sr Agnes Leddin |
| 1956 | Sr Emmanuel Lynch, Sr Regina O'Neill,<br>Sr Martin Doyle (Sr Treasa) |
| 1957 | Sr Joseph O'Connor,<br>Sr Benvenuta Brophy (Sr Catherine) |
| 1958 | Sr Joseph O'Connor,<br>Sr Benedict Lyons, Sr Martin Doyle. |

## HOLY SPIRIT SCHOOL, WEMBLEY DOWNS/CITY BEACH

When Archbishop Prendiville, in 1960, gave Father Tom Phelan the authority to establish a new parish at City Beach, a large portion of the district was still undeveloped. City Beach parish, a long, narrow coastal strip, not only took in a section of Wembley Downs on the eastern boundary, but also part of south Scarborough. Wembley Downs, a mixture of undulating land, sandy soil, limestone outcrops and low virgin scrub, was just then beginning to show promise as a popular locality for young families, although access to the area remained somewhat difficult. Empire Avenue ran only from Brompton Road to Weaponess Road and to reach their homes, without having to travel via Scarborough, residents used a rough track that cut through bushland, west of the present Wembley Downs golf course from the Boulevard in Floreat Park. Whilst the bushland setting was a naturalist's delight, the track was harsh on vehicles and not the easiest mode of travel to come to terms with for new home owners and visitors.

Parish negotiations to obtain a suitable block of land were held over until such time as the Perth City Council had completed their survey, and it was 1963 before the Archbishop of Perth, Dr Prendiville, purchased an ideal building site for the sum of £11,000. [1] Considering the future value of the land involved, this was a wise decision, although at the time, with a large parish debt to contend with, the small number of scattered parishioners living in Wembley Downs and City Beach might not have agreed. The construction of a village, built to accommodate athletes and officials taking part in the Empire Games held at Perth in 1962, was in many ways the catalyst responsible for improved conditions in these areas. Not only were roads completed, but the modern brick houses, built for the sporting event, were later sold by tender through the Rural and Industries Bank and purchased by eager buyers.

Until a presbytery was built in 1964, the parish priest had no permanent home and Mass for the newly-formed Holy Spirit Parish was celebrated in nearby government schools. At first, Father Phelan lived with the Dominican Fathers at St Dominic's in Innaloo, then at St Joseph's Orphanage (Catherine McCauley Centre), where he was chaplain. In 1963, he temporarily took charge of St Cecilia's parish, Floreat Park, and was assisted at weekends by a priest from the Societies of Missionaries to Africa. Father Thomas Phelan was born in County Kilkenny, Ireland, and studied for the priesthood at St Keiran's College, where he was ordained. After his arrival in Western Australia in 1949, he served as assistant priest at Northam and St Mary's Cathedral, Perth, and as administrator of the Cottesloe parish for six months. For a similar length of time, he also served at Armadale as *locum tenens*. A man of boundless enthusiasm, Fr Phelan was determined to provide a suitable primary school and church for Catholics living in the Wembley Downs/ City Beach parish.

At the same time as a site was surveyed for a presbytery, advice was also offered on the best possible location for future buildings. Young architect, Michael Fitzhardinge, generously drew up plans, free of charge, and to save costs, the building was sub-contracted. A group of committed parishioners, meanwhile, formed a working-bee to help lay the foundations of the presbytery. The Holy Spirit School was completed soon afterwards and, unlike traditional church-schools which were usually rectangular in shape, with classrooms divided by movable partitions, the innovative design was the result of careful planning. The building was constructed in the shape of a letter 'T', and according to a description given by Father Phelan, 'the top section of the T consisted of three rooms, the middle room being set up as a chapel, flanked by two classrooms with blackboards at extreme ends to minimise noise levels, the chapel acting as a noise-break. The stem of the T comprised a verandah and a third classroom'. To cater for the public, 'huge doors, one in the north wall of the chapel and the other as the south wall of the third classroom swung around on casters to open up the whole area for Sunday Mass in a cruciform shape of a church'.

The Holy Spirit Primary School in Brompton Road, opened for enrolments in February 1965, at the same time as the Dominican kindergarten in Doubleview. Sister Dominica Davis, a member of the Dominican community at Scarborough, was appointed Sister-in-Charge and because there was no direct public transport or vehicle available, arrangements had earlier been made for rostered parents to transport the principal each day from the Santa Sabina Convent in Lalor Street. School fees were 10 shillings a week and as the sole member of staff, Sr Dominica taught a combined class of 35 children from Years 1 and 2. Shortly after the opening of the primary school, a Parents' and Friends' Association was formed with Mr G. Brennan elected as president and Mrs W. Slaven as secretary. Parishioners, despite many of them having their own new homes and gardens to develop, helped establish the grounds, which became a mammoth task considering the winds that blew in from the ocean and the state of the poor sandy soil. Within a year, the number of pupils in attendance had risen to 49 with the Sister-in-Charge taking on the extra burden of a third class. Unfortunately, the Dominican community could not, at that time, spare another teacher to assist. [2]

Increased housing and major road works continued to improve conditions in the Wembley Downs and City Beach areas throughout the 1960s and, as a result, the influx of young families building or purchasing property had a marked effect on enrolments. By 1967, it became necessary to add a storeroom and two extra classrooms to accommodate the extra pupils attending the Holy Spirit Primary School. The school's first lay teacher, Mrs Kathleen Binks, a former government school employee, was engaged that year and later a young graduate, Miss Zeitlin, joined the teaching staff. The parish priest's successful involvement with real estate investments in 1967 and 1968, injected much-needed funds into the parish. In 1968, a larger storeroom was added to the school and part of the space utilised as a library. During that same year, a new car was purchased for Sister Dominica, the possession of which gave her a great deal more independence with regards to her school commitments. [3] When Sr Dominica was appointed principal of the Holy Rosary School in Woodlands in 1969, her place at the Holy Spirit School was taken by Sister Gemma Seaman, a gentle, conscientious person and a dedicated teacher. The following year, Sister Rosarii Keenan, who had recently returned to Western Australia from a teaching appointment in Canberra, succeeded her as principal. [4]

135. Pupils, Holy Spirit School, Wembley Downs/City Beach, 1969
L. to R. Back Row: P. McGurk, J. Clancy, S. Doherty, G. Snowden, A. Byrne, J. Thomas
Middle: F. McGurk, E. Thomas, P. Cowan, M. Brennan, E. Slavin, L. Still, K. Peel
Front: S. Good, ...., ...., K. Hall, M. Barrett, S. McGurk

The impressive, ultra-modern Holy Spirit Church, built in 1974 on high ground overlooking the school, has extensive views across the Indian Ocean and Rottnest Island. The building, designed by architects Forbes and Fitzhardinge and constructed by G. Robinson, is symbolic of the district's progress. By 1976, the Holy Spirit School had an enrolment of 240 children in co-educational classes from Years 1 to 3 and three teachers, Sister Rosarii Keenan, Sister-in-Charge, Sister Agnes Leeson and Sister Mary Ryan. At that stage, the girls continued their education at the school until Year 7, whilst boys, once having reached the higher level, transferred to other schools to complete their education. This policy changed in 1981, when Sr Rosarii introduced co-education from pre-primary classes to Year 7. [5]

136. Holy Spirit Church, City Beach

The official opening of the new Holy Spirit School hall took place on 20 April 1980 and, for the first time, pre-primary children were accepted as pupils. The outstanding success of this decision saw the erection of a modern pre-primary school centre three years later, with Miss Firth employed as teacher-in-charge. By then, Sister Imelda Ryan had taken up her appointment as principal of the school. Since its inception, the Holy Spirit Primary School has been blessed with an active group of parents and generous parishioners, whose contributions over the years was characteristic of the close-knit community. It was during Sr Imelda's principalship that further extensions were made to the building. These included an administration block in 1986, and a Year 7 classroom in 1989, which, apart from being functional, improved the appearance of the original buildings.

Sister Imelda Ryan was born in Melbourne, where she attended the Dominican Girls' College, Siena, at Camberwell, Victoria. Later, in 1970, she was accepted into the novitiate for the Western Australia Province and six years later made her final profession. Sister Imelda, dedicated teacher and fine administrator, remained principal of the Holy Spirit School at City Beach, for eight years. Her artistic flair in the area of fine handicrafts has been recognised by the many awards she has won at the Western Australian Royal Agricultural Show.

During the 1990s significant changes occurred in the administration of the Holy Spirit School, when, at the beginning of the decade, the Dominican Sisters withdrew from the school they had founded a quarter of a century earlier. The Sisters' departure in 1990, saw the appointment of the school's first lay principal, Mr Richard Cavanagh. A new vision to meet the demands of the current education system, eventually involved the employment of nine full-time teachers, three part-time teachers, two teaching assistants, a part-time librarian and assistant, a part-time Italian teacher and a school secretary. The school, ably managed by the City Beach Catholic

School Board and controlled by the Catholic Education Office, has been committed to upgrading the facilities. Although the primary school education provided is in keeping with the approach to the new century, the Dominican ethos, introduced by the Sisters in 1965, remains an integral part of the Holy Spirit School. [5]

137. Principals, Holy Spirit School.
L. to R.: Sisters Imelda Ryan, Rosarii Keenan, Gemma Seaman, Dominica Davis (inset)

# From Dunedin to Dongara and Doubleview

CHAPTER 8

## ST DOMINIC'S SCHOOL, INNALOO

Post-war development of Scarborough and its surrounds, following World War II, saw a huge increase in population, and the gradual formation of organisations and services such as a Progress Association, a public library, an infant health centre, a telephone exchange, shops, local halls, churches and schools. In the period between 30 June 1952 and 30 June 1953, when the value of building permits issued by the Perth Roads Board (City of Stirling) exceeded the £1,000,000 mark for the first time, it signalled a strong future for Scarborough and its environs. [1]

The Dominican Fathers arrived in Western Australia on 19 July 1954, and, during the months following their arrival, they were instrumental in establishing the parish of Innaloo, as well as a small Catholic primary school dedicated to St Dominic. Like their counterparts, the Dominican Sisters, the Dominican Fathers and Brothers were followers of St Dominic's way of life. Known universally as the Order of Preachers (OP), the order was founded in France in the 13th century, at a time when preaching was the prerogative of the bishop. Since then, the Dominican Fathers have carried out their apostolate 'to teach and preach' for more than seven centuries. In 1898, members of the Irish Province accepted an invitation from the Archbishop of South Australia to form a foundation in Adelaide. The number of Dominican Fathers coming from Ireland to Australia gradually increased until, in 1950, the Australasian Dominican Province was founded with the Provincial resident in Melbourne. It was from Victoria that a Dominican priest was assigned to Perth in 1954 and two years later that a foreign mission in the Solomons was established. [2]

On his arrival, Father Fintan Campbell OP, the first of the Dominican priests to settle in Perth, called on the Archbishop of Perth, accompanied by the Provincial of the Dominican Fathers, Father G. Cussen OP. During that visit he not only discussed his appointment as priest in charge of the future parish of Innaloo, but presented a set of sketch plans for a proposed four-room school in that suburb. In the meantime, Fr Campbell moved into the presbytery at Scarborough and temporarily took charge of that parish during Father McBride's absence through illness. Whilst there, he inspected a number of sites in the Doubleview area that might prove suitable for a church-school. On the basis of the approval he had already received, the priest contacted a recommended builder and, on 25 August, attended a meeting of the parishioners in the recently-opened Church of the Immaculate Heart of Mary in Scarborough to explain the proposal. Father Campbell informed those present that work would begin in October, and that the contractor intended to have the new classrooms completed in time for the start of school in February 1955. [3]

138. Father F. Campbell OP in front of St Dominic's School, Innaloo, 1955

After celebrating Mass at Scarborough, on 26 September 1954, Father Campbell further announced that the first liturgy to be held in the Innaloo district would take place at 7.00 a.m. on 3 October in the State School on the corner of Odin and Scarborough Beach Roads. The suburb of Innaloo (North Doubleview), situated on the northern side of Scarborough Beach Road, between Scarborough and Osborne Park, was once part of the Scarborough parish formed in 1948. An earlier proposal to separate the two localities became a reality when the parish of Innaloo was founded in November 1954.

Until the church-school was finished in the New Year, the priest continued to celebrate Mass in the local government school, and Mrs Hook, who lived opposite in Odin Road, kindly stored the altar and vestments used for the two early services held on Sundays. Mrs Grace Tyler, assisted at various times by other women and staunch parishioner, Mr Gerry Lyons, assembled each Saturday to set up the altar. A parish committee, consisting of George Tyler (president), Gerry Lyons (secretary) and members, Jim Hall and Gavin McMullen, was formed to raise funds.[4]

With so many young families living in the area, there was a great deal of interest shown in the progress of the new St Dominic's parish school being built on the corner of Beatrice Street and Phillip's Grove, Innaloo, and it was anticipated that, from the beginning, enrolment levels at the primary school would be exceptionally high. Archbishop Prendiville officially opened the building, constructed by Mr Stan Costello for approximately £9800, on Sunday, 6 February 1955. The original St Dominic's, which doubled as a parish church until a new place of worship was erected some 12 years later, consisted of three well-designed classrooms, with one room set aside for daily Mass. Mr Tony Kenny's firm, Supa Furn, supplied modern desks and chairs and a set of folding doors to divide two of the rooms. These dividers, when opened, provided extra space if the need arose.

The altarpiece in St Dominic's church-school, a wood-carved reproduction of Fra Angelico's fresco, *il Christo Pellegrino*, was the work of Mr de Jagar, who also made the wooden altar and communion rails. The wood-carving was an appropriate choice for a Dominican-based foundation, for the tomb of the renowned 15th century Dominican artist is near to that of St Catherine of Siena, in the Dominican church, San Maria sopra Minerva, in Rome. St Catherine of Siena, patroness of Italy, who died in 1380 at the age of 33, joined the Dominican third order in Siena at the age of 16 and spent much of her life caring for the sick. The name of the saintly Fra Angelico has since been given to a street in Doubleview, that of St Catherine to the neighbouring Dominican convent and Siena was the title under which the Dominican Girls' High School operated for a quarter of a century.[5]

139. Early days at St Dominic's

St Dominic's opened for enrolments on Monday, 7 February 1955, with a registration of 91 primary school pupils from Grade I to IV, and first term classes commenced the following day. Two Dominican Sisters, Sister Francis Huntsman (Sister-in-Charge) and Sister Martin Doyle (Sr Treasa), travelled each day from the Santa Sabina Convent in Scarborough to conduct classes. In May, Sr Francis was assigned to Dongara as Novice Mistress and Sister Dominica Davis took her place on the teaching staff at St Dominic's, [6] which, within a year, had increased enrolment to 157 pupils.

Sister Francis Huntsman was Victorian by birth. Born at Beulah on 16 April 1912 and christened Sheila, she attended the government primary school in that town and later received her secondary education at the Presentation Convent, Windsor, Melbourne. After gaining the appropriate qualifications, Sheila Huntsman entered the education system and taught in various government schools before entering the novitiate at Dongara in March 1944, and receiving her religious name, Sr Francis. A gentle, prayerful and patient person she was well-suited to primary school teaching and is lovingly remembered by those she taught at Mingenew, Three Springs, Cue, Scarborough and Innaloo. During her lifetime, Sr Francis was appointed to the roles of Novice Mistress, General Councillor, Prioress and Sister-in-Charge of schools, which prompted one of her religious companions to state, 'It was indicative of the confidence that the congregation had in her that she held a number of positions of responsibility'. Apart from these obvious qualities, Sr Francis also had a special rapport with small boys, which is evident from the remarks later made by one of her former pupils, 'Gee', he said when recalling the past some 40 years later, 'I loved that lady. I was always going to marry her!'

The Sisters in charge worked hard to establish the new foundation and they were grateful for the support given to them by caring parishioners. Both must have been greatly encouraged to read a Superintendent's assessment presented at the end of St Dominic's inaugural year. At the conclusion of the report he wrote, 'the school can be validly declared to be an efficient school and may be listed as approved. Teachers in the school are to be complimented on their enthusiasm and their success in stimulating the interest of a promising parent group'. [7]

Father Fintan Campbell was a tireless worker for the parish and a strong advocate of teamwork. No pupil's father could escape being involved in the regular busy-bees he organised for the benefit of the parish and school and he did not hesitate to let it be known that he expected all able parents to participate. A man of simple tastes, he lived in a caravan located close to St Dominic's school, which he shared for some time with the former Prior Provincial Father G. Cussen. It was said that 'he was indeed a mendicant friar after the manner of St Dominic'. In the early 1950s, a large proportion of the Doubleview district was still virgin bush and scrub, and although road construction was rapidly progressing in many areas, bush tracks between the main thoroughfares and new buildings were common. Visiting local homes was a top priority for the new parish priest and for several years he continued to ride his trusty push-bike around the parish, getting to know the people and ministering to their spiritual needs. A welcome visitor, Fr Campbell could always rely on the generosity of faithful parishioners for a daily meal. From December 1957, until he returned to Ireland in 1961, the Dominican Father combined his ministry at Innaloo with the duties of parish priest of the newly-created parish of Our Lady of the Rosary in Doubleview. [8] In this, he was given assistance when Father O'Sullivan arrived from Ireland, in February 1959, to join him in the recently-completed presbytery.

By 1958, the parish school at Innaloo had an enrolment of 222 children in all primary grades with seven teaching staff. Concerns regarding the size of enrolments at St Dominic's and St John's schools began to mount. Consequently, to satisfy the demands of parents living on the southern side of Scarborough Beach Road, and to lessen the problems associated with overcrowding, a decision was made to build a church-school in South Doubleview. Fortunately, most of these difficulties were quickly solved after the opening, in February 1959, of the Holy Rosary School. It was during the 1950s, that St Dominic's first lay teacher, Mrs Marjorie Dullard, was appointed to the staff. Dominican Sisters have not forgotten 'her generous financial contribution and loving faith, especially her teaching skills and bright, happy nature'.

140. St Dominic's School staff, Innaloo, 1965
L. to R.: Sisters Edith Murphy, Maria Power, Anne Costello, Mrs M. Dullard, Sisters Catherine Brophy, Bertrand O'Connor

On 11 July 1960, Father Foley OP took the place of Father O'Sullivan OP, who, after spending 18 months in Perth, was transferred to Queensland. At the same time, Brother Dominic returned from the Solomons to assist at the Priory, and the following year, Father F. X. Brown OP arrived from South Australia to take up the position of Prior at St Dominic's. Three years later, on 2 April 1964, the Dominican Fathers left St Dominic's to live in nearby Doubleview and Father G. O'Leary, a man renowned for his hearty laughter and good humour, was appointed to Innaloo. It was a position he held for 24 years and in gratitude for his long and caring service a stained glass window was placed above the altar in the parish church to commemorate his life's work. [9]

As a result of careful planning and enormous support from generous parishioners, a major development took place on 14 December 1966, when the Auxiliary Bishop of Perth, Myles McKeon, officially opened the new Church of St Dominic. The original building, built alongside the present church, remained in use as a school and during the 1970s and 1980s extensions to St Dominic's School took place on a site parallel to Beatrice Street. A new Year 1 classroom was completed in 1976 and four years later, on 24 April 1980, an office and an extra classroom for Year 7 pupils was opened. [10]

Several parents seeking the introduction of a co-education system, whereby boys could remain at St Dominic's until they had completed Year 7, made representation to the School Board in February 1977. When approached, the Prioress Provincial Sister Assumpta Moriarty, pointed out that she had no jurisdiction over parish school policy and therefore, the proposal for a change would have to be put before the Catholic Education Commission and members of the Dominican Sisters' Council before a decision could be made. Approval was duly granted and the new ruling was put into effect when classes resumed the following year. [11] In 1982, in line with the expansion taking place at St Dominic's, the School Board purchased a residence adjacent to the school in Beatrice Street and converted it into a kindergarten. The centre opened in 1983 and extra staff were employed to operate the kindergarten when enrolments revealed that there was a real need for this type of facility in Innaloo. Not only were the classes quickly filled, but also it became necessary to draw up a waiting list. Although disappointing to many parents, it was a promising sign that augured well for the success of future primary school enrolments.

St Dominic's School was ideally situated in the midst of several extensive Housing Commission (originally Worker's Home Board, now Homeswest) estates and, in view of the large concentration of children in these areas, it became necessary to regularly upgrade and expand the school over a period of several years. In 1983, the School Board agreed to upgrade the old toilet block, a decision that led to a major addition, in the form of a new two-storey wing and extensive refurbishing. The new building was completed in 1987 and, by February the following year, a total of 230 pupils, ranging from pre-primary to Year 7, were able to enjoy the use of a refurbished library, a multi-purpose area, a new classroom, a tuck shop and modern toilets. [12] Likewise, the opening of a new administration and staff block better advantaged the current staff. Computers, software and the appropriate furnishings had been purchased in advance by an active Parents' and Friends' Association, whose members had worked tirelessly to raise the amount required through numerous fund-raising events. On 20 March 1988, in a combined ceremony, Bishop R. Healy officially dedicated the Church of St Dominic and blessed the school extensions.

The newly-appointed first lay principal, Mr Paul Waddell, thanked all members of the Parents' and Friends' Association, the president of the School Board, Mr Vince Zappavigna, and especially the school's former principal, Sister Mary Ryan, for their generous contributions to St Dominic's over many years and also for their on-going support. [13] With fewer members to provide services, the Dominican Sisters no longer took an active part in St Dominic's Primary School after 1985. Instead the foundation continued as a diocesan school under the guidance of a highly-qualified and dedicated lay principal and staff. With the help of government grants, Stage One of an extensive building program commenced in 1996, followed by a second stage in 1997, and an official opening in 1998. Under principal Mr Darryl Winsor, appointed in 1994, St Dominic's continues, as in the past, to grow from strength to strength.

During the 32 years that the Dominican Sisters administered the school at Innaloo, the following religious held the position of principal:

| | |
|---|---|
| 1955 to May, | Sr Francis Huntsman |
| 1955 | Sr Dominica Davis |
| 1958 | Sr Assumpta Moriarty |
| 1961 | Sr Philomena Punch |
| 1962 | Sr Jerome O'Connor (Sr Helen) |
| 1964 | Sr Consillii Costello (Sr Anne) |
| 1967 | Sr Martin Doyle (Sr Treasa) |
| 1969 | Sr Francis Huntsman |
| 1970 | Sr Thomas Short |
| 1971 | Sr Anthony Sachse |
| 1972 | Sr Benevenuta Brophy (Sr Catherine) |
| 1973 | Sr Dolores Cummins |
| 1978 | Sr Mark Laracy (Sr Marlene) |
| 1983 | Sr Mary Ryan |

## HOLY ROSARY SCHOOL, DOUBLEVIEW

As its name suggests, residents occupying houses in the area known as Doubleview can lay claim to more than one fine view. From rising land, approximately two kilometres east of the coast, the sparkling blue Indian Ocean is visible in the west, while to the east it is possible to identify Perth and, in particular, the various high-rise buildings dominating the city skyline. Land developers recognised, as early as the 1930s, that this attractive tract of land close to the capital had the potential to become a select residential development. At that time, Dudley and Dwyer Ltd, one of Perth's best-known real estate firms, became seriously interested in establishing the Doubleview Estate. The parcel of land they acquired was subsequently sub-divided into 1700 residential blocks and over the ensuing years publicly promoted. [1]

In 1948, post-war investors and prospective home-owners could purchase a block of land in the Doubleview Estate for the average sum of £65. In the meantime, groups of War Service Homes and low-priced Housing Commission rental properties, financed by the State, were also built between 1944 and 1969 at Woodlands, Innaloo, Scarborough and South Doubleview, on land adjacent to that earlier acquired by Dudley and Dwyer. [2] Today, most Doubleview properties fetch extremely high prices, and, in retrospect, one has to admire the Dominican Sisters' and Fathers' foresight in selecting choice sites on which to build Siena Dominican Girls' High School, the Holy Rosary Primary School, St Catherine's Convent, Our Lady of the Rosary Church and the Dominican Fathers' Priory.

In 1957, Dominican Father Fintan Campbell OP celebrated the first Mass in the newly-established Holy Rosary parish at the home of Mr and Mrs D. Sydney-Smith. Prior to this, the Dominican Sisters, who had been teaching at St Dominic's, Innaloo since 1955, had displayed an interest in acquiring a suitable site in the Doubleview area on which to found a school. Initially, they were keen to obtain a plot of land with ocean views and with this in mind land was purchased, but later sold, in Queenscliffe Road, Doubleview. In October 1958, Fr Campbell showed the Sisters land held by the parish and Dominican Fathers in North Doubleview (Innaloo) and South Doubleview, including an elevated site overlooking Jackadder Lake. [3] Shortly afterwards, a decision was made to build a primary school in South Doubleview on a block of land facing, what is today, Williamstown Road. The Dominican Sisters were invited to staff the new foundation and it was hoped that on completion the Holy Rosary School would help relieve some of the pressure caused by overcrowding in St John's and St Dominic's schools.

The Holy Rosary Primary School, officially blessed and opened by Bishop Rafferty on Sunday, 8 February 1959, was built in a pretty bushland setting, which was originally approached by two well-defined bush tracks. One pathway ran from Coronation Street, the other from Queenscliffe Road and, so that the children might not become lost in the surrounding bush, a trail was blazed with yellow markings cut into the trunks of trees. This short-cut enabled pupils to safely find their way to Queenscliffe Road and Cobb Street. Those walking from Ewen Street, which was bituminised as far as Howie Street, had first to cross a limestone track, before following the marked bush track in the direction of the school. Parents with transport naturally drove their children and those pupils lucky enough to own a bicycle rode to school. [4]

Few residences existed close to the Holy Rosary School and for many years the adjacent suburb of Woodlands was no more than a recorded name on a map. Unfortunately, essential services were at first non-existent and the parish school lacked two main commodities – electricity and water. The situation regarding the supply of water, was overcome by having a quantity regularly carted and placed in two large tanks erected on the site of the future Siena Girls' High School and piped down to the primary school premises. The initial absence of school amenities was never a drawback, for parents willingly rallied to provide support in most areas that were wanting. With no corner shop in close proximity and no tuck shop at the school, one of the volunteer parents, Mrs Slavin, would take orders from the children in the morning and return home to make sandwiches and cakes, then return at midday to sell the prepared food and cordial in aid of school funds. [5]

141. Original Holy Rosary School, Doubleview, 1959

Although neat white cement slabs were later laid behind the building and the grounds were eventually beautified, the Holy Rosary playground originally consisted of loose black sand. Before the primary school was financially able to supply sporting equipment, parents kindly donated various activity items such as balls, skipping ropes and hoops. Having no suitable area within the school grounds for sporting activities, the first Holy Rosary Sports Day was held alongside Jackadder Lake, on a cleared section of land beside an old dairy (now the site of the Woodland Shopping Centre). Mass was held for the first time in the new school a week after it opened and the regular Sunday service that followed was always well-attended by Catholics living in the area. [6]

Sister Philomena Punch was appointed the school's foundation principal, with Sister Martin Doyle (Sr Treasa) assigned as a member of staff. Classes commenced in February 1959, with a roll call of 21 primary school pupils in Grades I and II, and also accommodated in the building were 27 First Year students (Year 8), relocated from St John's, Scarborough. These students and their teacher, Sister Regina O'Neill, were transferred from Scarborough to Doubleview after Father Campbell offered them temporary accommodation at Holy Rosary to relieve the overcrowding at St John's. His invitation was renewed in 1960 and extended again in 1961. In May 1960, a meeting was held in connection with the building of a secondary school at Doubleview and, after a favourable response from those involved, a decision was made to investigate the matter further. [7]

The early 1960s heralded a rapid growth in the number of children being enrolled at the Holy Rosary primary school and parishioners, recognising the need to increase the size of the building, managed to raise the extraordinary sum of £10,900 to cover the cost of erecting three additional classrooms. The extensions, completed by builder A. F. Peirl, were officially opened, on 30 September 1962, by the Archbishop of Perth, R. Prendiville, assisted by the parish priest, Father F. X. Brown OP. From the time of his appointment in 1961, Father Brown visited the school each week and displayed a great interest in its development and in the welfare of the students. Sadly, Father Fintan Campbell, who had ministered to the parishioners of Innaloo for some seven years and worked hard to establish a Dominican presence in the Doubleview district, was not present in 1962 to witness the opening of the new extensions to the primary school, or the erection of the Siena Dominican Girls' High School on an adjacent site. By then, Holy Rosary had a pupil intake from Years 1 to 7 with Sister Mercedes Clune (Sr Pauline) in charge as principal and Sister Maria Goretti Power and Sister Alice Wilkinson (Sr John) on the staff. [8]

142. Year 7 Captains, Holy Rosary, Doubleview, 1964
L. to R.: L. O'Sullivan, S. Austin, C. Walsh, J. Britten

In 1963, Mrs Snowdon, the school's first lay teacher, was employed to assist with the growing numbers. Some three years later, another dedicated lay teacher, Mrs Irene Grasso, was also appointed. A long-term staff member, Mrs Grasso remained at the school for over 30 years and is well-remembered by the many pupils she inspired. By 1964, a total of 240 primary school pupils were in attendance and the staffing was one lay teacher, Mrs Snowdon, and four Dominican Sisters, including Sister Thomas Short who lived at St Dominic's Priory in Bedford Park and travelled daily to Doubleview. In November that year, as a result of an earlier decision to increase the size of the building, construction began on two additional classrooms. [9]

Travelling each day from suburb to suburb was not only tiring, but also expensive and, so for convenience sake, on 20 January 1966, the principal of Holy Rosary, Sister Declan Callaly and another member of staff, Sister Eileen Leahy (Sr Reginald), moved into a community house built by the Dominican Sisters in Huntriss Road, Doubleview, initially to accommodate the staff teaching at Siena. From the time Sister Martin Doyle (Sr Treasa) was assigned to the school in 1959, both enrolments and improvements continued to grow under the following successive principals: Sisters Mercedes Clune (1961-62), Antoninus Campbell (1963-64), Declan Callaly (1965-68), Dominica Davis (1969-75), Anthony Sachse (1976-81), Rosarii Keenan (1982-87) and in 1988, Marlene Laracy (Sr Mark). Apart from supplying more classrooms and staff to ease the overflow of enrolments, the Sisters continued to uphold the original purpose of the founding Sisters. That was to provide an education which would best suit the children's needs in every aspect of their primary school lives and to prepare them for the next stage at secondary school level.

143. Winners of the Primary Schools' Choral Shield, WA Music Festival, 1968

The Sisters were particularly concerned about helping children with special needs. It was this concern that moved Sister Anthony Sachse, in 1978, to set up, in conjunction with Churchlands Teachers' College, a Special Education Unit for intellectually handicapped children, in which Mrs Pauline Hogan was employed as a teacher under a government-sponsored scheme. This arrangement continued until 1987 when, like the remainder of the Holy Rosary School classes, the Special Unit came under the auspices of the Catholic Education Commission. The following year, Mrs Evol Angelatos was appointed to take charge of the unit and for the next nine years was a highly-regarded and respected member of staff. [10] In 1983, Sister Rosarii Keenan introduced a pre-primary class for children turning five years of age during the year and Miss Linda Ingate was the first teacher appointed to care for the new group.

According to those who live and work with her, softly-spoken Sister Marlene Laracy is blessed with the ability to deal calmly with almost any situation. Born in Perth, Western Australia, she was enrolled by her parents, Veronica and Leo, an electrical engineer, at St John's primary school in Scarborough. Later, realising that she had a religious vocation, Marlene applied to the Dominican Congregation for entry and was consequently received into the congregational novitiate at Wahroonga, Sydney, New South Wales, on 10 December 1960. During that time she received the religious name Sister Mary Mark, but reverted several years later to her baptismal name. Sister Mark made her final profession on 29 December 1966 and studied successfully at both the Signadou Dominican Teachers' College in Canberra and the Churchlands Teachers' College in Perth. She was assigned, at various times during her religious life, to communities at Mingenew, Morawa, Bedford Park (St Peter's), Bentley, Morley Park, Dianella and Innaloo. When Sister Marlene completed five years as principal of St Dominic's, Innaloo, she had a year's study leave before being appointed to the

144. Principal, Sister Rosarii Keenan, with staff, Holy Rosary, Doubleview.1986

teaching staff at Holy Rosary in 1984, a position she retained until 1988, when she was appointed principal of the school. Sister Marlene also has a particular interest in the Special Education Unit and, in order to keep pace with the latest trends and methodology, she studied abroad. Through her natural compassion and the knowledge she has gained over many years, parents of these 'special' children have found in her a strong and understanding advocate.

The staff and pupils at Holy Rosary are extremely fortunate in having the strong support of Doubleview's parish priest Father Stephen Tarrant, as well as an active and enthusiastic Parents' and Friends' Association and a dedicated School Board. The first of several major projects to upgrade the school's facilities began in 1992 when, under a capital development plan earlier drawn up by the Board and approved by the Catholic Education Commission, the Special Education Unit was repositioned and upgraded and two new pre-primary centres were completed in time for the opening of school the following year. Stage Two of the program, which began soon afterwards, involved the relocating of Year 1 classes and the administration centre. These extensions were officially blessed by Archbishop Barry Hickey and opened by Mrs Therese Temby, Director of Catholic Education, on 8 April 1994. Present were the Hon. Mr George Strickland, member for Scarborough, representing the Minister for Education, Mrs Eoin Cameron, wife of the Federal Member for Stirling and invited councillors and members of the City of Stirling. The occasion was the culmination of more than a year's work and inspection of the building was a proud moment for all involved, especially for five of Holy Rosary's former principals, Sisters Pauline Clune, Antoninus Campbell, Declan Callaly, Anthony Sachse and Rosarii Keenan. [11]

Improvements to Holy Rosary did not cease there. In 1995, extra funds were provided through the School Board to replace the roof of the Year 2 classroom. The following year, the Board and the Parents' and Friends'

145. Principals, Holy Rosary School, Doubleview
L. to R.: Sisters Antoninus Campbell, Declan Callaly, Anthony Sachse, Rosarii Keenan, Marlene Laracy, (1999)

Association combined resources to upgrade the school's technology equipment. New IBM computers, printers, a scanner and appropriate software were purchased to suit each year level. Apart from successfully participating in a host of co-ordinated activities such as inter-school swimming, athletics and cross-country events, Holy Rosary consistently entered teams in the State Tournament of Minds, a competition, which among other objectives, aimed 'to encourage experimentation, to reward divergent thinking, to encourage team co-operation, to stimulate curiosity and to foster a love of learning'. In 1993 and 1994, Holy Rosary came first in the Social Science section and second in Language/ Literature. In 1995, the school team was placed first in Social Science and first in Mathematics/Engineering. This record was repeated the following year. In 1997, when Tournament Honours were introduced for the top 15 per cent of teams in each category, the Holy Rosary received Tournament Honours in all three categories – Social Science, Mathematics/Engineering and Language/Literature. [12]

As with all Catholic schools, Holy Rosary offered a wide range of cultural pursuits. Among the many opportunities available to students in later years, was the chance to become involved in Speak Up, a competition organised by the Penguin Club of WA and the Performing Arts Festival, held each August for Catholic Schools and Colleges. Teachers providing guidance in those areas during 1997 were Mrs Boaro, speech and drama, Mrs Martyn, choral singing and Sister Edith Murphy, who prepared girls for liturgical movement and choral singing. [13]

Sister Edith Murphy (Sr Andrew), like Sister Marlene Laracy, is a former Dominican pupil. Still a valued member of the Holy Rosary staff, she was born in Perth and was first educated by the Brigidine Sisters and then by the Dominican Sisters at St John's, Scarborough. In February 1960, she commenced her postulancy at Wahroonga, New South Wales, and later that year was accepted into the congregational novitiate established as a result of the amalgamation between the four autonomous Australian congregations. Before returning to Western Australia to take up her first position as kindergarten teacher at Bedford Park/Inglewood, Sr Andrew completed her teacher-training course. A friendly, outgoing person with a pleasant disposition, her great love and knowledge of music and dance has been obvious to all. Since her profession, Sister Andrew has held many teaching positions, including the Holy Rosary School in Canberra, St John's in Scarborough, Santa Clara in Bentley, St Joseph's in Perenjori and Marian School in Morawa, where for some years she was principal.

In 1998, a kindergarten class was commenced at Holy Rosary for those turning four years of age within the year. Mrs Rhiana Hornby was the inaugural teacher. The school has developed excellent facilities that include a hall and an up-to-date library, both of which are shared with the parish. From a simple structure with bare cement floors, no water or electricity and few facilities, the Holy Rosary primary school at Doubleview has developed into a fine, fully air-conditioned centre, which presently caters for two streams in all grades from kindergarten to Year 7 and a Special Education Unit which provides expert tuition for intellectually handicapped children. [14] A recent summary aptly described Holy Rosary, Doubleview as 'a Catholic School founded on the Dominican tradition of truth, love and knowledge'. [15]

## ST CATHERINE'S CONVENT AND NEWMAN SIENA COLLEGE, DOUBLEVIEW

During the 1960s, the continued growth of the northern parishes and the corresponding rise in school enrolments made the prospect of building a Dominican secondary school for girls an attractive proposition. In May 1960, the Prioress and members of the Dominican Council took the first step towards establishing a long-awaited high school when they met to discuss the viability of such a proposal. By then, the Holy Rosary primary school in Doubleview had been operating successfully for some 15 months and its future seemed assured. A Council decision was made to go ahead with plans to build, and, in June, Sister Laurence Prendiville was appointed to inspect and gather information about modern secondary schools and new trends in education. [1]

In 1961, there were 15 Dominican schools in existence in Western Australia with a total roll call of approximately 1500 children. Seven of these foundations existed in the metropolitan area, including one registered high school, St Thomas Aquinas, which catered for students living in the Bedford Park/Inglewood and Morley Park areas who wanted to complete their education at a Catholic secondary school. Towards the end of 1961, a newsletter, circulated to residents in Scarborough, Innaloo and Doubleview, informed the recipients that a new Dominican Girls' High School would be completed at Doubleview by 30 April 1962. [2] The elevated site on which the new high school was to be built was in a prime position, close to the city and rapidly developing suburbs, and relatively near to the existing convent at Scarborough. Perth architects, Summerhayes and Associates, contacted the Prioress Provincial at St Dominic's Priory, Dongara, on 5 December 1961, to inform her that the building site at Doubleview had been cleared and the foundations laid.

Siena Dominican Girls' High School, owned and run by the Sisters, was originally established as a five-year girls' secondary school. It was anticipated that, as well as drawing students from surrounding areas, Siena would have a natural intake of pupils from St John's, St Dominic's and Holy Rosary, the three primary schools in the area already administered and staffed by members of the Dominican community. [3] The name chosen for the new high school had, as one would expect, Dominican links. St Catherine of Siena, had spent the major part of her religious life in the service of the Church and mankind. She tended the sick, visited prisons, assisted the poor and, through her countless letters gave counsel to people from all walks of life. Recognising the need for reform in the Church, Catherine determinedly set about renewing it from within. She mediated peace between the cities of Italy and successfully negotiated the return to Rome of Pope Gregory XI, at that time in exile in Avignon. She died in 1380, at the age of 33 years, leaving behind a wealth of writings in her universally acclaimed *Dialogue* and extant letters. Catherine was canonised in 1461 and, in 1970, Pope Paul VI conferred on her the title, Doctor of the Church, a rank usually reserved for men. [4] It was appropriate therefore, that a Dominican centre for higher education be named in her honour.

146. Leaving Certificate candidates, R. Jermyn and J. MacRae outside the new Siena Girls' High School, Doubleview, 1962

Despite heavy rain, a large crowd attended when the first stage of the Dominican Girls' High School in Williamstown Road, Doubleview, was officially opened and blessed by Archbishop Redmond Prendiville on Sunday, 20 May 1962. The Prioress Provincial, Sister Emmanuel Lynch, and Sister Marie-Therese Sharman came from Dongara especially for the occasion and 86 foundation students, most of whom had transferred from Scarborough, assembled for the first time to form a guard of honour to greet the dignitaries. The new two-storey structure, completed by Brenton Buildings Pty Ltd and costing £38,000 to build and furnish, was capable of accommodating approximately 300 students. Shortly after opening day the *Catholic Record* reported:

*The school was built on a higher level than the ground floor, according to the slope of land. Students can enter the first floor by a short set of stairs, to the wide internal corridors. The entrance is completely glassed in and provides an attractive entry. The ground floor is also obtained from a doorway on the southern side of the building. The building is of bricks throughout with structural steelwork. The design has been completed with an eye to providing all modern facilities in school architecture and cloakroom and washing arrangements are well up to standard.* [5]

The upper level consisted of two classrooms on one side of the building, with a science laboratory and a domestic science room on the other side, divided by a wide central, passage. Similarly, on the ground floor, a broad corridor separated another set of classrooms from the office section and ablution facilities. Two of these ground floor classrooms were divided by concertina doors which, when required, were opened to provide the space for an assembly room. The six classrooms were airy and well-lit and, with one exception, all were furnished with single desks featuring up-to-date laminated tops. Each room had a walk-in cupboard for storage and the first floor domestic science room had the latest equipment, including new-style ironing boards that, when required for use, would slide out from beneath benches on the wall. [6] Tennis courts had been laid in the otherwise undeveloped grounds in readiness for use by students after the May holidays. Donations from parents, in the form of reference books, scientific apparatus and sports and general equipment, not only provided extra essentials but also offset some of the financial burden borne by the Sisters.

147. Leaving Class, Siena, Doubleview, 1965
L. to R.: C. Rinaldi, ...., M. Walsh, H. Kessler, Father F. X. Brown OP, M. Croy, E. Jacobs, S. Kempton

Although the construction of Williamstown Road, from Huntriss Road through to Siena, had been completed a week before the opening of the school, most of the existing streets were simply gravel tracks and in the beginning the suburb lacked a proper transport system. Siena's five foundation members, Sisters Assumpta Moriarty (principal), Dominic Galvin, Laurence Prendiville, de Sales Patterson (Sr Mary) and Margaret Mary Willmott (Sr Anita), continued to reside at the Santa Sabina Convent in Scarborough. At that stage, the community had only one car and a considerable amount of organisation was required to drive the group to and from Doubleview each day. In June 1962, Mr A. Boylen, Deputy Director of Secondary School Education, and a team of six Superintendents visited Siena to assess the standard of the new secondary school in terms of efficiency and scholarship. Coincidentally, on the same day, Monsignor J. Bourke, Director of Catholic Education in Western Australia, arrived to examine Christian Doctrine in all the classes. It was a great credit to the principal and the Sisters that very favourable reports were received from both the State Education Department and Catholic Education Office. As a result, the Dominican Girls' High School was registered as an efficient secondary school where government scholarships were tenable. [7]

A large proportion of Doubleview and Woodlands remained undeveloped and, for a time, some essential services were not available. Indeed, a submission, made on behalf of the Sisters, to have water supplied to their property was not successful until members of the Hale School Board of Governors later made a similar application. Fortunately, a decision to connect water to the new Church of England boys' boarding school meant that the same benefit was extended to the Dominican Girls' High School. [8] Improvements to the grounds and gardens were made easier when, in February 1963, a well was sunk and within nine months, after careful preparation, the school oval was planted with grass. [9] Much of the credit for the successful completion of this work must be given to several tireless workers, including Mr Jim Hopkins (President of the Parents' and Friends' Association), Mr Laurie Fisher and Sister Dominica Davis, who despite being Sister-in-Charge of St John's, Scarborough and teaching at that school full-time, faithfully tended the lawns in her spare time.

Since the opening of Siena in 1962, both the Parents' and Friends' Association, and members of the Ladies' Auxiliary have given freely of their time and expertise and shared in the development of the school. Serving on the Parents' and Friends' Association with the inaugural president, Mr Hopkins, were Mrs Joy Rodgers (secretary) and Mr Ed McGillivray (treasurer). It was due to Mrs Rodger's tenacity that the Roads Board finally constructed a road in front of the Dominican High School in time for the opening in May 1962. Likewise, foundation president of the Ladies' Auxiliary, Mrs Dorothy Boundy, headed a hard-working group of mothers who, among other works, organised the first school tuck shop. In those days, healthy salad trays were offered for two shillings. Also on sale were buttered bread rolls and sweet buns, but confectionery was never an option. [10] Over the years, both groups were responsible for raising funds which were generously contributed by the parents.

When the secondary school re-opened in February 1963, with an increased number of pupils, two extra Sisters were assigned to Siena. The group then consisted of Sisters Assumpta Moriarty (principal),

Laurence Prendiville, Baptist Robson (Sr Margaret), Concepta Flattery, Dominic Galvin and Catherine. Sister Cecilia Murphy, a member of the Holy Rosary staff, taught singing. At that time, there were approximately 104 students at Siena, 360 at St John's, 270 at St Dominic's and 172 at Holy Rosary. With 21 Sisters in residence at the Santa Sabina Priory to fill the teaching positions necessary for those numbers every available space was taken up in the convent. It was obvious that additional accommodation would have to be considered in the future. [11] In August that year, the Prioress Provincial, Sister Emmanuel Lynch, visited Scarborough and, among other items of interest, she discussed proposed extensions in connection with Siena. For the Sisters and students, 1963 was a busy and rewarding year – two students, Margaret Rogers and Elizabeth Berliat, were chosen to represent Siena at the Royal Garden Party held in honour of Queen Elizabeth II and Prince Philip during their visit to Perth. A Young Catholic Students (YCS) group was formed and a highly-successful and colourful pageant took place prior to the Christmas break. Finally, the results of the 1963 public examinations were gratifying. Both Leaving Certificate candidates passed, one with two distinctions, and 17 candidates successfully gained their Junior Certificates. [12]

In 1964, Sister Catherine was appointed principal and serving with her were Sisters Baptist Robson (Sr Margaret), Dominic Galvin, Ignatius Prendiville, Regina O'Neill and Lidwina de Groot (Sr Sophie). Both Sister Regina and Sister Lidwina resided at St Dominic's Priory in Bedford Park. Meanwhile, Sister Paschal Dowdall (Sr Kathleen) taught music and Sister Cecilia Murphy continued to take singing and music lessons. Once a week, on Wednesdays, a lay teacher was employed to take three separate sessions of callisthenics. The annual display was the culmination of these weekly lessons and was a feature of the school for many years. Held in the open air, they attracted a large number of parents and friends each year.

Besides being used as a school, the premises were occasionally utilised for other purposes during school holidays. In May 1964, the Dominican Sisters conducted a three-day seminar at the Siena Girls' High School with approximately 150 members of the teaching orders in attendance. The course of lectures, given on biblical catechesis, also touched on the Church's new direction which stated that Christian doctrine be taught with the Bible as the source book. The speakers were Sister Assumpta O'Hanlon OP, a member of the teaching staff form Santa Sabina, Strathfield, New South Wales and Monsignor J. Bourke, Director of Catholic Education in Western Australia. The exchange of ideas that followed was considered by most to be an enriching experience. Excavations for the extensions to Siena commenced on

17 August, 12 months after the Prioress Provincial first endorsed the school building program. By November 1964, the concrete slab for the second storey work had been poured. [13]

On 2 February 1965, a few weeks prior to the start of the new school year, Sister Baptist Robson (Sr Margaret) and Sister Antoninus Campbell moved from the Santa Sabina Convent into temporary premises in Doubleview. The new house, at 394 Huntriss Road, built by the Dominican community, had several advantages. The extra accommodation not only relieved some of the congestion

148. Sisters' house, 394 Huntriss Rd, Doubleview

in the convent at Scarborough, but because the property was in close proximity to the Holy Rosary Primary School and Siena it eliminated the need to acquire an extra car. The premature transfer to Huntriss Road took place before the builders had quite completed their work, and initially the occupants had to set up house without the use of electricity and water. The sparsely-furnished house began to present a slightly more domesticated appearance when a refectory table, custom built by Mr Harris, was delivered and when Sister Margaret Mary Willmott (Sr Anita) and Sister Lidwina de Groot (Sr Sophie) arrived at the convent the following day, bringing with them a table, a sewing machine and a borrowed desk. Chairs, however, were in short supply and, until the Sisters were properly settled, a number of seats were borrowed from the school and carried between different sections of the house as the occasion warranted. Within a few days, household articles, including crockery and cutlery, were delivered from Leonora – the Dominican school and convent in that town having closed at the end of 1963. The Ladies' Auxiliary, on their own initiative, contributed a number of very useful gifts to the Sisters' house. In the meantime, one of the rooms was set up as a chapel, using a wooden altar donated by Mr Harris which, whilst welcome as a donation, took up one-third of a very small room. It was a momentous occasion when Father Brown OP celebrated the first Mass in the tiny Huntriss Road chapel on Sunday, 21 February 1965. [14]

Sister Margaret (Sr Baptist), a foundation member of the new Doubleview community, was born at Ballarat in

Victoria, the daughter of John Robson and his wife Rita (née Casey). A happy person by nature, with a balanced approach to life, Margaret Robson, together with a second postulant from Victoria, Shelia Huntsman (Sr Francis), entered the novitiate at Dongara on 7 March 1944, and after making her final profession was assigned to schools in the Geraldton and Perth dioceses. Between 1963 and 1968, Sr Baptist specialised in teaching shorthand, typing and book-keeping at Siena, and later at St Thomas Aquinas Secondary School in Bedford Park. In the years 1970 and 1991, she accepted the added responsibility of the position of Congregational Bursar, a demanding task involving, among other duties, arranging the funding for various large community projects and ensuring that existing mortgages were duly met. It was Sr Margaret's careful management of funds that made possible many of the extensions to Siena and later Newman Siena.

Sister Antoninus Campbell was another member of the Huntriss Road community teaching at Siena. Born in Belfast, Northern Ireland, and christened Teresa at St Paul's Church in that city, she was the daughter of Francis Campbell, a civil servant, and his wife Rose (née McQuillan). A visit made to Ireland, in 1950, by Sister Laurence and her niece, Sister Ignatius Prendiville, precipitated the decision made by the future Dominican Sister to travel to Western Australia. After entering the novitiate at St Dominic's Priory, Dongara, and accepting her religious name, Sr Mary Antoninus, the young Sister made her final Profession of Vows on 16 December 1955. Sister Antoninus, a competent teacher and administrator, was appointed principal at Holy Rosary in 1963, a role she ably filled for two years. In 1973, she was appointed deputy principal at Newman Siena and five years later held the same position at St Thomas Aquinas College in Bedford Park. Mr Cooney, principal at St Thomas Aquinas, once described Sr Antoninus as 'indefatigable' – an opinion shared by many others. When she was transferred to Siena at the end of 1984, he paid a special tribute to his former deputy principal when he informed the audience on Speech Night, 'We have all learned to appreciate her deep faith, her cheerfulness and her total dedication to the welfare of your daughters'. [15]

A busy-bee, involving a group of willing helpers, was held at Siena on Saturday, 20 March 1965, in preparation for the official opening of the new wing, on 11 April, by Senator Dorothy Tangney. The combined effort put into tidying the grounds around the new building, was greatly appreciated by the Sisters who were delighted to see a large crowd join them on the opening day. Siena's new additions included an administration section with two adjoining classrooms on the ground floor and two more classrooms and a small library on the level above. All agreed that the impressive £35,000 extensions, designed by architect Mr Peter Arney, of Oldham, Boas, Ednie-Brown and Associates, gave the original building a more balanced look and ranked it among the more progressive schools in Perth. [16]

A spare room in the building was set aside for a privately-run kindergarten. The independent activity for four and five-year-olds, most of whom later enrolled at Holy Rosary to complete their primary school education, was accountable to the State Education Department, under the Early Childhood Education program. Surprisingly, over 100 applicants, some under four years of age were received, and it was decided that only those who turned five in 1965 would be accepted when St Catherine's Kindergarten opened in February. Thirty-three of the youngest children attended the morning session and the remaining 33 boys and girls were enrolled for afternoon classes at the Doubleview kindergarten conducted by Mrs Clare MacAnearney. [17] Her sister, Mrs Sadie Mulhern, ran a similar kindergarten at Bedford Park, and both teachers are remembered for their patience and the wonderful rapport they had with the young children in their care. Mrs MacAnearney's efforts were appreciated by the parents and a willing team of volunteers organised barbecues and games evenings, planted lawn in the playground area and set up kindergarten equipment. The end result was very impressive and, according to one supervisor from the Catholic Education Department, the kindergarten was 'the best-equipped in the Catholic schools system'. In 1970, when the venture closed through lack of space, the bulk of the equipment was donated to other Catholic schools.

149. St Catherine's Kindergarten, Doubleview
L. to R.: Mrs C. McAnearney, Mrs S. Hempsell

Several first-time events occurred in 1965. For example, Easter was made even more special than usual because, for the first time since their arrival at Greenough in 1899, the Sisters were able to celebrate Holy Week as a community in a Dominican parish, served by a Dominican priest. On a lighter note, the Sisters drove over to Bedford Park on St Dominic's Day, in August 1965, to field a team for a basketball (netball) match against the students and to everyone's delight the match was drawn. A few days later, on 12 August, Siena held its first school dance. The social function, held at the local RSL (Returned and Services League) Hall in Brighton Road, Scarborough, was such a resounding success that its future inclusion in the school calendar was a foregone conclusion. On 17 October, the school oval, by then ready for use, became the accepted venue for Siena's sports carnival.

The year ended on an equally pleasant note, not only because of Siena's successful academic results, but also because the Sisters were notified, in November 1965, that the Dominican Girls' High School had been allocated £8000 from the Commonwealth Activities in Education and Research Fund to assist in the construction and equipping of science facilities. The Prioress Provincial Sister Emmanuel, who was keen to take advantage of the grant, also recognised the wisdom of having the builders construct an additional room whilst they were on site. Consequently, in July the following year, she wrote to the Archbishop for permission to apply for a bank loan [18] and in October 1966, the construction of a commercial room, as well as a new laboratory, was commenced at the western end of the existing building. Another important milestone took place on 13 November 1966, when Father F. X. Brown celebrated the first Graduation Mass at the Holy Rosary church-school for 10 high school graduates, who were the first to complete the five-year course at Siena.

Until 1966, the Dominican High School was staffed entirely by Sisters, however, a marked increase in enrolments and falling numbers in the Dominican community saw Mrs Barbara Mulligan, the first of many dedicated lay teachers, appointed to the staff. Miss Anne Reynolds followed her in 1968. The number of lay staff grew steadily year by year and, although initially the female staff easily outnumbered the male staff, this situation gradually changed in the ensuing years. Their names, too numerous to include in this history, have been preserved in the Dominican archives. Mrs Cynthia Brown, the longest serving Dominican lay teacher, taught for a total of 24 years at Siena and St Thomas Aquinas. Recalling her enjoyable association with the schools and in particular with the Sisters, Mrs Brown wrote, 'As a non-Catholic teaching in a Dominican School in the Sixties, I had a lot to learn – I learnt especially about the Sisters' acceptance and appreciation of other religious faiths. I learnt also about the egalitarian nature of the schools – everyone was part of a team serving the students. People were not classified according to their positions; all were treated as valuable members of the family'. [19]

In keeping with the traditional Dominican colours of black and white, Siena's original sports uniform consisted of a short skirt with black and white pleats and a square-necked top. Later, a new sports uniform, designed by Mrs Beryl Kelly, was accepted and eventually used by many metropolitan Catholic schools. According to foundation student Elizabeth Ogden, Siena's sporting activities were initially limited to basketball, although tennis was available as an optional sport. In 1963, Siena

150. Siena sports team, 1967
L. to R.: Back Row: M. Crosby, C. Wilkins, E. O'Sullivan. C. O'Sullivan, M. O'Leary, M. Ryan, J. Chandler, H. Rogers, J. Breen, L. Ferguson, H. Crosby
Middle: W. Chandler, P. Lockyer, H. Ryan, ...., .... ,...., J. O'Reilly
Front: S. Hale, J. Newton, L. O'Sullivan, P. Kelly, R. Martino

entered and won its first tennis tournament and, in 1968, the basketball team won the Catholic Girls' Secondary Schools Association Basketball Competition. Eventually, the school was provided with the equipment needed to offer a whole range of organised sports. In this, the Sisters were assisted by members of the Parents' and Friends' Association, who at various times donated some of the more expensive sporting items such as tennis nets, hockey goals, hurdles and gym mats. Swimming and other competitive sports were introduced after the Catholic Girls Schools Sports Association (CGSSA) was formed in 1965. Although no convenient facilities were available for training, Siena entered the inaugural inter-school swimming competition and during lunch hour breaks contestants attended training sessions at Beatty Park. After Newman Siena College was established, Siena students made use of the Newman Senior College swimming pool at Churchlands. [20]

151. Siena Hockey Team
L. to R.: Back Row: S. Donnelly, Eric Pearce (coach), P. Hills, M. Callaghan, S. Pearce, P. Mann, Maureen Pearce (coach),
Middle: F. Malone, M. Herrera, J. Nice, S. O'Connor
Front: D. Tanham, C. Talati

Siena's first appointed sports mistress was Sister Margaret Mary Willmott (Sr Anita), and included among the teachers involved with Siena's early sporting activities were: Miss Peterson (sports mistress), Miss Debbie Craig (physical education and callisthenics), Miss Helen Magius (sports mistress), Mr Ted Hussey and Mr Bill de Gruchy (athletics coaches) and Mr Bruce Jones (netball coach). Sporting teams – Ferrer (gold), Penafort (red), Aquinas (green) and Prouille (blue), were appropriately given the names of Dominican saints – Vincent Ferrer, Raymund of Penafort, Thomas Aquinas and the birthplace of the Dominican Sisters in France, Prouille.

Music and the arts have always been an integral part of Dominican schools and Sisters teaching at the Siena Girls' High School continued to uphold the traditions of the past. This is attested to by the long list of successful music, speech and singing results achieved by their students over the years. Siena first entered the Musical Festival Eisteddfod in 1962 and, although not successful that year, later won the Junior Shield. Students have since recorded numerous successes in a variety of cultural events. In 1968, the Junior High School choral section of the Western Australian Music Festival was won by the Siena school choir conducted by Miss Marjorie Wyndham and trained by Sister Cecilia Murphy. Students were also encouraged and given many opportunities to test their talents in the Catholic Schools' Drama Festival, school concerts and music and dance. Among the many Siena students with extraordinary artistic talent was Miranda Coney, who, in 1980, at 15 years of age, gained entry into the Victorian College of the Arts and later became a principal dancer with the Australian Ballet Company.

152. Winners of Herbert Edwards Cup, 1978 and 1979
L. to R.: P. Colquhoun, J. Owens, J. Greig, J. Howlett

The third stage of a building program, directed by architects Oldham, Boas, Ednie-Brown and Associates, commenced towards the end of 1970, when an additional classroom was added to each of the three levels at the eastern end of the existing building. At the same time, the builders began to excavate for an undercroft. The extensions to Siena were timely, for during the 1960s there had been a rapid rise in population in the districts where the Dominican Sisters had established their schools. In 1971, it was estimated that 11,954 persons lived in Scarborough, 8277 in Doubleview, 6468 in Innaloo, 5869 in Wembley Downs and 4206 in Woodlands. The Churchlands district, which later played an important part in Siena's history, was just then beginning to develop. [21]

When Archbishop Launcelot J. Goody held a meeting at Victoria Square, on 5 March 1971, to discuss the advantages of establishing a Western Australian Catholic Education Commission, the Dominican Sisters were among those representing religious teaching orders. The state-wide closure of many small Catholic schools, due to fewer religious vocations and lack of finance, gave merit to the idea of forming such a body. Once the Commission was established a number of congregations ceased to operate the schools they had founded and the Catholic Education Commission assumed responsibility for them.

Members of the Dominican Council made two important financial decisions when they met in September 1971. First, the Sisters accepted a proposal to purchase a bus to transport fourth and fifth year students from Bedford Park to Siena in Doubleview. Secondly, arrangements were put in place to build a new Dominican Convent in the grounds behind the Siena Dominican Girls' High School. The damage caused by floodwaters at Dongara in March 1971, and the subsequent closure of the Dominican Sisters' principal Priory and major girls' boarding school in December that year, called for a forward planning scheme to assist with the community's resettlement in Perth. Fortunately, Sister Ignatius, the Provincial of the Sisters of Our Lady of the Mission in Highgate, graciously offered the use of their vacant convent at Maylands, to temporarily accommodate the elderly, retired Sisters who were the first to be transferred to Perth after the flood. [22]

After spending nine fruitful years in the neighbouring suburb of Innaloo, the Dominican priests settled into 4 Angelico Street, Woodlands (Doubleview) in April 1964. The occupants of this first small Priory in Woodlands included Fathers Francis Xavier Brown (1961-1967), Declan Gehring (1967-1970), Antoninus Costello (1970-1973) and Bernard Maxwell (1973-1979). The first of these, Father F. X. Brown achieved a great deal after his arrival in 1961 from Blackfriars, the Dominican Boys' College in Adelaide. He returned to assist in the Perth diocese in 1989 and has been appreciated as an active and well-known personality in the Doubleview area. In October 1976, a new, more spacious and comfortable Priory replaced the original house used by the Dominican Fathers. Built on the corner of Angelico and Sabina Streets, it is adjacent to the distinctive Church of Our Lady of the Rosary.

153. Our Lady of the Rosary Church, Woodlands

The church, completed in 1972 and officially opened by Archbishop Goody on 13 May 1973, stands in an attractive woodland setting against a backdrop of shady trees. The architect has utilised Toodyay stone for all of its masonry work and the unique style of the building, with its rich warm stonework and amber and cathedral green glass windows, presents a peaceful interior and an exterior that has become a landmark in the district.

Our Lady of the Rosary Church was designed by Father Bonaventure Leahy OP, with assistance from Messrs G. Thompson FRAIA, C. Garreffa, K. Gaynor, Father N. McDermott OP and countless people whose knowledge he tapped and advice he sought at all hours of the day and night. The building, which was financed with money derived from the sale of land at Ferrer Place, Woodlands, and the Wells fund-raising scheme, took two years to erect and seats 520 people. It is used extensively for the needs of the parish and by the staff and students of Holy Rosary Primary School, Newman Siena College and Newman College. [23]

Since 1980, three parish priests have been appointed to Woodlands – Fathers Denis Crowley (1980-1982), Kevin Condon (1983-1988) and Stephen Tarrant (1989-1999). Over the last 38 years, the Dominican family in Woodlands, Sisters, Fathers and Brothers have created an outstanding Dominican precinct from an isolated tract of virgin bush. During that time, they have established a community supportive of each other and of the school communities in the areas, encouraged by the prayers of the Tertiaries, a group of Dominican laity. Although the shortage of priests did not often allow it, the appointment of newly-ordained Dominican Fathers as chaplains of Newman Siena was always greatly appreciated by the college staff.

On 18 May 1972, the Dominican community, with the exception of those Sisters living at Scarborough, Bedford Park, Bentley, Morawa, Three Springs and Mingenew, moved into the modern bungalow-style St Catherine's Convent at Doubleview. The newly-completed Provincial House, which became the administrative centre for the Dominican Sisters in Western Australia, was blessed, on 10 June 1972, by Bishop Peter Quinn. [24] For its residents, including the Prioress Provincial, Sister Mary Patterson, and the Prioress of St Catherine's Convent, Sister Suzanne Vandeleur, the official opening was the fulfilment of a dream. Today, the peaceful St Catherine's Convent, built in spacious grounds behind the former Siena Girls' High School and the Holy Rosary Primary School and surrounded by attractive gardens, is a worthy successor to the original Priory established in the Irwin district just after the turn of the century.

Sister Julian (Sr Suzanne), who was the last Prioress to serve at Dongara and the first to be appointed in that role at Doubleview, was a trained nurse before entering the Dominican novitiate in 1955. A painting of the old Dongara Priory by her brother Michael, a talented West Australian artist, hangs in the entrance at St Catherine's Convent, Doubleview. Suzanne Vandeleur was born at Three Springs, the daughter of Peter Vandeleur and his wife Annie, and educated at the Dominican Ladies' College in Dongara. A person with a great sense of humour and 'a good head for business', Sr Suzanne, who was also appointed Prioress of Santa Sabina, Scarborough, in 1984, was a competent and efficient Superior during her terms of office. She subsequently served on the Archdiocesan Marriage Tribunal.

The fourth stage of the Siena's development program, earlier prepared by architects Oldham, Boas, Ednie-Brown and Associates, began to take shape in the third term of 1972. The new extension, constructed by Mr Alf Power, was erected at the western end of the building and comprised a library and classroom on the first floor, a laboratory on the ground floor as well as an undercroft. These additions were completed early in 1973 and, in that same year, Sister Perpetua Gill was appointed principal of the Siena Dominican Girls' High School, a position she held until her retirement in 1991.

The third of five children born to Norris and Bernadette Gill, Sister Perpetua, christened Bernice Linton, spent a happy childhood in the northern wheat-belt town of Morawa. With no local Catholic school available at that time, she attended the Morawa primary school and, to complete her secondary education, was enrolled as a boarder at the Dominican Ladies' College in Dongara. Later, as a qualified teacher, she taught for a number of years before entering the novitiate at Dongara on 15 August 1951. Apart from teaching at Siena, Sr Perpetua also taught at Dongara, Bedford Park and Scarborough and, in May 1971, she graduated with a Bachelor of Science Degree from The University of Western Australia. She was later given the opportunity to spend an enriching year at the International Casa di Studio in Rome to complete a course in Dominican spirituality. Despite the demanding nature of her work, Sr Perpetua's years at Siena were rewarding, particularly that aspect of her work which involved helping the less able students and the establishment of a special education centre for disabled students. Asked to reflect on Sister's life as a religious, one of her companions wrote:

*She was given the name Sister Mary Perpetua, under the special patronage of Mary, Mother of Perpetual Help. Her name in religious life was and is prophetic in that wherever she was called on to put her shoulder to the wheel to further the ministry of the Congregation she did so, cheerfully, willingly and most successfully. Of course her unfailing spirit of prayer underpinned her life and all the demands that religious life made on her. If those who knew her and lived with her over almost half a century were asked to name her special qualities, high on the list would be absolute trustworthiness, kindness, intelligence and courage. Sister Perpetua needed courage and faith to sustain her in all that she was asked to undertake and she was greatly blessed with both qualities. This was evident when the decision was taken to merge Siena Dominican Girls' High School with Marist College to create the co-educational Newman College. Sister Perpetua was closely involved in all the steps of that transaction and indeed to a large extent carried the practical burdens arising from it.* [25]

In February 1973, the Dominican Provincial Sister Assumpta Moriarty, met with the Brigidine Provincial, Sister Adrian Small, the Marist Provincial Brother Cletus Read, and the principal of the Marist College in Churchlands, Brother Timothy McDonald, to discuss the feasibility of an amalgamation and the problems that might arise if a co-education system were introduced. The Superiors of the three major Catholic secondary schools in the area, the Marist College principal Brother Timothy McDonald, the principal of the Siena Girls' High School, Sister Perpetua Gill, and the principal of the Brigidine College, Sister Christina O'Neill, continued to share ideas. Later, they were directed to set up a planning committee and a number of lay persons were invited to join the 12-member Interim Board chaired by Mr D. McBeath, a senior lecturer at the Western Australian Institute of Technology. Parents were later notified that a meeting would be held at the Brigidine College hall on 24 October 1973, to explain the rationale and philosophy behind the proposal to build a separate co-educational secondary school on Marist land at Churchlands. It was intended that the new establishment would cater for Year 11 and 12 students from the existing Siena, Brigidine and Marist Colleges, thus reverting the existing five-year secondary schools to three-year secondary schools. An application for government funding was not successful however, and although on-going discussions continued to take place, that particular aspect of the scheme was set aside and not considered again. [26]

Forward-planning was not the only major concern to be addressed by members of the Dominican Council during 1973 and it must have been a relief when the convent and college buildings at Dongara were finally sold by Kevin Sullivan and Associates in July and handed over to the purchaser, Mr A. Farnham of Perth. [27] A fifth extension to Siena, embodying an extra laboratory and a school canteen, was added to the building during the last term of 1973, to meet the needs of increased enrolments. By the end of 1974, Siena had some 400 students in attendance.

In the meantime, the Dominican Sisters had other issues to consider. The failing health of some of the elderly Sisters and the need for suitable long-term nursing home accommodation was a continuing concern. The Sisters' aim was to provide the best medical treatment available to those in need of extra attention, whilst at the same time keeping them within the community. A meeting with Mr K. Horgan, President of the Catholic Committee for Homes for the Aged, was therefore arranged, in May 1974, to discuss a proposal to build a special wing on vacant land adjoining the convent. Built in 1986, and now an integral part of St Catherine's Convent, the residential care centre is a place where the aged Sisters can return to familiar surroundings among the community's younger Sisters to receive the care they need.

Sister Rosarii Keenan, Prioress of St Catherine's Convent and the Sister-in-Charge of the care centre, together with a lay supervisor, have provided a pleasant environment and the physical and spiritual assistance necessary for the well-being of the Sisters during their latter years. Sister Rosarii was born in Narrandera, New South Wales and on the death of her father, moved with her family to Victoria. It was whilst living in that state that she met Father Packer CSSR, who encouraged her to follow her vocation to enter a religious life. After teaching in Victorian schools for a number of years, she entered the Dominican novitiate at Dongara in April 1952 and made her final profession in 1956. For the greater part of her life since then, she has occupied positions of principal at Perenjori, Bentley, Holy Spirit, Holy Rosary and Doubleview and for five years was a demonstration teacher at Signadou Teachers' College in Watson, Australian Capital Territory, earning a high reputation as teacher and principal. [28]

Architect Mr Peter Arney met the Sisters on 11 March 1977, to discuss plans to enlarge the convent and build a private chapel. As a result, an application was successfully made to the Metropolitan Building Authority in October 1977, for approval to begin substantial additions to St Catherine's Convent which embraced a visitor's flat and new chapel. [29]

The fine new chapel at St Catherine's was officially blessed and opened on 9 September 1978 and on Sunday, 19 November, the first Vigil Rosary was held in the chapel for the late Sister Pius Nolan, a respected member of the Dominican community and a pioneer in several foundations. The beautiful altar, once the focal point of the chapel in Dongara is now the centre-piece of St Catherine's chapel – a reminder of the Sisters' first Priory in Western Australia and the many Dominican Sisters who took their religious vows before the same altar. A striking circular stained glass window, bearing the Dominican crest

154. Sister Gemma and Year 8 class, 1980

< 155. Newman Siena College staff, with principal, Srister Perpetua Gill and deputies, Brother Joe Hughes and Mrs Shirley Voss, 1986

## GIRLS' SCHOOL TO CO-EDUCATION

156. Co-education group, Year 9 class, 1988 with teachers, Brother David Facci and Mr Gavin Knox, 1988

157. Special Education group with Sister Antoninus Campbell and Cardinal Larghi, 1995

158. First assembly of co-education students, 1983

and motto *Veritas*, was removed from the front door of the Dominican College at Dongara and reset in a recess in the wall of the new chapel's foyer. Likewise, several small stained glass windows, brought from the former Priory's chapel, have been placed in the southern wall of St Catherine's chapel. In the chapel are also eight wooden stalls from the chapel at Dongara – separate seating formerly used by the Sisters in a *chorus contra chorum formation* (one choir opposite the other) when saying the Divine Office, the common prayer of the ancient orders. These mementos provide a sense of atmosphere and help retain the present convent's links with the past.

Since 1978, St Catherine's has been fortunate enough to have a resident chaplain. The following priests have served in this role: Fathers Sean Bredin OS CAM, Peter Slattery O CARM, Michael Cave OSB, Nino Vinciguerra and Oliver Plunkett, the current chaplain.

Acting on a decision made the previous year, the first move made by the Dominican Sisters towards Siena becoming a co-educational school took place in February 1976, when girls in Years 11 and 12 from Siena attended the Marist College for Mathematics II and III, Physics and Chemistry, whilst the Year 11 and 12 Marist boys came to Siena to study Human Biology and French. A similar arrangement had existed for some years between the Brigidine and Marist Colleges. By November 1976, the sixth and final extension to the Siena Dominican Girls' High School took place when two additional classrooms were built at the end of the western wing at a cost of $50,000. [30]

Newman College, named after the eminent English Cardinal, theologian and scholar John Henry Newman (1801-1880), was inaugurated in 1977. In that year, all girls from Years 11 and 12 were transferred from Siena to the Newman Marist College at Churchlands. Meanwhile, the former Siena Dominican Girls' High School continued to accept girls from Years 8 to 10 under its new title Newman Siena College. At that stage, boys in equivalent years were being taught at the Newman Middle School, established in the former Brigidine College in Peebles Road, Floreat Park, and administered by the Marist Brothers. Members of the 1976 Interim Board of the co-educational College were Judge D. Heenan (acting chairperson during Mr D. McBeath's absence overseas), Sister Perpetua Gill OP, Sister Helen Maher CSB, Miss M. Lynch, Father B. Maxwell PP, Brother Timothy McDonald and Messrs G. Brennan, G. Overman, R. Firth, D. Elliot and A. Brady. [31]

In view of the additional enrolment of girls at the Newman Marist College, the staff for Years 11 and 12 was increased by a further six teachers, including two full-time Dominican staff members, Sister Declan Callaly and

Sister Anita Wilmott, and one part-time religious education teacher, Sister Helen O'Connor, who also taught at Newman Siena. Sister Declan, who had majored in English at The University of Western Australia and later obtained a Masters Degree in English Literature from Trinity College, Dublin, became co-ordinator of upper school English at Newman College in 1977. An artistic, studious person in tune with teaching, Sr Declan has a great love of the English language and the written word. The daughter of James and Mary Callaly of Dublin, Lucy arrived in Western Australia in 1950 and entered the novitiate the following year. Apart from teaching in the country and city, Sr Declan also served as Sister-in-Charge at the Huntriss Road and St Dominic's Priory, Bedford Park. In 1992, she resigned from her position at Newman College Senior School and accepted an offer to join the staff of the Christian Brothers' Agricultural College at Tardun. From her store of memories Sr Declan recently recalled:

*I can remember once teaching Sean O'Casey's play* Juno and the Paycock. *One of the characters, a Mrs Tankrid, mourns the loss of her son, who's been killed in an ambush and she says, "The pains I suffered bringing you into the world are nothing to the pains I'm suffering now, seeing you out of the world". I can remember, one day, quoting that to the students and saying that the pains I suffered bringing them in to high school were nothing to the pains I was suffering trying to get them out of high school. At the end of the year they gave me a book in which they inscribed, 'Thank you for the pains you suffered', and added the quote from the play, and their names.* [32]

It was during this period that Mrs Noeline Cooney, as deputy principal, remained in charge of the college while Sister Perpetua was absent overseas on a year's study leave. Mrs Cooney continued to hold that position in 1978. In the following years, the position of deputy was held by Mrs Colleen Kirkman (1978 and 1980), Mr Ron Powell (1981) and then by Mrs Shirley Voss (1982 to 1990).

In 1977, a second patron, Cardinal Newman, was chosen to share the name of the college with St Catherine of Siena, and in that same year, as well as advancing a new title, a new uniform was introduced at Newman Siena College. The girls wore grey skirts, sky blue shirts and light blue jumpers with two dark blue armbands and a dark blue blazer bearing the Newman logo. The boys wore identical coloured shirts and jumpers, with a pale blue tie and grey shorts or trousers. Newman Siena College in Williamson Road, Doubleview, owned by the Dominican Congregation and administered through the Newman Siena Board, was staffed by the Dominican Sisters, Marist Brothers and lay staff. In 1979, the staff consisted of seven Dominican Sisters – Perpetua Gill, Mary Patterson, Helen O'Connor, Gemma Seaman, Augustine Corbett, Francis Huntsman and Joseph Connor – as well as 25 lay teachers,

159. Aerial view, Dominican complex, Doubleview.
Top left: St Catherine's Convent. Top right: Newman Siena College. Lower left: Our Lady of the Holy Rosary Church. Lower Right: Holy Rosary School.

15 of whom were full-time teachers, three office staff, one laboratory assistant and one groundsman.

When the co-education system was totally introduced to both schools in February 1983, Sister Perpetua Gill continued as principal and Brother Joseph Hughes, who had previously been principal of Newman Middle College, was appointed deputy principal. Brother Joe, who played an important role in the smooth transition of Newman Siena from a girls' only school, has since been described as 'the right man for those times'. During this period, Marist Brothers Domnus and Thomas Horgan, each in his own way, contributed to the welfare of the students in a situation that was new to all of them. In keeping with the new development, Year 10 girls from Siena Newman College were transferred to Newman Senior School in Empire Avenue, Churchlands, and, for the first time, both boys and girls were accepted at Newman Siena in Years 8 and 9. [33]

The money raised through the Newman College Building Fund, established in 1981, made it possible to develop new projects and to extend existing buildings. Successive Board members, and others who undertook the task of following-up the pledges made by numerous donors, must have felt their efforts were justified when on Sunday, 20 February 1983, significant extensions to Newman Siena College were officially opened by the Hon. Andrew Mensaros MLA and blessed by the Auxiliary Bishop of Perth, Bishop Robert Healy. The new works, consisting of additional classrooms equipped to allow for teaching a range of elective subjects, a multi-purpose hall and an upgrade of existing facilities, were designed by architects Oldham, Boas, Ednie-Brown and Associates and the contract was let to Woodland Constructions. Seven days later, the first of many additional buildings completed at Newman Senior School were officially opened by the Hon. Ian Viner MP and blessed by the Archbishop of Perth, Sir Launcelot Goody KBE. In their wisdom, the Boards of the two colleges established a Building Trust Fund in 1987 and, a year later, funds from the Trust were used to complete a Special Education Centre at Newman Siena, a much-needed facility for intellectually handicapped students of the central-west region of the Archdiocese. Under the guidance of Sister Assumpta Moriarty, followed in turn by Sister Antoninus Campbell and Mrs Sophie Bogoias, the new centre rapidly became a valuable addition to the college. [34] In December 1990, the John Broderick Theatre Arts Building was blessed by Father Slattery O CARM and officially opened by Mr N. Catania MLC.

160. Sister Assumpta Moriarty

This new centre gave the long-serving Theatre Arts teacher, Mrs Jenny Lindsay and the large number of students who chose to enrol in this popular subject, the luxury of more space and improved conditions of light and sound. [35]

Early in 1990, a Review Committee, comprising representatives of the two orders, the Dominican and Marist and the Catholic Education Commission, undertook a comprehensive assessment of the two colleges since the introduction of co-education in 1983. One of the significant recommendations of the committee was that the Newman College Senior School and Newman Siena combine to form one school under one principal. It was also suggested that the implementation of that recommendation occur at the earliest feasible opportunity. [36]

It was at the end of 1991, that Sister Perpetua Gill resigned from the principalship of Newman Siena after 19 years in that role. The three years that followed her departure were years of further change and as the college moved towards amalgamation her successor, Sister Mary Ryan, must have often been sustained and encouraged by the words attributed to John Henry Newman, 'Where there is change, there is life'. During this period, two Marist Brothers were transferred to the eastern states. Brother Terrence Orrell, who made a considerable contribution during his eight years as principal of Newman College and was highly regarded by the staff of both colleges, left in 1992. In the following year, Brother David Facci, deputy principal at Newman Siena since 1987, resigned to take up another teaching position and his cheerful presence and pastoral care of all students was sorely missed. Brother Austin Redden, who departed in 1995, was the last of the Marists to serve at Newman Siena.

161. Sister Perpetua Gill

162. Sister Mary Ryan

Sister Mary Ryan's three years as principal concluded with all the necessary documentation for amalgamation completed by the end of 1994. She had every reason to feel satisfied with what had been accomplished in those years and looked forward to the challenge of a new and different apostolate. In January 1995, the opening of the new amalgamated college under one principal took place. To bring this vision to fruition, the newly-appointed head, Marist Brother Stephen Bugg, had worked tirelessly in unison with Sr Mary Ryan, the two religious orders and with chairman, Dr Tony Ryan, and members of the Board. It had been decided that the Dominican Sisters and Marist Brothers would be the co-governors of the two campuses and that the title Newman College would be retained with the component parts named according to their locations – Newman College (Doubleview campus) and Newman College (Churchlands campus). In 1997, the Dominican Sisters found it necessary to withdraw from the ownership and administration of the Doubleview campus, the last remaining school owned by the congregation in Western Australia. The paraliturgy on 25 June 1997, which marked the occasion, was offered in gratitude for the past and in faith and hope for the future direction of the congregation.

Just as Dominican students in this state have lived and studied for almost a century under the ancient Dominican motto *Veritas*, meaning Truth, so Newman College students aspire to follow Cardinal Newman's motto *Ex umbris et imaginibus in veritatem*, 'to move through shadows and images to truth'. Contemplation and teaching have been the hallmarks of the Dominican Sisters from Dominic's time, and although the contemporary religious have taken on new challenges to meet the needs of a changing world, the Dominicans' place in history reflects their contribution to education and learning over seven centuries. Pope John Paul II once stated, 'As teachers you kindle in your students a thirst for truth and wisdom'. [37] The Dominican Sisters in Western Australia, who have dedicated their lives to truth and imparted wisdom through their study and contemplation to thousands of students since 1899, have more than justified the pontiff's words.

163. Brother Stephen Bugg

164. Paraliturgy to mark Dominican Sisters' withdrawal from Newman College, 1997

CHAPTER 9

# A Rich Inheritance

'Since the Second Vatican Council religious orders have had to face diminishing numbers, changes in community life, the selling or conversion of property, erected, lived in and held beyond the lifetime of most of the inhabitants', wrote Catholic author D. O'Murchu. [1] Confronted by the changing times, the Dominican Sisters, along with other religious congregations entered a new cycle in their lives.

Although the winds of change blew slowly over the 700 centuries of Dominican existence, it was not uncommon throughout the order's history for communities to meet new challenges by making and accepting sensible adaptations to the rule to suit a particular situation. This was evidenced in Ireland when, along with two other ancient orders, the Poor Clares and Carmelites, the Dominicans survived harsh, tyrannical years by either temporarily dispersing or going into exile until social conditions had improved. Western Australia's founding

Dominican Sisters also readily accepted change when, in 1899, they agreed to relax the strict rule of enclosure to avoid problems associated with Australian conditions. The foundress, Mother Gabriel Gill, had already been through that exercise, for she had earlier raised the subject of adapting their constitutions to suit a new environment when she confided some of these concerns to Dr Kirby in Rome in April 1884:

*Our numbers are so limited and our works so heavy and important in the cause of religion that I have no scruple in giving orders contrary to the rule of enclosure in my desire to restore the failing health of three valuable and holy teaching nuns. Did I do right? Of course I had the Bishop's sanction, but I should feel most grateful if you could procure me for my lifetime, or rather my present and future terms of office (should I have any) full authority to exercise my judgement and power to change, according to circumstances, for health as well as school duties the Sisters of our various Convents, also to visit the Convents myself when a necessity occurs.* [2]

From the 1930s, due to modern demands in education, there was again an awareness of the need to change. The number of Sisters studying, part or full-time, increased during the inter-war and post-war periods and many Sisters attached to religious teaching orders were exempted from full-time duties in order to complete their studies at the Teachers' Training College or at The University of Western Australia. A number of noticeable community changes also took place in the Dominican Congregation in the 1950s. In 1955, lay Sisters exchanged the black scapular for the white scapular, thus abolishing the last distinction between choir Sisters and lay Sisters. In December that same year, permission was given for the Sisters to wear soft head-dress until a final decision was made about the introduction of a new style of habit more in keeping with Australian conditions. [3]

165. Sisters leaving for Teachers' College or University, 1950s
L. to R.: Sisters Gemma Seaman, Declan Callaly, Dolores Cummins, Antoninus Campbell, Gerard Lilley

An important year in the history of the Dominican Sisters in Australia was 1958 and new ground was broken when, on 11 March, the four separate congregations – one in New South Wales, two in South Australia and one in Western Australia were amalgamated into one national body under one Mother Prioress General residing in the Generalate in Canberra. Mother Philomena Waite was appointed the first Mother Prioress General of the newly-formed congregation and the former congregations became Provinces, each with their own Mother Prioress Provincial. The titles chosen were Holy Name Province (New South Wales), Holy Cross Province (Adelaide), Corpus Christi Province (North Adelaide) and Holy Family Province (Western Australia). In December 1960, the first Provincial Chapter was held at Bedford Park and Mother Emmanuel Lynch was elected Prioress Provincial. Sister Emmanuel's background has been described in an earlier chapter. Now in her 80s, the former Provincial is remembered, in particular, for her warm-hearted approach to others, her hospitality and her spontaneous sense of fun.

166. Mother Philomena Waite, first Prioress General of the Congregation of the Dominican Sisters of Australia, 1958

A decision was made on 27 December 1957, to ask the Dominican Sisters in South Australia if they would accept two postulants from Western Australia until such time as a larger group of novices entered novitiate at Dongara. [4] Sisters Francesca (Frances) Haddock and Lidwina (Sophie) de Groot moved to South Australia in 1958 to join the Dominican novitiate at Mt Lofty. A common novitiate was later set up at Wahroonga, New South Wales, and postulants from all Provinces, if they wished to continue, went there for their novitiate training and then to Signadou, the Dominican Teachers' College in Canberra, for their teacher preparation. The practical decision to have novices trained in a common novitiate was taken in an effort to rationalise the resources of the congregation and to provide the opportunity for them to experience and be faithful to their living heritage of common life, common prayer, study and service. Sisters Francesca and Lidwina were the first West Australian members to have this opportunity, followed in 1960 by Sisters Marlene Laracy, Edith Murphy, Sally Leeson and Myrtle Anstey.

167. Dominican Sisters at Signadou, Teachers' College, Canberra, ACT
L. to R.: Sisters Myrtle Anstey, Agnes Leeson, Edith Murphy, Anita Willmott, Marlene Laracy, Francesca Haddock

The second Vatican Council 1962-1965 was the catalyst for a new beginning and over the ensuing years the changes introduced into the majority of religious orders were slow, but marked. The most obvious of these was the disappearance of the symbolic habit worn by members of the different orders. Over the years, the former conventual lifestyle and strict rules have been adapted and the Sisters' lives have become more relevant to the times in which they live. Larger convents became expensive to maintain and it was not uncommon for some members of the community to move into smaller residences. After Vatican II, the role of the laity expanded and people previously drawn to structured religious orders in their desire to perform good works were given wider options. Consequently, as other avenues became available, it became more difficult to attract young women to join teaching and nursing orders. On a personal level, one of the more rewarding changes to take place within the community during the 1960s was the introduction of home visits for the Sisters. The first Dominican group, most of whom had been absent from Ireland for many years, arrived at Dublin on 22 November 1967, in time to spend a joyful Christmas with family and friends.

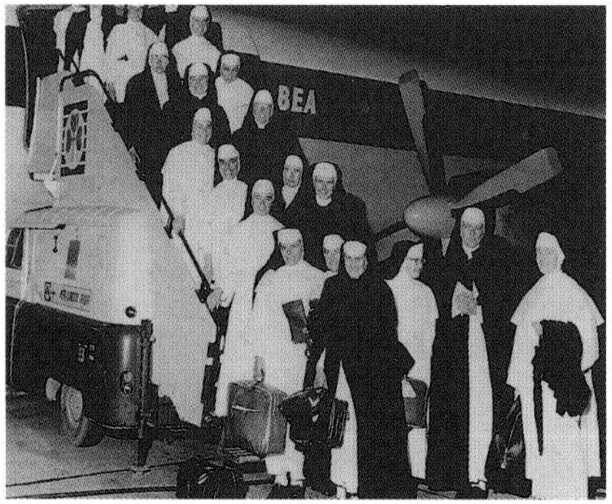

168. Irish Sisters on their first home visit, 1967

For any organisation to succeed, it is imperative that the top echelons exhibit an exemplary attitude as a benchmark for associated members and future leaders. The successive women who have led the Western Australian Dominican Sisters from their foundation through to present times have been worthy examples. The Sisters elected by members of the community over the years obviously displayed the desired qualities considered necessary for good leadership. They were women of courage and vision, of integrity and compassion, sustained by a deep faith and prayer life and a desire to spread the word of God. Meeting these criteria were Dominican leaders Mothers Gabriel Gill, Bonaventure McEntyre, Dominica Murphy, Vincent Colgan, Laurence Prendiville, Ceslaus Freed, Aquin Inglis, Emmanuel Lynch, Mary Patterson, Assumpta Moriarty, Concepta Flattery and today's Prioress of the Congregation, Sister Joan Carville.

Sister Mary Patterson, (the former Sr de Sales) was born in Dumfries, Scotland and as a child of eight years migrated with her family to New South Wales in 1927. The Pattersons later took up residence in South Perth and Mary attended St Columba's School conducted by the Sisters of the Sacred Heart in that suburb. Although the future Sister de Sales at first had no inclination to join a religious community, a meeting with Mother Laurence Prendiville at Bedford Park, led her to apply for acceptance as a Dominican Sister. Mary Patterson entered the Dongara novitiate on 6 January 1942 and made her final profession on 18 July 1946. Since then she has occupied many positions of authority, including that of principal, Prioress and Prioress Provincial.

A conscientious person and independent thinker, who has always lived by the precept 'peace', Sister Mary was described by one of her companions as 'a dour Scot famous for her unconditional generosity and down-to-earth practicality'. One of the Sisters illustrated the practical side of her nature with the following anecdote. The story centred on the small well-worn convent car, Sister Marie-Therese Sharman at the wheel and Sister de Sales Patterson (Sr Mary) as passenger. It seems that whilst out driving, the steering wheel came out of its socket and Sr Marie-Therese was left with the unenviable task of controlling the steering without a wheel. 'What will I do?', she asked in panic. Without the slightest sign of agitation, the ever-practical passenger Sr Mary advised, 'put it back', a suggestion the driver immediately obeyed. The car apparently continued its journey back to the convent without further incident. [5]

169. Prioress Provincials (WA) Sister Mary Patterson and Sister Kath Levitzke

Sister Assumpta Moriarty, a diligent and skilful primary and secondary school teacher, remained the Principal of Siena until 1972, when she was elected Prioress Provincial of the Dominican Sisters in Western Australia. Born in County Kerry, Ireland, where her parents had a small farm, Kathleen Moriarty received her primary school education locally before being enrolled as a boarder at Colaisde Ide. On the completion of her tertiary education, she studied primary school teaching at Carysfort Training College, Dublin, and later taught at rural and city schools. It was a meeting with Mother Laurence Prendiville, who was visiting Ireland in July 1950, that precipitated the young teacher's decision to leave her homeland four months later with 11 other Dominican postulants bound for Western Australia. A conscientious religious with a zest for learning, Sr Assumpta had the capacity to demand and obtain high standards from her pupils. Early in her religious life, Sister Assumpta studied for, and gained, an Arts Degree at The University of Western Australia with a double major in English and History as well as the Associate Diploma in Art of Speech. She taught for a time at Dongara, Bedford Park and Innaloo, but mostly at Siena in Doubleview. Throughout her eight-year term of office as Prioress Provincial,

170. Sisters Assumpta Moriarty and Josephine Compton, third Prioress General of the Australian Congregation

Sr Assumpta displayed the compassion required in that position and constantly encouraged members of her community to participate in both educational and spiritual studies. She had the ability to listen and her response was always a reflection of her wisdom and deep faith. [6]

A native of Ireland, Monica Clare Flattery (Sr Concepta), was born in Dublin, the daughter of civil servant Patrick Flattery and his wife Frances. She came to Western Australia and was received in to the Dominican community on 2 February 1952. True to the Dominican tradition of further study, she completed an Arts degree at The University of Western Australia, followed by a degree in Theology and Scripture from the Pontifical College, Regina Mundi, in Rome between 1964 and 1967. Sister Concepta, a reliable person, who according to her contemporaries excelled in all that she undertook, had her teaching career interrupted in 1970, when she was appointed Novice Mistress of Santa Sabina in Sydney. In 1985, Sr Concepta was elected Prioress Provincial of the Dominican Sisters of Western Australia and when the four Provinces reverted that year to congregations, she continued as Prioress General of the Western Australian congregation until the next election took place. A keen student with a strong sense of social justice, the strength of her convictions were often revealed in her willingness to take a firm stand on social and moral issues. Sister Concepta displayed a strong Dominican spirit, a keen interest in and a good knowledge of liturgy and theology. The Sisters have always been appreciative of the selfless service she has given to the congregation.[7]

171. Sister Concepta Flattery

Charged with selecting a Prioress to take them into the 1990s, members of the Western Australian Dominican community chose well when they elected Sister Joan Carville to lead them. The youngest of four surviving children of seven infants born to John and Josephine Carville of Belfast, Northern Ireland, Joan and her family had a long and close association with the Dominicans. The girls were educated at both primary and secondary levels by the Dominican Sisters and in their adult years the Carville men and women were members of the Third Order of St Dominic. Mother Laurence Prendiville's visit overseas in search of vocations in the early 1950s was timely, for Joan, who had been seriously contemplating a religious career, volunteered in 1952 to become a Dominican postulant. On entering the novitiate at Dongara the following year, she was given the name Sr Damian and after obtaining her teaching qualifications was assigned to schools at Bedford Park, Innaloo, Bentley,

172. Sister Joan Carville, Prioress General of the Dominican Sisters of WA, 1992-1999

Morawa, Dongara and Siena College, Doubleview. In 1974, she took a renewal course in Theology at the National Pastoral Institute in Melbourne. This was followed in 1975 by post graduate studies in Theology and Psychology at Fordham University, New York. On her return in 1985, Sister Joan, a staff member of the Catholic Pastoral Institute, lectured at the Nedlands campus of the then Secondary Teachers' College and later at Edith Cowan University. Between 1994 and 1998, as an elected member of the Co-ordinating Committee of the Dominican Sisters International, based in Rome, she forged invaluable links with the world-wide Dominican family.

Under Sister Joan Carville's leadership, members of her council have not only been responsible for the successful selling and acquisition of Dominican properties to suit contemporary accommodation needs, but also the renovation and refurbishment of all congregational convents. In the design and interior decorations, the Prioress has used her artistic talents to introduce an atmosphere of tasteful tranquillity. A personal communication from a member of Sr Joan's community drew an analogy between the first and current leaders of the Dominicans in this state. Her precis cleverly links characteristics shared by the two women:

*Mother Gabriel Gill was Prioress of the fledgling Dominican Congregation of Sisters in Western Australia one hundred years ago and Sr Joan was Prioress in the centenary year of 1999. Between both Dominicans parallels can be drawn.*

*Both were blessed with many sterling qualities, high among them resourcefulness and courage. Both, within the context of their times, respected the old values while ready to accept the new, when appropriate. While elegance and decorum were not an end in themselves, they were integral to the characters of both women. Difficulties that faced them were challenges to be overcome, not insurmountable obstacles. But, what marked both those leaders of the congregation most strongly was the spirit of faith and prayer that sustained them in good times and bad, in their dealings with people in many walks of life and with their Sisters.*

*Of both it can be truly said that their lives speak for them.* [8]

When one reflects on the characteristics of any group of people, even those who to all intents and purposes appear to be living the same kind of lifestyle, it becomes obvious that each group is quite different or unique.

Dominic, the founder of the Order of Preachers, was known as a man who wanted to respond to the needs of the time, which was for him to preach the Word of God in a period when false doctrines were being promoted. Dominicans today, as has been evidenced throughout the ages, take their preaching role very seriously. This takes many forms in many countries throughout the world because the seeds of the tradition from the time of Dominic entered into the heart of the Dominican vocation. So long as there are people searching for truth or who have obvious mystical yearning or seek a deeper social commitment, a Dominican can hardly stand idly by and yet still claim to be in the tradition of Thomas Aquinas, Catherine of Siena or any other Dominican Saint.

This dynamism of preaching demands relevancy, and requires from the preacher an openness to changing circumstances if the Word of God is to be heard in every age. The Dominican women in Western Australia, through discernment and prayer have adapted not only their style of dress and their lifestyle, but also the way in which the message is preached. As a result, it has been necessary for the Sisters, who formerly taught in schools and colleges, to undertake studies and retraining courses for ministries more suited to their age and the call of Spirit at this time in their histories. Areas to which the Sisters have responded are:

Chaplaincy in hospitals
Counselling in schools and colleges
Spiritual direction and retreats
Visitation
Visitation of the sick and elderly
Hospital visitation
Gaol visitation
Tutoring students
Catechetical work
Voluntary work in Church and State organisations
Craft work to aid the Missions
Justice and peace work
Legion of Mary
Household duties – cooking and hospitality
Welfare work

Although no longer having foundations in the Geraldton diocese, the Dominican Sisters continue to maintain a presence in the area. Sister Mary Ryan, having completed a psychology degree after a busy and fruitful teaching and counselling career, was offered an appointment as the Geraldton diocese's first Director of Centacare Family Services. Her background and ability to listen and relate to people, made her the ideal person to take up such a position. Working with Sister Mary at Centacare is Sister Patricia Robinson, a Dominican

Sister from New Zealand, who provides support services for victims of crime. Since 1992, Sister Declan Callaly has also been teaching at St Mary's Christian Brothers' Agricultural School in the Geraldton diocese at Tardun. She holds the position of Religious Education Co-ordinator and is the only religious Sister on the staff. It was not the first time that the Dominican Sisters had accepted an invitation to work at Tardun. In 1950, Sisters Teresa McQuillan, Dominic Galvin and Raphael Wood, took charge of the Pallottine Mission and established a fine working relationship with the Aboriginal children in their care. Later, in 1990, Sisters Margaret Scharf and Eileen Leahy, with lay principal Mr Andrew Jago, taught at the mission, during which time the new Wandalgu Catholic primary school was blessed and opened.

Locally-born, Sister Margaret Scharf, who had earlier taught at Holy Rosary, Doubleview, and been involved in the Motor Mission and mission work at Tardun and in the Solomon Islands, later obtained a Master of Arts degree in Spirituality at Gonzaga University, Spokane, Washington State, United States of America. She has since become a member of staff at the Center for Spiritual Development in Orange, California, where her ministry involves teaching, preaching, giving retreats, spiritual direction and liturgy preparation for the Center. Several other Sisters continue to provide valuable work outside of

173. Dominican Sisters International. Group taken at Conference in Rome, 1997

Western Australia. In Victoria, two members, Sisters Helen O'Connor and Margaret Vance, keep alive the Western Australian Dominican spirit in Melbourne. Both are employed as parish associates and Sister Helen currently combines that work with hospital chaplaincy at Heidelburg Hospital.[9]

As preachers of truth and women called to contemplation and prayer, the Sisters live in the communities suited to their ministry. St Catherine's Convent in Doubleview is regarded as the mother-house of the congregation. In Scarborough, the Sisters live in a number of small houses clustered around the original convent in that area, Santa Sabina, and meet regularly for prayer and community gatherings.

The Dominican Sisters living in Australia are a federated group and support the work of each of the four congregations across the continent. This is achieved through yearly meetings of representatives. Each of the congregations is also affiliated with the world-wide network of Dominican women through membership of the Dominican Sisters International, which has as its objectives:

*to support one another in living out the Dominican charism and to claim and promote their identity as women preachers*

*to facilitate communication and networking among Dominicans at both regional and international levels to foster a more compassionate world order through promoting peace and justice, integrity of creation and human rights especially those of women*

*to explore and foster collaborative initiatives among the Dominican family.* [10]

In line with the Dominican Sisters who reside in almost every country in the world, working through their preaching and teaching in schools, colleges, universities and hospitals often in the most deprived circumstances and in a variety of church and state agencies, the Western Australian Dominican Sisters continue the work of their founder with courage and dedication.

Having achieved the work they set out to accomplish in the distant goldfields and extensive wheat lands, north and east of Perth, the Dominican Sisters have left the fields of gold and put down new roots. Proud of their rich inheritance, the Sisters, in the true spirit of the order, have since grasped new-found opportunities to reach out in all directions to sustain and offer guidance to people of all ages, creeds, and nationalities. Given that the Dominican Sisters education program remained essentially constant over the years, it stands to reason that, despite the present absence of Dominican schools in Western Australia, a litany of tributes will be evoked from friends, clergy and grateful pupils during the congregation's year long centenary celebrations in 1999.

As the present members of the Dominican Congregation approach the 21st century, they see their future roles not as educators in the school system, but as continuing their journey through preaching and by reflecting gospel living, imbued by the spirit of St Dominic. As they look to this 'new set of challenges the Dominican Sisters' vision of their vocation remains inspired by St Dominic's – *Contemplari et contemplata aliis tradere* – to contemplate and give to others the fruits of their contemplation'.[10]

# VERİTAS

**A Tribute to the Dominican Sisters of WA**
**Composed by Gerry Crooks**

1. From soft and gentle rains they came,
From lands of misty skies,
From ancient stories carved in time and hope
that never dies;
The call they heard in fields of green,
Their journey thus begun.
They left, in faith, for fields of gold blown dry
by scorching sun.

**REFRAIN**

We celebrate a story of wisdom from above,
Of faithful lives and patient dreams,
A simple song of love;
Its melody compassion, a deeply-felt unrest,
Its wondrous call of *veritas* through which
we all are blest.

2. At Greenough and then far beyond
The seed was gently sown.
Through courage in adversity they made
this land their own.
With open hearts they freely gave,
Their talents freely shared;
They brought their skills and learning
to all for whom they cared.
(Refrain)

CODA

And still today the memory of those courageous few
Who journeyed to those fields of gold
Is now our story too.
Through friendships formed and lasting
And forged through prayer and pain,
Their spirit will forevermore
In our hearts remain.

# Appendix

PROFESSED SISTERS WHO SERVED THE CHURCH IN WA BETWEEN 1899 AND 1999

| RELIGIOUS NAME | BAPTISMAL NAME |
|---|---|
| Sr M. Alacoque Culhane | Mary |
| Agnes Leeson | Sally |
| Agnes Leddin | Elizabeth |
| Albertus Bain | Rosalind |
| Aloysius O'Neill | Mary |
| Aloysius Pickerd | Catherine |
| Alphonse Marie de Kuyer | Elizabeth |
| Alphonsus O'Connor | Mary |
| Ambrose Bernet | Annette |
| Anastasia Byrne | Annie |
| Andrew Murphy | Edith |
| Anne Graham | Agnes |
| Annunciata Kelly | Mary |
| Antoninus Campbell | Teresa |
| Antoninus Houlahan | Ellen |
| Anthony Sachse | Patricia |
| Aquin Inglis | Mary |
| Assumpta Moriarty | Kathleen |
| Augustine Corbett | May |
| Augustine Lane | Andrea |
| Baptist Hall | Jessie |
| Baptist Robson | Margaret |
| Benedict Lyons | Mary |
| Benignus O'Connor | Mary |
| Benvenuta Brophy | Catherine |
| Berchmans Wilson | Jean |
| Bernadette Punch | Joan |

| RELIGIOUS NAME | BAPTISMAL NAME |
|---|---|
| Bernard Larney | Anne |
| Bernard Rogers | Mary |
| Bernardine Hanafin | Margaret |
| Bertrand O'Connor | Gladys |
| Bonaventure McEntyre | Anne |
| Brigid Kelly | Mary |
| Carmel Keeley | Florence |
| Catherine Kenny | Mary |
| Cecilia Murphy | Brigid |
| Ceslaus Freed | Alice |
| Christine Fogarty | Winifred |
| Christopher Sachse | Pauline |
| Clement Hughes | Ellen |
| Columba Wilkinson | Joan |
| Concepta Flattery | Monica |
| Concepta Waterson | Margaret |
| Consilii Costello | Anne |
| Damian Carville | Joan |
| Declan Callaly | Lucy |
| de Montfort Evans | Barbara |
| de Porres Anstey | Myrtle |
| de Sales Patterson | Mary |
| di Pazzi Miscall | Mary |
| di Ricci Levitzke | Kathleen |
| di Ricci Kirby | Ellen |
| Dolores Cummins | Mary |
| Dolores Lloyd | Sarah |
| Dominic Galvin | Catherine |
| Dominica Davis | Dorothy |
| Dominica Murphy | Margaret |

| RELIGIOUS NAME | BAPTISMAL NAME |
|---|---|
| Elizabeth McKenzie | Denise |
| Emmanuel Lynch | Mary |
| Evangelist Graham | Mary |
| Eymard Regan | Irene |
| Felicitas Plunkett | Margaret |
| Francesca Haddock | Frances |
| Francis Huntsman | Sheila |
| Gabriel Barden | Teresa |
| Gabriel Gill | Victoria |
| Gemma Seaman | Margaret |
| Gerard Lilley | Jeanette |
| Gerard Milligan | Catherine |
| Gertrude Dominish | Dorothy |
| Gonzales Wall | Maria |
| Hyacinth Carroll | Mary |
| Ignatius Prendiville | Hannah |
| Imelda Buckley | Mary |
| Imelda Heron | Mary |
| Imelda Ryan | Imelda |
| Immaculate Ashleigh | Gladys |
| Jacinta Vance | Margaret |
| Jerome O'Connor | Helen |
| John Wilkinson | Alice |
| Jordan Leddin | Marnie |
| Jordana Mackey | Judith |
| Joseph O'Connor | Mary |
| Josephine Hanafin | Agnes |
| Josephine Kenny | Ellen |
| Julian Vandeleur | Suzanne |
| Laurence Prendiville | Ellen |
| Lidwina de Groot | Sophie |
| Magdalen Lewis | Dorothy |
| Maria Goretti Power | Patricia |
| Marie-Therese Sharman | Violet |

| RELIGIOUS NAME | BAPTISMAL NAME |
|---|---|
| Margaret Mary Willmott | Anita |
| Margaret Scharf | Margaret |
| Mark Laracy | Marlene |
| Martin Doyle | Treasa |
| Mary Ryan | Mary |
| Mercedes Clune | Pauline |
| Michael Ryan | Patricia |
| Norbert Burke | Pauline |
| Paschal Dowdall | Kathleen |
| Patrick Doyle | Amy |
| Paul Hutton | Amelia |
| Paul O'Connor | Hanora |
| Perpetua Gill | Bernice |
| Peter Geeson | Margaret |
| Philomena McGrath | – |
| Philomena Punch | Mary |
| Pierre Ross | Diane |
| Pius Nolan | Catherine |
| Raphael Wood | Gertrude |
| Raymund Creed | Margaret |
| Regina O'Neill | Anna |
| Reginald Leahy | Eileen |
| Reginald Rice | Mary |
| Rosarii Keenan | Mary |
| Rose McCusker | Mary |
| Stanislaus McDonough | Mary |
| Stephen Hulbert | Ann |
| Teresa McQuillan | Rose |
| Thomas Short | Rita |
| Vianney O'Brien | Esther |
| Veronica Ryan | Mary |
| Vincent Colgan | Susanna |
| Xavier Ryan | Anne |

# Abbreviations

| | |
|---|---|
| ACAP | Archdiocesan Catholic Archives Perth. |
| BL | Battye Library. Alexander Library, Perth. |
| DAD | Dominican Archives Doubleview. |
| GDA | Geraldton Diocesan Archives. |
| MOM | Mother of Missions. |
| RWAHS | Royal Western Australian Historical Society. |
| SITS | Star in the South. |
| WACR | Western Australian Catholic Record. |
| WAN | West Australian Newspapers. |
| OP | Order of Preachers. |
| PBVM | Presentation Sisters. |
| Pers. Comm. | Personal communication. |
| RSM | Sisters of Mercy. |
| RSJ | Sisters of St Joseph of the Sacred Heart. |

# Reference Notes

## CHAPTER ONE
## AOTEAROA, LAND OF THE LONG WHITE CLOUD

1. Sr Augustine McCarthy, SITS, p. 22. See MOM, pp. 1–5.
2. Sr Augustine McCarthy, MOM, pp. 2, 4.
3. ibid., p. 5.
4. ibid., p. 6.
5. SITS, pp. 9-12.
6. MOM, pp. 9, 10.
7. SITS, pp. 22, 23. The Romans numbered the days after the Ides.
8. ibid., pp. 26, 27, 34.
9. ibid., p. 35. Te Deum, 'Thee God we praise', sung on special occasions as a thanksgiving.
10. MOM, p. 19. Fr Moreau earlier attempted to get French Sisters to work in Dunedin. In fact, one newspaper reported: 'French Sisters of the Mission on the way'.
11. ibid., p. 21.
12. SITS, pp. 31, 37, 38.
13. ibid., pp. 30, 31.
14. ibid., pp. 38, 39.
15. ibid., p. 38. See MOM, p. 22.
16. MOM, p 27.
17. ibid., p. 24.
18. SITS, p. 48.
19. ibid., pp. 50, 51. See MOM, p. 40, 41.
20. ibid., pp. 53, 56.
21. ibid., pp. 58, 59.
22. MOM, p. 44.
23. SITS, p. 63.
24. ibid., p. 72.
25. MOM, p. 46.
26. SITS, pp. 81, 82.
27. ibid., p. 89.
28. DAD, T. Kirby, Rome, copy of letter to M. Gabriel Gill, 3.12.1884. M. Gabriel received an Apostolic blessing from Pope Leo XIII as well as approval to found a novitiate in Ireland.
29. SITS, p.100. Beaumont was originally owned by the Guiness family.
30. ibid., p.101.
31. ibid., pp. 102, 103.
32. DAD, Dom Columba Marmion OSB, Maredsous, copy of letter to M. Gabriel Gill, Beaumont, 11.9.1888. It appears that M. Gabriel was not then on the best of terms with her landlord Edward O'Malley, which put the length of her stay at Beaumont in jeopardy.
33. SITS, p.106.
34. ibid., pp.106, 107.
35. MOM, pp. 66, 67.
36. SITS, p. 116.
37. MOM, p. 82.
38. ibid., p. 102, 103.
39. *Veritas* 1949.
40. ibid., pp. 104-106, 115, 116. Some Sisters believed that Sr Agnes Rooney, the eldest of the New Zealand foundation group, should have been made Superior because of her age and experience. It was also alleged that originally Sr Agnes herself shared this opinion.
41. ibid., p. 116. See SITS, p. 167. The status of foundations originating from Cabra, Dublin, such as Sion Hill, was challenged. This was due to a controversial declaration in 1895, which insisted that Cabra ceased to be a Dominican convent after it was placed under the jurisdiction of the Archbishop of Canterbury in 1832. Sr Catherine Hughes died at Sydney in Jan. 1902.
42. WACR, 8.9.1898.
43. R. Marchant James, *Cork to Capricorn*, pp. 134, 139-144.
44. SITS, p. 166. See DAD, Archbishop T. Carr, Melbourne, copy of letter to M. St Peter Slattery, Dunedin, 15.10.1896.
45. ibid., p.167.

46. MOM, pp. 117, 118.
47. ACAP, Bishop Kelly, letter to M. St Peter Slattery, Dunedin, 5.1.1899.
48. MOM, p.122.
49. ibid., pp. 124, 125.

## CHAPTER TWO
## TO SIN, SAND, SORROW, SORE EYES AND SARDINES

1. M. Gabriel Gill's diary, entry, 24.4.1899.
2. Sr di Ricci Kirby's diary, 24.4.1899.
3. M. Gabriel Gill's diary, 24.4.1899.
4. Sr di Ricci's Kirby's diary, 25.4.1899.
5. M. Gabriel Gill's diary, 26.4.1899.
6. *NZ Tablet,* 1915. See SITS, pp. 168, 169. Sr di Pazzi was born 8 December 1877.
7. M. Gabriel Gill's diary, 27.4.1899. See Sr di Ricci's diary, 27.4.1899.
8. ibid., 28.4.1899.
9. ibid, 29.4.1899.
10. ibid.
11. ibid., 1.5.1899. See di Ricci's diary, 1.5.1899.
12. Sr di Ricci's diary, 1.5.1899. Spelling of vessel's name differs in M. Gabriel's diary.
13. *Veritas* 1899-1949. Sr Gonzales Wall was born 19.7.1865.
14. Ibid.
15. Ibid.
16. Ibid.
17. M. Gabriel's diary, 4.5.1899.
18. ibid., 6.5.1899. The Sisters did not own anything. Everything was in common, hence the expression *ad usum* [for the use of] was generally used.
19. ibid., 7.5.1899.
20. ibid., 23.5.1899. During the $19^{th}$ and early part of the $20^{th}$ century 'Loreto' was spelt with two 't' s.
21. ibid., 25.5.1899.
22. ibid.
23. Sr di Ricci's diary 27.5.1899.
24. ibid., 29.5.1899. See Sr Gonzales's diary 28.5.1899. Also MOM, pp.136, 137.
25. ibid., 4.6.1899.
26. ibid., 6.6.1899.

## CHAPTER THREE
## ... AND THEY CAME TO THE GREENOUGH

1. WACR, 16.6.1899, p. 15. *Cathedral Chronicle,* June 1950, *Geraldton Express,* 16.6.1899.
2. ibid.
3. ibid., See Sr di Piazzi Miscall's diary, 7.8.1899. Today's spelling of the word 'Mille' omits the 'l' and in the word 'failthe', the 'h'.
4. ibid.
5. DAD, Sr di Piazzi Miscall's diary, 7.6.1899.
6. Ibid.
7. WACR, 22. 2.1894. See *Geraldton Advertiser*, 12.2.1894.
8. DAD, Sr di Pazzi Miscall's diary, 19.6.1899.
9. DAD, annals, Holy Rosary, Greenough, 14.6.1899.
10 Sr di Pazzi Miscall's diary, 12.6.1899.
11. *Cathedral Chronicle*, January 1950, article, 'Mr Clune's Tribute'. See *Veritas* 1899-1949.
12. Sr di Pazzi Miscall's diary, 14.6.1899.
13. ibid., 20. 6.1899.
14. SITS, pp.175, 176.
15. M. Gabriel Gill's diary, 12.6.1899.
16. Sr di Pazzi Miscall's diary, 30. 6.1899.
17. ibid., 13.6.1899, 20.6.1899, 3.9.1899.
18. DAD, annals, Holy Rosary, Greenough, 1.7.1899.
19. DAD, Sr Albertus Bain, interview notes.
20. DAD, annals, Holy Rosary, Greenough, 23.7.1899.
21. WACR, 29.7.1899.
22. *Geraldton Express-Murchison, Yalgoo Goldfields Chronicler*, 4. 8.1899. See Sr di Pazzi Miscall's diary, 26.7.1899.
23. M. Gabriel's Gill's diary, 4.8.1899. Fr McCabe commenced the first St Peter's Church in 1864 and Fr Lecaille completed it in 1867.
24. Sr di Pazzi Miscall's diary, 22.7.1899, 1.8.1899, 5 and 23 Sept. 1899.

25. ibid., 12.7.1899, 12 and 28. Sept. 1899.
26. D. F. Bourke, op cit., p. 78.
27. ACAP, McCarthy, thesis.
28. Sr di Pazzi Miscall's diary, 3., 5 and 30 Aug. 1899. Possibly the land settlement arranged by Bishop Kelly and Fr Ryan on 27.7.1899.
29. ibid., 5.9.1899.
30. ibid., 3. 9.1899.
31. ibid.
32. DAD, Sr Anastasia Byrne, interview notes.
33. DAD, annals, Holy Rosary, Greenough, 27.7.1899. See SITS, p.176.
34. Sr di Pazzi Miscall's diary, 19.9.1899.
35. ibid., 20.9.1899.
36. ibid., 25.9.1899.
37. ibid., 28.9.1899.
38. ibid.
39. ibid., 29.11.1899.
40. ibid., 30.11.1899.
41. ibid.
42. ibid., 8.1.1900.
43. ibid., 20.12.1899.
44. R. Marchant James, *Cork to Capricorn*, pp. 146-150.
45. DAD, *Book of Permissions*.
46. D. F. Bourke, op.cit., p.181.
47. R. Marchant James, op.cit., p. 140. *Ad limina* refers to a visit made by a bishop to Rome every five years.
48. ACAP, Catholic Year Book, 1902, p.85. Figures based on year prior to publishing date. Mixed schools taught children of both sexes. Catholic schools worked reasonably well under the Elementary Education Act of 1871, but became dissatisfied when the controversial Assisted Schools Abolition Act was passed in Oct. 1895. The Public Education Amendment Act passed in 1899, meant that secular education at government schools was provided free of charge to children under 14 years. Education became compulsory and the Efficient School system was also introduced, whereby non-government schools could be examined on request and declared efficient.
49. Sr di Pazzi Miscall's diary, 3 and 4 Jan. 1900.
50. The site of the new dormitory is unknown. The description could refer to a temporary building, or renovations to Goodwin's house.
51. WACR, 31.3.1900.
52. DAD, Box 310., vol. I., 18.8.1900.
53. DAD, Sr di Ricci Kirby's diary, 20.8.1900.
54. ibid., 21.8.1900.
55. ibid.
56. ibid.
57. ibid., 23.8.1900. Kate obviously left the order and details of her life after returning to New Zealand are unknown.
58. *Sower*, 1.5.1909.
59. WACR, 8.12.1900.
60. ibid., 12.1.1901.
61. Book of the Clothing of Professions, Holy Rosary Convent, Greenough. A Choir Sister's main ministry was education in some form. A lay Sister's duties involved domestic and outside work.
62. WACR, 17.8.1901, p.10. Also 3.8.1901, p. 8.
63. DAD, cutting, paper not identified, 27.12.1901.
64. ACAP, Catholic Church Directory, 1904, p. 86.

## CHAPTER FOUR
## CUE, QUEEN OF THE MURCHISON

1. P. Heydon, *Just A Century Ago*, p. 4.
2. *Veritas*, 1899-1949, J. C., article, 'Reminiscences'.
3. P. Heydon, *Just A Century Ago*, p. 7.
4. *Murchison Times and Day Dawn Gazette*, 8.2.1900. See P. Heydon, op cit., p 33.
5. ibid., 19.9.1899.
6. ibid., 3.10.1899. Kitchens in colonial buildings were often detached from the main building in case of fire.
7. ibid., 23.9.1899.
8. ibid., 3.10.1899.
9. ibid.,11.11.1899.
10. ibid., 21.11.1899. See Sr di Pazzi Miscall's diary, 10.11.1899. Newspaper report should have read Greenough, not Geraldton.
11. ibid.

12. DAD, Sr di Pazzi Miscall's diary, 17.1.1900. See annals, Holy Rosary, Greenough, 9.6.1900.
13. *Murchison Times and Day Dawn Gazette*, 18.1.1900.
14. ibid., 8.2.1900, 16.2.1900.
15. D. F. Bourke, op. cit., p.171.
16. DAD, annals, Holy Rosary, Greenough, 20.1.1902.
17. *Murchison Advocate*, 13.7.1901.
18. DAD, M. Gabriel Gill, letter to Convent, Cue, 1.11.1901.
19. DAD, Book of Permissions, Holy Rosary, Greenough, January 1900.
20. DAD, annals, Holy Rosary, Greenough, 30.6.1900.
21. *Murchison Times and Day Dawn Gazette*, February 1903.
22. MOM, pp. 164, 165.
23. ibid., p.165.
24. DAD, Sister's description of fire, 2.12.1903. See D. F. Bourke, op.cit., p.178.
25. DAD, Sr Joseph O'Connor, notes. A Portress was a Sister whose duties included answering the convent door.
26. M. Grey, née Healey, interviewed by Srs Margaret Scharf and Perpetua Gill, June 1992. See Sr Joseph O'Connor's notes.
27. *Murchison Times and Day Dawn Gazette*, February 1904. See MOM, pp. 161, 169.
28. MOM, pp. 171, 172.
29. ibid.
30. DAD, M. Gabriel Gill, letter to Sr Aquinas Gawne, 10.9.1904. See MOM, p.169.
31. DAD, Sr di Pazzi Miscall, letter to Sion Hill, Dublin, 1905.
32. ibid.
33. ibid.
34. ibid.
35. DAD, Sr Philomena McGrath, letter to Priory, Dongara, April 1905.
36. Sr di Pazzi Miscall, letter to Sion Hill, April 1905. No mention of M. Gabriel's death appeared in the annals, Priory, Dongara.
37. ibid. A soutane is a priest's cassock. A rochet, a surplice worn by a bishop.
38. MOM, p.152.
39. *Sower*, 1.6.1908, p. 5.
40. ibid., 1.3.1909, pp. 1-11.
41. ibid., 1.2.1909, p. 4. See *Sower*, 1.3.1909, p. 1.
42. ibid., 1.7.1909, pp. 9, 10.
43. ibid., February, 1910, pp. 4, 5. See *Murchison Times and Day Dawn Gazette*, January 1910.
44. ibid., March 1910, p. 5.
45. ibid., 1.11.1910, pp. 7, 8. See *Sower*, August 1910, p. 8.
46. Census, 1911. See D. F. Bourke, p. 178.
47. *Sower*, June 1910, pp. 4, 5. See R. Marchant James. op. cit., pp. 223, 224.
48. ibid., January 1911, p. 7.
49. ibid., September 1911, p. 6. The date of arrival was possibly 22.9.1911.
50. *Mt Magnet Miner and Lennonville Leader*, 30.9.1911. Most students enrolled at the Adelaide University as The University of WA did not open until 1913.
51. *Sower*, December 1911, p.14.
52. ibid., January 1912, p.12.
53. ibid., September 1913, p. 11.
54. P. Heydon, *Gold on the Murchison*, p.106.
55. Bishop Kelly, letter to Mr Colgin, Cue, 3.10.1916.
56. *Sower*, February 1919, p. 18.
57. GDA, Fr O'Connor, letter to Bishop Gummer, 2.5.1943.
58. ibid.
59. DAD, Sr Dominic Galvin, notes.
60. ibid.
61. DAD, Education Department, Inspector's report, July 1954.
62. *Catholic Chronicle*, November 1967.

**CHAPTER FIVE**
**ON THE BANKS OF THE IRWIN**

1. Irwin Historical Society, S. Scotter, notes. See Sr Albertus Bain's interview with L.Classon, daughter of Mary Ann Nairn.
2. D. F. Bourke, op. cit., p. 173. See *Cathedral Chronicle*, December 1948. The date of her arrival is often questioned.
3. Irwin Shire Library, C. Penny, handwritten memoirs.
4. WACR, 1.1.1902.

5. DAD, annals, Priory, Dongara, 25.1.1902.
6. WACR, 22.2.1902.
7. *Geraldton Express*, 21.2.1902. See WACR, 1.3.1902.
8. WACR, 2.11.1901, 15.3.1902. The Dominicans took the name 'St Joseph's' with them to Dongara intending to use it for their primary school.
9. DAD, J. Nairn, typescript, 'First School Days at Dongara'.
10. Irwin District Historical Society, S. Scotter notes. S. Moore's site listed as Location 933.
11. J. Nairn, op.cit., Additional comments, not in the original, have been added to the typescript.
12. DAD, annals, St Dominic's, Dongara, 8.1.1902.
13. ibid., 25.1.1902.
14. ibid., 20.1.1902, 25.1.1902.
15. *Victoria Express*, 27.1.1902. See DAD, Book of Admissions, Holy Rosary, Greenough.
16. DAD, annals, Holy Rosary, Greenough, 24.1.1902.
17. DAD, 'Outline of the History of the Holy Family Province'. See MOM, p. 160.
18. MOM, pp. 160-162.
19. DAD, 'Outline of the History of the Holy Family Province'. See MOM, p. 162.
20. SITS, p. 177. See MOM, p. 162.
21. *Victoria Express,* June, 1902.
22. ibid., 13.11.1902.
23. DAD, J. Nairn, op.cit.
24. DAD, annals, Priory, Dongara, 28.1.1903.
25. GDA, document, Victoria Location, Block No. 1057.
26. WAN, 3.8.1903. See DAD, J. Nairn, op.cit.
27. DAD, annals,, Priory, Dongara, 8.1.1904.
28. DAD, M. Gabriel, letter to Mr Herbert, 2.7.1904.
29. DAD, Appointment book, St Dominic's 14.7.1905.
30. WACR, cutting, January 1908.
31. DAD, J. Nairn, op. cit.
32. *Sower,* January 1909.
33. DAD, annals, Priory, Dongara, 2.1.1910, 30.6.1910.
34. *Sower,* p. 7, 1.10.1909.
35. DAD, annals, Priory, Dongara, 21.1.1910, 30.6.1910.
36. ibid., April 1910. See *Sower*, p. 8, December 1910.
37. *Sower*, January 1911, February 1911, pp. 4, 5. See January 1918.
38. ibid., June 1911, p. 6.
39. DAD, Sr Joseph O'Connor, notes.
40. *Sower*, September 1913, pp. 8, 16.
41. ibid.
42. ibid., June 1917, p. 8.
43. ibid., August 1917, p. 6.
44. DAD, annals, Priory, Dongara, 20.12.1919, 12.4.1921, 25.9.1923.
45. ibid., 20.5.1924.
46. ibid., 30.9.1926.
47. ibid., 17.5.1927, 9.1.1928.
48. *Geraldton Express,* 9.5.1928.
49. WACR, 18.5.1928. See *Geraldton Express*, 9.5.1928.
50. DAD, annals, Priory, Dongara, 9.1.1928.
51. E. Marshall, pers. comm., 1997.
52. DAD, Sr Joseph O'Connor, notes.
53. ibid.
54. DAD, Sr Teresa Martelli, interview with Sr Imelda Heron, March 1992.
55. *Veritas,* 1934-1942.
56. ibid., vol. III., 1937, 1938.
57. DAD, 'History of the Bushies' Schools', 1938-1988.
58. *Veritas* 1934-1942, B. Gill, article.
59. I. Gallop, notes, 1998.
60. *Cathedral Chronicle*, February 1942.
61. *Veritas* 1934-1942.
62. *Heritage Views*, October 1996, vol. 2, no. 4. J. Rowland, article 'From Dublin to Dongara and Beyond'.
63. *Cathedral Chronicle*, January 1965, article, 'Ideals', p. 4.
64. ibid., p. 5.
65. W. Sullivan, pers. comm., 14.4.1998.
66. *Cathedral Chronicle*, December 1969, p. 7.
67. DAD, Sr Jordana Mackey, notes.
68. DAD, Sr Kath Levitzke, notes.

69. DAD, Register of Mother Provincial, January 1955-1978.
70. V. Fienberg, letter to Prioress, Dongara, December 1971.
71. DAD, Sr Bernadette Punch, notes.

## CHAPTER SIX
## FOOTPRINTS IN THE SANDS OF TIME

### DAYDAWN

1. F. K. Crowley, *A Short History of Western Australia*, p. 34.
2. P. Heydon, *Gold on the Murchison*, p. 12.
3. ibid., p. 162.
4. DAD, Book of Permissions, Holy Rosary, Greenough.
5. *Murchison Times and Day Dawn Gazette*, 4.2.1902.
6. P. Heydon, *Just a Century Ago*, pp. 39, 43.
7. *Murchison Times and Day Dawn Gazette*, 28.6.1902, 1.7.1902.
8. ibid., 23.8.1902, 4.9.1902.
9. R. Hutchison MLA, letter to Sr Francis Huntsman, Priory, Dongara. 5.6.1964.
10. *Sower*, February 1911. Same advertisement appeared earlier.
11. ibid., 1.3.1909, p. 1, 1.6.1909, p. 5.
12. ibid., December 1910.
13. ibid., January 1911.
14. ibid., March 1911, p. 6.
15. ibid., August 1911, p. 7.
16. ibid., October 1911.
17. DAD, Sr Joseph O'Connor, notes.
18. DAD, annals, Priory, Dongara, 3.1.1913.
19. Sower, January 1918, p. 10. See P. Heydon, *Gold on the Murchison*, p.108.
20. ibid., April, 1918. p. 16.
21. DAD, Sr Joseph O'Connor, notes.
22. R. Hutchison MLA, letter to Sr Augustine Corbett, 1960. See R. Hutchison MLA, letter to Sr Francis Huntsman, Dongara, 5.6.1964.

### LEONORA AND GWALIA

1. *Back to Leonora-Gwalia*, souvenir brochure, September 1948. See DAD, Chronological Table of events, Leonora District.
2. ibid.
3. *Back to Leonora-Gwalia*, op. cit.
4. M. Gabriel Gill, letter to Fr O'Malley, Leonora, 11.2.1903.
5. ibid.
6. *Kalgoorlie Miner*, 28.9.1996, article 'On the Road to the Centenary, Leonora-Gwalia 1986-1996'.
7. ibid. See *Back to Leonora-Gwalia,* op cit.
8. *Sower*, January 1909, p. 1.
9. ibid., 1.3.1909, p. 1.
10. ibid., 1.4.1909, p. 5.
11. ibid. See *Sower*, 1.2.1909, p. 4.
12. ibid.
13. ibid., 1.7.1909, p. 5. See *Sower*, 1.12.1909, p. 6.
14. ibid., January 1910, p. 15.
15. ibid., January 1911, p. 20.
16. ibid., February 1910, p. 7.
17. ibid., July 1910, p. 11.
18. ibid., March 1911, p. 8. See *Sower*, February 1911, p. 6.
19. ibid., March 1912, p. 10.
20. ibid., June 1917, p. 8.
21. DAD, Archbishop Prendiville, Perth, letter to Bishop O'Collins, Geraldton, 16.8.1939. See Bishop O'Collins letter to Archbishop, 7.7.1939 and A. McLay, *Women out of their Sphere*, pp. 230, 231.
22. Sr Vincent Colgan, letter to Bishop O'Collins, Geraldton, 18.7.1939.
23. Sr Augustine Corbett, Leonora, letter to Bishop O'Collins, 28.4.1940.
24. DAD, Sr Xavier Ryan, notes. Sr Augustine Corbett, Leonora, letter to Bishop O'Collins, 28.4.1940.
25. DAD, Sr Xavier's Ryan, notes. See *Veritas* 1949.
26. ibid.
27. DAD, Education Department, Inspector's report, September 1953, 1954.
28. ibid.

29. DAD, Sr Xavier Ryan, notes.
30. ibid.
31. *Sower*, December 1996, p. 4. See WAN, 27.4.1964.

**MEEKATHARRA**

1. P. Heydon, *Gold on the Murchison*, p 163.
2. *Sower*, 1.2.1909, pp. 4, 5. See *Sower* 1.3.1909, p. 10, April 1909, p. 4.
3. ibid., 1.6.1909, pp. 5, 6.
4. ibid., 1.4.1909.
5. ibid., August 1910, p. 8.
6. ibid., February 1911, p. 6, March 1911.
7. ibid., July 1911, pp. 7, 10.
8. ibid., August 1911, p. 9.
9. ibid., May, 1913, p. 11.
10. ibid., March 1917.
11. DAD, school concert programme, 18.3.1918.
12. DAD, Appointment Book, Priory, Dongara, 25.5.1918.
13. DAD, Sr Joseph O'Connor, notes, 17.6.1992.
14. DAD, Sr Bertrand O'Connor, notes.
15. ibid.
16. DAD, Sr Dominic Galvin, notes.
17. *Sunday Times*, M. McGann, article, 'The Last Bell To Ring for a Little School', 6.12.1970.

**THREE SPRINGS**

1. *Sower,* 1.4.1909, p. 3.
2. ibid., See DAD, Sr Xavier Ryan, notes.
3. ibid. September 1911.
4. *Cathedral Chronicle*, October 1958, p. 1.
5. DAD, Sr Xavier Ryan, notes. See *Veritas*, 1949.
6. *Sower*, January 1918, p. 7.
7. ibid.
8. *Our Heritage in Progress,* brochure, Parish of Three Springs, 1959.
9. DAD, miscellaneous, Three Springs Convent.
10. ibid.
11. Sr Dominic Galvin, notes.
12. *Cathedral Chronicle*, October 1958.
13. ibid., March 1964. See DAD, Fr Maurice Carse, letter to Bishop Hickey, 24.9.1987.
14. Father, F. X. Brown, notes on Sr Xavier Ryan.
15. Sr Perpetua Gill, pers. comm., 1998.
16. *Cathedral Chronicle*, October 1966.
17. ibid, September 1967.

**YALGOO**

1. Heritage Council of Western Australia, *Yalgoo, Heritage Trail,* p. 1.
2. ibid., pp. 2, 3.
3. A. Palmer, *Yalgoo*, p. 21.
4. *Sower*, 2.8.1909, p. 8. See 1.10.1909, p. 6. 1.12 1909, p. 5. October 1910, p. 14.
5. P. Anson, *Hermit of Cat Island,* p. 50.
6. A. Palmer, op. cit., p. 56.
7. DAD, Fr J. Hawes, Yalgoo, letter to M. Prioress, Dongara, 12.10.1919. Dean Hawes was appointed Monsignor on 28.11.1937.
8. ibid.
9. ibid., 26.10.1919.
10. ibid.
11. ibid., Mullewa, letter to M. Prioress, Dongara, 22. 7.1921.
12. ibid., Yalgoo, letter to M. Prioress, Dongara, 7.8.1921.
13. ibid.
14. ibid., 11.9.1921. Harry Jermy later assisted Hawes when he built the Mullewa Church.
15. ibid., 14.9.1921.
16. ibid., 24.9.1921.
17. ibid., 11.9.1921.
18. ibid., 27.10.1921.
19. ibid., 24.11.1921.
20. ibid., 3.1.1922.
21. ibid., 19.1.1922.
22. ibid., Willy-willy, Aboriginal for spiralling wind.
23. J. Taylor, notes, 'The Art and Architecture of John Cyril Hawes', unpublished manuscript.

24. Fr J. Hawes, letter to M. Prioress, Dongara, 19.1.1922.
25. WACR, 23.3.1922, Kate O'Connor, letter to 'Aunt Bessie's Children's Column'.
26. DAD, Sr Joseph O'Connor, notes.
27. DAD, Sr Dominic Galvin, notes.
28. ibid.
29. D. Gerrans, pers. comm., 1998.
30. *Cathedral Chronicle*, August 1980. Vol. 51, no. 8.
31. ibid., June 1981. The date of the school's closure is often incorrectly cited. The last Education report was submitted in 1950.

**MINGENEW**

1. J. T. Reilly, *Reminiscences of 50 Years in WA,* quotation from obituary for S. Phillips, *Northam Advertiser*, June 1901.
2. E. M. Halley and H. H. Wilson, *Roundabout Geraldton*, p. 43.
3. Mingenew Historical Society, *Mingenew, 1846-1986,* p. 42.
4. R. Stephens, *The Mingenew Story,* p. 16. [page numbers calculated, not printed]
5. *Sower*, 1. 4. 1909.
6. *Sower,* November 1910, p. 11.
7. DAD, *Geraldton Express,* cutting n.d., March 1912.
8. J. Newton, notes, St Joseph's Church, Mingenew, March 1998.
9. ibid.
10. Mingenew Historical Society, op.cit., pp. 68, 70.
11. Sr Bertrand O'Connor, notes, Mingenew.
12. ibid.
13. DAD, Education Department, school reports, D. McDonald, 30.11.1945, S. F. Thornbury, 17.6.1947.
14. *Greenough Sun,* 28.9.1950. See Education Department, school report, A. Dineen, 24.4.1950.
15. Education Department, school report, D. McDonald, 11.8.1952.
16. ibid., A. H. Trotman, 3 .6.1953. See *Greenough Sun,* 10. 2. 1954.
17. ibid.
18. DAD, Sr Dominic Galvin . See *Cathedral Chronicle*, November 1954.
19. ibid., August 1957, October 1958, p. 2.
20. J. Newton, op.cit. See R. Stephens, p 110.

**REEDY**

1. P. Heydon, *Just a Century Ago,* p. 2.
2. DAD, Sr Bernadette Punch, notes.
3. ibid.
4. *Murchison Times and Cue–Big Bell–Reedy Advocate*, p. 1.
5. P. Heydon, op. cit., p. 92.
6. ibid., p. 93.
7. DAD, Sr Xavier Ryan, notes.
8. ibid.
9. Education Department, Inspector's school report, S. F. Thornbury, 30.7.1947.
10. DAD, Sr Xavier Ryan, notes.
11. P. Heydon, *Just a Century Ago*, p. 101.

**MORAWA, PERENJORI and MOTOR MISSION**

1. *Cathedral Chronicle*, June 1983, p. 2.
2. ibid.
3. ibid.
4. ibid.
5. ibid., July 1933, p. 2, article, 'Morawa's New Church', p. 2. See parish brochure, *Golden Jubilee of the Holy Cross Church, Morawa, July 1933-July 1983.*
6. ibid.
7. RWAHS, brochure, *Morawa Heritage Walk*, 1997.
8. Parish brochure, *Golden Jubilee of the Holy Cross Church, July 1933-July 1983.*
9. *Cathedral Chronicle*, April 1955.
10. DAD, Sr Declan Callaly, notes on Morawa and Perenjori.
11. ibid.
12. DAD, Sr Bernadette Punch, notes on Motor Mission.
13. WACR, 8.5.1986.
14. *Cathedral Chronicle*, July 1983, p. 7.
15. DAD, Appointment Book.
16. DAD, Class Teacher evaluation sheet, Marian Convent, Morawa, 18.7.1985.
17. DAD, annals Morawa, 1986.

CHAPTER SEVEN
REAPING THE HARVEST

BEDFORD PARK

1. F. D. Bourke, op. cit., p. 208.
2. WACR, March 1938.
3. DAD, Sr Marie-Therese Sharman, notes on Bedford Park.
4. DAD, Fr McBride, copy of letter to Archbishop Prendiville, 4.8.1940.
5. DAD, Archbishop Prendiville, letter to M. Vincent Colgan, 6.8.1940. Revised Constitutions came in to force on 15.9.1941 when M. Vincent was in charge. She was formally elected as the first Prioress General in January 1942.
6. DAD, Sr Marie-Therese Sharman, notes on Bedford Park.
7. ibid.
8. ibid.
9. ibid. See D. Popham, *Reflections*, p. 230. Sr Albertus wrote three well-known books on WA history, *Ancient Landmarks, Full Fathom Five,* and *A Place of their Own.* She was recently elected a Fellow of the Royal Western Australian Historical Society.
10. Sr Marie-Therese Sharman, notes.
11. ibid.
12. ibid.
13. ibid.
14. Sr Marie-Therese Sharman, notes on Bedford Park.
15. ibid. The Dominican Sisters were in fact a Pontifical Order. To please Bishop Kelly and subsequent bishops, the early Sisters, however, did not press the issue and for many years were regarded as diocesan.
16. DAD, Register of the Provincial, February 1955. See St Thomas Aquinas School Annual 1983, article, 'Beginnings', p. 6.
17. Sr Albertus Bain, *All Our Yesterdays*, p. 20. See DAD, annals.
18. DAD, Register of M. Prioress Provincial, January 1955-December 1978.
19. DAD, report, J. West, Superintendent, Education Department, 25.9.1967.
20. St Thomas Aquinas College Annual, 1978.
21. ibid. 1981.
22. DAD, Sr Perpetua Gill, notes.
23. DAD, G. Cooney, letter to Bro. Faulkiner, 6.8.1984.
24. DAD, Sr Concepta Flattery, response to work party recommendations, 24.7.1988.
25. DAD, Sr Perpetua Gill.
26. C. Brown, notes January 1999.
27. Sr Assumpta Moriarty, pers. comm., 1999.

BENTLEY

1. Sr Albertus Bain, *From Drifting Sand to Glistening Marble,* pp.1-3.
2. ibid., pp. 6, 8.
3. DAD, E. Logan, Santa Clara report, 30.6.1954. Education Department reports, 1945-1955.
4. Sr Albertus.Bain, op. cit., p.10
5. DAD, annals, Siena Convent, Bentley, 1961.
6. Sr Albertus Bain, op. cit., pp.12, 13.
7. DAD, annals February, 1967.
8. School Annual, article, 'History', p. 3. See staff notes, 'Bentley Highlights, 1991'.
9. Sr Anne Larney, notes on Bentley.

MORLEY PARK

1. Infant Jesus Primary School Annual, 1991, article, 'From the Beginning', p. 2.
2. ibid.
3. ibid., article by Beverley Parry, p. 3.
4. Dad, Sr Helen O'Connor, notes on Morley Park.

DIANELLA

1. Register of M. Prioress Provincial, January 1955-1978.
2. Church of Our Lady's Assumption, Dianella Silver Jubilee Celebration brochure, 1965-1990, p. 2.
3. ibid., p. 3.
4. DAD, Sr Maria Goretti Power, notes on Dianella.
5. Silver Jubilee Brochure, op. cit., p. 5.
6. St Thomas Aquinas Annual 1982, p. 1, article by Dr W. E. Moore in Centre for Research in Evaluation, Education Department of NSW, 1973.

ST JOHN'S SCARBOROUGH

1. L. Easton, *Stirling City* p. 31. See M. Thomas, (compiler), *Along the Plank Road*, pp. 48, 49.
2. WAN, 18.1.1886.
3. M. Thomas (compiler), *Along the Plank Road*, p. 46.
4. Brochure, *History of Immaculate Heart of Mary, Golden Jubilee 1948-1998*, p. 37. See Silver Jubilee 1948-1973.
5. DAD, Sr Celine O'Farrell RSM, notes on St John's, Scarborough.
6. ibid.
7. DAD, Sr Joseph O'Connor, notes on Scarborough. See 'History of Scarborough'.
8. ibid.
9. DAD, annals, Scarborough 1952. See Sr Joseph O'Connor, notes on Sisters.
10. E. Dragun, pers. comm., 1999.
11. Sr Perpetua Gill, notes 'Recollections of Early Days', September 1993.
12. DAD, annals 1953.
13. Brochure, *History of Immaculate Heart of Mary, Golden Jubilee 1948-1998.*
14. T. Willesee, pers. comm., May 1998.
15. DAD, annals 1954. See WACR, 25.2.1954.
16. ibid., 1955, 1956.
17. ibid., 1955, 1956, 1959. See Inter Dominican School Sports Programmes.
18. ibid., 1958.
19. DAD, 'History of Scarborough', p. 41.
20. DAD, 1959. According to the Dominican Rule a convent with more than 12 Sisters in residence was entitled to be called a Priory. The title Prioress applied to the person in charge.
21. ibid., 1961. See Sr Perpetua Gill, notes.
22. DAD, Sr Dominica Davis, interview by Sayers 1988.
23. DAD, Sr Anthony Sachse, notes on St John's.
24. DAD, Jan Ibbotson, notes on St John's.
25. DAD, notes on St John's.

ST THERESA'S, GWELUP

1. Sr Anne McLay, *Women Out of Their Sphere*, p. 162.
2. ibid., p. 163.
3. DAD, Archbishop Prendiville, letter to M. Laurence Prendiville, 1.1.1951.
4. DAD, annals, 1950-1970. See Sr Joseph O'Connor, notes on Gwelup.
5. Sr Joseph O'Connor, notes on Gwelup.
6. ibid. See Sr Declan Callaly, notes on Gwelup.
7. DAD, W. Rourke, inspector's report, 30.7.1953.
8. Sr Declan Callaly, notes on Gwelup.

OUR LADY OF GRACE, NORTH BEACH

1. L. Newell (compiler), *Along a Shore Line*, p. 39. See R. Erickson, *Dictionary of Western Australians, Vol. 3.* pp. 351, 352, the Castle Hotel was demolished in 1973. Streets named for members of the Hamersley family are: Elvire, Flora, Margaret, Ada, Mary, Edward (now Hale) and Hugh.
2. WAN, 17.8.1911.
3. L. Easton, *Stirling City*, p. 1.
4. Oral History brochure, Our Lady of Grace, *A lifetime by the Sea, 1920-1989*, p. 11.
5. L. Newell, Freda Carmody, article on North Beach Church, p.133.
6. *A Lifetime by the Sea,* p. 4.
7. Sr Bernadette Punch, notes on North Breach, 1998 'History of Our Community'.
8. ibid.
9. ibid.
10. ibid.
11. DAD, notes on North Beach.
12. Register of Mother Prioress Provincial, January 1955-December 1978.
13. *A Lifetime by the Sea,* p. 6.

HOLY SPIRIT, WEMBLEY DOWNS

1. Fr T. Phelan, notes on Holy Spirit Parish, 1998.
2. DAD, Sr Rosarii Keenan, notes, 'History of Holy Spirit School'.
3. ibid., See Fr T. Phelan, notes.
4. Fr T. Phelan, notes. See DAD, History of Catholic Schools of Scarborough, Doubleview Regions.
5. Sr Rosarii, notes.

CHAPTER EIGHT
FROM DUNEDIN TO DONGARA TO DOUBLEVIEW

ST DOMINIC'S, INNALOO

1. L. Easton, *Stirling City,* p. 194.
2. DAD, Dominican Newsletter, No 21, September 1954, article 'Westward Ho!', September 1954. See Sr Perpetua Gill, interview notes, Fr F. X. Brown.
3. DAD, annals, Santa Sabina, Scarborough, 1954. See WACR, 29.7.1954.
4. WACR, 13.9.1954.
5. DAD, clipping, n.d. See DAD parish notes.
6. DAD, annals, Santa Sabina, Scarborough, 1955.
7. DAD, Education Department Inspector's report, December 1954-1955. See also St Dominic's Bicentennial Annual 1988, p. 3., article, 'A Brief History'.
8. DAD, Sr Assumpta Moriarty, notes on Fr F. Campbell.
9. DAD, annals Santa Sabina, Scarborough, 1960-61.
10. St Dominic's Bicentennial Annual 1988, p. 3.
11. G. Cooper, St Dominic's School Board, letter to Catholic Education Commission, 22.2.1977.
12. ibid.
13. ibid.

HOLY ROSARY, DOUBLEVIEW

1. L. Easton, *Stirling City*, p. 75.
2. ibid., p. 194. Between 1944-1969 the list of new housing units included: Woodlands (44), Innaloo (863), Scarborough (988), Churchlands (91), Doubleview (1,030).
3. DAD, Register of M. Prioress Provincial, January 1955-December 1978, entry October 1958.
4. DAD, 'History of Our Community', p. 103. See DAD, Fr F. X. Brown, notes.
5. ibid., pp. 103-105.
6. ibid.
7. DAD, Register of M. Prioress Provincial, January 1955-December 1978, entry May 1961.
8. DAD, notes on Holy Rosary. See 'History of Our Community'.
9. DAD, Register of M. Prioress Provincial, January 1955-December 1978.
10. DAD, Sr Perpetua Gill, notes.
11. Holy Rosary Year Book 1994, p. 2.
12. ibid., 1997, p. 9.
13. ibid.
14. DAD, Sr Perpetua Gill, notes on Holy Rosary.
15. DAD, notes on Holy Rosary.

SIENA

1. Register of Prioress Provincial, January 1955-December 1978, entries, May, June, 1960.
2. DAD, brochure to residents 1961, and Summerhayes letter to M. Provincial, Dongara, 5.12.1961. See History of Siena pp. 15, 16.
3. DAD, Newman College Review, p. 9.
4. Newman Siena College Prospectus 1986. See History of Siena, p. 2.
5. WACR, 24.5.1962. See Santa Sabina annals 1950-1964, entry May 1962.
6. ibid.
7. DAD, Santa Sabina annals, entry June 1962.
8. DAD, History of Siena, p. 19.
9. DAD, Santa Sabina annals, entry February 1963.
10. History of Siena, p. 38. See DAD, list of members.
11. DAD, annals, Santa Sabina Scarbrough, entry February 1963.
12. ibid., entry December 1963.
13. ibid., entries May, August, November, 1964. See WACR 14.5.1964.
14. DAD, annals, Priory, Dongara, 1965-1969, entry February 1965.
15. St Thomas Aquinas, Bedford Park Year Book 1983.
16. DAD, annals, Priory, Dongara, April 1965.
17. DAD, annals, Santa Sabina, Scarborough, entry December 1964.
18. DAD, Register of M. Prioress Provincial January 1955-1978, entry November 1965, July 1966.
19. C. Brown, pers. comm., notes 1999.
20. DAD, 'History of Siena', pp. 39, 40.
21. Census 1971.

22. Register of M. Prioress Provincial, January 1955-December 1978, entry Nov. 1971.
23. Holy Rosary Church brochure. Fr Leahy, a formal student of building sciences, spent most of his 24 years in Australia and NZ designing buildings. Holy Rosary was his first church.
24. DAD, Dongara Priory annals, entry 18 May 1972.
25. DAD, notes on various Dominican Sisters.
26. DAD, notes on 'Historical Development of Siena', pp. 3, 4.
27. Register M. Prioress Provincial, January 1955-December 1978, entry July 1973.
28. Sr Perpetua Gill, notes Sr Rosarii Keenan, February 1999.
29. Register of M. Prioress Provincial January 1955-December 1978, entries 31.10.1977, 12.10.1977.
30. ibid., entry November 1976.
31. DAD, 'History of Siena', p. 58.
32. Sr Declan Callaly, notes.
33. Newman College Review, p. 7.
34. ibid., p. 14.
35. ibid., p. 17.

## CHAPTER NINE
## A RICH INHERITANCE

1. D. O'Murchu, *A Religious Life: A Prophetic Vision: Hope and Promises for Tomorrow,* p. 31.
2. MOM, M. Gabriel Gill, letter to Dr Kirby, April 1884 p. 59. See SITS, p. 140.
3. Register of M. Prioress, January 1955-December 1978.
4. Dominican annals, Priory Dongara, 27.12.1957.
5. DAD, notes on various past Sisters.
6. ibid.
7. ibid.
12. ibid.
13. ibid.
14. ibid.
15. ibid.
16. Sr Joan Carville, notes.

# Bibliography

## PUBLISHED WORKS


Anson P., *The Hermit of Cat Island,* Burns & Oats, 1958.

Bain, A., *All Our Yesterdays, History of St Thomas Aquinas 1941-1988.* Dominican Sisters, Perth, 1989.

Bain, A., *From Drifting Sand To Glistening Marble, A History of Santa Clara, Bentley, 1954- 1988,* Dominican Sisters, Perth, 1989.

Bourke D. F., *History of the Catholic Church in Western Australia 1829-1979,* Vanguard Service Print, Perth, 1979.

Crowley, F. K., *A Short History of Western Australia,* MacMillan, Melbourne, 1959.

Easton, L., *Stirling City,* University of Western Australia Press, Nedlands 1971.

*Encyclopedia Brittanica* 1999, Chicago, Illinois, 1999.

Erickson R. (compiler), *Dictionary of Western Australians, Vol. 3, Free 1850 –1868,* University of Western Australia Press, Nedlands, 1979.

Halley E. M. and Wilson, H. H., Reprint 1978, *Roundabout Geraldton and the Victoria District,* Regency Print, Perth, 1978.

Heydon P. R., *Just A Century of Gold,* Hesperian Press, Victoria Park, Perth, 1987.

Heydon P. R., *Gold on the Murchison,* Hesperian Press, Victoria Park, Perth, 1986.

Heydon, P. R., *Meekatharra, End of the Earth,* Hesperian Press, Victoria Park, Perth, 1994.

Jaggard, E., *A Challenge Answered, A History of Surf Lifesaving in Western Australia,* The Surf Life Saving Association of Australia (WA), Perth, 1979.

Jarrad, B., *Life of St Dominic,* Blackfriars, London, 1955.

Marchant James, R., *Cork to Capricorn. A History of the Presentation Sisters in Western Australia 1891-1996,* The Congregation of the Presentation Sisters of Western Australia, 1996.

McCarthy, Sr A., *Mother of the Missions,* Dominican Sisters, Dunedin, New Zealand, 1989.

McCarthy, Sr A., *Star in the South,* Dominican Sisters, Dunedin, New Zealand. 1970.

McLay, A., *Women out of their Sphere,* Sisters of Mercy, Western Australia, 1992.

Mingenew Historical Society, *Mingenew Story, 1846-1896,* Hesperian Press, Victoria Park, Perth, 1960.

L. Newell (co-ordinator), *Along a Shoreline,* North Beach Historical Society, Artlook, 1980.

O'Murchu, D., *Religious Life: A Phophetic Vision: Hope and Promises For Tomorrow,* Ave Maria Press, USA, 1991.

Palmer, A., *Yalgoo.* Lap Industries, Fremantle, 1985.

Popham, D. *Reflections,* Carroll's Pty Ltd, Perth, 1978.

Reilly, J. T., *Reminiscences of Fifty Years Residences in WA,* Sands & McDougall, Perth, 1903.

Stephens, R.. *The Mingenew Story,* Geraldton Newspapers Ltd, 1960.

Thomas M. (co-ordinator), *Along The Plank Road –Through Njookenbooroo to Scarborough Beach,* self published, Copyspot, Perth, 1989.


## ARCHIVAL SOURCES


Archdiocesan Catholic Archives, Perth.

Battye Library, Alexander Library, Perth.

Dominican Archives, Dunedin, New Zealand.

Dominican Archives, Doubleview.

Geraldton Diocesan Archives.

Geraldton Regional Library.

Irwin District Historical Society.

Three Springs Shire Library.


## OFFICIAL PUBLICATIONS AND REPORTS


Blue Book, Ecclesiastical Returns, BL.

Catholic Directory, ACAP.

Catholic Year Book 1902, ACAP.

Newman College Review 1990s.
Census reports, BL.
Weather reports, BL.
*A Brief History of the WA Government Railways*, Government publication (n.d.).

## UNPUBLISHED REPORTS, ANNALS

Education Department, various school reports between 1940-1960s.
Dominican annals, Holy Rosary, Greenough, 1899-1902.
Dominican annals, Santa Sabina, Scarborough, 1950-1964.
Dominican annals, St Catherine's, Doubleview.
Dominican annals, St Dominic's, Dongara, 1901-1971.
Dominican Book of Permissions.
Dominican Book of the Clothing of Professions.
Register of Mother Prioress Provincial, 1928-1963.

## SECONDARY SOURCES, PAMPLETS, OCCASIONAL PUBLICATIONS

Abbot, L., 'History of Dominican Sisters WA', BL Q271-972 ABB.
Brennan, L. and D. (compilers), oral history brochure, 'A Lifetime By The Sea 1920-1989, Our Lady of Grace Parish, North Beach', Crystal Printing, Perth, 1989.
Gwalia, souvenir brochure 'Back to Leonora'.
Chronological Table of Events in Leonora District.
Contemporary Restorationism, an Anthropologist comments.
Dominican Sisters International, 'Reflections on the Feast of St Catherine of Siena', April 1997.
DAD, Dominican Congregation, 'The Dominican Way'.
DAD, 'Dominican Spirituality'.
Heritage Council of WA 1989, 'Yalgoo Heritage Trail'.
DAD, 'History of Bushies' School'.
DAD, International Dominican Information.
Mingenew Shire, 'A History of Districts Schools' (held in Mingenew Shire Library).
DAD, 'Outline of the Holy Family Province'.
Rose, P. J. 'History of Scarborough', 1960, BL HS/PR/1400.
DAD, various school, sports and concert programmes.
Souvenir Brochure, 'Back to Leonora-Gwalia'.
DAD, The Congregation of Dominican Sisters in WA, Constitutions and Directory.
DAD, 'The Dominican Sister'.
DAD, 'The Dominican Sisters, National'.
Three Springs Parish, brochure 1959, 'Our Heritage in Progress'.

## DIARIES

DAD, Gill, M. Gabriel, 1899, Also BL 1325A.
DAD, Kirby, Sr di Ricci, April 1899 and 20 August 1900-September 1900.
DAD, Miscall, Sr di Piazzi, April 1899 to January 1900.
DAD, Wall, Sr Gonzales.

## SCHOOL AND COLLEGE ANNUALS

Chisholm College.
Siena Girls' College.
St Dominic's School.
St Thomas Aquinas College.
Newman College, Mission Statement.
Newman College Prospectus.
Our Lady's Assumption.
Santa Clara.
*Veritas* 1899-1949, Jubilee edition.
*Veritas* 1934-1936.
*Veritas* 1937-1938.
*Veritas* 1939-1943.

## TYPESCRIPT

Canonical Status of Dominican Sisters, Holy Family Province.
Dominican Policy.
Newman Siena Enrolment Policy.
Nairn, J. 'First School Days at Dongara'.
Phelan, Fr Tom, notes on Holy Spirit parish, City Beach.

## NEWSPAPERS, JOURNALS

*Cathedral Chronicle*
*Cue Black Range Courier and Sandstone Observer*, 1907-1915

*Day Dawn Chronicle,* 1902-1909
*Diocesan News*
*Geraldton Advertiser*
*Geraldton Express*
*Greenough Sun*
*Kalgoorlie Miner*
*Leonora Miner*
*Morawa Advertiser*
*Mt Magnet Miner and Lennonville Leader*
*Mt Magnet and Yalgoo*
*Murchison Advocate*
*Murchison Miner* 1911
*Murchison Times and Day Dawn Gazette*
*Murchison Times and Cue-Big Bell-Reedy Advocate*
*Murchison Yalgoo Goldfields Chronicler*
*New Zealand Tablet*
*Northern Advertiser*
*Reedy Advocate*
*Sower*
*Sunday Times*
*The Mt Magnet Leader and Youanmi Miner*
*The West Australian*
*Victoria Express*
*West Australian Catholic Record*

**LETTERS (original and copied) NOTES AND PERSONAL COMMUNICATIONS**

Boyle, Ann, letter to author.
Archbishop Prendiville, Perth, DAD.
Bishop O'Collins, Geraldton to Prioress, DAD.
Brown, Cynthia, notes, DAD.
Brown, Fr F. X., DAD.
Carville, Sr Joan, notes to author.
Criddle, Lionel, interview and letter to author.
Dawson, Joan, notes.
Dragun, Estelle, notes to author.
Gallop, Ida, letter to author.
Gerrans, Dorne, notes to author.
Hall, Bro T., Sydney Archdiocese archives, letter to author.
Hurrell, Gwen, interview.
Hutchison, Ruby MLC, DAD.
Kelly, Mary, interview.
Marshall, E. (Nell) and Jenny, to author, interview, letters to author.
D, Marmion, Dom Columba, Maredsous, DAD.
McCarthy, Sr Augustine OP, New Zealand, letter to author.
McGinley, Sr Judith OP, New Zealand, letters to author.
McGrath, Sr Philomena OP to Ireland, DAD.
Miscall, Sr di Pazzi.
Moore, Colin.
Newton, Jean.
Punch, Sr Bernadette OP, interview and notes.
Rowlands, letter to author notes.
Scotter, Shirley, letters to author.
Staples, Joy, interview.
Stokes, Jean, interview.
Sullivan, W., letter to Sisters, Doubleview.
Willesee, Terry, notes to author.

**SISTERS' REMINISCENCES**

Callaly, Sr Declan OP.
Galvin, Sr Dominic OP.
Gill, Sr Perpetua OP.
Keenan, Sr Rosarii OP.
Levitzke, Sr Kath OP.
Mackey, Sr Jordana OP.
Moriarty, Sr Assumpta OP.
O'Connor, Sr Bertrand OP.
O'Connor, Sr Joseph OP.
O'Farrell, Sr Celine RSM.
Punch, Sr Bernadette.
Ryan, Sr Xavier OP.
Scarf, Sr Margaret OP.
Sharman, Sr Marie-Therese OP.
Aborigines

# Index